HIGHWAY TO HEAVEN SERIES
EDWARD A. FITZPATRICK, *Editor*
Institute of Catechetical Research, Marquette University

THE HIGHWAY TO GOD

HIGHWAY   TO   HEAVEN   SERIES
_____

BOOK OF THE HOLY CHILD (Grade One)

LIFE OF MY SAVIOR (Grade Two)

LIFE OF THE SOUL (Grade Three)

BEFORE CHRIST CAME (Grade Four)

THE VINE AND THE BRANCHES (Grade Five)

THE MISSAL (Grade Six)

HIGHWAY TO GOD (Grades Seven and Eight)

———

Accompanying this Series is the RELIGION IN LIFE CURRICULUM for grades one to six and PRACTICAL PROBLEMS IN RELIGION for grades seven and eight.

HIGHWAY TO HEAVEN SERIES VII-VIII

The Highway to God

Prepared (in co-operation with a group of priests
and sisters teaching in elementary schools)
IN THE CATECHETICAL INSTITUTE OF
MARQUETTE UNIVERSITY

GEORGE H. MAHOWALD, S.J., PH.D., *Chairman*
RAPHAEL N. HAMILTON, S.J., PH.D.
GERARD SMITH, S.J., M.A.

By
EDWARD A. FITZPATRICK, PH.D.
Director of the Catechetical Institute

ST. AUGUSTINE ACADEMY PRESS
HOMER GLEN, ILLINOIS

Nihil obstat:
H. B. RIES,
Censor librorum

Imprimatur:
✝ SAMUEL ALPHONSUS STRITCH,
Archiepiscopus Milwaukiensis

February 23, 1933

This book was originally published in 1933 by The Bruce Publishing Company.
This edition reprinted in 2017 by St. Augustine Academy Press
based on the 1936 second printing.
Some of the illustrations were replaced due to deterioration of the originals.

Softcover ISBN: 978-1-64051-042-5
Hardcover ISBN: 978-1-64051-043-2

INTRODUCTORY WORD TO THE TEACHER

This book concludes the "Highway to Heaven" series. It organizes for the student the material he has covered in various ways, from various angles in the preceding six years. It organizes the course in religion. The process of integration which was carried on throughout the course, and notably in the third grade, for the doctrine taught up to that time, is in this book done for the whole course.

It gives unity and organization to the curriculum in religion. It emphasizes doctrine. It includes the entire *Baltimore Catechism* with its questions and answers. It brings into sharper relief the religious principles which have been implicit and have become more explicit in the development of the course.

The most striking immediate characteristic of the book is undoubtedly its size. This is due to the "enriched materials" that are included in the text, both as a foundation for the doctrine and as superstructure of its application to life. It grows out of our conception that the curriculum in religion must be a Catholic culture as well as Catholic knowledge. It grows, too, out of our conception that religion is at least as important as any other subject or all other subjects in the curriculum and should have textbooks as worth while in comprehensiveness, in richness of material, in make-up, in size, as other textbooks. The richness of the subject calls for an "enriched" textbook.

There is a fundamental architectonic idea underlying this book. It has been characteristic of the Religion-in-Life curriculum. It figures man's spiritual progress under the image of progress on a highway — the Highway to Heaven. It follows the historical order. The beginning of the journey for the human race is after the expulsion from Paradise as a result of the Fall of Man. How that came about for the human race and the individual man requires that the story of the Creation be told. That constitutes the first unit. God's first actual help for man came in those familiar guideposts on the Highway to Heaven, the Commandments of God. They constitute the second unit of the book. The long-expected Messiah promised in the Garden of Eden came. Who He is; what He did on earth; what He did for man's progress on the Highway and the achievement of his destiny constitute the third unit of the book. The fourth unit of the book deals with the means by which Christ continued Himself and His work in the world for the salvation of men — the Roman Catholic Church. The fifth and sixth units deal more specifically with the means by which Christ continues His work in the world through the Church — the seven sacraments, and the commandments of the Church. The concluding unit of the book deals with several topics, prayer, angels, and as a formal conclusion of book and of curriculum, the Apostles' Creed.

This historical development will prove to be a fruitful, logical organization for the individual. The whole plan is knit together. It is interrelated. It is coördinated. It is unified. It is the natural cumulative integration of the various elements, the knowledge of doctrine, of liturgy, of Christian hymns and poems, the attitudes toward life and eternity, the practical problems of everyday life, and the religious life of grace of the individual. Religious knowledge is not unrelated to the day-to-day life of the individual. Religion is in life. And life is swallowed up in eternity.

EDWARD A. FITZPATRICK

CONTENTS

		PAGE
	Introductory Word to the Teacher	v

CHAPTER

I.	God the Creator	1
II.	The Story of the Creation	8
III.	Adam and Eve	15
IV.	Why God Made Man	22
V.	The Commandments of God	28
VI.	The First Commandment of God	38
VII.	The Second Commandment of God	50
VIII.	The Third Commandment of God	59
IX.	The Fourth Commandment of God	70
X.	The Fifth Commandment of God	80
XI.	The Sixth and Ninth Commandments	87
XII.	The Seventh and Tenth Commandments	92
XIII.	The Eighth Commandment	98
XIV.	Sin	104
XV.	The Messiah	115
XVI.	Prepare Ye the Way of the Lord	121
XVII.	The Early Life of Christ	128
XVIII.	The Divinity of Christ: The Miracles	137
XIX.	The Public Life of Christ: The Parables	144
XX.	Some Memorable Sayings of Christ	154
XXI.	Christ and the Holy Eucharist	161

CONTENTS

XXII.	THE CRUCIFIXION	173
XXIII.	HE IS RISEN	183
XXIV.	MARY, FULL OF GRACE	193
XXV.	CHRIST AND THE APOSTLES	203
XXVI.	THE HOLY GHOST ON PENTECOST	217
XXVII.	THE ROMAN CATHOLIC CHURCH	225
XXVIII.	GRACE AND THE SACRAMENTS	240
XXIX.	BAPTISM	254
XXX.	THE FORGIVENESS OF SINS	263
XXXI.	THE CONFESSION OF SINS	270
XXXII.	THE PUNISHMENT OF SIN	281
XXXIII.	THE SACRAMENT OF THE HOLY EUCHARIST	287
XXXIV.	THE REAL PRESENCE	298
XXXV.	THE EUCHARIST AS A SACRIFICE: THE HOLY MASS	306
XXXVI.	CONFIRMATION	318
XXXVII.	MATRIMONY	329
XXXVIII.	EXTREME UNCTION	335
XXXIX.	HOLY ORDERS	341
XL.	PRAYER	349
XLI.	THE COMMANDMENTS OF THE CHURCH	358
XLII.	THE SAINTS	383
XLIII.	THE ANGELS	391
XLIV.	THE END OF THE JOURNEY	399
XLV.	THE APOSTLES' CREED	407
	INDEX	413

Chapter I

GOD THE CREATOR

Who is God?

God is the Creator of heaven and of earth and of all things.

> In heaven, up above,
> Dwells the Father, God of love,
> He made the earth, He made the sky,
> The ocean wide, the mountains high,
> He made each flower and bird and tree,
> He made you, and He made me,
> He sends the snow, He sends the rain,
> He makes the flowers bloom again,
> And when the earth is bleak and bare,
> He feeds the birdies, everywhere.
> — *Berdice Moran*

God is Love. The finest and most beautiful things on earth help us to get some idea of God. When we say God is Love, we must try to think of a love more perfect than any human love — more perfect even than the love of a mother for her child. God is Love. We must love God above all things.

God Our Father. We think of God, too, as our Father. He loves us, His children, white or black, yellow or red, rich or poor, wise or ignorant. We are all God's children, no matter where we were born or what our condition of life may be.

Since we are all God's children, we should remember that God loves us all, and that He wants us to love and help one another. We must avoid quarreling, avoid hatred, avoid bad or evil thoughts about others, avoid saying evil things to others. If we love one another, we shall deserve to be called the children of God, and we may joyfully call God our Father, as we do when we say the prayer taught by Christ Himself.

King David's Praise of God. Some of the greatest poems ever written were composed by the Jewish king, David. Before Jesus was born on earth, the Jews were the only people who had a true knowledge of God. David never grew tired of singing the praises of God. His poems are called the Psalms, and he himself is called the Psalmist. There are, in the Bible, one hundred and fifty of these Psalms, over half of which were written by David himself. Here is one of them:

> Out of the mouth of infants and sucklings Thou hast perfected praise, because of Thy enemies, that Thou mayest destroy the enemy and the avenger.
> For I will behold Thy heavens, the works of Thy fingers: the moon and the stars which Thou hast founded.
> What is man that Thou art mindful of him? or the son of man that Thou visitest him?
> Thou hast made him a little less than the angels, Thou hast crowned him with glory and honor: and hast set him over the works of Thy hands.
> Thou has subjected all things under his feet, all sheep and oxen: moreover the beasts also of the fields.
> The birds of the air, and the fishes of the sea, that pass through the paths of the sea.
> O Lord, our Lord, how admirable is Thy name in all the earth! (Psalm viii.)

There are many beautiful thoughts in these Psalms. Turn to them often in your Bible, even when you have only a few minutes; on every page you will find something worth while. Here are some lines from them worth learning by heart:

> The heavens show forth the glory of God, and the firmament declareth the work of His hands.
> Day to day uttereth speech, and night to night showeth knowledge.
> There are no speeches nor languages, where their voices are not heard. (xviii. 2–4.)

> The earth is the Lord's and the fullness thereof: the world, and all they that dwell therein.
> For He hath founded it upon the seas; and hath prepared it upon the rivers.

Who shall ascend into the mountain of the Lord: or who shall stand in His holy place?

The innocent in hands, and clean of heart, who hath not taken his soul in vain, nor sworn deceitfully to his neighbor.

He shall receive a blessing from the Lord, and mercy from God his Savior. (xxiii. 1-5.)

Lord, Thou hast been our refuge from generation to generation. Before the mountains were made, or the earth and the world was formed; from eternity and to eternity Thou art God.

Turn not man away to be brought low: and Thou hast said: Be converted, O ye sons of men.

For a thousand years in Thy sight are as yesterday, which is past. . . .

And let the brightness of the Lord our God be upon us: and direct Thou the works of our hands over us; yea, the work of our hands do Thou direct. (lxxxix. 1, 2, 3, 4, 17.)

Sing joyfully to God, all the earth: serve ye the Lord with gladness. Come in before His presence with exceeding great joy.

Know ye that the Lord He is God: He made us, and not we ourselves. We are His people and the sheep of His pasture. Go ye into His gates with praise, into His courts with hymns: and give glory to Him.

Praise ye His name: for the Lord is sweet, His mercy endureth forever, and His truth to generation and generation. (lxxxix. 2-5.)

Unless the Lord build the house, they labor in vain that build it.
Unless the Lord keep the city, he watcheth in vain that keepeth it. (cxxvi. 1.)

God the Creator. Everything in the world was made by God. God existed before the world was created and He shall live on after it is destroyed. God always was and He always will be: He had no beginning and He will have no end. He is, the Psalmist says, "from eternity to eternity." The world and everything in it, as well as all other parts of the universe — the sun, the moon, the stars — are God's creation. He made the angels, men, animals, and plants. He can do all things, and nothing is hard or impossible to Him.

We can make things, but we cannot create, in the sense we mean when we say God creates. The most we can do is to cause great changes in things, changes that other people have not made. The poet puts words and thoughts together in new ways; the musician makes wonderful new combinations of the notes in our scales; a sculptor makes a beautiful statue from a block of marble. We sometimes say that these men have *created* poems, songs, or statues, when they use in new ways materials, or things which already exist.

Only God can create. When God creates, behold, there is something where there was nothing. We shall try to understand this great truth a little more clearly later. Let us often recall to our minds the fact that God is the Creator. He created heaven and earth and all things; He created us; we are His creatures. No wonder King David sings forth his faith in God, his trust in God, his love for God, and his thankfulness to God. Follow the example of David. Love God. Every day, at any time of the day, say just a word to God, or, at least, think of Him. Use the language of the Psalms or use your own little prayer.

A.M.D.G. It is a good practice to put at the head of all your school papers, the letters A.M.D.G., which are the initial letters of four Latin words which mean "For the greater glory of God." Do this to show your gratefulness to God, your willingness to serve Him, and your love for Him whose creature you are.

God is Eternal. God is the Creator of heaven and earth and of all things. He exists from eternity to eternity, from everlasting to everlasting. He is, we say, eternal. He had no beginning, and He can have no end. "Before the mountains were made, or the earth and the world was formed, from eternity to eternity Thou art God," as the Psalmist says. God had no beginning. He always was and He always will be.

God and Man. God is the Creator; man is the creature of God. Man comes from God. Man has a beginning, but God has given him a soul which will never be destroyed. The fact that he has a soul which will never die makes a human being somewhat like God, but God is not like a human being. God is the Creator; man is the creature. God is eternal, without beginning and without end. "All things were made by Him," says St. John, "and without Him was made nothing that was made." So said the Apostle, and we repeat: "I believe in God, the Father Almighty, Creator of heaven and earth."

God is Perfect. God is perfect in every way. Man is imperfect. Some men, because of love of God and willingness to do what He has commanded, are less imperfect than others, but no man is perfect, God is infinitely perfect, perfect in every way. God is all just, all holy, all merciful as He is infinitely perfect. God can do all things and nothing is hard or impossible to Him.

God is Love, Justice, Mercy. God is Love. God is just, and merciful, too, and forgiving. God is holy. David sings about God:

For the Lord is just, and hath loved justice: His countenance hath beheld righteousness. (x. 8.)

My God is my helper, and in Him will I put my trust. (xvii. 3.)

The Lord hath heard, and hath had mercy on me: The Lord became my helper. (xxix. 11.)

He loveth mercy and judgment: the earth is full of the mercy of the Lord. (xxxii. 5.)

O praise ye the Lord, for He is good: for His mercy endureth forever. (cxvii. 29.)

I will praise Thee, O Lord, with my whole heart: for Thou hast heard the words of my mouth.
I will sing praise to Thee in the sight of the angels: I will worship toward Thy holy temple, and I will give glory to Thy Name.
For Thy mercy, and for Thy truth: for Thou hast magnified Thy holy name above all. (cxxxvii. 1–2.)

God is a Pure Spirit. God is not a human being. He is a spirit. He is a spirit infinitely perfect. God can do all things, and He knows all things, even our most secret thoughts, words, and deeds. But God is a pure spirit, and cannot be seen with our bodily eyes. It is difficult for us to think just what a spirit is.

What is God? God is a spirit infinitely perfect. This is God's world; it was created by Him. Everything was created by Him. He is everywhere in the world, but we do not and cannot see Him because He is a pure spirit, and we know pure spirits cannot be seen with our bodily eyes. God watches over His children. He loves us. He is Love Itself. Being God, He knows all things, even our most secret thoughts, words, and actions. Being God, too, He can do all things, and nothing is hard or impossible to Him. He is Love; He is merciful; He is holy; He is the sum of all perfection; He is infinitely perfect. He sees us and watches over us.

Questions from the Catechism

Q. Who is God?
A. **God is the Creator of heaven and earth and of all things.**

Q. What is God?
A. **God is a spirit infinitely perfect.**

Q. Had God a beginning?
A. **God had no beginning; He always was and He always will be.**

Q. Where is God?
A. **God is everywhere.**

Q. If God is everywhere, why do we not see Him?
A. **We do not see God, because He is a pure spirit and cannot be seen with bodily eyes.**

Q. Does God see us?
A. **God sees us and watches over us.**

Q. Does God know all things?
A. **God knows all things, even our most secret thoughts, words, and actions.**

Q. Can God do all things?
A. **God can do all things, and nothing is hard or impossible to Him.**

Q. Is God just, holy, and merciful?
A. **God is all just, all holy, all merciful, as He is infinitely perfect.**

Questions for the Pupil

1. Did you think of God today? When?
2. Did you today do something out of love for God?
3. Do you thank God for His kindness to you?
4. Are you grateful for the beautiful things in the world about you?
5. How do you show your love of God?
6. How do you praise God in word? in thought? in deed?
7. How may you become more pleasing to God?
8. How do you show respect for the name of God?
9. Are you careful not to offend God by any of your words?

GOD THE CREATOR

10. Can you give up those faults that make your soul less lovely in God's sight, such as quarreling and unkindness?
11. Does the fact that you are a child of God help you:
    a) To keep good thoughts in your mind?
    b) To prevent any bad thoughts?
    c) To help another child; your mother?
12. Put the above questions in the first person. Copy them into your notebook. Return to them occasionally and answer the questions for yourself.

Problem Questions

1. What would you say to a boy if you heard him misuse the name of God?
2. What is the best reparation to God you can make when you hear someone using His name in vain?
3. A boy carelessly endangers his life and when warned says, "God is good, He will protect me." Do you think he is right?

Quotations from the Bible

To what incident does the following description refer?
Who was present?
What is the significance of the event?

"In the beginning God created heaven and earth" (Gen. i. 1).

"All things were made by Him; and without Him was made nothing that was made" (John i. 3).

Suggestive Assignments

1. Enumerate some of the things God does for you, in one column, and in a parallel column enumerate the things you do for God.
2. Make a little prayer of your own in praise of God.
3. Look in the Book of Psalms for some brief prayers that you may like to repeat.
4. Learn the hymn of praise, "Holy God We Praise Thy Name."
5. Find several stories in the Bible that illustrate the mercy, the love, or the justice of God.

Chapter II
THE STORY OF THE CREATION

God is the Creator of heaven and earth and of all things.

Genesis. How God created the heavens and the earth is told us in an interesting way in the very first book of the Bible. Because it tells us of the beginnings of things, the generation of things, how things came to be, the first book of the Bible is called Genesis. The author of the book tells us, as God inspired him, the story of the creation.

Genesis and the Jews. The story was told to the Jews of that day, who lived among idolaters. Idolaters were people who paid to creatures the worship which belongs to God alone. This worship due to God alone they gave to animals, the sun and moon, to plants, and even to statues of wood and stone. To warn the Jews against such evils, the inspired writer told the story, pointing out in a manner that the people could easily understand, the great fact that there is but one God and that He is the Creator of the whole universe, and that to Him only is due divine worship. The Jews did not always listen to this warning. We read, later on in the Old Testament, that they did not always keep this pure faith, but became idolatrous; i.e., they sometimes gave the worship due to God alone to His mere creatures; they even went so far as to worship a golden calf.

Genesis and Science. The story of the creation told in the Book of Genesis of the Old Testament gives the main facts of the creation put in a way that the people could easily understand. It is important that you understand the order and the facts, and then you will see that there is no conflict between the facts as told in the Book of Genesis and what scientists today have learned about the development or evolution of the world. The story of the creation as found in Genesis is as follows:

In the Beginning: There was nothing except God; then there were heaven and earth. God willed it and they were created. This is the story in Genesis:

In the beginning God created heaven and earth. And the earth was void and empty, and darkness was upon the face of the deep; and the spirit of God moved over the waters (Gen. 1. 1–2).

Creation of Light. And moving on the waters, the Spirit of God created light.

And God said: Be light made. And light was made. And God saw the light that it was good; and He divided the light from the darkness. And He called the light Day, and the darkness Night (i. 3–5).

Creation of Heaven. There was heaven and earth, and the light and the darkness created by God's act. And notice that God saw that it was good. And the waters were great, and God made the firmament or the sky and called it heaven.

And God said: Let there be a firmament made amidst the waters: and let it divide the waters from the waters. And God made a firmament, and divided the waters that were under the firmament, from those that were above the firmament, and it was so. And God called the firmament, heaven (i. 6–8).

Creation of Earth. Having made the heavens, the waters under the firmament were divided and the earth was created. And this is the way the inspired writer of Genesis tells us of what happened:

God also said: Let the waters that are under the heaven, be gathered together into one place: and let the dry land appear. And it was so done. And God called the dry land, Earth; and the gathering together of the waters, he called Seas (i. 9, 10).

And then the comment:

And God saw that it was good.

The Earth Bringeth Forth Herbs. And the land was separated from the heaven and the waters. But now there were to be added to the land trees and herbs of many kinds, having seed each one according to its kind. And this is what the inspired writer tells us of what happened:

And He said: Let the earth bring forth the green herb, and such as may seed, and the fruit tree yielding fruit after its kind, which may have seed in itself upon the earth. And it was so done.

And the earth brought forth the green herb and such as yieldeth seed according to its kind, and the tree that beareth fruit, having seed each one according to its kind. And God saw that it was good (i. 11, 12).

Sun and Moon and Stars. Now that the earth showed the work of God, so the heavens would show it with the two great lights and the stars. The inspired writer of Genesis says:

And God said: Let there be lights made in the firmament of heaven, to divide the day and the night, and let them be for signs, and for seasons, and for days and years:

To shine in the firmament of heaven, and to give light upon the earth. And it was so done.

And God made two great lights: a greater light to rule the day; and a lesser light to rule the night; and the stars.

And He set them in the firmament of heaven to shine upon the earth.

And to rule the day and the night, and to divide the light and the darkness (i. 14–18).

And again the comment:

And God saw that it was good.

Creatures of the Waters. The heavens and the earth and the waters were created, and herbs and trees covered the earth, and the sun and moon and stars were in the firmament. And then God created the living creatures in the waters; moving creatures, fowls that fly above the earth, great whales, and the like:

God also said: Let the waters bring forth the creeping creature having life, and the fowl that may fly over the earth under the firmament of heaven.

And God created the great whales, and every living and moving creature, which the waters brought forth, according to their kinds, and every winged fowl according to its kind (i. 20, 21).

And again the comment:

And God saw that it was good.

Creatures of the Earth. God having created the heaven, the earth, and the waters, and the living creatures of the waters, then created the living creatures on the earth, cattle and creeping things and beasts of the earth:

And God said: Let the earth bring forth the living creature in its kind, cattle and creeping things, and beasts of the earth, according to their kinds. And it was so done.

And God made the beasts of the earth according to their kinds, and cattle, and everything that creepeth on the earth after its kind (i. 24, 25).

And as with all creation, "God saw that it was good."

Creation of Man. And God placed on the earth at this time man, who was made in the image and likeness of God, and ruled over everything on the earth. The inspired writer of the first chapter of the Book of Genesis said:

And He said: Let Us make man to Our image and likeness; and let him have dominion over the fishes of the sea, and the fowls of the air, and the beasts, and the whole earth, and every creeping creature that moveth upon the earth.

And God created man to His own image: to the image of God He created him: male and female He created them;

And God blessed them, saying: Increase and multiply, and fill the earth, and subdue it, and rule over the fishes of the sea, and the fowls of the air, and all living creatures that move upon the earth.

And God said: Behold I have given you every herb bearing seed upon the earth, and all trees that have in themselves seed of their own kind, to be your meat:

And to all beasts of the earth, and to every fowl of the air, and to all that move upon the earth, and wherein there is life, that they may have to feed upon. And it was so done (i. 26–30).

And looking at the whole creation:

And God saw all things that He made, and they were very good.

And we look at the creation, the wonder, the mystery, the beauty, and the intelligence and plan of it, and we say only God could create it. All of man's works are nothing compared to it.

The Steps in the Creation. The steps in the Creation were therefore six:

1. *a)* Creation of heaven and earth and the waters (without form).
   b) Creation of the light.
2. *a)* Creation of the firmament, the heavens.
3. *a)* Creation of the earth.
   b) Creation of the herbs and fruits of the earth.
4. Creation of the sun, the moon, and stars in the heavens.

5. Creation of the creatures of the waters.
6. *a*) Creation of the creatures of the earth, the creeping things, cattle, and the beasts of the field, and
    b) Creation of man, the lord of creation.

God Resteth. And the story of the creation closes with what God did on the seventh day.

So the heavens and earth were finished, and all the furniture of them.

And on the seventh day God ended His work which He had made; and He rested on the seventh day from all His work which He had done.

And He blessed the seventh day, and sanctified it: because in it He had rested from all His work, which God created and made (ii. 1–3).

What is a "Day"? These are the six steps in the story of the creation. In the English translation of this old inspired Hebrew book, the Bible, the length of time of each of these steps in the creation is called one "day." Men differ as to just what the word *day* means in the story of the creation. Some think that it means a day in the usual sense of that word; namely, twenty-four hours; some think it means an indefinite period of time, as when we say, "in our *day,* men have solved some of the most difficult problems of science." The Church has never said what we must believe as to the time of the creation. But it is important for us to know these six stages in the creation of the world.

Nothing is Impossible to God. God could have made these different creatures in a day, or in an instant, or over a longer period of time. He is almighty and all powerful. He willed that they should be, and they existed. This is the power of God, unlike any human power. Nothing is impossible to God.

Some say that the events told in Genesis are really eight different works, as follows:

1. Creation of the firmament, the heavens.
2. Creation of the earth.
3. Creation of light.
4. Creation of the herbs and fruits of the earth.
5. Creation of the sun, the moon, and stars in the heavens.
6. Creation of the creatures of the waters.
7. Creation of the creatures of the earth, the creeping things, cattle, and the beasts of the field, and
8. Creation of man, the lord of creation.

THE STORY OF THE CREATION

God's Power. God made all things, both those which we can see and those which we cannot see, the visible as well as the invisible. As we learn more about God's creation we wonder as to its order and the extraordinary intelligence that we see in it. We begin to appreciate somewhat God's power, God's wisdom, God as Creator. How true is David's song of God's power and God's love of us. The more we learn the more wonderful and mysterious does God's power seem. It is easy to understand the first article of the Apostles' Creed.

I believe in God, the Father Almighty, Creator of heaven and earth.

Questions from the Catechism

Q. Who made the world?
A. **God made the world.**

Q. Who created heaven and earth, and all things?
A. **God created heaven and earth, and all things.**

Q. How did God create heaven and earth?
A. **God created heaven and earth from nothing by His word only; that is, by a single act of His all-powerful will.**

Questions for the Pupil

1. In what book is the story of the creation told?
2. What is the Bible?
3. What is the Old Testament?
4. Describe the steps in the creation of the world.
5. In the language of the Book of Genesis, tell the story of the Creation of Man.
6. What was to be man's relation to all other creatures? Can you quote the exact words from the Book of Genesis?

Problem Questions

1. What part should creatures play in your life? Can they help you to heaven? Can they hinder you?
(The teacher will tell you what St. Ignatius of Loyola says in a great book he wrote, called the *Spiritual Exercises*, in answer to this question.)
2. In what ways does the creation of the world reflect the greatness of God?

Quotations from the Bible

For each of the following quotations:

a) Identify the speaker.
b) State the conditions under which the statement was made.
c) Give the meaning.
d) Tell its significance.

"Be light made" (Gen. i. 3).

"Let the earth bring forth the green herb, and such as may seed, and the fruit tree yielding fruit after its kind, which may have seed in itself upon the earth" (Gen. i. 11).

"Let Us make man to Our image and likeness; and let him have dominion over the fishes of the sea, and the fowls of the air, and the beasts, and the whole earth" (Gen. i. 26).

Suggestive Assignments

1. Find any poems that tell about Creation in a way that pleases you. Copy them neatly in your notebook.

2. Learn as much of Chapter I of the Book of Genesis as relates to the Creation.

3. Find beautiful pictures of the Creation by God. Paste them in your notebook.

Chapter III
ADAM AND EVE

The story of the making of man by God was told in general terms in the preceding chapter. You will recall the words:

And He said: Let Us make man to Our image and likeness: and let him have dominion over the fishes of the sea, and the fowls of the air, and beasts, and the whole earth, and every creeping creature that moveth upon the earth.
And God created man to His own image: to the image of God He created him, male and female He created them (i. 26, 27).

The Making of Man. Man is made up of the dust of the ground and a living *soul*. The words of the second chapter telling the story, state it more clearly:

And the Lord God formed man of the slime of the earth: and breathed into his face the breath of life, and man became a living soul (ii. 7).

The dust of the ground we know as our body, and the spirit or breath that God breathed into the body became the soul. And we know that the image and likeness of God in which man is created is in this living soul. The soul being like unto God, we should be especially careful about it, and guard its welfare. How we can do this we shall see in detail later. We shall take more care of the soul for it is that which makes us different from all other things, and especially because it is directly the creation of God Himself — it is the very breath of God. It is a spirit that will never die, and has understanding and free will. If we should lose our soul, we would lose, as we shall see, God and everlasting happiness.

Man in the Garden of Eden. A man, with a living soul, the likeness and image of God, was placed in the Garden of Eden planted by God Himself. Every tree that was pleasant to the sight and good for food was provided. Here are the words of the inspired writer of Genesis:

And the Lord God had planted a paradise of pleasure from the beginning: wherein He placed man whom He had formed.

And the Lord God brought forth of the ground all manner of trees, fair to behold, and pleasant to eat of: the tree of life also in the midst of paradise: and the tree of knowledge of good and evil.

And the Lord God took man, and put him into the paradise of pleasure, to dress it, and to keep it (ii. 8, 9, 15).

The Tree of Knowledge. In the midst of the beautiful Garden of Eden was the tree of knowledge of which God had told Adam he must not eat:

And He commanded him, saying: Of every tree of paradise thou shalt eat:

But of the tree of knowledge of good and evil thou shalt not eat. For in what day soever thou shalt eat of it, thou shalt die the death (ii. 16–17).

The Making of Woman. There was found no helper suitable for Adam in all the creatures which had been formed out of the ground. And the story of Genesis runs as follows:

And the Lord God said: It is not good for man to be alone: let Us make him a help like unto himself. . . .

Then the Lord God cast a deep sleep upon Adam: and when he was fast asleep, He took one of his ribs, and filled up flesh for it.

And the Lord God built the rib which He took from Adam into a woman: and brought her to Adam.

And Adam said: This now is bone of my bone, and flesh of my flesh: she shall be called woman, because she was taken out of man.

Wherefore a man shall leave father and mother, and shall cleave to his wife: and they shall be two in one flesh (ii. 18, 21–24).

The Fall of Man. And the woman, who had not yet been named Eve, was tempted and led astray by the devil in the form of a serpent. God had said "Ye shall not eat of the fruit of the tree which is in the midst of the garden, nor touch it, lest you die." But Eve listened to the serpent who said then, "You shall not surely die — when you eat of it your eyes will be opened, and you will become as gods, knowing good and evil." And so the story is told:

And the woman saw that the tree was good to eat, and fair to the eyes, and delightful to behold: and she took of the fruit thereof, and did eat, and gave to her husband who did eat (iii. 6).

ADAM AND EVE DRIVEN FROM PARADISE
By Gustave Doré, nineteenth century.

The Free Will of Man. God had given Adam the power to choose to do or not to do a thing as Adam willed. He could obey God's command, or he could disobey. "God made man from the beginning and left him in the hands of his own counsel," says the Psalmist. This power which men have to choose to do one thing or another, or not to do at all, we call free will. It raises man above all the other creatures of the earth that God made. It is part of the likeness of man to God. It makes man's service to God a willing service. It also makes possible the acts of disobedience and the sins of men.

The Punishment. And for disobeying the command of God, the sorrows of the woman would be made great. The serpent was forced to go on his belly and eat the dust of the earth all his life. And to Adam the Lord said:

Because thou hast hearkened to the voice of thy wife, and hast eaten of the tree, whereof I commanded thee that thou shouldst not eat, cursed is the earth in thy work; with labor and toil shalt thou eat thereof all the days of thy life.

Thorns and thistles shall it bring forth to thee; and thou shalt eat the herbs of the earth.

In the sweat of thy face shalt thou eat bread till thou return to the earth, out of which thou wast taken: for dust thou art, and into dust thou shalt return (iii. 17–19).

And Adam tilled the ground whence he was taken.

The Result of Adam's Sin. The prospect before Adam was truly great. He had been placed in a garden planted by God Himself. It contained "every tree that was pleasant to the sight, and good for food." And God said it was not good for man to be alone, and finding in all the creation no suitable helpmate for him, He created woman. And the prospect for Adam as for his future was a glorious one. "In his flesh was perfect health; and in his soul perfect peace."

All was lost by the sin of disobedience; by the act of rebellion against God's sovereignty. Adam and Eve were forever cast out of the Garden of Eden, and with this sin came all the ills that flesh is heir to — sorrow, pain, death.

Original Sin. And man's soul was affected, too. It suffered a loss of God's grace, which loss we call original sin. This act of

ADAM AND EVE

Adam's was a sin because it was a violation of the command of God. It is called "original," which means the first or the beginning, because it was caused by the act of Adam and Eve, the parents of the human race, the first man and woman. We begin life not as Adam was before the fall, but in the weakened condition caused by his fall. That is the result of Adam's disobedience. Original sin is not due to any fault of ours; it is not a sin which we ourselves commit. When we talk of "original sin" in the descendants of Adam, including ourselves, we do not speak of the actual sin of Adam, but of the effect on our human nature in its weakened and unhappy state due to his sin. It is the condition of our human nature which we inherit from Adam. It comes down to us from Adam. Original sin is not a positive or an actual sin of mine or yours, but it is negative, it means the absence of something in our soul, that something we call the grace of God. It is fortunate for us that this grace is easily and simply given back to our soul, ordinarily by baptism.

Effect on Human Nature. But our nature is not like that of Adam and Eve as they came, innocent and holy, direct from God. It is like their corrupted or weakened nature after the *act* of disobedience. It left in us a tendency to evil.

God, however, did not leave man to himself, but held out hope to him. He promised him help. He would open again to man the gates of heaven. And in the last book of the New Testament we learn something of what that means:

And God shall wipe away all tears from their eyes: and death shall be no more, nor mourning, nor crying, nor sorrow shall be any more, for the former things are passed away (Apoc. xxi. 4).

Questions from the Catechism

Q. What is man?
A. **Man is a creature composed of body and soul and made to the image and likeness of God.**

Q. Is this likeness in the body or in the soul?
A. **This likeness is chiefly in the soul.**

Q. How is the soul like to God?
A. **The soul is like God because it is a spirit that will never die, and has understanding and free will.**

Q. Of which must we take more care, our soul or our body?
A. **We must take more care of our soul than of our body.**

Q. Why must we take more care of our soul than of our body?
A. **We must take more care of our soul than of our body, because in losing our soul we lose God and everlasting happiness.**

Q. Who were the first man and woman?
A. **The first man and woman were Adam and Eve.**

Q. Were Adam and Eve innocent and holy when they came from the hand of God?
A. **Adam and Eve were innocent and holy when they came from the hand of God.**

Q. Did God give any command to Adam and Eve?
A. **To try their obedience, God commanded Adam and Eve not to eat of a certain fruit which grew in the garden of Paradise.**

Q. Which were the chief blessings intended for Adam and Eve had they remained faithful to God?
A. **The chief blessings intended for Adam and Eve, had they remained faithful to God, were a constant state of happiness in this life and everlasting glory in the next.**

Q. Did Adam and Eve remain faithful to God?
A. **Adam and Eve did not remain faithful to God; but broke His command by eating the forbidden fruit.**

Q. What befell Adam and Eve on account of their sin?
A. **Adam and Eve on account of their sin lost innocence and holiness, and were doomed to sickness and death.**

Q. What evil befell us on account of the disobedience of our first parents?
A. **On account of the disobedience of our first parents, we all share in their sin and punishment, as we should have shared in their happiness if they had remained faithful.**

Q. What is the sin called which we inherit from our first parents?
A. **The sin which we inherit from our first parents is called original sin.**

Q. Why is this sin called original?
A. **This sin is called original because it comes down to us from our first parents, and we are brought into the world with its guilt on our soul.**

Q. Does this corruption of our nature remain in us after original sin is forgiven?
A. **This corruption of our nature and other punishments remain in us after original sin is forgiven.**

ADAM AND EVE

Q. Did God abandon man after he fell into sin?

A. **God did not abandon man after he fell into sin, but promised him a Redeemer, who was to satisfy for man's sin and reopen to him the gates of heaven.**

Q. Did the Son of God become man immediately after the sin of our first parents?

A. **The Son of God did not become man immediately after the sin of our first parents, but was promised to them as a Redeemer.**

Questions for the Pupil

1. How do you take care of your body?
2. How do you take care of your soul?
3. Why should you take better care of your soul than of your body?
4. Does your soul help your body?
5. Does your body help your soul? May it hinder it?
6. Find the passage in the Apocalypse which is given at the end of the chapter.
7. How can you take better care of your soul in the future than you have in the past?

Problem Questions

1. In the life of any saint, find out how he or she took care of her soul. Has this any suggestion for us?

Quotations from the Bible

For each of the following quotations:
a) Identify the speaker.
b) State the conditions under which the statement was made.
c) Give the meaning.
d) Tell its significance.

"Of every tree of paradise thou shalt eat: But of the tree of knowledge of good and evil, thou shalt not eat. For in what day soever thou shalt eat of it thou shalt die the death" (Gen. ii. 16–17).

"It is not good for man to be alone: let Us make him a help like unto himself" (Gen. ii. 18).

"I will put enmities between thee and the woman, and thy seed and her seed: she shall crush thy head, and thou shalt lie in wait for her heel" (Gen. iii. 15).

Chapter IV
WHY GOD MADE MAN

What is Man? Let us go back to Chapter I and read again the eighth Psalm; or better still, if we learned it by heart, let us write it out. The Psalmist, after he beholds the heaven and the earth, the moon and the stars, wonders why God was so good to man, and marvels at the place of man in creation. Man is only a little lower than the angels. What is man?

Thou hast made him a little less than the angels, thou hast crowned him with glory and honor: and hast set him over the works of Thy hands.

Thou hast subjected all things under his feet, all sheep and oxen: moreover the beasts also of the fields.

The birds of the air, and the fishes of the sea, that pass through the paths of the sea.

O Lord our Lord, how admirable is Thy name in all the earth! (Ps. viii. 6–10.)

The Wonder of Man. Even though we know that man is made in the image and likeness of God, and is created by God and is a living soul, it is natural to wonder at the goodness and mercy of God. "What is man that Thou art mindful of him and the son of man that Thou visitest him?" But that prompts another question: What is it all for? A poet mourning over the death of a friend says:

> Whence are we, and why are we,
> Of what scene the actors or spectators?

A Paradise for Man. If we call to mind the facts about Adam and Eve in the Garden of Eden, perhaps we will be helped to understand the purpose in the creation of man. By God's act man has a living soul. He has power to understand, to reason, and to will. God made a most beautiful and lovely place for Adam, in the Garden of Eden. It was called a paradise — which means a park, a very beautiful place. But more important than this was the beauty of Adam's soul. He had grace and in a very real sense his soul was made to the image and likeness of God. He was not only man in the natural state that we know him but in a supernatural state. God had given him graces and blessings greater than those really belonging to human nature.

The Punishment of Disobedience. This paradise Adam would have continued to enjoy if he had not disobeyed. God, as a test of his love and his service, told him not to taste of the fruit of the Tree of Knowledge. He willed or decided to eat the fruit. And because Adam consented God cast him and Eve out of Paradise, and they felt in their nature an inclination to evil which we inherit. Man lost grace; and suffering, disease, and death is his lot.

Obeying God's Commands. So God expects obedience to His commands and His laws. He makes it possible for man to obey of his own free will. Man can, but he may not, do as he wills, except at his peril. If he wills not to obey, punishment is sure to follow, as it did in the case of Adam.

Serve God. We should serve God as God wishes and not as we may choose to serve Him. We should carry out faithfully the commandments He has given, and we should avoid the things God commands us not to do. From Adam we can learn, at least, the lesson that man should serve God, keep His commandments, and avoid the things He has forbidden.

Love God. As God's creatures we should love Him, because we are His creatures and He is the Creator, and because everything we have comes from Him, who is the Giver of all good gifts. He gives us all our gifts of body and soul. He always watches over us. The love of God should be the reason for our service to God. Love God. He loved us first. He loves us always. His great love of us is the greatest reason for our service to Him.

Know God. But our love of God, as a great saint said, should abound more and more in knowledge. We must know God in such ways as we can. We see Him in His creation: the earth, and the heavens, sun and moon and stars. "The heavens declare the glory of God and the firmament showeth His handiwork." We see Him in our fellow human beings. We see Him in ourselves. We see Him in our human nature which Christ took on earth.

The Duty of Man. The duty of man is to know God, to love Him, and to serve Him. We must believe in Him, hope in Him, and love Him. Our love will abound or grow more and more as we know God in His great love for men, and as we realize the truth more and more in its fullness that we learned in the primary grades: God is Love. Knowing God better, and loving Him more deeply, we are the more ready and willing to serve Him, to say as President McKinley said when he was dying, repeating the words of Christ: "Not my will, but Thy will be done." This should be our thought not only in our dying hour, but each day of our lives.

Whither? What is my destiny? For what was I created? Whither am I going? are questions that man often asks and more often thinks of in his own mind. These are other forms of the questions: Why did God make man? What for? Whither?

From God to God. God must have had a purpose in the creation of man. He made man only a little lower than the angels, and all things are made to serve Him. Perhaps the simple answer to the problem of man's destiny is from God to God — to spend not time but all eternity with God, to see Him face to face, not as through a glass, darkly.

The Destiny of Adam Before the Fall. Adam was placed in his earthly paradise — a mark of the goodness of God. This was given with but one command — not to eat of the fruit of the Tree of Knowledge. Thus God wished to test Adam who had the power of free will. Had Adam for the time, which in the wisdom of God was enough, not been tempted himself, or had he refused the fruit of the forbidden tree when offered it by Eve, then what was to be the reward? From all that we know the reward would have been the taking of Adam to heaven, there to see God face to face and to enjoy this beatific vision for all eternity. There would have been no death, and this change from paradise to heaven would have come, we do not know just how, but perhaps in the form of the Ascension of Christ, or, as in a passage in St. Paul, which it is hard to understand:

> Behold, I tell you a mystery. We shall all indeed rise again, but we shall not all be changed.
> In a moment, in the twinkling of an eye, at the last trumpet: for the trumpet shall sound, and the dead shall rise again incorruptible: and we shall be changed.
> For this corruptible must put on incorruption; and this mortal must put on immortality (I Cor. xvi. 51–53).

Man's Destiny. To be with God in heaven is still man's destiny. As great St. Augustine said: "For Thyself, O God, Thou hast made us, and our hearts will not rest until they rest in Thee." He goes to his home which is God. His destiny is in heaven to which he will go if he merits or deserves it. To return to his Divine Father, the world prodigal returning home, that is man's destiny. But it is no longer the simple taking of a creature worthy through obedience to God's command of passing from an earthly, natural paradise to supernatural happiness forever and ever, there to be with God.

The Long Journey to Man's Final Home. Not only is the journey of man's life to his final home not so simple and direct as it would have been had Adam not disobeyed God's command, but man is less able to travel the way. Adam was a creature, but in a special sense, God's. His soul had the likeness of God, but the effects of the disobedience was to dim this likeness; in fact, the soul was robbed of the Godlike quality, which we call sanctifying grace, until it could be given back. It will be for us to follow man on his journey to his final home.

Heaven. We have described this destiny of man as to be at home with God, the prodigal returning to his Father's mansion. We call it heaven. How glorious it is, we cannot imagine. We try to picture it in terms of the best things of earth, but we have but a faint likeness. The truth is in the Apostle's words: "Eye hath not seen, nor ear heard, neither hath it entered into the heart of man, what things God hath prepared for them that love Him" (I Cor. ii. 9).

Question from the Catechism

Q. Why did God make you?
A. **God made me to know Him, to love Him, and to serve Him in this world, and to be happy with Him forever in the next.**

Questions for the Pupil

1. Why was man created?
2. What is man's final end?
3. What is meant by "Man can, but he may not do as he wills except at his peril"?
4. How did you exercise your free will today?
5. Did it help you on the road to God?
6. How do you show your love for God?
7. Explain the statement: "We see Him [God] in our fellow human beings."
8. List acts that show we do not realize the full meaning of this statement.
9. List acts that show our love of our neighbor and our love of God.
10. What can you do to know God better, and to learn more about Him?

Problem Questions

1. Find in the New Testament any descriptions of life with God or heaven (see Vaughn, *The Divine Treasury of Holy Scripture*).
2. Write a paragraph telling what you understand by the quotations from St. Augustine.
3. Show from the life of any saint, his or her love of God.
4. Show from the life of any person not a saint his or her love of God (e.g., Lincoln).

Quotations from the Bible

For each of the following quotations:
a) Identify the speaker.
b) State the conditions under which the statement was made.
c) Give the meaning.
d) Tell its significance.

"In the sweat of thy face shalt thou eat bread till thou return to the earth, out of which thou wast taken: for dust thou art, and into dust thou shalt return" (Gen. iii. 19).

"Let Us make man to Our image and likeness" (Gen. i. 26).

"What doth it profit a man, if he gain the whole world, and suffer the loss of his own soul? Or what exchange shall a man give for his soul?" (Matt. xvi. 26.)

WHY GOD MADE MAN

"Thou hast made him a little less than the angels, thou hast crowned him with glory and honor: and hast set him over the works of thy hands" (Ps. viii. 6).

To what incident does the following description refer?
Who was present?
What is the significance of the event?

"The Lord God formed man of the slime of the earth" (Gen. ii. 7).

Chapter V
THE COMMANDMENTS OF GOD

On this journey of man from birth to his heavenly home with God, there are many stumbling blocks in the way.

A Heavenly Reward. Just as Adam was tried in the Garden of Eden, so man is tried during his life on earth. Man is given the choice of doing what God has commanded or doing otherwise. If he keeps faithfully all the commandments of God, he will return to his Father in heaven, and receive the place which was prepared from the beginning of the world.

The Punishment of Disobedience. If he deliberately breaks these commandments and shows no sorrow, then he shall suffer forever in the place of the wicked, called hell. How we live here on earth is, therefore, very important to us after we die. We may not do as we please, or neglect God's law, or drift, for we shall have to meet the punishment no matter what we think about it. It will do no good to say, "I won't count it this time." Every time counts. And every time we slip, makes it all the more difficult to get back on God's Highway.

The Master of men has put this very clearly and briefly:

Enter ye in at the narrow gate: for wide is the gate, and broad is the way that leadeth to destruction, and many there are who go in thereat.

How narrow is the gate, and straight is the way that leadeth to life: and few there are that find it! (Matt. vii. 13-14.)

God's Love of Man. To help him keep on God's Highway, God has at different times shown His love for man by pointing out the way man should go. God has told him exactly how to keep the road, avoiding detours and crossroads and blind alleys.

The first ten guideposts on the Highway of Life, which is God's way, are the Ten Commandments, which God gave to Moses on Mount Sinai.

The Jews in Egypt. The Jews were in Egypt and suffered much under Pharaoh, the King of Egypt. He would not let them go to their own land. Ten plagues were sent on Egypt, and Pharaoh allowed the Jews to leave Egypt, and Moses led them from the land of bondage. In the third month after the departure of the Jews out of the land of Egypt, they reached Mount Sinai.

Moses on Mount Sinai. Moses went up into the mountain and heard God.

And Moses went up to God: and the Lord called unto him from the mountain, and said: Thus shalt thou say to the house of Jacob, and tell the children of Israel:

You have seen what I have done to the Egyptians, how I have carried you upon the wings of eagles, and have taken you to Myself.

The Commandments of God

I. I am the Lord thy God, who brought thee out of the land of Egypt, out of the house of bondage. Thou shalt not have strange gods before me. Thou shalt not make to thyself a graven thing, nor the likeness of any thing that is in heaven above, or in the earth beneath, nor of those things that are in the waters under the earth. Thou shalt not adore them, nor serve them.

II. Thou shalt not take the name of the Lord thy God in vain.

III. Remember that thou keep holy the Sabbath day.

IV. Honor thy father and thy mother.

V. Thou shalt not kill.

VI. Thou shalt not commit adultery.

VII. Thou shalt not steal.

VIII. Thou shalt not bear false witness against thy neighbor.

IX. Thou shalt not covet thy neighbor's wife.

X. Thou shalt not covet thy neighbor's goods.

If therefore you will hear My voice, and keep My covenant, you shall be My peculiar possession above all people; for all the earth is Mine.

And you shall be to Me a priestly kingdom, and a holy nation. These are the words thou shalt speak to the children of Israel.

Moses came, and calling together the elders of the people, he declared all the words which the Lord had commanded.

And all the people answered together: All that the Lord hath spoken, we will do (Exod. xix. 3–8).

The Ten Commandments. And when Moses went up into the mountain the third day, this is what the Lord God said:

I am the Lord thy God, who brought thee out of the land of Egypt, out of the house of bondage.

Thou shalt not have strange gods before Me.

Thou shalt not make thyself a graven thing, nor the likeness of anything that is in heaven above, or in the earth beneath, nor of those things that are in the waters under the earth.

Thou shalt not adore them, nor serve them: I am the Lord thy God, mighty, jealous, visiting the iniquity of the fathers upon the children, unto the third and fourth generation of them that hate Me:

And showing mercy unto thousands of them that love Me and keep My commandments.

Thou shalt not take the name of the Lord thy God in vain: for the Lord will not hold him guiltless that shall take the name of the Lord his God in vain.

Remember that thou keep holy the Sabbath day.

Six days shalt thou labor, and shalt do all thy works.

But on the seventh day is the Sabbath of the Lord thy God: thou shalt do no work on it, thou nor thy son, nor thy daughter, nor thy manservant, nor thy maidservant, nor thy beast, nor the stranger that is within thy gates.

For in six days the Lord made heaven and earth, and the sea, and all things that are in them, and rested on the seventh day: therefore the Lord blessed the seventh day, and sanctified it.

Honor thy father and thy mother, that thou mayest be long lived upon the land which the Lord thy God will give thee.

Thou shalt not kill.

Thou shalt not commit adultery.

Thou shalt not steal.

Thou shalt not bear false witness against thy neighbor.

Thou shalt not covet thy neighbor's house: neither shalt thou desire his wife, nor his servant, nor his handmaid, nor his ox, nor his ass, nor anything that is his.

The Commandments of Love

"And thou shalt love the Lord thy God, with thy whole heart, and with thy whole soul, and with thy whole mind, and with thy whole strength. This is the first commandment. And the second is like to it: Thou shalt love thy neighbor as thyself." *Mark XII, 30-31.*

And all the people saw the voices and the flames, and the sound of the trumpet, and the mount smoking: and being terrified and struck with fear, they stood afar off (Exod. xx. 2-18).

How to Love God. And Moses' words to his people should be borne in the mind and in the heart of all people, always, and should be remembered by you and me:

Hear, O Israel, and observe to do the things which the Lord hath commanded thee, that it may be well with thee, and thou mayest be greatly multiplied, as the Lord the God of thy fathers hath promised thee a land flowing with milk and honey.

Hear, O Israel, the Lord our God is one Lord.

Thou shalt love the Lord thy God with thy whole heart, and with thy whole soul, and with thy whole strength.

And these words which I command thee this day, shall be in thy heart:

And thou shalt tell them to thy children and thou shalt meditate upon them sitting in thy house, and walking on thy journey, sleeping and rising.

And thou shalt bind them as a sign on thy hand, and they shall be and shall move between thy eyes.

And thou shalt write them in the entry, and on the doors of thy house (Deut. vi. 3-9).

Ordinances of the Lord. On the mountain the Lord gave Moses a great many laws for the Jews to keep. Some of them had to do with the sacrifices expected of the Jews, their ceremonials, and manners, others related to the matter in the Ten Commandments. In relation to the commandments, some of these more detailed instructions will be very interesting.

And the people stood afar off. But Moses went to the dark cloud wherein God was (Exod. xx. 21).

He that striketh a man with a will to kill him, shall be put to death (Exod. xxi. 12).

He that striketh his father or mother, shall be put to death (Exod. xxi. 15).

He that curseth his father or mother, shall die the death (Exod. xxi. 17).

An Eye for an Eye. It will be noted how severe the punishments are and how often the penalty is death. One notes, too, the spirit which seems to underlie so much of this law, which Christ later changed:

Eye for eye, tooth for tooth, hand for hand, foot for foot. Burning for burning, wound for wound, stripe for stripe (Exod. xxi. 24–25).

Sealing the Covenant with Blood. In accordance with the sacrifice of the Old Law which has been described in your Bible History and which will be taken up later in this book, the agreement or covenant with God that the Jews would keep the commandment of God and obey His laws was sealed with the blood of animals. Here is the detail as it is given in the Book of Exodus.

And He said to Moses: Come up to the Lord, thou, and Aaron, Hadab, and Abiu, and seventy of the ancients of Israel, and you shall adore afar off.
And Moses alone shall come up to the Lord, but they shall not come nigh: neither shall the people come up with him.
So Moses came and told the people all the words of the Lord, and all the judgments: and all the people answered with one voice: We will do all the words of the Lord, which He hath spoken.
And Moses wrote all the words of the Lord: and rising in the morning he built an altar at the foot of the mount, and twelve titles according to the twelve tribes of Israel.
And he sent young men of the children of Israel, and they offered holocausts, and sacrificed pacific victims of calves to the Lord.
Then Moses took half of the blood and put it into bowls: and the rest he poured upon the altar.
And taking the book of the covenant, he read it in the hearing of the people: and they said: All things that the Lord hath spoken we will do, we will be obedient.

And he took the blood and sprinkled it upon the people, and he said: This is the blood of the covenant which the Lord hath made with you concerning all these words (Exod. xxiv. 1–8).

This was what we have come to call the Old Testament or Covenant ratified with the blood of animals. We shall see what the New Testament is and how it, too, was sealed with blood.

The Importance of the Commandments. The importance of the commandments as a means of pleasing God and being saved is pointed out unmistakably in the story of Christ and the rich man.

If thou wilt enter into life [eternal life] keep the commandments, says Christ.

The story is simple and the lesson it has to teach is clear as it is given to you in Christ's words:

And behold one came and said to Him: Good master, what good shall I do that I may have life everlasting?

Who said to him: Why askest thou Me concerning good? One is good, God. But if thou wilt enter into life, keep the commandments.

He said to Him: Which? And Jesus said: Thou shalt do no murder, thou shalt not commit adultery, thou shalt not steal, thou shalt not bear false witness.

Honor thy father and thy mother: and, thou shalt love thy neighbor as thyself.

The young man saith to Him: All these have I kept from my youth, what is yet wanting to me?

Jesus saith to him: If thou wilt be perfect, go sell what thou hast, and give to the poor, and thou shalt have treasure in heaven: and come follow Me.

And when the young man heard this word, he went away sad: for he had great possessions.

Then Jesus said to His disciples: Amen, I say to you, that a rich man shall hardly enter into the kingdom of heaven (Matt. xix. 16–23).

What would we do in that case? Would we go away sad, or should we instantly do as Jesus directed? Do we care more for our possessions or riches than we do for God? What little sacrifice did we make for God this month?

The Greatest Commandment. An excellent general view of the law of God is contained in Christ's answer to the question of the doctor of law, who himself was supposed to know such things.

. . . A doctor of the law asked Him, tempting Him: Master, which is the great commandment in the law? Jesus said to him: Thou shalt love the Lord thy God with thy whole heart, and with thy whole soul, and with thy whole mind.
This is the greatest and the first commandment.
And the second is like this: Thou shalt love thy neighbor as thyself.
On these two commandments dependeth the whole law and the prophets (Matt. xxii. 35–40).

If you will take your Bible and look at (1) Deuteronomy, Chapter vi, Verse 5, (2) Leviticus, Chapter xix, Verse 18, you will find that Christ was quoting the words of the Old Testament.

The Two Tables of Stone. When Moses came down from the mountain, Mount Sinai, he brought two tables of stone, the tables of the covenant, written with the finger of God, and containing the word which God had spoken "in the Mount from the midst of fire." On one of these stones were the first three commandments, on the other were the remaining commandments. The first contained the commandments of the love of God, and the second the commandments of the love of the neighbor.

Numbering the Commandments. Sometimes we hear the fourth commandment called the fifth, the second, the third, and the like, and we may have wondered how such confusion comes about. There is, too, a famous picture representing the two tables of stone of Moses that has four Roman numerals on one, and the remaining six on the other. In either case, however, the contents are the same.

This confusion is due to the fact that Catholics in numbering the commandments follow the original Hebrew text, and the practice of the early Church. Some Protestants divide the first commandment in two parts; and combine the ninth and tenth into one.

THE COMMANDMENTS OF GOD

Catholic	Other
The First Commandment	is divided into the First Commandment and the Second Commandment
The Second Commandment	is called the Third Commandment
The Third Commandment	is called the Fourth Commandment
The Fourth Commandment	is called the Fifth Commandment
The Fifth Commandment	is called the Sixth Commandment
The Sixth Commandment	is called the Seventh Commandment
The Seventh Commandment	is called the Eighth Commandment
The Eighth Commandment	is called the Ninth Commandment
The Ninth and Tenth Commandments	are included in the Tenth Commandment

Even if it had not been the way it is, it would seem better to keep the ninth and tenth commandments separate, for the ninth forbids sins against purity, and so is very like to the sixth commandment, and the tenth forbids sins against justice and is more closely joined to the seventh commandment. In our later discussion, because of this fact, we shall study the sixth commandment along with the ninth and the seventh with the tenth.

Division into Ten Commandments by God. The division into ten commandments is contained in the Bible itself. In Exodus we read, "and He wrote upon the table the ten words of the covenant" (xxxiv. 28). In Deuteronomy we find these words: "And He showed you His covenant which He commanded you to do, and the ten words that He wrote in two tables of stone" (iv. 13).

Questions from the Catechism

Q. What must we do to save our souls?
A. **To save our souls we must worship God by faith, hope, and charity; that is, we must believe in Him, hope in Him, and love Him with all our heart.**

Q. Which are the commandments that contain the whole law of God?
A. The commandments which contain the whole law of God are these two: First, Thou shalt love the Lord thy God with thy whole heart, with thy whole soul, with thy whole strength, and with thy whole mind; second, Thou shalt love thy neighbor as thyself.

Q. Why do these two commandments of the love of God and of our neighbor contain the whole law of God?
A. These two commandments of the love of God and of our neighbor contain the whole law of God because all the other commandments are given either to help us to keep these two, or to direct us how to shun what is opposed to them.

Q. Which are the commandments of God?
A. The commandments of God are these ten:
1. I am the Lord thy God, who brought thee out of the land of Egypt, out of the house of bondage. Thou shalt not have strange gods before Me. Thou shalt not make to thyself a graven thing, nor the likeness of anything that is in heaven above, or in the earth beneath, nor of those things that are in the waters under the earth. Thou shalt not adore them, nor serve them.
2. Thou shalt not take the name of the Lord thy God in vain.
3. Remember thou keep holy the Sabbath day.
4. Honor thy father and thy mother.
5. Thou shalt not kill.
6. Thou shalt not commit adultery.
7. Thou shalt not steal.
8. Thou shalt not bear false witness against thy neighbor.
9. Thou shalt not covet thy neighbor's wife.
10. Thou shalt not covet thy neighbor's goods.

Q. Who gave the Ten Commandments?
A. God Himself gave the Ten Commandments to Moses on Mount Sinai, and Christ our Lord confirmed them.

Questions for the Pupil

1. What little sacrifice did you make for God today? this week? this month?
2. What commandment did God give Adam?
3. What was the result of Adam's disobedience?
4. What commandments did God give for all men?
5. What may be the result of your disobedience of these commandments?

THE COMMANDMENTS OF GOD 37

6. Discuss the statement, "I won't count it this time."
7. Explain the meaning of the phrase, "An eye for an eye."
8. Explain the meaning of the words: (1) "The way that leadeth to destruction," and (2) "the way that leadeth to life."
9. What is meant by "If thou wilt enter into life, keep the commandments"?

Quotations from the Bible

For each of the following quotations:
a) Identify the speaker.
b) State the conditions under which the statement was made.
c) Give the meaning.
d) Tell its significance.

"Not everyone that saith to Me, Lord, Lord, shall enter into the kingdom of heaven; but he that doth the will of My Father who is in heaven, he shall enter into the kingdom of heaven" (Matt. vii. 21).

"I am the Lord thy God, mighty, jealous, visiting the iniquity of the fathers upon the children, unto the third and fourth generation of them that hate Me: And showing mercy unto thousands to them that love Me, and keep My commandments" (Exod. xx. 5–6).

"Thou shalt love the Lord thy God with thy whole heart, and with thy whole soul, and with thy whole strength" (Deut. vi. 5).

"Thou shalt not steal" (Exod. xx. 15).

"Honor thy father and thy mother, that thou mayest be longlived upon the land which the Lord thy God will give thee" (Exod. xx. 12).

"All the law is fulfilled in one word: Thou shalt love thy neighbor as thyself" (Gal. v. 14).

"Master, which is the great commandment in the law? Jesus said to him: 'Thou shalt love the Lord thy God with thy whole heart, and with thy whole soul, and with thy whole mind.' This is the greatest and the first commandment. And the second is like to this: 'Thou shalt love thy neighbor, as thyself.' On these two commandments dependeth the whole law and the prophets" (Matt. xxii. 36–40).

Suggestive Assignments

1. Give a full account from the early books of the Old Testament of Moses on Mount Sinai.
2. Show that the commandments are all summed up in the two commandments of the love of God and the love of neighbor.
3. What do the words "Highway to God" suggest to you? Write an allegory of human life using this as a basis. Perhaps your teacher will read you parts of an old morality play called "Everyman."

Chapter VI
THE FIRST COMMANDMENT OF GOD

How to Love God. It was true of the Jews of old as it is with all of us today, that on a man's journey through life he often forgets or disregards his Creator. One of the surest aids to help man on the road to life is the statement of Moses to the people of Israel:

Thou shalt love the Lord thy God with thy whole heart, with thy whole soul, and with thy whole strength.

If we keep in mind that it is from Him that we come and that it is to Him that we go, we are not likely to get off the direct path.

What the First Three Commandments Command. To remind us of God as the Guide of our life is the purpose of the first three commandments. These commandments more particularly require:

1. That we shall worship God only.
2. That we shall worship no one else.
3. That we shall not worship nor adore nor serve any graven image nor anything whether in the heavens above, or on the earth below, or in the waters on the earth.
4. That we shall not take the name of God in vain.
5. That we shall always remember Him, but particularly by keeping holy the Sabbath day.

The Lord is My Shepherd. We can in many ways in our daily life keep before our minds the Lord God. As we are favored in life we must remember that the Lord God is the Giver of all good gifts. As we have time during the day we might call to mind a little prayer or a psalm such as the twenty-second Psalm:

The Lord ruleth me: and I shall want nothing. He hath set me in a place of pasture.

He hath brought me up, on the water of refreshment: he hath converted my soul.

He hath led me on the paths of justice, for His own Name's sake.

For though I should walk in the midst of the shadow of death, I will fear no evils, for Thou art with me.

Thy rod and thy staff, they have comforted me.

Thou hast prepared a table before me, against them that afflict me.

Thou hast anointed my head with oil; and my chalice which inebriateth me, how goodly is it!

And Thy mercy will follow me all the days of my life.

And that I may dwell in the house of the Lord unto length of days.

As we look about us everywhere and see the signs of God's creation we shall remember that we, too, are His creatures. He is *my* Shepherd. Whenever we can, we should gladly profess our belief in and love of God. We must never fail to do what God commands us because we see others breaking the commandments.

Love of Our Fellow Man and of All Creatures. One of the best ways to show our sincere love of God every day is to show love for people generally, and even for the birds and beasts. You will often see quoted a passage from Coleridge's *The Ancient Mariner,* which you should learn:

> He prayeth well who loveth well,
> Both man, and bird, and beast.
>
> He prayeth best who loveth best,
> All things both great and small,
> For the dear Lord, Who loveth us,
> He made and loveth all.

When this love of neighbor and of all God's creatures is practiced for the love of God, you are keeping the First Commandment.

Even when life is not pleasant, and when things seem hard, you must show in these times, too, a faith and hope in God. Prayer will help you at such times. No Christian ever loses hope, because many of these unpleasant things pass soon, and others that are pleasant last longer and will give strength and hope. In addition to faith and hope we will have a very real love of God. Love God always.

To Worship God Alone. It follows from what we have just learned that God alone deserves your worship; that no human being, or no thing, nor any creature should ever in thought or word or deed receive the worship which is due God alone. Hence, in this First Commandment there is the statement: "Thou shalt not have strange gods before Me." This was particularly necessary to state to the Hebrew people. Though they kept the worship of the one true God, they often fell into false worship, even to the worship of a golden calf.

And the people seeing that Moses delayed to come down from the mount, gathering together against Aaron, said: Arise, make us gods, that may go before us: for as to this Moses, the man that brought us out of the land of Egypt, we know not what has befallen him.

And Aaron said to them: Take the golden earrings from the ears of your wives, and your sons and daughters, and bring them to me.

And the people did what he had commanded, bringing the earrings to Aaron.

And when he had received them, he fashioned them by founders' work, and made of them a molten calf. And they said: These are thy gods, O Israel, that have brought thee out of the land of Egypt.

And when Aaron saw this, he built an altar before it, and made proclamation by a crier's voice, saying: Tomorrow is the solemnity of the Lord.

And rising in the morning, they offered holocausts, and peace victims, and the people sat down to eat, and drink, and they rose up to play.

And the Lord spoke to Moses, saying: Go, get thee down: thy people, which thou hast brought out of the land of Egypt, have sinned.

They have quickly strayed from the way which thou didst shew them: and they have made to themselves a molten calf, and have adored it, and sacrificing victims to it, have said: These are thy gods, O Israel, that have brought thee out of the land of Egypt.

And when he came nigh to the camp, he saw the calf, and the dances: and being very angry, he threw the tables out of his hand, and broke them at the foot of the mount:

And laying hold of the calf which they had made, he burnt it, and beat it to powder, which he strewed into water, and gave thereof to the children of Israel to drink (Exod. xxxii).

Worship of Creatures — Evil. We might not be so foolish as to worship a golden calf as these Hebrews did. But we see around us men and women who have *forgotten* or given up God for money, position, or social standing. This is their "golden calf." We are in danger of giving to creatures or things the honor which belongs to God alone; we attribute to these same creatures a perfection which belongs to God alone. And generally we worship creatures or forms of man-made religion which is a false worship. Creatures may be properly used for our salvation, but we must always remember they are merely creatures. They are not God.

Fortune Tellers, Spiritualists, Dreams. We must be very careful ourselves not to give worship or even honor or homage to things which do not deserve them, even though they may be associated with religion. We should be careful, too, to see that we do not thoughtlessly or willfully violate this commandment by going to fortune tellers who cannot know the future, or believing in spiritualism, or having faith in charms or signs, or even in dreams. From human beings, as such, the future of one's individual life is hidden. In the early part of the Bible we find these practices forbidden:

Neither let there be found among you any one that shall expiate his son or daughter, making them pass through the fire: or that consulteth soothsayers, or observeth dreams and omens, neither let there be any wizard.

Nor charmer, nor any one that consulteth pythonic spirits, nor fortune tellers, nor that seeketh the truth from the dead.

For the Lord abhorreth all these things, and for these abominations He will destroy them at thy coming (Deut. xviii. 10–12).

Vain Observance. There are a number of things which boys and girls hear or do that in the beginning may be innocent enough because they are done thoughtlessly which when continued in, are violations of the First Commandment. We hear boys say:

I found a horseshoe and I'll have good luck.
I saw a black cat this morning. I'll have bad luck.
She broke a mirror yesterday. She'll have seven years' bad luck.
Oh, there are thirteen at table. One of us is going to die suddenly or other misfortunes will come upon us.

Much like this are the superstitions about Friday, especially Friday the thirteenth. Some people say that to start something on Friday is a sign of bad luck, and Friday falling on the thirteenth is sure to bring bad luck to everyone.

There is no connection whatever between these events and what is supposed to follow from them. These things couldn't under any circumstances cause such results good or bad as are predicted. Some very simple-minded people imagine that in some mysterious way the devil has a connection with these events. That is absurd, and that is the worst form of these superstitions or as they are called, *vain* observances. St. Chrysostom's words apply not only to those things that are listed, but to such things in general:

A day is not lucky or unlucky of its own nature (for one day differs not from another), but it becomes such by our industry, or our sloth; if you employ it in virtue, it will be a lucky day, and merit a reward from God; if you spend it in wickedness, it will be an unlucky day, and deserves His anger and punishment.

The important thing is what we do; these things have no meaning in themselves. We are in God's hands, and we are under His Providence. Our free will gives us the chance to serve Him.

Faith, Hope, and Love of God. We must have faith in God. We must hope in Him. We must love Him. We show our reliance on God, too, by lifting up our souls to Him in prayer, and offering as the Jews did of old, a sacrifice. This last you do in your regular attendance at Church. In what service?

David's Attitude Toward God. Open the Book of Psalms almost anywhere and see what faith and hope and trust in God is.

In the twenty-third Psalm we read:

Who shall ascend into the mountain of the Lord: or who shall stand in His holy place?

The innocent in hands and clean of heart, who hath not taken his soul in vain, nor sworn deceitfully to his neighbor.

He shall receive a blessing from the Lord and mercy from God his Savior.

In the twenty-fourth Psalm we read:

To thee, O Lord, have I lifted up my soul. In Thee, O my God, I put my trust; let me not be ashamed.

Let all them be confounded that act unjust things without cause.

Shew, O Lord, Thy ways to me, and teach me Thy paths.

Direct me in Thy truth, and teach me; for Thou art God my Savior: and on Thee have I waited all the day long.

Remember, O Lord, Thy bowels of compassion; and Thy mercies, that are from the beginning of the world.

The sins of my youth and my ignorances do not remember.

According to Thy mercy remember Thou me: for Thy goodness' sake, O Lord.

Keep Thou my soul, and deliver me: I shall not be ashamed, for I have hoped in Thee.

In the twenty-fifth Psalm we read:

Judge me, O Lord, for I have walked in my innocence: and I have put my trust in the Lord, and shall not be weakened.

Prove me, O Lord, and try me; burn my reins and my heart.

I will wash my hands among the innocent; and will compass Thy altar, O Lord:

That I may hear the voice of Thy praise: and tell of all Thy wondrous works.

I have loved, O Lord, the beauty of Thy house; and the place where Thy glory dwelleth.

My foot hath stood in the direct way: in the churches I will bless Thee, O Lord.

In the twenty-sixth Psalm we read:

The Lord is my light and my salvation, whom shall I fear? The Lord is the protector of my life: of whom shall I be afraid?

One thing I have asked of the Lord, this will I seek after; that I may dwell in the house of the Lord all the days of my life.

That I may see the delight of the Lord, and may visit His temple.

I will sing, and recite a psalm to the Lord.

Hear, O Lord, my voice, with which I have cried to Thee: have mercy on me and hear me.

My heart hath said to Thee: My face hath sought Thee: Thy face, O Lord, will I still seek.

Be Thou my helper, forsake me not; do not Thou despise me, O God my Savior.

In the twenty-seventh Psalm we read:

The Lord is my helper and my protector: in Him hath my heart confided, and I have been helped.

And my flesh hath flourished again, and with my will I will give praise to Him.

The Lord is the strength of His people, and the protector of the salvation of His anointed.

Save, O Lord, Thy people, and bless Thy inheritance: and rule them and exalt them forever.

Our Faith in God. Let us pray to God in the same spirit and with the same fervor. Let us make use of every opportunity to learn about God (1) in His creation, (2) in our attendance at Church, (3) in reading good religious books, (4) in talking to pious men, (5) in studying this and other books on religion, (6) in reading the Bible, and (7) learning what God has taught through the teachings of the Church. Of course this means that we will avoid all false teaching, and avoid those who do not believe in God or what God has taught, whom we call heretics or infidels. We will avoid books, plays, or movies that may teach false doctrine or bad morals. We will, too, express publicly our faith in God, and acknowledge His Providence by word or deed whenever honor to God, our neighbor's good, or our own requires it.

We can sin against this commandment by not trying to know what God has taught, by refusing to believe all that God has taught, and by neglecting to profess our belief in what God has taught. We must not by our silence in our "gang," at our club, on the playground, or in a game permit dishonor or disrespect to God, when a word or act could stop it, or would prevent its happening again. Let us daily by brief quotations from the Psalms or from the prayers of Holy Mass make reparation for such disrespect or dishonor.

Presumption and Despair. We must all try to keep God's commandments, and to use every means we can for our salvation; i.e., to stay on God's Highway. To expect rashly to gain salvation and to neglect or refuse the means of salvation is presumption. "He that loves the danger shall perish in it." And that is the certain end of the presumptuous man. On the other hand, to distrust God by giving up hope of salvation is the sin of despair. The words of the prophet Isaiah should be recalled to man:

If your sins be as scarlet, they shall be made as white as snow.

Each of us might write out our own attitude. It might run like this: "I will trust and hope in the Lord. I will avoid every occasion that might lead me to do something that would be displeasing or disrespectful to God. I will make use of every chance to do Him honor and respect, to praise Him, to show my love for Him. I will never rashly (i.e., presumptuously) fail to use every means to keep on God's Highway. I know that I must be always on guard in this life, and presumption is too dangerous and too conceited an attitude to take. I will not give up in despair. I shall always hope in His mercy. To whom else can I look?"

All Religions Not the Same. It also follows from the First Commandment that we should not confuse the worship of the one true God with any compromise or any merely human institution. All religions cannot have the same amount of truth. There must be a true religion. We must be careful not to seem to give any approval to other religions. To attend a wedding or a funeral service in another church just to show our personal interest or regard is permissible but we must not join in their prayers. To attend other religious services is not permissible. To pick this doctrine, and refuse that, and not to take the whole teaching of God, which we know to be His teaching is to set up oneself against God.

Avoiding Temptation. In our everyday life in anger or in temper or without thought, we may do a number of things that are against this Commandment and show the lack of a live faith and hope in God. When other boys and girls do something we know to be wrong, we may be tempted to fall in with them. When they do not speak the way they should about God or the Church, or religious things, they may think that we approve of it, because we are afraid to speak out against them. We should in a quiet way whenever there is real necessity, profess our faith in God, and show our displeasure with what is wrong.

Divine Worship to God Only. To God alone belongs divine honor and worship. We beg pardon for our sins from God only. We ask grace from God only. We offer the Sacrifice of the Mass to God only. We may pay honor and respect to those great souls who love God and gave their lives whole-heartedly in His service. They are the chosen friends of God whom we call, on earth, saints. We can honor them ordinarily by imitating their virtues, learning about their lives, by keeping their feast days. This is especially true of Mary, the Mother of Christ.

Sacrilege. We should be respectful and reverent toward consecrated persons, such as bishops or priests (or Sisters), toward consecrated places such as churches or cemeteries, and toward consecrated things such as chalices used in the Mass, or other sacred vessels or relics. Any malicious striking or injury to a consecrated person is a sacrilege. The pollution by bloodshed, the desecration by theft or otherwise, the using for secular purposes of a consecrated place is a sacrilege. So is the seizure, unworthy use, or disrespect for consecrated things, a sacrilege. These are all forbidden by the First Commandment.

Simony. A terrible sin, too, is the buying or selling of spiritual things, or the performing of spiritual services for money. This is called *simony*. If you will turn to the Acts of the Apostles (viii. 18), and read about Simon Magus, you will find out how the word *simony* came to be used for this form of sacrilege. A voluntary offering to priests when they perform services is lawful and is a means of fulfilling the Fifth Commandment of the Church which we shall speak of later.

The Worship of God. We should in every practical way show our belief in God, and pay homage of worship to Him, and Him only, as the Ruler of the universe, our Creator, and the Lord of heaven and of earth. On every occasion we will express this firm belief of ours. Naturally we would never express any denial of it, even in jest. We should make use of every chance to learn all we can about God, and our duties toward Him. When we read books on religion and morality we will naturally read only those that are good. We will take part in our Church services whenever we can, to show our belief and our love of God and of our desire to worship Him.

Little Prayers of the Love of God. We will memorize little prayers and quotations about the mercy, love, and power of God, and will call them to mind during the day if only for a minute. We will realize that we depend on God, and will pray

THE FIRST COMMANDMENT

to Him for strength, for hope, for faith. We will pray to Him also so we will not despair at any time during our life, and particularly during periods of sickness or trial. We will never trust to ourselves alone to win over the problems of life, but always ask for God's aid.

He that dwelleth in the aid of the Most High shall abide under the protection of God (see Ps. xc. 1).

And so we may end this chapter by asking the question, "If God be for us, who can be against us?"

Questions from the Catechism

Q. What is the First Commandment?
A. **The First Commandment is: I am the Lord thy God; thou shalt not have strange gods before Me.**

Q. How does the First Commandment help us to keep the great commandment of the love of God?
A. **The First Commandment helps us to keep the great commandment of the love of God because it commands us to adore God alone.**

Q. How do we adore God?
A. **We adore God by faith, hope, and charity, by prayer and sacrifice.**

Q. How may the First Commandment be broken?
A. **The First Commandment may be broken by giving to a creature the honor which belongs to God alone; by false worship; and by attributing to a creature a perfection which belongs to God alone.**

Q. Do those who make use of spells and charms, or who believe in dreams, in mediums, spiritists, fortune tellers, and the like, sin against the First Commandment?
A. **Those who make use of spells and charms, or who believe in dreams, in mediums, spiritists, fortune tellers, and the like, sin against the First Commandment, because they attribute to creatures perfections which belong to God alone.**

Q. Are sins against faith, hope, and charity, also sins against the First Commandment?
A. **Sins against faith, hope, and charity are also sins against the First Commandment.**

Q. How does a person sin against faith?
A. **A person sins against faith, first, by not trying to know what God has taught; second, by refusing to believe all that God has taught; third, by neglecting to profess his belief in what God has taught.**

Q. How do we fail to try to know what God has taught?
A. **We fail to try to know what God has taught by neglecting to learn the Christian doctrine.**

Q. Who are they who do not believe all that God has taught?
A. **They who do not believe all that God has taught are the heretics and infidels.**

Q. Which are the sins against hope?
A. **The sins against hope are presumption and despair.**

Q. What is presumption?
A. **Presumption is a rash expectation of salvation without making proper use of the necessary means to obtain it.**

Q. What is despair?
A. **Despair is the loss of hope in God's mercy.**

Q. How do we sin against the love of God?
A. **We sin against the love of God by all sin, but particularly by mortal sin.**

Problem Questions

1. You find a poor man alone in a hut. He is very ill and you advise him to make his peace with God. He tells you that his sins are too great to be forgiven. What sin does he commit by entertaining such thoughts? What would you tell him? Could you give him an example of great sinners who were forgiven by God because they repented sincerely?

2. Your parents attend a funeral service at a Protestant church and wish you to go along. May Catholics attend such services? Would they be allowed to attend any Protestant services? Catholics are eager to have Protestants come to their church; why should they not return the courtesy?

3. A young man is leading a very sinful life. He realizes that he should change his ways and make his peace with God, but he always tells himself that there will be time enough tomorrow. What sin does he commit?

4. Mary is in serious trouble and becomes discouraged. She wishes that she would die. May she entertain such a wish? May people ever wish to die? Under what circumstances?

5. Henry and George are walking along the street when they suddenly meet a gang of rough boys. The boys stop them and ask them whether

THE FIRST COMMANDMENT

they are Catholics. Must the two tell them? What is the reason for your answer?

6. Sue and Jane go to the fortune teller "just for fun!" The fortune teller tells Sue something which really comes to pass shortly afterwards. Sue asks you what you think about it. What would you tell her?

7. Jack never went to any other but a good Catholic school. He seemed to be a good boy, but shortly after he went to work he lost his faith. What, do you think, might have been the cause?

8. Someone sends you a chain prayer and tells you that you will be visited by some terrible calamity if you do not say it and help to circulate it. What should you do about it? What sin do you commit by believing in such things? Mention other superstitions you know about.

9. You have a rosary that was blessed by the Holy Father. It is valued at 50 cents, but a friend offers you $5 on account of the blessings it bears. May you accept the money for the rosary? May you accept any money? May you give it to your friend as a gift?

10. Louis wears a four-leaved clover for good luck. You laugh at him, but he says you are just as bad, for you wear a medal and believe it is going to keep away all harm. How will you explain the difference?

11. A thief steals some money from church. Later he repents. In confessing his thefts, must he make any distinction between what he took from church and what he stole elsewhere? Suppose the money he took from church amounted to very little? What do we call such a sin? What other sins are called sacrileges?

12. John's mother advises him not to go with certain companions because they are harmful to him. He tells her not to worry, for he knows how to take care of himself and will not follow their bad example. Is John right?

Quotations from the Bible

For each of the following quotations:
a) Identify the speaker.
b) State the conditions under which the statement was made.
c) Give the meaning.
d) Tell its significance.

"Thou shalt not have strange Gods before Me."

"I have loved, O Lord, the beauty of Thy house; and the place where Thy glory dwelleth" (Ps. xxv. 8).

"If your sins be as scarlet they shall be made white as snow" (Isa. i. 18).

Chapter VII
THE SECOND COMMANDMENT OF GOD

The Second Commandment. The second signpost on the road which man travels from life to death, is, *Thou shalt not take the name of the Lord, thy God, in vain.*

This is the second of the Ten Commandments given to Moses on Mount Sinai. It concerns itself, as does the First Commandment, with our relation to God. It forbids us to use His name in a way that would dishonor it. Of course the best way to keep this commandment is to have a strong love of God, to keep in mind, as in the First Commandment, that He is our Creator, and that it is from Him that we came and to Him that we go. Filling our minds with the praise of God is the surest way to avoid taking His name in vain. "Blessed be God. Blessed be His holy name," should ever be on our lips. We should know well the Divine Praises said after Benediction of the Blessed Sacrament, and call them to mind if we are ever tempted to break the Second Commandment or if we hear people speak about God and religion in an irreverent way.

The Divine Praises are:
- *a)* Blessed be God.
- *b)* Blessed be His holy Name.
- *c)* Blessed be Jesus Christ, true God and true man.
- *d)* Blessed be the Name of Jesus.
- *e)* Blessed be His most Sacred Heart.
- *f)* Blessed be Jesus in the most holy Sacrament of the Altar.
- *g)* Blessed be the great Mother of God, Mary most holy.
- *h)* Blessed be her holy and immaculate conception.
- *i)* Blessed be the name of Mary, virgin and mother.
- *j)* Blessed be St. Joseph, her most chaste spouse.
- *k)* Blessed be God in His angels and in His saints.

THE SECOND COMMANDMENT 51

Punishment. And with this Second Commandment goes a threat, very real even though the exact nature of the punishment is not told. "For the Lord will not hold him guiltless that shall take the name of the Lord his God in vain" (Exod. xx. 7). This is the only commandment with a threat.

Irreverence. People show irreverence in many ways. They call on God's name in every other sentence without cause, without serious intention, and because they have thoughtlessly acquired the habit. Worse than this, however, is the calling of God's name in anger or in jest. We call such needless reference to God irreverence.

* Blasphemy. Some people with no love of God, with no respect for their Creator, are sometimes heard to laugh at God, religion, and the Church, and to use contemptuous and abusive language against God and holy persons and holy things. Such language, and even when not expressed, such thoughts, are called blasphemy. Any thought, word, desire, or act insulting to God is a blasphemy. This is a great violation of the Second Commandment. So great is it that in the Old Testament blasphemy was punished by death:

He that blasphemeth the name of the Lord, dying let him die: All the multitude shall stone him (Levit. xxiv. 16).

Vows. We often promise ourselves or make resolutions to amend our lives — to do better. We even think we shall do this or that because of some good fortune we have had, or because of a sermon that we heard, or a mission that we attended. We sometimes carry them out, and sometimes, too often, we do not have the *stick-to-it-iveness* to carry out these intentions or resolutions. Sometimes, more deeply impressed by our dependence on God we willingly promise to do something for His honor and glory that is pleasing to Him. The Old Testament tells us God accepted such promises or, as we shall now call them, vows. To voluntarily make a vow to God (and vows can be made only to God), and not to keep it, would be, as it were, mocking God, and breaking the Second Commandment. But to be a valid vow:

1. It must have been voluntarily and deliberately made by the person.

2. It must have been pleasing to God — not displeasing, unjust, or sinful.

3. It must have been possible for the person to do it.

Keeping Vows. With these conditions present, the failure to carry out the vow once made is a sin, grievous or slight according to the nature of the vow and the intention we had in making it. We should not make vows hastily or too readily and it would be well to consult our confessor before making any vow. We might keep in mind the statement God made in the Book of Deuteronomy:

> When thou hast made a vow to the Lord thy God, thou shalt not delay to pay it: because the Lord thy God will require it. And if thou delay, it shall be imputed to thee for a sin.
>
> If thou wilt not promise, thou shalt be without sin (Deut. xxiii. 21-22).

Oaths. In courts of law it is the custom for people to swear or take an oath, calling on God to witness the truth of what they say. In such cases it is lawful to take the oath. Needless to say, such calling of God to witness the truth of what we say should not become common, nor should it be done without necessity. It must be clear to anyone that the duty always to tell the truth must be even greater when we especially ask God to witness the truth of what we say. To take a false oath, which is called perjury, is the same as to deny the power and knowledge of God and His justice. It is inspired by a lack of faith in God, or a belief that He can be deceived, or it is done to gain some little earthly good, or to escape some earthly trouble. We willfully call on God, who is Truth itself, to witness our lie. Thus, we deliberately insult God.

Perjury in Courts of Justice. We use oaths in courts of justice because the welfare of society is at stake and we believe that men will tell the truth under oath; i.e., when they call God to witness the truth of what they say. While modern society does not punish false oaths as severely as the Jews did of old, those who make false oaths commit perjury; i.e., call God to witness a statement they know to be a lie, and are severely punished. Any system of courts which does its work well, must depend upon the

THE SECOND COMMANDMENT

oaths being considered seriously. To destroy the binding quality of oaths is to build our courts and systems of justice on a foundation of sand, or on no foundation at all.

Rash and Unnecessary Oaths. A more general consideration of oaths makes it clear under what conditions oaths may be taken. When the truth of a statement needs to be discovered to justify oneself against false charges, or to correct an error in a serious matter, or where a neighbor's life or his property or his good name or his welfare are at stake, an oath is permitted: this in addition to any requirement by lawful authority as in taking some public office, or in the courts. But in general, oaths should not be taken unless they are absolutely necessary. Certainly one should not rashly take oaths on small matters or without full consideration. Rash oaths and unnecessary oaths are violations of the Second Commandment.

False and Unjust Oaths. There may be sins against the Second Commandment on the matter or content of oaths. An oath may deal with either a statement of fact or a promise. Clearly, when we call on God to witness a statement it must be true, or, if we make a promise, we must intend to carry it out. If the person taking an oath knows that what he says is false, or is doubtful, or if he does not intend to carry out the promise, then he violates the Second Commandment by a false oath. If what he takes an oath to do is an evil or an injustice, then the oath is a violation of the Second Commandment because it is unjust. And, of course, such an oath has no binding force because of its evil or unjust character, and an effort to carry it out is another sin. The kind of sin committed in any one of these cases will depend on the character and form of the oath — grievous or venial as the case may be.

There is another way of looking at oaths, and that is from the viewpoint of a famous sentence of Jeremiah (iv. 2): "Thou shalt swear: As the Lord liveth, in truth, and in judgment, and in justice."

Swearing. We seem to be growing careless as a people in reverence and respect for the holy name of God. While the Church is growing in numbers, still there are many who know not God. They are careless, or neglectful, or ignorant. But it is surprising the number of boys and girls and men and women who too often in everything they say must have an oath or a curse. We call these acts of calling on God to witness the truth of our statements swearing. It includes promises, threats, oaths and vows. Swearing seems to be a habit with too many, even in the most unimportant and small matters. So much of this is done without thought and carelessly that when the attention of the offending person is called to it, he is likely to correct his ways. Certainly we should avoid it as if it were the plague. It is, in fact, a moral plague. With the prophet let us rather say "Bless the Lord, O my soul, and never forget all He hath done for thee" (Ps. cii. 2). Let the praise and thanksgiving be our part — and reverence too. "Blessed be the name of the Lord," as Job said.

Cursing. Another form of sin against this commandment that we hear often on the street and sometimes on the school playground, is calling God to do some evil to ourselves or our neighbors. "May God strike you blind." "May you have seven years' hard luck." There are many forms of cursing which we do not include here because they are curses. But we can see, in our hearts, that the calling upon God to do evil to His creatures is a violation of this commandment and shows a woeful condition of the soul of the person cursing, and a very queer idea of God's justice and God's love for His creatures.

Even men with no religion look down upon and condemn cursing and the uttering of profane words. It is bad taste, bad judgment, bad manners, as is indeed every violation of God's law. Profane words very properly go along with cursing.

Let Us Honor the Name of God. Let us call upon the Lord in prayer. Let us respect always the word of God, especially His commandments, meditate upon them, read and hear them as often as possible.

Questions from the Catechism

Q. What is the Second Commandment?

A. **The Second Commandment is: Thou shalt not take the name of the Lord thy God in vain.**

THE SECOND COMMANDMENT

Q. What are we commanded by the Second Commandment?
A. **We are commanded by the Second Commandment to speak with reverence of God and of the saints, and of holy things, and to keep our lawful oaths and vows.**

Q. What is an oath?
A. **An oath is the calling upon God to witness the truth of what we say.**

Q. When may we take an oath?
A. **We may take an oath when it is ordered by lawful authority or required for God's honor or for our own or our neighbor's good.**

Q. What is necessary to make an oath lawful?
A. **To make an oath lawful it is necessary that what we swear to be true, and that there be a sufficient cause for taking an oath.**

Q. What is a vow?
A. **A vow is a deliberate promise made to God to do something that is pleasing to Him.**

Q. Is it a sin not to fulfill our vows?
A. **Not to fulfill our vows is a sin, mortal or venial, according to the nature of the vow and the intention we had in making it.**

Q. What is forbidden by the Second Commandment?
A. **The Second Commandment forbids all false, rash, unjust, and unnecessary oaths, blasphemy, cursing, and profane words.**

Problem Questions

1. During the day, so often, children, you think of your parents, your home, the baseball game. How often do you think of Jesus? Your mother loves you when you say, "Mother, dear," and such loving words sincerely. Wouldn't Jesus love you much, too, if during the day you would often say to Him, "Jesus, Jesus"? How often do you think you could easily do so? Try it this day at every change of lessons.

2. How could you show reverence to the holy name of Jesus? (Bowing my head slightly when it is pronounced, taking off my hat, never using His name vainly.)

3. What do you think of a child who laughs upon hearing another child say the name of God in an angry or irreverential tone? Which child, do you think, has committed the graver sin?

4. You are a young boy. You hear one of the big boys using very bad language and often saying the Holy Names in a shocking way. Would you

let him talk like that, or would you have courage enough to tell him not to speak so? Tell the class what you would really say to him.

5. How would you make good the wrong you have done by using the name of God in anger before a group of children? (Confession and apology publicly given.)

6. The priest has given the order that the next one he hears cursing on the playground will be expelled. You hear a boy who always used bad language when no teacher or priest is near, do so. What would you do or say to him?

7. A boy thinks it is smart to imitate the bad language he hears from grown-up people. He shows off before his friends through cursing. What kind of sin do you think he is committing and how many?

8. Why should such expressions as "Cross my heart, I'm telling the truth," and "Sure as heaven," very seldom be used?

9. What is the best act of reparation to God you make when you hear someone using His name in vain? (Pronounce the name devoutly, make an act of sorrow for him.)

10. How could a group of boys prevent one or more boys from using the Holy Names profanely or from using vulgar expressions on the playground, without telling the teacher on them?

11. A little boy or girl has come to school with the evil habit we are discussing. The parents thought it "cute" when the little one would use these words. How could the children at school help the child to break this habit without offending the parents?

12. How would you act toward a child who is trying to overcome his vicious habit, but who very often does forget himself?

13. Should your father at times say very unbecoming and even sinful words, could you tell him it is wrong and you do not like it? If he gets angry with you for telling him could you show him some other way that you don't want him to talk like that?

14. I know of a certain child who was purposely taught to curse by another person. The parents are much grieved, but again and again the child will forget himself. What do you think of the guilt of the person who is responsible?

15. A little boy has followed the example of his father in cursing. When the mother corrects him, he says: "Daddy does it, why can't I?" What do you think that mother ought to do?

16. Some men so readily curse their horses, or cars, or what not. What do you think of such ingratitude to God?

17. What can you do in your own families, even though you are quite young, and even though your family never uses coarse and sinful language, to raise its moral standard still higher in reference to the Second Commandment?

THE SECOND COMMANDMENT

18. What do you think a good Catholic young person would do, should he find that his friends, time and again, use profane language or speak deridingly of holy things?

19. Some young men commonly indulge in (as one writer puts it) "deviled" language. They frequently use words that refer to hell, Satan; this is often called "swearing," but it is only vulgar. Although these words in themselves are not sinful, what about the scandal given to bystanders and especially to children?

20. Very often Catholics themselves, by their free and jocose way of speaking, are the cause of others deriding religion. What should these Catholics do to overcome their habit?

21. What do you think of a magazine which will permit cartoons that put some one or other teaching of the Church or some member of the clergy, perhaps the Pope, in a ridiculous light? If you are subscribing to such a magazine and in general it is a good paper, what will you do?

22. What do you think of the Holy Name Society?

23. Why are such expressions as "God is cruel, unjust"; "God doesn't care for me"; "What good is praying anyway?" etc., in time of trial or sorrow, so grievously sinful?

24. If any expressions like the above are made without due deliberation, and the person is immediately sorry, what do you think of the sin?

25. You are called upon the witness stand. Your own good name will be tarnished and perhaps your money lost if you tell the whole truth about the defendant, who is your business partner, your relative, or your friend. You have sworn "To tell the truth, the whole truth, and nothing but the truth; so help me God!" Regardless of your loss, what must you do?

26. On the witness stand you have become all muddled in a cross-examination. You tell an untruth. Have you committed perjury?

27. A man swears never to forgive his wayward son or daughter. What do you know about such an oath?

28. Why does the Church forbid secret societies like the Free Masons?

29. Such expressions as "God knows," "God is my witness," "Before God," can be oaths or not. What does this depend upon? (Intention of both parties.) Why should you avoid such strong language as "I swear," or "Upon my soul!" even though they do not mean an oath?

30. A girl twelve years old became mortally sick. She promised to consecrate her life to God should she recover. This was some years ago. She recovered but has not kept her promise. What have you to say about this?

Quotations from the Bible

For each of the following quotations:
a) Identify the speaker.
b) State the conditions under which the statement was made.

c) Give the meaning.
d) Tell its significance.

"Thou shalt not take the name of the Lord thy God in vain" (Exod. xx. 7).

"Thou shalt swear: as the Lord liveth, in truth, and in judgment, and in justice" (Jer. iv. 2).

"Bless the Lord, O my soul: and let all that is within me bless His holy name" (Ps. cii. 1).

"Blessed be the name of the Lord" (Job).

Chapter VIII
THE THIRD COMMANDMENT OF GOD

The Third Commandment. On the road of life we must keep in mind Him whose creatures we are. We must have deep in our hearts the love of Him as a child devoted to his father. We must show this in outward acts. The Third Commandment lays down a special time for it to take place — this exterior worship of God. Among the Jews under the Old Law it was the Sabbath day, the seventh day, the day of rest. The commandment is briefly: *Remember that thou keep holy the Sabbath day*. Or more fully:

> Remember that thou keep holy the Sabbath day. Six days shalt thou labor, and shalt do all thy works. But on the seventh day is the Sabbath of the Lord thy God: thou shalt do no work on it, thou nor thy son, nor thy daughter, nor thy manservant, nor thy maidservant, nor thy beast, nor the stranger that is within thy gates.
>
> For in six days the Lord made heaven and earth, and the sea, and all things that are in them, and rested on the seventh day: therefore the Lord blessed the seventh day, and sanctified it (Exod. xx. 8–11).

A Definite Time for Special Worship. It is but natural that sincerely and devoutly worshiping God, and guided by the faith and hope we have in Him, we should honor Him with outward worship and thanksgiving. It is good practical sense that some certain time should be set aside for this worship, amid the many everyday duties of life. It will serve to call us back to the main purpose of our journey at regular times, so that we do not get mixed up too completely with the cares and pleasures of the world, or the side trips from our main highway, perhaps even to get lost in one of these, and never find the main road again.

The Law in Man's Heart. In the sense which we have just defined the Third Commandment, it is closely related to the First and Second Commandments. The prayers of homage and worship to God grow out of the fact that He is the Lord our God. In that way this commandment is, like the others, a part of the moral law. It would have been felt by man even if God had not revealed it to Moses on Mount Sinai. It is written in the very nature of the universe, or as we say, in the heart of man. But whether we should pay this homage or worship of God at any one time more than at another is not a matter of nature, but is part of the ceremonial law as given by God to the Hebrews, and as such it could be changed if the purpose were fulfilled. If you look in the early books of the Old Testament, you will find a number of other changes that were made by the coming of Christ. Note particularly the change in the form of sacrifice to God.

The Sabbath in the Old Testament. The observance and keeping holy the day of the Lord God was of very great importance as may be seen by the many times it is spoken of in the Old Testament. Read the prophets, particularly Ezekiel, to find out how God thundered against the Jews for defiling the sanctuaries and profaning the Sabbath. In the passages, note that the punishment for failing to keep holy the Sabbath was death. A few of the passages follow:

Speak to the children of Israel, and thou shalt say to them: See that thou keep My Sabbath: because it is a sign between Me and you in your generations: that you may know that I am the Lord, who sanctify you.

Keep you My Sabbath: for it is holy unto you: he that shall profane it, shall be put to death: he that shall do any work in it, his soul shall perish out of the midst of his people.

Six days shall you do work: in the seventh day is the Sabbath, the rest holy to the Lord. Every one that shall do any work on this day, shall die.

Let the children of Israel keep the Sabbath, and celebrate it in their generations. It is an everlasting covenant (Exod. xxxi. 13–16).

Six days you shall do work: the seventh day shall be holy unto you, the Sabbath, and the rest of the Lord: he that shall do any work on it, shall be put to death.

You shall kindle no fire in any of your habitations on the Sabbath day (Exod. xxxv. 2–3).

Blessed is the man that doth this, and the son of man that shall lay hold on this: that keepeth the Sabbath from profaning it, that keepeth his hands from doing any evil.

THE THIRD COMMANDMENT

And the children of the stranger that adhere to the Lord, to worship Him, and to love His Name, to be His servants: every one that keepeth the Sabbath from profaning it, and that holdest fast My covenant (Isa. lvi. 2, 6).

Thus saith the Lord: Take heed to your souls, and carry no burdens on the Sabbath day: and bring them not in by the gates of Jerusalem.

And do not bring burdens out of your houses on the Sabbath day, neither do ye any work: sanctify the Sabbath day, as I commanded your fathers.

But they did not hear, nor incline their ear: but hardened their neck, that they might not hear Me, and might not receive instruction.

And it shall come to pass: if you will hearken to Me, saith the Lord, to bring in no burdens by the gates of this city on the Sabbath day: and if you will sanctify the Sabbath day, to do no work therein:

Then shall there enter in by the gates of this city kings and princes, sitting upon the throne of David, and riding in chariots and on horses, they and their princes, the men of Juda, and the inhabitants of Jerusalem: and this city shall be inhabited forever.

And they shall come from the cities of Juda, and from the places around about Jerusalem, and from the land of Benjamin, and from the plains, and from the mountains, and from the south, bringing holocausts, and victims, and sacrifices, and frankincense, and they shall bring in an offering into the house of the Lord.

But if you will not hearken to Me, to sanctify the Sabbath day, and not to carry burdens, and not to bring them in by the gates of Jerusalem on the Sabbath day: I will kindle a fire in the gates thereof, and it shall devour the houses of Jerusalem, and it shall not be quenched (Jer. xvii. 21-27).

Keep ye My Sabbaths, and reverence My sanctuary. I am the Lord (Levit. xix. 30).

Keep My Sabbaths and reverence My sanctuary: I am the Lord (Levit. xxvi. 2).

Saturday or Sunday. In the Old Law the particular time of giving in a formal manner this worship of God, which should fill our whole life was the seventh day. The Apostles changed the time of observance, but not the requirement or spirit of the commandment, from the seventh day (Saturday) to the first day (Sunday), because on this day Christ rose from the dead and it was on this day the Holy Ghost descended on the Apostles. It must be remembered too that Our Blessed Savior accepted public homage on Palm Sunday.

Other Holydays Among the Jews. The Jews, of course, kept other festivals or feast days holy besides the Sabbath, which indeed we can see in our city today. They abstain from servile works and otherwise keep holy these days, sometimes as on their day of atonement, among orthodox Jews, remaining all day in prayer. It was at the Jewish feast of the Passover (the Pasch) or the feast of the Unleavened Bread, as it is called, that Christ instituted the Holy Eucharist. The establishment of the Passover by God Himself is thus told in Chapter 23 of the Book of Leviticus which describes the "holydays to be kept." It begins by reminding them of the Sabbath and then goes on to the feast of the Solemnity of the Lord, and then to the Passover.

And the Lord spoke to Moses, saying: Speak to the children of Israel, and thou shalt say to them: These are the feasts of the Lord, which you shall call holy.

Six days shall ye do work: the seventh day, because it is the rest of the Sabbath, shall be called holy. You shall do no work on that day: it is the Sabbath of the Lord in all your habitations.

These also are the holydays of the Lord, which you must celebrate in their seasons.

The first month, the fourteenth day of the month at evening, is the phase of the Lord:

And the fifteenth day of the same month is the solemnity of the unleavened bread of the Lord. Seven days shall you eat unleavened bread.

The first day shall be most solemn unto you, and holy: you shall do no servile work therein:

But you shall offer sacrifice in fire to the Lord seven days. And the seventh day shall be more solemn, and more holy: and you shall do no servile work therein (Lev. xxiii. 1–8).

And in the same chapter the feast of the Atonement is prescribed.

And the Lord spoke to Moses, saying: Upon the tenth day of this seventh month shall be the day of atonement, it shall be most solemn, and shall be called holy: and you shall afflict your souls on that day, and shall offer a holocaust to the Lord.

You shall do no servile work in the time of this day: because it is a day of propitiation, that the Lord your God may be merciful unto you (27–28).

Christian Holydays. With the coming of Christ and His life

THE THIRD COMMANDMENT

on earth there were a number of great events which should be commemorated. What these are we shall see in the First Commandment of the Church.

The Four Parts. The Third Commandment of God may be divided into four parts.

1. Remember, thou keep holy the Sabbath day.
2. Six days shalt thou labor, and do all thy works; but on the seventh day is the Sabbath of the Lord thy God.
3. Thou shalt do no work on it, thou, nor thy son, nor thy daughter, nor thy manservant, nor thy maidservant, nor thy beast, nor the stranger that is within thy gates.
4. For in six days the Lord made heaven and earth, and in the seventh He ceased from work.

Holiness of the Sabbath. In the first place, we are commanded to remember the Sabbath day and to keep it holy. Beginning the commandment with the word *Remember* is meant to impress upon us in a special sense the need for keeping the commandment before our minds; that we must not forget it, nor neglect its observance because of worldly affairs or any other interest whatever. It is from the very meaning of the word, Sabbath, a day of rest, a day for the stopping of work — that the command comes "Thou shalt do no work on it." But there is not merely this negative requirement, that is, there is not only something that we must *not* do; it must be kept holy. Just as the Jews went to the synagogue on Saturdays in order to carry out this commandment, so we go to Mass on Sunday. It is to be a day to offer works of piety, of devotion, and of religion. It is to be a day to do works of mercy. It is to be a day of reading religious books. It is to be a day of prayer and other good works. By keeping ourselves free, doing no work such as takes up our time on other days, and giving ourselves up entirely to the religious service of God, we shall receive the reward of which the prophet Isaias tells us:

If thou turn away thy foot from the Sabbath, from doing thy own will in My holyday, and call the Sabbath delightful, and the holy of the Lord glorious, and glorify Him, while thou dost not thy own ways, and thy own will is not found, to speak a word:

Then shalt thou be delighted in the Lord, and I will lift thee up above the high places of the earth, and will feed thee with the inheritance of Jacob thy father. For the mouth of the Lord hath spoken it (Isa. lviii. 13-14).

The Day of the Week. The second part of the commandment is:

Six days shalt thou labor, and do all thy works; but on the seventh day is the Sabbath of the Lord thy God.

It brings out the first part by saying it again with the strong division between the six days of the week in which we are to work, and the seventh day, which is the Lord's. Certainly no works, or occupation with the daily grind of affairs shall make us forget, or neglect, or even make small of the fact that the seventh day is the Sabbath of the Lord. All our works must be done on other days. In the Old Testament this choosing of a day for the special worship of God was called a sign:

And sanctify My Sabbaths, that they may be a sign between Me and you: and that you may know that I am the Lord your God (Ezech. xx. 20).

It was a sign too ". . . that man should dedicate and sanctify himself to God, since even the very day is devoted to Him. For the holiness of the day consists in this, that on it men are bound in a special manner to practice holiness and religion" (*Catechism of the Council of Trent,* p. 401).

No Servile Works on the Lord's Day. The third part of the commandment is:

Thou shalt do no work on it, thou, nor thy son, nor thy daughter, nor thy manservant, nor thy maidservant, nor thy beast, nor the stranger that is within thy gates.

It goes further and is more specific. Not only must the head of the household but everyone connected with the household, even the stranger within the gates, and what seems more strange, the beasts, keep holy the Sabbath day. Nothing is to be permitted to stand in the way of worship of God on the Lord's day. Some works of necessity will need to be done on the Sabbath; e.g., the sick may be nursed and policemen and firemen must perform their

THE THIRD COMMANDMENT

duty. If a man's ox shall fall into a pit, it shall be taken out. Servile works are lawful on the Lord's day when the honor of God, the good of our neighbor, or necessity require them.

The cattle and beasts of the field are forbidden to work because some person would have to guide and direct them, and so far as possible, every human being is to be free to give God the honor and worship which the love of Him in our hearts prompts. And so some excuses or reasons are removed before they can be given.

Single Devotion to God. Servile works are forbidden on the Lord's day. They are not forbidden because they are improper or evil in themselves, for they are not, but because they withdraw or distract the attention from the worship of God, which is the great object of the commandment. Some servile works are permitted, for example any works that are necessary in regard to the celebration of divine worship, any work that is for the good of our neighbor, or any work of necessity. Christ brings out these points by appeal to the Old Testament and to the Jews of His own day.

At that time Jesus went through the corn on the Sabbath: and His disciples being hungry, began to pluck the ears, and to eat.

And the Pharisees seeing them, said to Him: Behold Thy disciples do that which is not lawful to do on the Sabbath day.

But He said to them: Have you not read what David did when he was hungry, and they that were with him:

How he entered into the house of God, and did eat the loaves of proposition, which it was not lawful for him to eat, nor for them that were with him, but for the priests only?

Or have ye not read in the law, that on the Sabbath days the priests in the temple break the Sabbath, and are without blame? (Matt. xii. 1-5).

And when He had passed from thence, He came into their synagogues.

And behold there was a man who had a withered hand, and they asked Him, saying: Is it lawful to heal on the Sabbath days? that they might accuse Him.

But He said to them: What man shall there be among you, that hath one sheep: and if the same fall into a pit on the Sabbath day, will he not take hold on it and lift it up?

How much better is a man than a sheep? Therefore it is lawful to do a good deed on the Sabbath days.

Then He saith to the man: Stretch forth thy hand: and he stretched it forth, and it was restored to health even as the other (Matt. xii. 9–13).

Works Proper for the Lord's Day. Needless to say, to give oneself up to sin is a special desecration of the day, not only because of the sin itself, but because at a time we should be especially devoted to God, we insult Him. The Sabbath is profaned by intemperance, by revelry, and by public scandal. It is, on the other hand, consecrated or made holy by our going to church and with heartfelt piety and devotion assisting at divine worship, by meditation on the purpose of the day, by frequent prayer or ejaculations and praise of God, by giving alms to the poor and needy, by visiting the sick, by consoling the sorrowful and the afflicted, and in general by the corporal and spiritual works of mercy. Reasonable recreation is, of course, permissible and desirable.

Remember the Sabbath Day to Keep it Holy!

The Analogy of the Creation. And so the Lord rested on the seventh day, blessed it and sanctified it. So must we in like manner. We must give ourselves up with whole hearts during the religious services to the love and veneration of God. We must pray. Every act of mercy or love to our neighbor for God's sake is especially fitting for the day.

Keeping on God's Highway. We do not point out here what a great benefit it has always been to mankind from the merely physical and social point of view to have the one day's rest in seven. It is from the moral and religious point of view, even more important. Periodically, that is once a week, to be recalled to the main purpose of life and the reason for our being on earth, is a remarkable way to keep us on God's Highway to our long home. To spend a day in a manner to recall particularly the fact that we are on God's Highway, would seem to be all that would be needed to keep those of good intentions and good will, on the highway, making gains at all times toward our final destiny. We do become wrapped up in the cares and riches of this life, and seem to lose our way, but every week we are sure to have one reminder, the Lord's day.

THE THIRD COMMANDMENT

Questions from the Catechism

Q. What is the Third Commandment?
A. **The Third Commandment is: Remember thou keep holy the Sabbath day.**

Q. What is forbidden by the Third Commandment?
A. **The Third Commandment forbids all unnecessary servile work and whatever else may hinder the due observance of the Lord's day.**

Q. What are servile works?
A. **Servile works are those which require labor rather of body than of mind.**

Q. Are servile works on Sunday ever lawful?
A. **Servile works are lawful on Sunday when the honor of God, the good of our neighbor, or necessity requires them.**

Problem Questions

1. Grandmother is very ill and cannot be left alone. You are asked to remain at home with her while the rest go to Sunday's Mass. May you do so if there is no other Mass? What reason can you give for your answer?

2. Your father takes you on a fishing trip early Sunday morning. You plan on stopping at the next town to hear Mass, but by the time you get there Mass is over. Are you excused?

3. A railroad man has to work on Sundays and cannot hear Mass. May he keep his job? Every few weeks he gets off Sunday mornings just at the time when Mass is half over. He reasons that as long as he could not get a whole Mass there is no need of his going to church. Is he right?

4. A young man is out all Saturday night. Before returning home on Sunday morning he enters church to hear Mass. He sleeps during the greater part of the service. Has he fulfilled his obligation? What must one do in order to fulfill the obligation of hearing Mass on Sundays?

5. A group of boys plan to go camping for three weeks. Fred is sent to select the place and the boys remind him that he must make sure that they will be able to hear Mass on Sundays. Fred returns and says that there is a Catholic church two miles distant. When they arrive, they find that this is not a Catholic church and that there is none near by. Suppose Fred knew all the time that this was not a Catholic church, how much of the blame must he take upon himself? Would it be enough for him to confess that he missed a Sunday's Mass? Suppose he really thought he was right, would the matter be different? Should the boys remain at the camp?

6. A working girl receives the news that her mother is very ill and she is needed at home. It is Sunday, and in order to be ready for the journey, she will have to do some laundering and sewing. May she do so?

7. Six girls are invited out to a camp for a week-end. They know there is no Catholic church in the vicinity. Several of the girls say that since it is impossible for them to attend Mass they are excused. Are they right?

8. You are on your way to Mass on Sunday. A car ahead of yours is turned over and the driver is injured. If you stop to help him you will miss the only Mass there is at your church. Should you offer your help or go to Mass?

9. Since Mr. Grey owns a radio he does not go to Mass on Sundays. He says he hears Mass and a good sermon every Sunday over the radio and really gets more out of it than when he goes to church. Is he in the right?

10. Jack stays home from Mass on Sunday in order to shovel snow. He says the janitor shovels snow in front of church and if he has a right to do so, so have other people. What will you tell Jack?

11. A farmer and his family were just ready to start for Mass on Sunday morning when they noticed that a heavy storm was threatening. In order to save his crops the farmer went out into the field and also ordered his hired men to do the same. They all missed Mass. Were they justified in doing so? Give reason for your answer.

12. Don wanted to paint the garden fence on Sunday afternoon, but his father would not permit him to do so, as that is servile work and therefore sinful. Don says that their neighbor paints pictures every Sunday and says that it is no sin. Is there any difference?

13. Mary and Jane live on a farm. They have to remain home from Mass every other Sunday to take care of the children and the house. Mother tells them they ought to recite the Mass prayers at home, but Mary says that will do no good as long as they cannot attend Mass. What do you think about the practice?

14. Mr. Daly goes to a low Mass every Sunday and then goes out fishing or hunting. Mr. Smith, his neighbor, tells him that hearing a Mass is not enough to "keep holy the Sabbath." If you were Mr. Smith, how would you explain the case to Mr. Daly?

15. "You are not keeping the word of God" says a non-Catholic to you. "The Bible says 'Remember thou keep holy the Sabbath day,' and you Catholics keep Sunday instead." Is there a difference between Sabbath and Sunday? How would you explain the position of Catholics?

16. Mr. Blake is a Catholic, but he does not attend Sunday Mass. He says he will work while he is young and strong and will devote a great deal of time to his soul when he is old and can no longer work. What would you tell him?

17. Marie would not get up at once when her mother called her on

THE THIRD COMMANDMENT

Sunday morning. Because of this she came to Mass after the Offertory. What must she do? Why? Suppose there is no other Mass, what obligation has she?

18. Mr. Payne goes to Mass and other devotions every Sunday. During the week, however, he is engaged in a dishonest business. What do you think of him as a Christian?

19. What does the Consecration of the Mass mean to you? Why do you look at the Host and whisper, "My Lord and my God"?

Quotations from the Bible

For each of the following quotations:
a) Identify the speaker.
b) State the conditions under which the statement was made.
c) Give the meaning.
d) Tell its significance.

"Remember that thou keep holy the Sabbath day" (Exod. xx. 8).

"Therefore, it is lawful to do a good deed on the Sabbath days" (Matt. xii. 12).

Chapter IX
THE FOURTH COMMANDMENT OF GOD

The Commandments of Love of Neighbor. The first three commandments deal with our relationship to God. In keeping them we show our love of God. The other seven commandments deal more with our relationship to our fellow men. They tell us how, on the Highway of Life, we should treat our fellow men in such a way as to show our love of God, whose creatures they are. This love of neighbor and our fellow man is the love of God's creatures. It is done for the love of God. In this way our service on the Highway of Life helps us to keep in mind our journey's purpose, and to arrive triumphantly at its end.

Father and Mother. The first of these commandments that deal with the love of our neighbor relates especially to those human beings who are closest to us, our mother and father, and, as we shall see, it goes even further than that. We are given to our parents who guide us during the helpless days of infancy and early childhood, and love and protect us during the period of youth. Their love and their interest and their concern for us extends even beyond that to the time when we ourselves may be heads of families, or have gone out from the parental home. We have watched them make little and great sacrifices for us, to protect us from every harm and injury or danger, to keep us away from evil companions, bad shows, or bad books. We have seen them save money, or deny themselves things to get us the things within their means that we needed or thought we wanted. They give us an education, see that we are instructed in religion and in other knowledge, and try to give us all that is necessary for our future here and hereafter, and a full life now.

Honor Our Parents. The first thing which the Fourth Commandment requires is that we honor, love, and obey our parents in all that is not sin. The word used in the commandment is *honor*, but honor includes these other terms. "To honor is to think respectfully of anyone, and to hold in the highest esteem all that relates to him." It includes love, respect, obedience, and reverence!

How We May Honor. If we really love our parents, all the other things will follow. We will respect them and reverence them, and even when we do not understand fully the reasons for their advice or correction, we will accept it cheerfully and promptly because we know they intend it for our welfare, and by it show their love for us. We will gladly show our response to that love by not waiting to be told what should be done, but by foreseeing things our parents want, by praying for them, and by striving in every way to please them. If they have some little fault or weakness, special care should be taken not to provoke them or anger them in this particular.

In Old Age and Sickness. We should also remember that as our parents grow old we should do everything possible to make their old age happy and contented and gladly accept the chance of taking care of them, or helping in their support in every way possible. In time of sickness we should be a consolation to them and provide them support if they need it. And this is especially true at the time of death, when we should see that they have the consolations of religion.

The Honor We Owe Others. The honor and obedience which we owe to our parents is a symbol of the honor and obedience which we owe to all persons who have rightful authority, or are our lawful superiors. We must consider them as the representatives and helpers of our parents and we owe them honor like the honor we owe our parents. These persons are the bishops and pastors in the Church, judges and officers in our civic life, teachers in our schools, and other lawful superiors. Whenever these persons are acting within their power and ask us to do things not against the law of God, we should obey them; but, needless to say, if anyone in authority should ask us to do something contrary to the law of God, he should not be obeyed, for as we read in the Bible: "We ought to obey God rather than man."

Honor for Our Spiritual Superiors. To those who give their lives for the love of God, to preach the word of God, and serve God, we gladly give obedience, listen to their words of advice, and seek their help in time of trouble, at all times especially on moral and religious questions. The priest wishes to live the simple life of ready service to God, and has the right to receive whatever is necessary for his support. We are expected to contribute to the support of our pastors, and are glad to do so.

Our Duty as Citizens. Under this commandment comes also our duty as citizens; that is, our duty to the government. We must obey all just laws. We should carry out all our duties of voting, of paying taxes, of rendering military service if required of us, and other public duties. We should gladly do a little more than this by looking for chances to help and serve, and to make life better for our neighbors. We should do this for the love of God, which perhaps will direct others on Life's Highway to look to Him for guidance, and perhaps kindle their love of God. It will help all of us to be better prepared for the journey's end.

The Promise of the Fourth Commandment. If we read the stories of the Old Testament, we must be struck by the blessings and happiness and long life on earth that came to children who honored and obeyed their parents, and likewise by the misfortune and shame and disgrace that came to children who did not obey their parents.

The Fourth Commandment is the first commandment with a promise "that thou mayest live a long time," and it is added in the Book of Deuteronomy, "it may be well with thee" (Deut. v. 16). Those who keep this commandment are promised a long life. "Children who honor their parents and gratefully acknowledge the blessing of life received from them, are deservedly rewarded with the protracted enjoyment of that life to an advanced age." They receive not only length of days, but peace and safety to live well.

Why It Is Not Given Sometimes. But sometimes the dutiful child is not longlived. What the Providence of God is we may not always understand. But we read in the Book of Wisdom something that may help us to understand these cases. This book says, "He was taken away lest wickedness should alter his understanding, or deceit beguile his soul." (Wisd. iv. 11.) The prophet Isaias says something that may help us to understand: "The just man is taken away from before the face of evil." Or as it is elsewhere explained, "He is spared the bitter anguish of witnessing the calamities of his friends or relations in such evil days."

Violations of the Fourth Commandment. We violate the Fourth Commandment, when we are disobedient to our parents, refusing or willfully neglecting to do what our parents ask or tell us to do. We violate this commandment, too, when we treat our parents with disrespect, despise their commands, are ashamed of them because they are old-fashioned, or not stylish, or for other foolish reasons. We violate this commandment through stubbornness, or willfulness, refusing to take their advice and suggestions, or rebelling at their correction. We violate this commandment, too, when we show the same spirit or act in the same way to other lawful superiors as well — bishops, priests, teachers, and other superiors within the limits of their authority.

The Punishment. After reading the Old Testament one cannot help but realize what a terrible sin and injustice a lack of respect or gratitude or love for the parents whose children we are, is. Here are some of the statements we find:

He that curseth his father or mother shall die the death (Exod. xxi. 17; Lev. xx. 9).

He that afflicteth his father, and chaseth away his mother, is infamous and unhappy (Prov. xix. 16).

He that curseth his father, and mother, his lamp shall be put out in the midst of darkness (Prov. xx. 20).

The eye that mocketh at his father, and despiseth the labor of his mother in bearing him, let the ravens of the brooks pick it up and the young eagles eat it (Prov. xxx. 17).

Love of God Supreme. We owe the highest honor and homage to God alone, who is the Father and Creator of all. No creature is worthy of the same love we give to God. But to our earthly parents, to whom God gave us, we owe our finest human love, because in a sense they represent God. To them was given the duty to care for us and guide us. We love them for themselves and for their love of us, but also for the love of God. If, as not often happens, parents forgetting their duty should command anything contrary to God's law, the supreme love of God will guide us, and we will remember that "we ought to obey God rather than men."

Responsibility of Parents. It is to our parents that God has given us. During our early years it is for them to decide what kind of education we shall have, where we shall go to school, what we shall study, as well as to have general care over us. It is a great duty to which God holds parents. They must see to the bodily and spiritual welfare of their children. They should deal with them sensibly, making them obey, but being neither too harsh nor too easy. They should keep before the child that he was made to serve God and they should help him in that way above all. Failure to carry out this duty may mean the loss of their own soul. Children should work together in every way with their parents in living a good Christian life for the welfare, especially the spiritual welfare, of both.

The Responsibility of Superiors. The authority given to parents is for the welfare of the child. Parents are to provide for the children, to instruct them, to correct them in justice and prudence, to give them a good education to prepare them for life duties, to love them, and to pray for them. So superiors have a very great duty to those under their charge. The authority given to superiors, whether spiritual or civil superiors, is not for themselves, but for the good of those under them. The example for all parents and superiors is Christ. Although He had all power in heaven and on earth, He died on the cross for His charges — you and me — for our eternal welfare. Power is always given to be used for love. The good Shepherd dies for His sheep. Explain this.

A Parent to His Son. The way the parent should think of his sons, and the way practical parents feel about it, is shown

THE FOURTH COMMANDMENT

clearly in the advice which Tobias gave to his son when he was about to die.

Therefore when Tobias thought that his prayer was heard that he might die, he called to him Tobias his son,

And said to him: Hear, my son, the words of my mouth, and lay them as a foundation in thy heart.

When God shall take my soul, thou shalt bury my body: and thou shalt honor thy mother all the days of her life:

For thou must be mindful what and how great perils she suffered for thee in her womb.

And when she also shall have ended the time of her life, bury her by me.

And all the days of thy life have God in thy mind: and take heed thou never consent to sin, nor transgress the commandments of the Lord our God.

Give alms out of thy substance, and turn not away thy face from any poor person: for so it shall come to pass that the face of the Lord shall not be turned from thee.

According to thy ability be merciful.

If thou have much give abundantly: if thou have little, take care even so to bestow willingly a little.

For thus thou storest up to thyself a good reward for the day of necessity (Tob. iv. 1–10).

Never suffer pride to reign in thy mind, or in thy words: for from it all perdition took its beginning (Tob. iv. 14).

See thou never do to another what thou wouldst hate to have done to thee by another.

Eat thy bread with the hungry and the needy, and with thy garments cover the naked (Tob. iv. 16–17).

Bless God at all times: and desire of Him to direct thy ways, and that all thy counsels may abide in Him (Tob. iv. 20).

Fear not, my son: we lead indeed a poor life, but we shall have many good things if we fear God, and depart from all sin, and do that which is good (Tob. iv. 23).

Questions from the Catechism

Q. What is the Fourth Commandment?

A. **The Fourth Commandment is: Honor thy father and thy mother.**

Q. What are we commanded by the Fourth Commandment?

A. **We are commanded by the Fourth Commandment to honor, love, and obey our parents in all that is not sin.**
Q. Are we bound to honor and obey others than our parents?
A. **We are also bound to honor and obey our bishops, pastors, magistrates, teachers, and other lawful superiors.**
Q. Have parents and superiors any duties toward those who are under their charge?
A. **It is the duty of parents and superiors to take good care of all under their charge and give them proper direction and example.**
Q. What is forbidden by the Fourth Commandment?
A. **The Fourth Commandment forbids all disobedience, contempt, and stubbornness toward our parents or lawful superiors.**

Problem Questions

1. Did you ever hear a little boy or a little girl call his father by a name that was not nice? Maybe he did not call his father that name so he could hear it, but you heard it. What would you do?

2. I know a little girl who will not talk to her mother for a long time, even for a whole hour, because mother punished her. What should this girl do to get over her nasty feelings?

3. Sometimes a little boy will talk real meanly about his father because his father will not give him a dime to spend for a movie. What do you think of a boy like that? I wonder if you ever did that? Let's tell Jesus today we will never do that again.

4. I once saw a little boy run out and slam the door when his father refused to let him stay on the street with the other boys until nine o'clock. What should that boy do to make up for this act?

5. When you meet your mother on the street, how should you show your respect to her? I think your mother would almost weep if her little boy would run away when he sees her coming, don't you?

6. If mother sometimes does things you know are wrong, for instance, suppose she tells you to stay home from school to help her with the washing and to tell the teacher you were sick, what would you say to mother about it?

7. If mother dresses in an old-fashioned way, would you be ashamed of her when you are with your friends in a crowd?

8. Who knows what contempt means? If a child thinks himself so much better and smarter than his parents and acts that way (contempt), he is sinning against the Fourth Commandment through contempt. What does that mean?

THE FOURTH COMMANDMENT

9. What do you think of your big sister who says to mother: "Oh, shucks! you're an old-timer"?

10. Why do you love your mother? Your father?

11. What do you think of a little girl your age who often says, "Mamma, I love you so much," but always gets pouty when her mother says she should wash the dishes or take care of the baby?

12. When father and mother are old and perhaps poor and you are grown up, what will you do for them?

13. If mother is very sad because you are not a very good boy or girl, and is worried because you have not been good at school, or have had a fight with the boys, or have taken some money, what do you think you ought to do to make her happy again?

14. What do you think of your big sister if she tells your mother to go away for the evening because she intends to have *swell* company and is afraid your mother won't be swell enough? Will you ever do that?

15. George is a little boy who thinks he knows better than his father. His father says to him: "George, I don't want you to go with Billy Jones any more; he's not the kind of boy I want you to be with." But George knows better and won't take his father's advice and goes with Billy Jones. Do you think George loves his father if he won't listen to him?

16. Mother has made you a new dress but you don't like it; how would you show your love and gratitude to her in spite of your feelings?

17. Mother is sick and very tired. What will you do when you come home from school to show her that you love her?

18. What are some of the jobs you can do at home to show you love your parents?

19. Father says, "You stay home tonight. No movies." Dad and mother go away for the evening and you know it. Joe E. Brown is on just around the corner and you can get back long before your parents come home and they will never know anything about it. Will you go to that movie? What do you think of one who would go after his father has said this?

20. Mother wants you to eat spinach and to drink milk. You don't like it and begin to grumble and get stubborn at the table. You know that is wrong, but you always do it. How can you get over that habit?

21. Mother has told her little girl to watch the baby on the lawn. The fire engine comes by and she runs along, forgetting all about the baby. After an hour she comes back. A little voice had whispered to her after a little while that she is disobedient, but she would not listen. Baby is still safe on the lawn. Should the girl tell mother what she had done or should she say nothing about it because the baby's all right? What would you do?

22. Sunday afternoon there are services at church. Dad says, "Son, you go to church this afternoon, and then you may go to the park." You run

off to church, kneel about two minutes in the back, then run out to the park. Were you obedient?

23. Father says, "You mow the lawn this morning." You obey but you are grumbling and grouching the whole morning. How are you sinning against the Fourth Commandment?

24. Do you see any rewards God has promised in the Fourth Commandment to children who obey? What are they?

25. What punishments has God made ready for those children who are disobedient to their parents in very important cases? Can you tell the class how a big man might commit a mortal sin against his parents?

26. How long must a boy or girl obey parents?

27. If a boy of your age usually is disobedient, how can he learn to become obedient?

28. You don't like your teacher sometimes because you think she is cross. You try to tease her by being naughty and when she calls on you, you get saucy. Why must you obey even a teacher whom you do not like?

29. A girl is stubborn because she thinks she did not deserve to be scolded. Even if she didn't deserve it, what else might she do to show the teacher that she is innocent instead of becoming stubborn?

30. If you have said something that is very disrespectful about your teacher and which would lower her in the minds of the other children, making them act naughtily, what would you have to do to make up for this?

31. You may not take books home from a shelf. You started a story and want to finish it, so you slip the book between your other ones and go off with it, intending to return it in the morning. Is that right?

32. How do you like this resolution: I am going to obey the rules of the school to keep out of trouble?

33. Dad has given you five cents to put into the collection box. On the way you buy four cents' worth of candy and put one cent into the box. Besides deceiving, how would you be failing in your duty toward the Church?

34. You know you should not talk in church when the Blessed Sacrament is there, but your friend next to you starts talking; what will you do about it?

35. Some little boy says very bad things about the priest which he has heard his father say. He is saying this to a crowd of boys and you also hear him. Have you any duty to stop him and how would you do it?

36. To be a good citizen a boy or girl must always obey the traffic rules; besides running the risk of being hurt, aren't children disobeying at such times if they run their own way as they please? Is that a sin?

37. You must help keep the streets clean. After school you have banana peelings, paper bags, etc., which you throw into a back street when

THE FOURTH COMMANDMENT

nobody sees you. What kind of boy might such continued action make you?

38. You have chicken pox but you play with the neighbor children anyway when their mother and your mother don't see you. Are you disobeying a law?

Quotations from the Bible

For each of the following quotations:
a) Identify the speaker.
b) State the conditions under which the statement was made.
c) Give the meaning.
d) Tell its significance.

"Honor thy father and thy mother, that thou mayest be longlived" (Exod. xx. 12).

"We ought to obey God, rather than men" (Acts v. 29).

Chapter X
THE FIFTH COMMANDMENT OF GOD

The life that was given to us by God we must take care of. The life that was given to our neighbor we must respect.

Thou Shalt Not Kill. The journey on Life's Highway to God would be strange indeed if the life that was given us by God could be lawfully destroyed by ourselves or by others. Taking one's own life, suicide, is a violation of God's will in the creation of each of us. The love of neighbor would certainly be violated by killing him. Even without the special commandment of God, it would be a strange life — like a nightmare — if life could be destroyed at will. And it is strengthened by the specific commandment, the fifth — which is, *Thou Shalt Not Kill.*

Love, Peace, and Friendship. The Fifth Commandment has a broader meaning and wider scope than perhaps appears upon first sight. It forbids killing or murder, but its aim is to protect the life of each person. It holds life sacred, and it would prevent anything that would lead to the injury or the destruction of life. Besides its negative side which forbids us to kill, and anything that might lead to anger, fighting, hatred, revenge, and murder, it has a positive meaning, which is that we are to "cherish sentiments of charity, concord, and friendship toward our enemies, to have peace with all men, and finally, to endure with patience every inconvenience" (*Catechism of the Council of Trent*, p. 421). In short, we must love our neighbor.

Preservation in Security of Human Life. If we keep in mind that the purpose of the commandment is to preserve human life and to make it secure, we may be better able to understand certain exceptions, especially that one, where the state sentences to death men who have no respect for human life themselves, as shown by their killing a person or committing some other great

THE FIFTH COMMANDMENT

outrage. The sentence of death was often used in olden days, but has been slowly done away with until today it is used largely as a punishment for crimes of killing or murder. The state has the right to kill in such cases because by this it gains the very purpose of the commandment. It should be noted that even in this extreme case, life imprisonment is taking the place of killing by electrocution or hanging.

War. In like manner, the soldier who takes the life of an enemy in a just war, because of his duty to his country, and not because of cruelty or ambition, is not guilty of a violation of this commandment. But good men everywhere are hoping that men may be able to live together in peace so that wars may become few until finally they are stopped entirely. The love of God in men's hearts, and the love of the neighbor for the love of God, will bring that day about.

Accidents. Even in the earliest time it is shown that where death was caused by accident, there was no guilt. In the Book of Deuteronomy we read: "He that killeth his neighbor, ignorantly, and who is proved to have gone with him to the wood to hew wood, and in cutting down the tree the ax slipt out of his hand, and the iron slipping from the handle struck his friend and killed him, shall live" (Deut. xix. 4–5). But where an accidental death is caused by an unlawful act, or by neglect, or want of due care, there is guilt. There is no guilt when a person is forced to kill a person in self-defense, where every means has been used to protect himself otherwise.

The Sacredness of Life. And *The Catechism of the Council of Trent* — a great authority — after pointing out these exceptions, goes on to say:

> The above are the cases in which life may be taken without violating this commandment; and with these exceptions all other killing is forbidden, whether we consider the person who kills, the person killed, or the means used to kill.
>
> As to the person who kills, the commandment recognizes no exception whatever, be he rich or powerful, master or parent. All, without exception or distinction, are forbidden to kill.
>
> With regard to the person killed, the law extends to all. There is no

individual, however humble or lowly his condition, whose life is not shielded by this law.

It also forbids suicide. No man possesses such power over his own life as to be at liberty to put himself to death. Hence we find that the commandment does not say: Thou shalt not kill another, but simply: *Thou Shalt Not Kill*.

Finally, if we consider the numerous means by which murder may be committed, the law admits of no exception. Not only does it forbid the taking away of the life of another by laying violent hands on him, by means of a sword, a stone, a stick, a halter, or by administering poison; but also strictly prohibits the accomplishment of the death by another by counsel, assistance, help, or any other means whatever (p. 423).

We Must Not Contribute Directly or Indirectly. We are forbidden not only to kill but forbidden to do anything that leads to murder or puts human life in danger or makes it less safe. It is a violation of this commandment to order or direct or command a person to do anything that leads to death or makes life unsafe. We are forbidden to do anything by encouragement or supply the means, for in these ways we would be contributing to murder and the other things forbidden by this commandment. We sin in our hearts if we desire any of these things. We must, too, do certain things to prevent violation of this commandment.

The surgeon whose patient dies because of his gross ignorance or gross neglect violates this commandment.

If it is possible for us, we must give warning to those in danger, or if it is possible to give help, it is our duty to do so. Where we can prevent or lessen murder, hatred, quarreling, revenge, or scandal, we should do so out of love for our neighbor.

Quarreling, Anger, Hatred, Revenge Forbidden. We must beware of every feeling and passion leading to destruction or injury to human life; quarreling, wrangling, and fighting are forbidden. The advice to "let not the sun go down upon your anger" if followed will save you from breaking this commandment. If we control our anger, we can perhaps control those dangerous feelings which sometimes give rise to it: envy, jealousy, and pride. Anger is justifiable sometimes, for example, in our refusal to be led into temptation by anyone. If anger generally is forbidden, how much more is hatred. We read in the Bible: "Whoso hateth his brother is a murderer." A very dangerous feeling or passion, indeed, is revenge. How quickly it rushes into our mind. How evil are its results. We must remember our prayer in the "Our Father": We hope to be forgiven our trespasses as *we forgive* those who trespass against us. If we keep in mind the example and words of Christ dying on the cross, we can do our share in keeping this commandment of God. You remember what Christ's words were: "Father, forgive them for they know not what they do."

Bad Example and Scandal. We may injure that spiritual life in our neighbor which makes him "an image of God" as well as his physical life. Bad example of every kind is also forbidden by this commandment because it kills or injures the life of the soul. On the other hand, we should "let our light so shine before men that they may see our good works and glorify our Father who is in heaven." Not only is bad example forbidden but every form of scandal: immoral words or cursing, bad books or bad pictures, indecent dress, or any words, deeds, or omissions leading others to sin. Do you remember that quotation which Abraham Lincoln used in his second inaugural address as President of the United States: "Woe to the world because of [offenses] scandals. For it must be that scandals [offenses] come: but nevertheless woe to that man by whom the scandal [offense] cometh" (Matt. xviii. 7)?

The Love of Neighbor. We are commanded by the Fifth Commandment not only not to kill, but to avoid everything that may put human life in danger. We are commanded by the Fifth Commandment to live in peace and union with our neighbor, to respect his rights, to seek his spiritual and bodily welfare, and to take care of our life and health. God's Highway becomes truly a place for God's creatures. We shall live on, helping everyone along and keeping ourselves fit for the journey. We use the gifts of God, especially the gift of life, for the arrival at the end of our journey — the salvation of our soul, and we will lend a helpful hand to other human beings.

Charity. On this highway to our home with God, it is fitting that this love of the neighbor for the love of God should be shown by all of us. To keep it in mind, we should memorize what St. Paul says about charity, think about it often, and try to live it as we proceed on the Highway of Life.

If I speak with the tongues of men, and of angels, and have not charity, I am become as sounding brass, or a tinkling cymbal.

And if I should have prophecy and should know all mysteries and all knowledge, and if I should have all faith, so that I could remove mountains, and have not charity, I am nothing.

And if I should distribute all my goods to feed the poor, and if I should deliver my body to be burned, and have not charity, it profiteth me nothing.

Charity is patient, is kind: charity envieth not, dealeth not perversely; is not puffed up;

Is not ambitious, seeketh not her own, is not provoked to anger, thinketh no evil;

Rejoiceth not in iniquity, but rejoiceth with the truth;

Beareth all things, believeth all things, hopeth all things, endureth all things.

Charity never falleth away whether prophecies shall be made void or tongues shall cease, or knowledge shall be destroyed.

For we know in part, and we prophesy in part.

But when that which is perfect is come, that which is in part shall be done away.

When I was a child, I spoke as a child, I understood as a child, I thought as a child. But, when I became a man, I put away the things of a child.

We see now through a glass in a dark manner; but then face to face.

Now I know in part; but then I shall know even as I am known.

And now there remain faith, hope, and charity, these three: but the greatest of these is charity (I Cor. xiii).

Unstained Hands, Undefiled Hearts. It must be clear, therefore, that all willful murder, fighting, anger, hatred, revenge, and bad example, are forbidden by this commandment, and that love and charity, forgiveness and mercy are commanded. We must not only keep our hands unstained, but our hearts pure and undefiled.

Questions from the Catechism

Q. What is the Fifth Commandment?
A. **The Fifth Commandment is: Thou shalt not kill.**
Q. What are we commanded by the Fifth Commandment?

THE FIFTH COMMANDMENT

A. **We are commanded by the Fifth Commandment to live in peace and union with our neighbor, to respect his rights, to seek his spiritual and bodily welfare, and to take proper care of our own life and health.**

Q. What is forbidden by the Fifth Commandment?

A. **The Fifth Commandment forbids all willful murder, fighting, anger, hatred, revenge, and bad example.**

Problem Questions

1. What do you think is the chief reason we may not kill our neighbors or ourselves?

2. Our body is like a rented house. The owner of the house can do what he wants to with it, but the renter may not. How does a renter treat the house? How, then, should we treat our body?

3. Many of you have seen a drunken man on the street. What do you think of such a man? Would you like to be a man like that? If not, what must you start doing today already? (Mortification in small things.)

4. Some children think it is "smart" to hang on cars, to run in front of coming automobiles or trains. Are these acts sinful? (They expose themselves unnecessarily to fatal accidents.)

5. A friend has told you that swimming is fine. Your father said the water is still too cold. The boy calls you a coward because you tell him the water is too cold. What will you do about it?

6. A friend tells you in the presence of a group of younger children, that one of your classmates has cheated in an examination, has stolen something, has lied. He is not absolutely sure, but he tells it anyway. How can you prevent the sin of scandal with these younger children?

7. If you told others the same stories about this boy, and they in turn told others, what do you think of the guilt in your case?

8. Even if you know these things to be true about him, why should you refrain from telling your friends about them? Whom should you tell?

9. At times girls are very jealous of one another. When another person receives a reward, how can you overcome your feeling of envy or jealousy? Often say, "Jesus help me to become a noble child."

10. I have often heard children say, "I just hate John. I can't stand him." If these children hate the evil qualities of John, does that prove that they hate John himself? In what does the sin consist?

11. What do you think a good way of treating a child who always picks a quarrel on the playground or in the games?

12. Do you think it is a joke to trip anybody purposely? Mention some of the results to such a thoughtless act.

13. When you cause suffering through such a foolish joke, are you obliged to pay the bills due to doctors, hospitals, etc.?

14. Sometimes groups of boys or girls talk indecently. You don't want that to continue. How will you try to stop it?

15. If you have vexed your parents or your schoolmates, what will you do to make up for this?

16. What do you think of a boy who is always calling others names, but who gets very angry as soon as he thinks he is offended?

17. What do you think of a boy or a girl who becomes angry very easily?

Quotation from the Bible

For the following quotation:
a) Identify the speaker.
b) State the conditions under which the statement was made.
c) Give the meaning.
d) Tell its significance.

"Thou shalt not kill" (Exod. xx. 13).

Chapter XI

THE SIXTH AND NINTH COMMANDMENTS

The Sixth and Ninth Commandments. The sixth commandment of God is: *Thou Shalt not Commit Adultery.* Very much like the sixth commandment is the ninth commandment: *Thou Shalt not Covet Thy Neighbor's Wife.*

The Great Importance of Marriage, Family, and Home. These two guideposts on the highway to our home with God are meant, in the first place, for the protection of home and family and the marriage relation. No one relationship is more important than the relationship in the home growing out of the marriage relationship. The welfare of husband and of wife, and of children and of parents, are bound up with the home. To permit impurity or immodesty to enter it would in the end affect all the community. To keep it pure and modest helps to make our neighborhood and our larger communities better. It keeps the road clear and open to our Father's house.

Impurity Destroys Home. These commandments are directed against sins of thought and word as well as sins of deed. We must resist every temptation toward impurity of thought and word as well as immodesty in act, of dress, of manner, of reading. The commandment is directed by name against the sin of adultery, which is an improper relationship between married people. It is directed, too, against every impure or immodest relation between human beings whether married or not. Such a relationship by the evil that results therefrom, will destroy the marriage relationship and home. But the surest way of keeping such a disorder from coming into one's life is to grow up with fixed habits of life that regulate a pure and modest way of living. Now is the time to begin.

Interests and Hobbies. We should build up a number of good habits now. Have a number of wholesome interests and hobbies, things worth while in themselves, and useful, such as stamp collections, mechanics, nature study, drawing, and the like. Perhaps no greater safeguard against violations of this commandment and many other troubles in later life is the habit of reading worth-while books, and the refusal to read trash or immoral or suggestive books or articles. This habit also protects us against one of the great temptations to all sins and especially impurity; i.e., a habit of indolence. There is a famous proverb that the devil finds things for idle hands to do. Do not let yourself drift into habits of idleness. Have so many worth-while things you want to do, or books to read that you are always ready to make use of any spare time you may have, even ten or fifteen minutes. Be interested in sports so that you can play at least fairly well.

The Golden Mean. Another habit to start now as a protection against sins in the future is a habit of temperance, what the old Greeks called, "the golden mean." Be temperate in dress, in food, in language, in all your habits. Avoid extremes. Avoid showiness in dress, in food, in manners.

Immodest Books, Conversations, Pictures, Plays. These two habits, of keeping busy and of being temperate, as they develop will help you to avoid impure or immodest conversation, reading immodest books and especially newspapers, looking at bad pictures, going to see immodest moving pictures and plays. You should be too interested in worth-while things to waste your time with these. You will think too well of yourself to do the evil things listed above. Your self-respect and your love of God will forbid that.

Time and Life. Perhaps a word may be added about time. Time is one of the most precious things you have. It is your own life. To waste time is to waste your life. It passes and can never be recalled. Use it now for wise and good and pure purposes, and you will make sure the happiness of your future life.

A Motto for You. If there is one motto that you should keep in mind and follow today, tomorrow, and as long as you live, it is this:

SIXTH AND NINTH COMMANDMENTS

For the rest, brethren, whatsoever things are true, whatsoever modest, whatsoever just, whatsoever holy, whatsoever lovely, whatsoever of good fame, if there be any virtue, if any praise of discipline, think on these things (Phil. iv. 8).

Frequent the Sacraments. These suggestions will be a great protection against sins of thought, word, or deed. But, in addition to them, boys and girls should use the most important means of keeping in God's friendship; namely, prayer and the sacraments. Go often to confession and Holy Communion, and pray to God regularly and devoutly. Prayer and the sacraments will feed the spiritual life of the soul and keep you pure and modest. Practice, too, a special devotion to the Blessed Virgin Mary. Pray also to those two saints so noted for their purity, St. Aloysius and St. Agnes. Love God with your whole heart and your whole soul and your whole mind.

A Beatitude. The strongest reason or motive you can have is the statement in those beautiful sayings of Jesus Christ, called the Beatitudes:

Blessed are the pure [clean] of heart, for they shall see God.

Questions from the Catechism

Q. What is the Sixth Commandment?
A. **The Sixth Commandment is: Thou shalt not commit adultery.**

Q. What are we commanded by the Sixth Commandment?
A. **We are commanded by the Sixth Commandment to be pure in thought and modest in all our looks, words, and actions.**

Q. What is forbidden by the Sixth Commandment?
A. **The Sixth Commandment forbids all unchaste freedom with another's wife or husband; also all immodesty with ourselves or others in looks, dress, words, or actions.**

Q. Does the Sixth Commandment forbid the reading of bad and immodest books and newspapers?
A. **The Sixth Commandment does forbid the reading of bad and immodest books and newspapers.**

Q. What is the Ninth Commandment?
A. **The Ninth Commandment is: Thou shalt not covet thy neighbor's wife.**

Q. What are we commanded by the Ninth Commandment?

A. **We are commanded by the Ninth Commandment to keep ourselves pure in thought and desire.**

Q. What is forbidden by the Ninth Commandment?

A. **The Ninth Commandment forbids unchaste thoughts, desires of another's wife or husband, and all other impure thoughts and desires.**

Q. Are impure thoughts and desires always sins?

A. **Impure thoughts and desires are always sins, unless they displease us and we try to banish them.**

Problem Questions

1. There are three saints always pictured with a lily. Do you know who they are? Why do they carry a lily? Of what is the lily a symbol?

2. What is meant by the proverb: Birds of a feather flock together. Do you believe the saying always true? James goes with bad companions, but he says the boys can't harm him; in fact, he is doing his best to make them better. Do you think he will succeed? What comparison could you make to prove your point to James?

3. You and your little sister are out in the country for a walk. Your sister is very thirsty and wants to take a drink from the river. Would you allow her to do that? Why not? Would that be worse than to take her to a show that is not good? Or to hear a wicked story, or read a bad book? What difference is there? Do you know of a Scripture text that would apply here?

4. Ben takes you to his home for the first time and shows you his room. The walls are filled with indecent pictures. Could you judge from them what kind of companion Ben is? Would the pictures be a sure sign that he is bad or could there be another reason for his having them? What should you do in either case?

5. Ann and her sister go to a party. They soon learn that the people at the party are not behaving decently. Ann wants to go home, but her sister says they would offend their friends by leaving now, and furthermore they would be laughed at. What would you do under the circumstances?

6. Jack was sitting by the window and reading. All of a sudden he caught himself in the act of daydreaming and realized that his thoughts had drifted to forbidden things. Had Jack committed a sin up to this time? What should he do now? He takes up his book and begins to read again, but finds that he cannot get rid of his evil thoughts. Can you suggest other remedies?

7. Frank is a lazy boy who spends most of his time in idle dreaming or lying around doing nothing. Joseph, his brother, is always occupied with something. He is always reading, or working, or playing. Which of the two

SIXTH AND NINTH COMMANDMENTS

boys has the better chance of remaining morally good? Why? Can you find a proverb that will answer this question?

8. Dorothy is not careful about dressing modestly. Her mother tells her she is doing wrong, but Dorothy answers that she is only doing what other girls are doing and that it has not harmed her yet, nor will it harm her. Do you agree? Do you know that the *Sunday Visitor* is carrying on a crusade for modesty in dress? Look it up and see whether you would like to join.

9. Grace's older sister wants her to go along to a dance. Grace knows that the place has a very bad reputation, but her sister says that they will stay with their own group and that, after all, it's up to a girl to keep her place. Do you think Grace should go?

10. If your parents or your pastor warned you that the water you were about to drink is poisoned, would you drink the water anyway, just because you could see nothing wrong with it? Do you think people who want to poison others through bad reading would be foolish enough to label the books "Poison"? Do they want you to see that they are bad? Then do you think it wise not to listen to the warnings of your parents or your pastor in regard to dangerous amusements, such as dances, movies, etc.?

11. Why did God choose Mary as His mother and St. Joseph as His foster father? Why was He particularly fond of St. John and of little children? Do you know what special favor virgins will enjoy in heaven? Who were the Vestal Virgins, and what favors did they enjoy?

12. Do you know of any great sinners who have become saints? The act of consecration to the Blessed Virgin has been highly recommended by priests to those who wish to free themselves from sins against the Sixth Commandment or to protect themselves against such sins. Say it every day with all your heart, especially when you find yourself in danger.

Quotations from the Bible

For each of the following quotations:
a) Identify the speaker.
b) State the conditions under which the statement was made.
c) Give the meaning.
d) Tell its significance.

"Thou shalt not commit adultery" (Exod. xx. 14).

"Thou shalt not covet thy neighbor's house: neither shalt thou desire his [neighbor's] wife" (Exod. xx. 17).

"Blessed are the clean of heart; for they shall see God" (Matt. v. 8).

Chapter XII
THE SEVENTH AND TENTH COMMANDMENTS

Man's Helpfulness on the Highway. Man's journey, as we have seen, can be helped best by the love of God and the love of neighbor. It is especially true that all of us who are pilgrims on the road should have a fine sense of justice. We should be satisfied with what is our own and be happy in our enjoyment of it. Naturally we shall want to share some of the good things of life with our friends, and, inspired by holy charity, give freely to less fortunate human beings who are with us on the same journey to eternal life.

The Seventh Commandment. The Seventh Commandment helps our progress on the Highway of Life by its command: *Thou Shalt not Steal.* It aims to promote justice among men and to prevent or discourage every injustice. What is forbidden by the commandment is more than the taking of property from its rightful owner, without his freely given consent. Any desire for, or consent to, the taking of the property of another without his consent is forbidden by this commandment and the Tenth Commandment. The possession of the property of another without his consent is a violation of this commandment.

What is Forbidden. If we make a list of the ways men have done injustice to one another, we shall know some of the ways the commandment is broken, and what is forbidden by it. The buying of stolen goods is forbidden as well as the stealing of goods, for the former only encourages the latter. The finder of goods belonging to another must try to find the owner and restore the lost thing. We can see, too, that not only is he a thief who goes and steals a woman's pocketbook, but also he who lies about the goods he sells, he who adulterates his goods, or he who sells adulterated goods as genuine, or he who defrauds by false weights or measures, or he who obtains money under pretense of poverty. Those who do not give full service for their pay in public or private employment "steal," as well as those who do not pay the laborer or worker his hire. Those who defraud their creditors or deny their just debts, steal. But to be too hard on those who owe us or to press men who really cannot pay their debts, leads to rapacity, a serious violation of this commandment. Other forms of stealing will suggest themselves to you, perhaps even among boys or girls.

Why We Must Make Restitution. We cannot be forgiven any of these sins unless we give back, or make restitution of, what we have unjustly taken or possessed to the person whose property we have taken or to his heirs. In case this cannot be done, we must give an equal amount in alms to the poor. "Without restitution," says St. Augustine, "the sin is not forgiven." This duty of restitution is placed not only on the person who did the stealing, but on everyone who coöperated or helped in his sin; the one who may have ordered it, or encouraged it, or remained silent when he could have prevented it, or who gained something from it, or who guarded, defended, or received the thief. All these are responsible for restoring ill-gotten goods or their value, as far as they are able, otherwise they cannot be forgiven. If restitution cannot be made in full, it should be in part — as much as possible. If restitution cannot be made all at once, it should be made as soon as possible. The property stolen may be given back through the priest who is bound to secrecy.

Almsgiving. On the other hand, this commandment, as the prophets and leaders in the Old Testament and in the New Testament teach us, implies an obligation that we sympathize with the poor and needy, and relieve their needs and distress both by our means and by our services. A very practical way to do this, today, is by active service in, or help to the Society of St. Vincent de Paul; as well as by direct service or aid where we know there is need. This side of the commandment is a positive aid to the life of our neighbor on the road we all travel, and it may lift him out of his sorrow, and may restore or strengthen his faith in God, which will be a greater service than the mere giving of alms.

The Occasions of Sin. We should do everything we can to keep ourselves from the occasions of this sin. We should be industrious and regular in our work, preparing ourselves to give better service, and receive, thereby, perhaps promotion. We should be careful not to go with companions or groups who have more money than we have, or who spend it faster and more showily. We should beware of that which the comics in our newspapers call "Keeping up with the Joneses." We should avoid all tastes for clothes, or forms of amusements, or sports, beyond our normal means. Such things are too likely to lead us into temptation, and finally to sin, and perhaps even to prison and disgrace. A good, decent life within our means, with simple pleasures, will give us a contentment of life which the "highflier," the "spendthrift," and the like, will never know.

The Seventh and Tenth Commandments. The Tenth Commandment which is *Thou Shalt not Covet Thy Neighbor's Goods* is a strengthening of the Seventh. It emphasizes not the act of stealing, but all unlawful desire for the neighbor's property. The good man will be satisfied with what he has. He will not desire what belongs to others, and he will rejoice in others' welfare as he is content with his own. The temptations to violate the Seventh Commandment are removed at their source, and the same thing is true as we have seen in the relation of the Ninth Commandment to the Sixth.

Concupiscence. Disorderly and vicious desires, concupiscence, which is the penalty of original sin, are forbidden because they are the fuel of sin. They are evil. They are wrong. They lead to injustice. They destroy the peace of man's inner life. They lead to sin. Whereas we should be glad over our neighbor's welfare, we make our neighbor our enemy because he stands in the way of our desire. Whereas we should be satisfied with what we have, we become dissatisfied even unto sin. Whereas we know that our neighbor has a right to what is his, we desire to take or keep wrongfully what belongs to him. It is for these reasons that

SEVENTH AND TENTH COMMANDMENTS

covetousness is especially forbidden by the Tenth Commandment in addition to the prohibition of the Seventh Commandment.

Questions from the Catechism

Q. What is the Seventh Commandment?
A. **The Seventh Commandment is: Thou shalt not steal.**

Q. What are we commanded by the Seventh Commandment?
A. **By the Seventh Commandment we are commanded to give to all men what belongs to them and to respect their property.**

Q. What is forbidden by the Seventh Commandment?
A. **The Seventh Commandment forbids all unjust taking or keeping what belongs to another.**

Q. Are we bound to restore ill-gotten goods?
A. **We are bound to restore ill-gotten goods, or the value of them, as far as we are able; otherwise we cannot be forgiven.**

Q. Are we obliged to repair the damage we have unjustly caused?
A. **We are bound to repair the damage we have unjustly caused.**

Q. What is the Tenth Commandment?
A. **The Tenth Commandment is: Thou shalt not covet thy neighbor's goods.**

Q. What are we commanded by the Tenth Commandment?
A. **By the Tenth Commandment we are commanded to be content with what we have, and to rejoice in our neighbor's welfare.**

Q. What is forbidden by the Tenth Commandment?
A. **The Tenth Commandment forbids all desires to take or keep wrongfully what belongs to another.**

Problem Questions

1. Mother has given you a dollar to buy groceries. The sale today saves you ten cents. What will a truly honest boy do? What do you say about the boy who would spend it for candy without his mother's knowledge?

2. What would you say about putting that money into the mite box in school without your mother's knowledge?

3. Even though stealing a pencil or some paper from a friend is not a serious sin, still you know that it is wrong. Why should you not take it? (It offends God venially.)

4. What may happen to a child who has the habit of taking little things from his neighbor in school without asking his permission?

5. If you know that a certain girl is taking things from the other pupils, will you keep still about it as long as your things are not taken? Whom should you tell?

6. Tell the children what you would say to a pupil in your class who took your pencils a number of times and has not returned them.

7. You know your little friend has taken a quarter from his home and bought some candy. He offers to treat you. Are you stealing by taking some of it? How would you make him realize that this is very wrong?

8. You read or hear so often about robberies, especially in the large cities. What is robbery and what kind of sin is it?

9. What is the difference between robbery and theft?

10. This last Christmas robbers broke into an orphanage and stole the orphans' gifts and goodies, even some of their clothes. Did they commit a graver sin than if they had stolen from other children?

11. What kind of sin is it to steal from the Church, something that belongs to the Church? (Sacrilege.) Is it always a mortal sin? (No.)

12. Very often when people go traveling, they will take towels, napkins, spoons, and suchlike, as souvenirs from places they visit. Is this stealing?

13. Just a few years ago many babies died in New York. It was proved that the milk which the mothers bought for them was not pure and nutritious enough. It had been adulterated and so the mothers were cheated. Who is guilty before God for so many deaths?

14. A merchant has been using incorrect weights for defrauding the people. What can you say about such methods?

15. You have a counterfeit dollar and know it. You got it from somebody else in change. You will be the loser if you do not use it to pay your debt. What will you do in the case?

16. The conductor has forgotten to collect your fare. Should you pay him of your own accord?

17. Many men make money by gambling. They are Catholics and go to Church regularly. What might Protestants say on this point about the Catholic Church? What do you say?

18. Mr. Frank is always grumbling about paying his school taxes and assessments, saying he has no children in school. Why do you think he is doing wrong?

19. In a very famous letter to the world, called an encyclical, Pope Leo XIII, Our Holy Father, said, "Every wage earner is entitled to a just wage." What do you think he meant? Explain also how the wage earner must be just to his employer.

20. Whenever you have found something of great or small value, what should you do?

21. You and another boy have been trying to win the highest honors in your class. Both of you have worked very, very hard. He wins. A

SEVENTH AND TENTH COMMANDMENTS

temptation to wish him all kinds of bad things comes upon you, but you heroically overcome it and are kind and good to him. Who is the greater hero in God's eyes?

22. How do you think a child will grow up who is never satisfied with what he has but always wants more and more?

23. When you are tempted to desire something unlawfully, how about thinking like this: "No person knows my thoughts, but there is One who examines my mind and heart — God"?

24. Does the Tenth Commandment forbid one to desire great advancement in one's work or in acquiring property?

25. John has cut a little hole in his school desk. Day by day it gets a little larger. Is he committing sin?

26. You see a boy marking up some of the schoolbooks with ink. What are you going to do about that, or isn't it any of your business?

27. On your way home from school every evening a group of boys do something wrong and think it is a good joke; for instance, they mark up or smear walls of buildings, steal fruit from a stand or from an orchard, tear each other's clothing, break down fences. You know all these things are wrong. What could you do about it?

28. At times a child is found in school who is happy when he can damage property. He lets the faucet open, writes on the walls, breaks locks, etc. How could you other boys help him to stop this?

29. You have borrowed a book from your friend. Of course, you mean to restore it, but months have slipped by and the book is showing pretty hard use. How are you failing in showing respect to your neighbor's property?

Quotations from the Bible

For each of the following quotations:
a) Identify the speaker.
b) State the conditions under which the statement was made.
c) Give the meaning.
d) Tell its significance.

"Thou shalt not steal" (Exod. xx. 15).

"Thou shalt not covet thy neighbor's house: neither shalt thou desire his wife, nor his servant, nor his handmaid, nor his ox, nor his ass, nor anything that is his" (Exod. xx. 17).

Chapter XIII
THE EIGHTH COMMANDMENT

Excuses for Lies. Another of the signposts on the highway leading to God warns us against lies and the father of lies who is the devil. For human beings this is a very wise provision. Nothing is so easy, so simple, and seems so unimportant as lies to change our direction from God, who is Love, to the devil, who is the father of lies. We are always so ready to make excuses. We call our false witness only a "white lie." We excuse ourselves on the ground that certain worldly wise people lie, as if we should not trust in God instead of such. We excuse ourselves in telling lies for revenge, hurting ourselves as well as our enemy. We seem to think it right to return evil for evil when as true Christians and sons of God we should rather return good for evil. We make such other excuses for our falsehoods and perjuries as our human weakness or inconvenience, or perhaps we say it helps us in our business.

The Eighth Commandment. The Eighth Commandment, which is, *Thou Shalt not Bear False Witness Against Thy Neighbor,* forbids all these things. In the passage in the third book of the Old Testament (Leviticus), where the commandments are repeated, the Eighth Commandment is thus worded: "You shall not steal. You shall not lie, neither shall any man deceive his neighbor" (Lev. xix. 11).

In Courts of Justice. It especially forbids that false witness or testimony which is given on oath in a court of justice. In this case we call, as it were, God to witness the truth of what we say. To lie in such a case is to tell a falsehood to God who is Truth itself, and who cannot be deceived. Because men give special trust and regard to statements made under such conditions, evil-minded people may use it, and thus defy God to deceive men. Men, of course, punish severely by imprisonment and fine those who are known to lie under oath; i.e., commit perjury. This is, of course, as it should be, because our system of courts of justice is based on trust in statements made under oath.

Who is My Neighbor? Who is the neighbor against whom false witness must not be borne? If we consider the case carefully, it forbids all deceit, lying, or perjury. In the parable of the good Samaritan, Christ Himself tells us who our neighbor is. He is the one who shows mercy, or the one who needs our help whether he be fellow citizen or stranger, friend or enemy — in other words, every other human being.

"Let no one," says the great St. Augustine, "who bears false testimony against himself think that he has not violated this commandment, for the standard of loving our neighbor is the love which we cherish toward ourselves."

No Lies For or Against Our Neighbor. Nor is false witness, or false testimony in lies or deceit permitted *in favor of* our neighbor, whoever he is, or of ourselves. Detraction — making known the secret faults or sins of another — is forbidden by the Eighth Commandment. We must not exaggerate the faults of others; we must not sow discord or take pleasure in sowing discord. We must not be a whisperer of gossip or rumor or falsehood. Flattery, fawning, and insincere praise for any purpose and particularly for favor or money or honor is forbidden. *Calumny,* to charge a person with faults of which he is not guilty, is forbidden. It is always a sin, for it is always a lie.

Negative Commands. Thus, false witness or testimony of every kind, against, or even in favor of anybody including oneself, is forbidden by the Eighth Commandment. While the commandment is directed against false witness or testimony in the courts, it applies just as well to all the relations of life.

Reputation. This commandment aims to prevent injury to the honor or reputation of all other human beings. "A good name is better than great riches." It aims to prevent any injuring of another person's name by suspicion, detraction, slander, or abuse; or from any motive whatever — malice, revenge, hatred, ingratitude, or envy — which increases the enormity of the sin, or from thoughtlessness, carelessness, or idle gossip. The poet Shakespeare has put the case very well:

> Who steals my purse, steals trash.
> 'Tis something, nothing,
> 'Twas mine, 'Tis his, and has been slave to thousands,
> But he that filches from me my good name, robs me of that
> Which does not enrich him and makes me poor indeed.

Positive Commandment. The commandment besides forbidding certain things, commands certain things. It requires that justice be done: that the innocent shall not be condemned nor the guilty set free, and the decision shall not be influenced by money or favor, hatred or friendship. While the commandment is aimed directly at witnesses, it also applies to all persons involved — judges, lawyers, plaintiffs, and defendants. All must speak truthfully and in charity.

Love of Truth for Love of God. People should be taught to tell the truth because of love of God and love of their neighbor. They can see too, practically, that it prevents injustice being done to them. They should see first how grievously lies offend God. Six things there are which the Lord hateth, and the seventh, His soul detesteth: haughty eyes, a *lying tongue,* hands that shed innocent blood, *a heart that deviseth wicked plots,* feet that are swift to run into mischief, *a deceitful witness that uttereth lies,* etc.

The Wings of a Lie. One cannot hope for pardon for lies, or detraction, or calumny, against another until he has repaired as far as possible the injury done whether this was done in a court of justice, or in private and familiar conversation. It is almost impossible ever to catch up with a lie. It seems to have wings as swift as light and as evil as darkness. While remorse may come, and sorrow, it is hardly ever possible fully to repair for the injury done.

Effect of Lies on Society. Moreover, our relations with all our fellow men in government, in our neighborhood, in our social relations depend on truth and trust and confidence in these relations. By lying and deceit, these ties are broken and the very cement which holds society together is loosened.

What Charity Prevents. Charity is the best guide on God's Highway. "Charity thinketh no evil," as the Apostle says. It never harms our neighbor in his honor. It guards his reputation. It does not willingly listen to any unjust condemnation of a neighbor, to slander or gossip or idle rumor. It changes the direction of such evil talk. It expresses disapproval or at least displeasure at hearing violations of this commandment. It keeps in mind the words "Every idle word that men shall speak, they shall render an account for it in the Day of Judgment" (Matt. xii. 36).

What Charity Promotes. Charity finds good in the neighbor — at least some good. It confirms a habit of St. Teresa always to tell a good point about a person of whom evil was spoken. It follows the preference of St. Anselm, "I would far rather err by thinking good of a bad man than of thinking evil of a good man." It prefers silence to much speaking, or useless and idle words. It fills the mind with happy quotations from great literature — little prayers, expressing love of God, or love of neighbor. It spreads news and approval of the actual good that men do — little acts of kindness, of thoughtfulness, of love; it takes pleasure in praising justly and often in an act showing love of neighbor; it makes contagious the spirit of neighborliness, by loving the good and finding pleasure in it, and discovering the good of the neighbor and finding more pleasure in that. "Love your enemies. Bless them that curse you, do good to them that hate you, and pray for them that despitefully use you and persecute you." Then truly will you be children of God. You will show it perhaps best by doing the spiritual works of mercy: which are (1) to instruct the ignorant, (2) to counsel the doubtful, (3) to admonish sinners, (4) to bear wrongs patiently, (5) to forgive offenses willingly, (6) to comfort the afflicted, and (7) to pray for the living and the dead.

Questions from the Catechism

Q. What is the Eighth Commandment?
A. **The Eighth Commandment is: Thou shalt not bear false witness against thy neighbor.**

Q. What are we commanded by the Eighth Commandment?
A. **We are commanded by the Eighth Commandment** to speak the truth in all things, and to be careful of the honor and reputation of everyone.

Q. What is forbidden by the Eighth Commandment?
A. **The Eighth Commandment forbids** all rash judgment, back-biting, slanders, and lies.

Q. What must they do who have lied about their neighbor and seriously injured his character?
A. **They who have lied about their neighbor** and seriously injured his character, must repair the injury done so far as they are able, otherwise they will not be forgiven.

Problem Questions

1. A friend of yours is passing notes to others and does not pass them to you. You feel sure that she is telling things about you. Are you justified in drawing such conclusions? What sin do you commit? Can you give other examples of rash judgment.

2. A boy in your class has been found guilty of stealing. A few days later you miss some money out of your desk. You and your classmates conclude that the same boy stole your money. What should you do about it? Discuss fully.

3. Your mother sends you to the door to tell an agent that she is not at home. Should you obey?

a) Must children obey their parents in all things? Can you give an example of a case in which a child need not obey its parents?

b) Do you think there is any difference between lies that are harmless and those that are not? What would you consider a harmless lie? A harmful lie?

4. The teacher leaves the classroom and asks all the children to keep on working quietly. As soon as she is out you turn around and laugh and talk. When she returns you quickly get back to your work. Is there any wrong in that? What should you call such action?

5. Mary knows that Ethel is in bad company and is deceiving her teacher and her parents. Should she tell anyone? Should we always tell when we know something about another person?

6. You have a chance to look into your book during examination. May you do so?

7. The girl sitting behind you in school does not know her lesson. You can help her out by opening your book and placing it so that she can see the lesson. May you help her? Who do you think would be wronged more by such an action, the teacher or the girl?

8. One of the boys in your school is arrested for forgery. Everybody knows about it. May you discuss the matter?

9. You play sick so that you don't have to go to school. Is there any wrong in that?

10. Elsie has a new dress. She asks you how you like it. You do not like it at all, but do not wish to hurt her feelings. How would you answer her?

11. Your friend Margaret tells you a secret and asks you never to tell. You promise. Must you keep your word?

12. Your chum received a letter which she does not show you. You go to her desk later and read the letter without her consent or knowledge. Had you a right to do so?

13. A boy asks you where you are going. You tell him you are going to the North Pole. Is that a lie?

14. You listen with pleasure to an evil story about someone else. Do you commit any wrong?

Quotations from the Bible

For each of the following quotations:
a) Identify the speaker.
b) State the conditions under which the statement was made.
c) Give the meaning.
d) Tell its significance.

"Thou shalt not bear false witness against thy neighbor" (Exod. xx. 16).

"Charity thinketh no evil" (I Cor. xiii. 5).

"Love your enemies: do good to them that hate you: and pray for them that persecute and calumniate you" (Matt. v. 44).

Chapter XIV
SIN

Failure to Keep the Commandments. The soul's Highway to God is the road we travel when we keep the commandments. But though this is the road to true happiness, man sometimes loses his way. He violates these laws of God in many ways:

He does not pay proper respect to God.
He curses and uses profane language.
He is disobedient to and dishonors his parents.
He kills and murders.
He commits adultery.
He steals.
He lies and bears false witness against his neighbors.
He covets his neighbor's wife and his neighbor's goods.

We call such violations of the law of God sins. Any of the acts which have been listed here and described in the last few chapters, are violations of God's law. Sin is any violation of the law of God. Its nature is shown clearly in the violation of these commandments of God. There are other parts of God's laws which we must obey under pain of sin, as we shall see later. How really bad and terrible sin is can be seen from the punishment of Adam and Eve for their violation of God's command in the garden of Eden.

Actual Sin. While original sin is due to a willful violation of the command of God by our first parents, and we suffer because of it, as has already been shown, it is not a sin that we personally committed. In our case, original sin describes the condition of our soul as a result of the sin committed by Adam and Eve, which we call original sin. Our own violation of God's law, that which we ourselves willfully commit by thought or word or deed or omission or failure to do what we ought, is called "actual sin."

Actual sins are our personal sins — actually ours. Original sin is not for each of us an actual sin; it was, however, an actual sin of Adam. We inherit its effects.

Our Responsibility for Sins of Another. The sins we ourselves commit are actual sins. We shall point out later that because of what we do we may become responsible for the sins of other persons. In both these cases our sins are actual sins due to our personal act, word, or thought.

When We Are Responsible for Our Sins. There is an important point to remember about actual sins. If we should violate God's law (1) through mistake or misunderstanding, or (2) because we were so ill mentally or physically that we did not know what we were doing, or (3) because we were physically forced into it, then, of course, such a violation of God's law would not be a sin because we did not do the act willingly. If we do an evil act, it is not counted as a sin if we did not know that it was sinful, or if it was done through no fault of our own, or if our will did not consent to the act. A violation of the law of God knowingly, without force in any way, is a sin. We say, it must be deliberate or willful. We must know what we are doing and consent to it of our own free will. A person who willingly and knowingly violates one of God's commandments is guilty of sin.

Important and Less Important Matters. Wherever, then, man violates any of the laws or commands of God of his own free will, he commits a sin. If this violation of the law of God is in an important or grievous matter, and if deliberate, we say it is a mortal sin. When it is in a less important or slight matter, or if in a more important matter without sufficient reflection, it is a venial sin. Mortal means deadly, fatal. It kills the spiritual life of the soul; that is, it leaves the soul without sanctifying grace. It separates man from God so long as he is in that state of sin. If he should die in that state, he would suffer eternal punishment.

Examples of Mortal Sin. A violation of the law of God is a mortal sin if (1) it is in a grievous matter, (2) if the person gives it sufficient reflection so that he understands what he is doing, and (3) if he agrees or consents to do it; i.e., if there is full consent of his will. The sin happens at the moment of consent, whether the act itself is ever carried out. What goes on in your mind and conscience is most important. You and God are the only ones who really know your thoughts and motives.

Examples of mortal sin are as follows: Whenever there is a violation of God's laws in a grave matter, with the knowledge and consent of the doer, there is mortal sin. Willful murder is a mortal sin; robbery, burglary, and theft of considerable amounts are mortal sins. So is willful withholding of a laborer's pay. Willful disrespect to parents may be a mortal sin. To take a small amount from a very poor person may be a mortal sin. Willful sins against modesty and purity are always mortal sins. We have repeated the words "willful" in the description of these mortal sins to bring out this factor and the malice in the act.

Venial Sins. Where any of the three conditions for a mortal sin are not found in an act of man violating a law of command of God, we have venial sins. If we violate God's law in the less important matters, it is a venial sin. If we did not know or understand, or we did not know sufficiently the evil of what we were doing, we committed a venial sin; or if we did not fully consent to the violation of God's law, it was a venial sin, even in an important matter.

Examples of Venial Sins. It is difficult to give examples of venial sins because it is difficult to tell in any one case how clearly the person knew what he was doing, how he deliberated and how fully or partially he gave his consent. But these may be taken as examples:

Theft of a small amount.
Taking a pencil.
Keeping an umbrella you have borrowed.
Referring to God's name irreverently in passion.
Going to Mass late, before the Offertory, through carelessness.

Love of God Will Save Us. God gave us free will that we might serve Him if we will, and take punishment if we do not. We understand that and yet men violate the laws of God. We excuse ourselves by saying we are human. But we remember the command: "Thou shalt love the Lord thy God with thy whole heart, with all thy soul, and with all thy strength." If we do that, we can be sure of the final outcome.

The Seven Capital Sins. But there are certain qualities in human beings which lead man off God's Highway of a holy and blessed and good life, to what we might call the devil's highway to everlasting fire.

These tendencies of human nature which are likely to lead us into sin are: (1) Pride, (2) Covetousness, (3) Lust, (4) Anger, (5) Gluttony, (6) Envy, (7) Sloth.

Perhaps one way to get an idea of these sources of sins is to list their opposites with them. These sources and their opposites are:

1. Pride   Humility
2. Covetousness   Liberality
3. Lust   Chastity
4. Anger   Meekness
5. Gluttony   Temperance
6. Envy   Brotherly Love
7. Sloth   Diligence

These are not so much sins in the sense in which we have defined sin, as they are the sources or conditions of sins, the fountains from which sins come, they are the *capital* of sins. They are usually referred to as the capital sins.

Pride. Pride is an inordinate love of our own greatness. It is a false sense of our own importance compared to others, especially in relation to God. There can be no comparison, but man sets up his own will against God in his false pride. This leads him to violations of the command to worship God and Him only, not to take the name of the Lord in vain, to honor father and mother. There are a number of sayings in the Book of Proverbs that are interesting here:

Pride goeth before destruction: and the spirit is lifted up before a fall (xvi. 18).

In the mouth of a fool is the rod of pride: but the lips of the wise preserve them (xiv. 3).

Humiliation followeth the proud: and glory shall uphold the humble of spirit (xxix. 23).

Covetousness. "Lead me into the path of Thy commandments; for this same I have desired. Incline my heart unto Thy testimonies and not to covetousness" (Ps. cxviii. 35–36).

In these verses from Psalm cxviii we see the contrast between the path of the commandment and covetousness. Covetousness leads us from the path of the commandments. It is the desire for things not our own. It is a strong or disorderly desire for what belongs to our neighbor. It is specifically forbidden by the Ninth and Tenth Commandments. It also leads to violation of the commandment *not to steal*. It prevents charity entering our hearts; it prevents us from doing the deeds of mercy.

Lust. Lust is an inordinate appetite for sexual gratification. To seek this gratification outside of matrimony is against God's law. It applies to the desire as well as to the act. When yielded to unlawfully it shows a lack of self-control. The effects of lust are thus described:

Lust leads to excessive fondness for amusement, dissipation, neglect of duties, shameless excesses, seduction of innocence, enmity, duels, suicide, madness, despair.

Anger. "The patient man is better than the valiant: He that is slow to anger is better than the mighty, and he that ruleth his spirit, than he that taketh cities" (Prov. xvi. 32).

This passage from the Book of Proverbs is a good introduction to a few remarks on anger. Anger, like all the qualities we are considering, is a lack of self-control. We are easily annoyed by what displeases us, and we fly into a passion. This kind of lack of control leads us to hatred, quarreling, cursing, blasphemy, and even to murder.

Gluttony. Gluttony also takes us from the path of God's ways. In Proverbs we read:

Hear thou, my son, and be wise: and guide thy mind in the way.
Be not in the feasts of great drinkers, nor in their revelings, who contribute flesh to eat:
Because they that give themselves to drinking, and that club together shall be consumed; and drowsiness shall be clothed with rags (xxiii. 19–21)

SIN

The gluttonous person eats and drinks too much and too often. St. Paul says, "Their god is their belly." This habit leads to idleness, drunkenness, quarreling, destruction of home, and even murder.

Envy. In the Book of Wisdom we read, "By the envy of the devil, death came into the world: and they follow him that are of his side" (Wisd. ii. 24–25).

The envious person is pleased at his neighbor's misfortune or sadness, and is sad because of his spiritual or temporal joy. Envy must not enter into the good man's life. He must not envy even his enemy but love him as indeed he must love all men. "Envy not the unjust man" we read in Proverbs "and do not follow his ways." And again, "Let not thy heart envy sinners, but be thou in the fear of the Lord all day long." Or if we realize how unjust and, it would seem, almost unpardonable envy is, we would understand a final passage from Proverbs (xiv. 30): "Soundness of heart is the life of the flesh; but envy is the rottenness of the bones."

Sloth. The slothful are those who refuse to exert themselves and thus neglect their duties. The author of Proverbs describes the slothful man thus: "The slothful hideth his hand under his armpit, and it grieveth him to turn it to his mouth" (Prov. xxvi. 15). But the worst sloth is in spiritual things. God said, "I would that thou were cold or hot. But because thou art lukewarm and neither cold nor hot I will vomit thee out of My mouth." Sloth leads to ruin of property, lying, deceit, neglect of religion, and infidelity.

Cultivate the Virtues. The remedy to cure us of these vices or sources of sin is the building up of the opposite virtues: humility, the opposite of pride; liberality and generosity, the opposite of covetousness; chastity, the opposite of lust; meekness, the opposite of anger; temperance, the opposite of gluttony; brotherly love, the opposite of envy; and diligence, the opposite of sloth.

The Four Cardinal Virtues. These virtues which also are the opposite of the seven capital sins are included under another classification of virtues: the four cardinal virtues: prudence, justice, temperance, and fortitude. The Book of Wisdom says (viii. 7):

> And if a man love justice: her labors have great virtues; for she teacheth temperance, and prudence and justice, and fortitude, which are such things as men can have nothing more profitable in life.

Justice is the virtue by which we aim to give everyone his due, to do what is right, to be fair, to believe in the square deal. Prudence helps us to do justice by making us able to see what is truly good and pleasing to God, not to be deceived by false appearances, and to recognize whatever is evil and shun it. Fortitude keeps us in the way of virtue on God's Highway by making us able to bear whatever comes in the way of temptation, hardships, injustice, or persecution rather than to neglect our duty. And through temperance by avoiding extremes and holding to the golden mean of virtue we are able to overcome sensual or evil inclinations or desires when they come, and to resist all other allurements from virtue. Do you try to be prudent, just, strong, and temperate?

The Occasions of Sin. On the other hand, we may be lead into sin, or fall into sin, or be too weak to resist particular temptations, or occasions of sin. We may more readily fall into sin because of certain places, or of certain persons, or of other occasions. It is our duty to avoid such occasions of sins, for the simple reason as we are told that they who love the danger shall perish in it. Avoid persons, places, or things, or occasions or situations of any kind which have led you in the past or are likely to lead you into sin in the future.

Coöperating in Sin. We are, of course, responsible for our own sins. We may be responsible, too, for the sins of others when because of what we did or failed to do, we lead another person into sin.

We become responsible for another person's sin in many ways; nine especially have been noted:

1. **Counsel or Advice.** We become answerable for another person's sin when by our counsel or advice we urge a person,

especially one who is younger, or under our authority, or weaker, to do something which we know is evil.

2. **Command.** We become answerable for another person's sins if they are committed by our command, as for example to our younger brothers or sisters, to a servant under us, to an employee in our shop or factory, or to anyone under our authority or influence who obeys our commands.

3. **Consent.** We become answerable for any person's sin when, knowing its character, we consent to it. It will not do to think in your mind — "Well, it is his action, not mine, let him do it, if he wants to."

4. **Provocation.** We become answerable for another person's sin when we provoke it, when we keep "egging him on" as the boys say. When a person is weakening in his determination to do an evil and we add fuel to the fire by telling him he is "a fraid cat," "a quitter," "yellow," or that he can be leader of the gang, or he can get the new suit he wants, or whatever other means we use to provoke the individual to act.

5. **Praise or Flattery.** We become answerable for another person's sin when he does it through our praise or flattery. "Sure, now you're a man and you can do those things." "You can go to the movies with us tonight." Or to a superior, "That was cleverly done," or "You are so clever that you could get by without being caught."

6. **Silence.** We become answerable for the sins of another person when we stand by silent when a word from us could prevent the act when we are obliged to prevent it. Silence requires an act of mind and will and is just as real a sin as any which results in outward action.

7. **Connivance.** We become answerable for the sins of another person when we coöperate with the sinner either in ways mentioned above or by consenting to the act, or by failing to discover it when we could, or by profiting by it.

8. **Taking Part in Sin.** We become answerable for the sin of another person by taking a part in it, however small or slight it may seem.

9. **Defense of Sin.** We become answerable for another's sin by defense of it.

The Accessory Sin May be the Principal Sin. In these various ways we are the cause of another's sin, or actively take part in the sinning and therefore are as guilty as the person who did the act, or said the evil thing, or had the evil thought. The fact is that the main guilt may be ours, especially where the sin was committed by command, or with our help, or by provocation. We become guilty of sin ourselves in these ways even when the other person does not follow our advice, or give in to our flattery, or obey our command, or coöperate with our evil interest, whatever we may think of our responsibility. A leader of a boy's gang may injure his soul greatly unless he uses his power to prevent sins among the members. He cannot be careless or shirk his responsibility or say "I didn't do it."

The Old Adam in Man. It is the capital sins in the creature, man, that causes him at times to forget his Creator, and to violate deliberately the laws which God has commanded. These laws and commands are not only the ways of the Lord to heaven, they make the happiest paths on earth. But the old Adam in man, thinking in his pride to be greater than he is, shall lose also his Paradise — which he does every time he sins. He loses the spiritual life of the soul, which only a merciful God makes it possible to regain through a real repentance and a firm resolution not to sin again.

Sin is the enemy man meets on the paths of God's way. It is not, however, outside himself. It is in his heart, or, as we say, in his flesh. He has within himself both the power to control, and the principal sources of it — pride, covetousness, lust, anger, gluttony, envy, sloth. The mastery of these feelings and desires is called self-control, self-mastery. This comes about through self-denial for God's glory. Self-control is the supremely worth-while thing in life. It keeps us on God's path to our heavenly home. Sin came into the world through Adam, and it shall be mastered through Christ. One of the greatest of English poems, *Paradise*

Lost, written by John Milton, summarized this idea in its opening lines:

> Of man's first disobedience and the fruit of that forbidden tree,
> Whose mortal taste brought death into this world,
> And all our woe, until one great Man restored us,
> Sing Heavenly Muse.

Questions from the Catechism

Q. Is original sin the only kind of sin?
A. **Original sin is not the only kind of sin; there is another kind of sin, which we commit ourselves, called actual sin.**

Q. What is actual sin?
A. **Actual sin is any willful thought, word, deed, or omission contrary to the law of God.**

Q. How many kinds of actual sin are there?
A. **There are two kinds of actual sin — mortal and venial.**

Q. What is mortal sin?
A. **Mortal sin is a grievous offense against the law of God.**

Q. Why is this sin called mortal?
A. **This sin is called mortal because it deprives us of spiritual life, which is sanctifying grace, and brings everlasting death and damnation on the soul.**

Q. How many things are necessary to make a sin mortal?
A. **To make a sin mortal three things are necessary: a grievous matter, sufficient reflection, and full consent of the will.**

Q. What is venial sin?
A. **A venial sin is a slight offense against the law of God in matters of less importance, or in matters of great importance it is an offense committed without sufficient reflection or full consent of the will.**

Q. Which are the effects of venial sin?
A. **The effects of venial sin are the lessening of the love of God in our heart, the making us less worthy of His help, and the weakening of the power to resist mortal sin.**

Q. Which are the chief sources of sin?
A. **The chief sources of sin are seven: Pride, Covetousness, Lust, Anger, Gluttony, Envy, and Sloth; and they are commonly called capital sins.**

Problem Questions

1. What is the relation of sin to the commandments?
2. What is sin?
3. What are the occasions of sin?
4. In what ways may a person coöperate in the sins of another?
5. Give a concrete example.
6. Show in a particular case how the person who coöperates in a sin may be the real sinner.
7. What was Adam's sin in the Garden of Eden?
8. Is it in its nature the same kind of sin we commit when we sin?
9. What is actual sin? Was Adam's sin an actual sin?
10. What is original sin? What are its effects on us?
11. What is the difference between mortal and venial sin?
12. What three conditions of an act make it a mortal sin?
13. What are the seven capital sins? Are they sins in the same sense as we have been using the term?
14. Show how any (each) one of the capital sins leads to actual sins.
15. What do you mean by virtue?
16. What are the four cardinal virtues? Illustrate from your experience or reading.
17. Show how a real love of God in your heart will keep you from sin.
18. If you are deliberating on an act is it better to say "I won't do this because it is a sin," or "I will do the opposite because of love of God"?
19. Give from literature any character that illustrates the seven capital sins. How does the author make the character unlovely (repulsive)?
20. Report on Sargent's "Seven Capital Sins" from the frieze in the Boston Public Library.

Quotations from the Bible

For each of the following quotations:

a) Identify the speaker.
b) State the conditions under which the statement was made.
c) Give the meaning.
d) Tell its significance.

"They that are well have no need of a physician, but they that are sick" (Mark ii. 17).

"Thou shalt love the Lord thy God with thy whole heart, and with thy whole soul, and with thy whole strength" (Deut. vi. 5).

Chapter XV
THE MESSIAH

Signposts on God's Highway. The commandments are signposts on God's Highway to help man reach his home which is heaven. For years and generations the commandments guided the Jewish people in the way they should go. They still guide people everywhere in the world as to the right path.

A Promised Leader. But a greater thing was promised by God. He promised a great Leader who would show man the way of life. He was to be the Holy One, the Blessed God, the Anointed One, the Christ. He was to be the Savior, the Redeemer of mankind. He would wipe out the evils of Adam's sin. Sin came into the world through one man, Adam, and through sin, death, so through another Man, the Redeemer, would come grace and justice and life everlasting. The Son of God did not become man immediately after the sin of Adam and Eve, our first parents. The promise was made by God that the Redeemer or Savior of Mankind would come, but man did not know the time.

The Great Expectation. The Bible contains many prophetic sayings about Him. This expectation was alive in the time of Christ, for Andrew, after he stayed for a day with Christ, hastened to find his brother, Simon, whom Christ called Peter, to announce the great news: "We have found the Messias, which is, being interpreted, the Christ" (John i. 41). And Philip says of Jesus: "We have found Him of whom Moses in the law, and the prophets did write, Jesus, the son of Joseph of Nazareth" (John i. 45). And Nathaniel said to Him: "Thou art the Son of God, Thou art the King of Israel" (John i. 49). Surely according to this testimony, this is the Messiah. And the woman of Samaria at Jacob's well, to whom He spoke of a curing water, which, if men drink, they should not die, says prophetically enough:

The woman saith to Him: I know that the Messias cometh (who is called Christ): therefore, when He is come, He will tell us all things (John iv. 25).

Great was the expectation among the Jews of the Messiah who would save the world. Men could be saved before Christ the Son of God, became man, by believing in the Redeemer or Messiah to come, by keeping the commandments, and by being truly sorry for their sins.

The Prophecies of the Messiah. The statements regarding the Messiah in the Bible are:

He Shall be of the Seed of Abraham:

By My own self have I sworn, saith the Lord: because thou hast done this thing, and hast not spared thy only-begotten son for My sake:
I will bless thee, and I will multiply thy seed as the stars of heaven, and as the sand that is by the seashore: thy seed shall possess the gates of their enemies.
And in thy seed shall all the nations of the earth be blessed, because thou hast obeyed My voice (Gen. xxii. 16–18).

He Shall be of the Seed of David:

The Lord hath sworn truth to David, and He will not make it void: of the fruit of thy womb I will set upon thy throne (Ps. cxxxi. 11).

He Shall be Born in Bethlehem:

And thou, Bethlehem Ephrata, art a little one among the thousands of Juda: out of thee shall He come forth unto Me that is to be the ruler in Israel: and His going forth is from the beginning, from the days of eternity (Mich. v. 2).

He Shall be Born of a Virgin:

Therefore the Lord Himself shall give you a sign. Behold a virgin shall conceive, and bear a son, and His name shall be called Emmanuel (Isa. vii. 14).

Young Men Shall See Visions: Old Men Shall Dream Dreams:

And it shall come to pass, in the last days (saith the Lord) I will pour out My Spirit upon all flesh: and your sons and your daughters shall prophesy, and your young men shall see visions, and your old men shall dream dreams.
And upon My servants indeed, and upon My handmaids will I pour out in those days of My Spirit, and they shall prophesy.

THE MESSIAH

And I will show wonders in the heaven above, and signs on the earth beneath: blood and fire, and vapor of smoke.

The sun shall be turned into darkness, and the moon into blood, before the great and manifest day of the Lord come.

And it shall come to pass, that whosoever shall call upon the name of the Lord, shall be saved (quoted in Acts ii. 17–21, Douay Version of the Bible).

He is the Son of God:

The Lord hath said to Me: Thou art My Son, this day have I begotten Thee (Ps. ii. 7).

I will be to Him a father, and He shall be to Me a son . . . (II Kings vii. 14).

He Shall Sit on the Right Hand of God:

The Lord said to my Lord: Sit Thou on My right hand: Until I make Thy enemies Thy footstool (Ps. cix. 1).

He Shall be Rejected by Men:

The stone which the builders rejected; the same is become the head of the corner (Ps. cxvii. 22).

He Shall be Valued at Thirty Pieces of Silver:

And I said to them: If it be good in your eyes, bring hither My wages: and if not, be quiet. And they weighed for My wages thirty pieces of silver (Zach. xi. 12).

His Garments Shall be Parted:

They parted My garments amongst them: and upon My vesture they cast lots (Ps. xxi. 19).

He Shall be the Prince of Peace:

For a Child is born to us, and a Son is given to us, and the government is upon His shoulder: and His name shall be called, Wonderful, Counselor, God the Mighty, the Father of the World to Come, the Prince of Peace.

His empire shall be multiplied, and there shall be no end of peace: He shall sit upon the throne of David, and upon his kingdom; to establish it and strengthen it with judgment, and with justice, from henceforth and forever; the zeal of the Lord of Hosts will perform this (Isa. ix. 6–7).

He Shall be Priest After the Order of Melchisedech:

The Lord hath sworn, and He will not repent: Thou art a priest forever according to the order of Melchisedech (Ps. cix. 4).

The Expected King. There was among the Jews a strong expectation of this King or Messiah. But the Jews were looking for an earthly king, living in palaces, clothed in purple, appearing with great pomp, great dignity, and even greater pageantry. They would become a great people in a political sense, their kingdom would be restored.

My Kingdom Is Not of This World. But no such king came and no such kingdom was created or restored. This King even said: "My kingdom of God is not eating and drinking, but justness and peace and joy in the Holy Spirit."

Jesus Christ is the Expected Redeemer. The promise of God is Christ, the Son of God. The Child born of a virgin who shall be called the Wonderful, the Prince of Peace, is Jesus Christ our Lord. The Savior of Men, the Redeemer of Men, is the same Christ Jesus, our Lord.

His Appearance in the World. Nothing that these people who expected an earthly king, hoped for, came to pass. In fact, everything was just the opposite. God works in mysterious ways His wonders to perform. The Child was born in a stable, though He was of the line of David and of Abraham. For thirty years He lived with Joseph and Mary with practically no record, except what His Blessed Mother kept in her heart. He Himself said: "The foxes have holes, and the birds of the air have nests, but the Son of Man hath not where to lay His head." After a bloody sweat, a cruel scourging, and being crowned with thorns, He is led unjustly to what men would call a shameful and ignominious death — crucifixion between two thieves. A strange king this, as earthly kings go. But He is no earthly king. He is the King of kings, the Lord of lords. He is the Son of God. Let us learn more of His life on earth.

Questions from the Catechism

Q. Did God abandon man after he fell into sin?

A. **God did not abandon man after he fell into sin, but promised him a Redeemer, who was to satisfy for man's sin and reopen to him the gates of heaven.**

Q. Did the Son of God become man immediately after the sin of our first parents?

THE MESSIAH

A. **The Son of God did not become man immediately after the sin of our first parents, but was promised to them as a Redeemer**

Q. How could they be saved who lived before the Son of God became man?

A. **They who lived before the Son of God became man could be saved by believing in a Redeemer to come, and by keeping the commandments.**

Problem Questions

1. Make a list of the Old Testament prophecies that you know by heart, regarding the Messiah.
2. What does the word *Messiah* mean?
3. What did the Jews of Christ's day think the kingdom of God would be?
4. Did the people of Christ's day recognize Him as the Messiah?
5. Why was the coming of the Messiah a greater event even than the gift to Moses of the Ten Commandments?

Quotations from the Bible

For each of the following quotations:
a) Identify the speaker.
b) State the conditions under which the statement was made.
c) Give the meaning.
d) Tell its significance.

"I will bless thee, and I will multiply thy seed as the stars of heaven, and as the sand that is by the seashore: thy seed shall possess the gates of their enemies.

"And in thy seed shall all the nations of the earth be blessed, because thou hast obeyed My voice" (Gen. xxii. 17–18).

"The Lord hath sworn truth to David, and He will not make it void: of the fruit of thy womb I will set upon thy throne" (Ps. cxxxi. 11).

"And thou, Bethlehem Ephrata, art a little one among the thousands of Juda: out of thee shall He come forth unto Me that is to be the Ruler of Israel: and His going forth is from the beginning, from the days of eternity" (Mich. v. 2).

"Therefore the Lord Himself shall give you a sign. Behold a virgin shall conceive, and bear a son, and His name shall be called Emmanuel" (Isa. vii. 14).

"The Lord hath said to Me: Thou art My son, this day have I begotten Thee" (Ps. ii. 7).

"The Lord said to my Lord: Sit Thou at My right hand: Until I make Thy enemies Thy footstool" (Ps. cix. 1).

"The stone which the builders rejected: the same is become the head of the corner" (Ps. cxvii. 22).

"And I said to them: If it be good in your eyes, bring hither My wages: and if not, be quiet. And they weighed for My wages thirty pieces of silver" (Zach. xi. 12).

"They parted My garments amongst them: and upon My vesture they cast lots" (Ps. xxi. 19).

"For a Child is born to us, and a son is given to us, and the government is upon His shoulder: and His name shall be called, Wonderful, Counselor, God the Mighty, the Father of the World to Come, the Prince of Peace.

"His empire shall be multiplied, and there shall be no end of peace: He shall sit upon the throne of David, and upon his kingdom; to establish it and strengthen it with judgment and with justice, from henceforth and forever; the zeal of the Lord of hosts will perform this" (Isa. ix. 6–7).

"The Lord hath sworn, and He will not repent: Thou art a priest forever according to the order of Melchisedech" (Ps. cix. 4).

"The Voice of one crying in the desert: Prepare ye the way of the Lord, make straight in the wilderness the paths of our God" (Isa. xl. 3).

"Behold My Servant, I will uphold Him: My elect, My soul delighteth in Him: I have given My spirit upon Him, He shall bring forth judgment to the Gentiles" (Isa. xlii. 1).

"They shall not leave anything thereof until morning, nor break a bone thereof, they shall observe all the ceremonies of the phase" (Num. ix. 12).

"Jesus saith to him: I am the Way, and the Truth, and the Life. No man cometh to the Father but by Me" (John xiv. 6).

"This day, is born to you a Savior who is Christ the Lord" (Luke ii. 11).

"Thou shalt call His name Jesus. For He shall save His people from their sins" (Matt. i. 21).

To what incident does the following description refer?
Who was present?
What is the significance of the event?

"God so loved the world, as to give His only-begotten Son; that whosoever believeth in Him may not perish, but may have life everlasting" (John iii. 16).

Chapter XVI
PREPARE YE THE WAY OF THE LORD

The Acceptable Time Had Arrived. There was a rather wonderful series of events that happened in the year just before the birth of the Savior. God's angels came to announce the most important messages ever sent to man. This series of messages reached their highest point in the announcement: "Unto you is born a Savior who is Christ, the Lord." This series of messages is as follows:

1. Announcement by an angel to Zachary of the birth of his son, John the Baptist.

2. Annunciation by an angel to the Blessed Virgin Mary that she was chosen to be the Mother of Jesus.

3. Announcement by an angel to the shepherds of the birth of the Savior.

So truly might it be said, as indeed it was said: "Now is the acceptable time, now is the day of salvation."

The Angel's Announcement to Zachary. The message of the birth of John the Baptist was carried by the Angel Gabriel, who stands by the throne of God.

There was in the days of Herod, the king of Judea, a certain priest named Zachary, of the course of Abia; and his wife was of the daughters of Aaron, and her name Elizabeth. And they were both just before God, walking in all the commandments and justifications of the Lord without blame. And they had no son, for that Elizabeth was barren, and they both were well advanced in years. And it came to pass, when he executed the priestly function in the order of his course before God, according to the custom of the priestly office, it was his lot to offer incense, going into the temple of the Lord. And all the multitude of the people was praying without, at the hour of incense. And there appeared to him an angel of the Lord, standing on the right side of the altar of incense. And Zachary seeing him, was troubled, and fear fell upon him. But the angel said to him: Fear not, Zachary, for thy prayer is heard; and thy wife Elizabeth shall

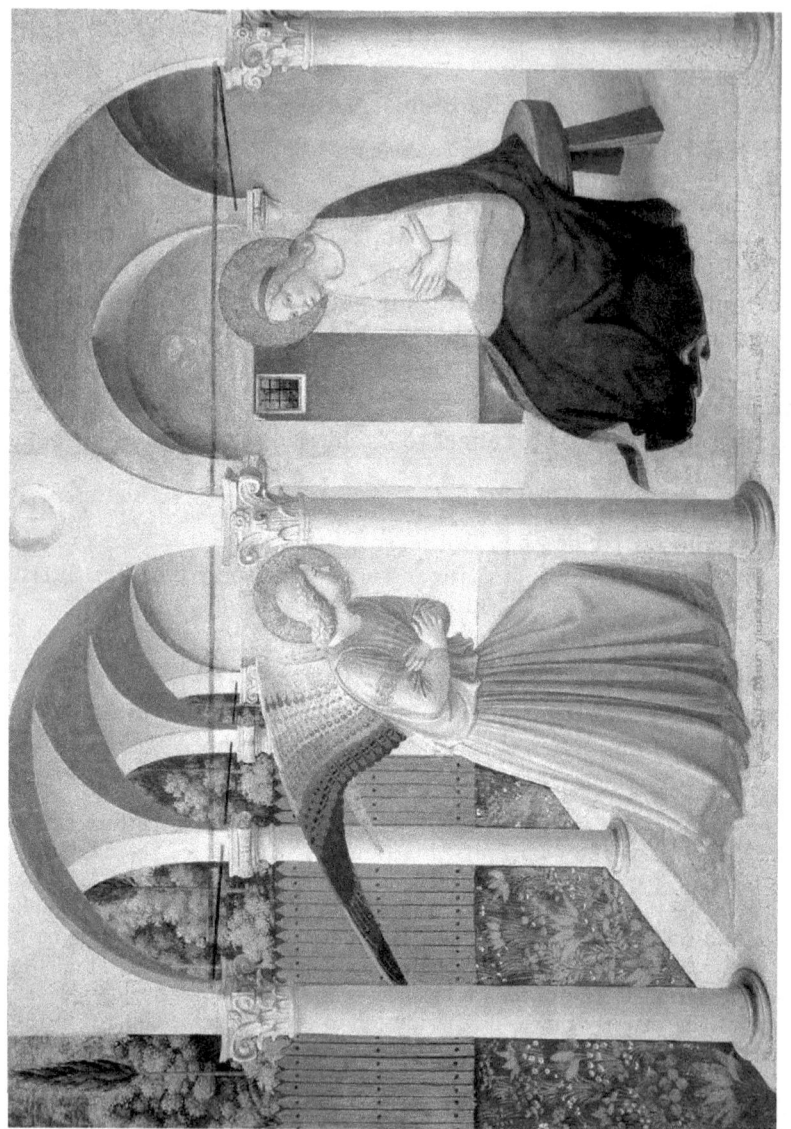

THE ANNUNCIATION

Painting by Fra Angelico, fifteenth century, in the chapel of convent, Monte Carlo.

bear thee a son, and thou shalt call his name John: And thou shalt have joy and gladness, and many shall rejoice in his nativity. For he shall be great before the Lord, and shall drink no wine nor strong drink: and he shall be filled with the Holy Ghost, even from his mother's womb. And he shall convert many of the children of Israel to the Lord their God. And he shall go before Him in the spirit and power of Elias: that he may turn the hearts of the fathers unto the children, and the incredulous to the wisdom of the just, to prepare unto the Lord a perfect people. And Zachary said to the angel: Whereby shall I know this? for I am an old man, and my wife is advanced in years. And the angel answering, said to him: I am Gabriel, who stands before God; and am sent to speak to thee, and to bring thee these good tidings. And behold, thou shalt be dumb, and shalt not be able to speak until the day wherein these things shall come to pass, because thou hast not believed my words, which shall be fulfilled in their time. And the people were waiting for Zachary; and they wondered that he tarried so long in the temple. And when he came out he could not speak to them: and they understood that he had seen a vision in the temple. And he made signs to them, and remained dumb. And it came to pass, after the days of his office were accomplished, he departed to his own house. And after those days, Elizabeth his wife conceived, and hid herself five months, saying: Thus hath the Lord dealt with me in the days wherein He hath had regard to take away my reproach among men (Luke i. 5–25).

Fulfillment of Prophecy. John the Baptist was the fulfillment of two prophecies of the Old Testament. In Malachias it was prophesied:

Behold I send My angel, and he shall prepare the way before My Face. And presently the Lord, whom you seek, and the angel of the testament, whom you desire, shall come to His temple. Behold he cometh, saith the Lord of Hosts (Mal. iii. 1).

In Isaiah it was said:

The voice of one crying in the desert: Prepare ye the way of the Lord, make straight in the wilderness the paths of our God (Isa. xl. 3).

The Annunciation. On March 25 of the year before Christ's birth, the announcement is made to Mary that she is to be the Mother of the Son of the Most High, conceived by the Holy Ghost:

And in the sixth month, the angel Gabriel was sent from God into a city of Galilee, called Nazareth. To a virgin espoused to a man whose name was Joseph, of the house of David; and the virgin's name was Mary. And the angel being come in, said unto her: Hail, full of grace, the Lord is with thee: blessed art thou among women. Who having heard was troubled at his saying, and thought with herself what manner of salutation this should be. And the angel said to her: Fear not, Mary, for thou hast found grace with God. Behold thou shalt conceive in thy womb, and shalt bring forth a son and thou shalt call His name Jesus. He shall be great, and shall be called the Son of the Most High; and the Lord God shall give unto Him the throne of David His father; and He shall reign in the house of Jacob forever. And of His kingdom there shall be no end. And Mary said to the angel: How shall this be done, because I know not man? And the angel answering, said to her: The Holy Ghost shall come upon thee, and the power of the Most High shall overshadow thee. And therefore also the Holy which shall be born of thee shall be called the Son of God. And behold thy cousin Elizabeth, she also hath conceived a son in her old age; and this is the sixth month with her that is called barren: Because no word shall be impossible with God. And Mary said: Behold the handmaid of the Lord; be it done to me according to thy word. And the angel departed from her (Luke i. 26–38). (See also Isa. vii. 14; Dan. vii. 14, 27; Mich. iv. 7.)

This day in which the Angel Gabriel announced to the Blessed Virgin Mary that she was to be the Mother of God is known as Annunciation Day.

The Birth of Christ. And the event for which the world had so long been waiting had taken place.

And it came to pass that in those days there went out a decree from Cæsar Augustus, that the whole world should be enrolled. This enrolling was first made by Cyrinus, the governor of Syria. And all went to be enrolled, everyone into his own city.

And Joseph also went up from Galilee, out of the city of Nazareth into Judea, to the city of David, which is called Bethlehem; because he was of the house and family of David, to be enrolled with Mary his espoused wife, who was with child.

And it came to pass, that when they were there, her days were accomplished, that she should be delivered. And she brought forth her first-born Son, and wrapped Him up in swaddling clothes, and laid Him in a manger; because there was no room for them in the inn (Luke ii. 1–7).

And this day is Christmas, December 25, that we all know so well, one of the most joyous days in all human history; the day on which Christ was born in a stable in Bethlehem. And that first Christmas occurred over nineteen hundred years ago. The Son of

God, as announced by the Angel Gabriel, became the Son of the Blessed Virgin Mary. So Mary is truly the Mother of God, because Christ is both the Son of God, and the Son of man. We call what happened at the birth of Christ the Incarnation; that is, the Son of God became man. At that time the Son of God, who existed as God from all eternity, became man.

The Angel's Announcement to the Shepherds. At the time when our Lord was born an angel appears to shepherds keeping the night watches, and brings them the good tidings of great joy, that shall be to all the people:

And there were in the same country shepherds watching, and keeping the night watches over their flock.

And behold an angel of the Lord stood by them, and the brightness of God shone round about them; and they feared with a great fear.

And the angel said to them: Fear not, for, behold, I bring you good tidings of great joy, that shall be to all thy people:

For, this day, is born to you a Savior, who is Christ the Lord, in the city of David.

And this shall be a sign unto you. You shall find the infant wrapped in swaddling clothes, and laid in a manger.

And suddenly there was with the angel a multitude of the heavenly army, praising God, and saying:

Glory to God in the highest; and on earth peace to men of good will.

And it came to pass, after the angels departed from them into heaven the shepherds said one to another: Let us go over to Bethlehem, and let us see this word that is come to pass, which the Lord hath showed to us.

And they came with haste: and they found Mary and Joseph, and the Infant lying in the manger.

And seeing, they understood of the word that had been spoken to them concerning this Child.

And all that heard, wondered; and at those things that were told them by the shepherds.

But Mary kept all these words pondering *them* in her heart.

And the shepherds returned, glorifying and praising God, for all things they had heard and seen, as it was told unto them (Luke ii. 8–20).

Who is Christ? The facts concerning Christ in this chapter are given briefly in the simple words of the Apostles' Creed:

I believe in Jesus Christ, His [God's] only Son, our Lord, who was conceived by the Holy Ghost, born of the Virgin Mary.

Questions from the Catechism

Q. Why is Jesus Christ true man?
A. **Jesus Christ is true man because He is the Son of the Blessed Virgin Mary and has a body and soul like ours.**

Q. How many natures are there in Jesus Christ?
A. **In Jesus Christ there are two natures, the nature of God and the nature of man.**

Q. Is Jesus Christ more than one person?
A. **No, Jesus Christ is but one Divine Person.**

Q. Was Jesus Christ always God?
A. **Jesus Christ was always God, as He is the second Person of the Blessed Trinity, equal to His Father from all eternity.**

Q. Was Jesus Christ always man?
A. **Jesus Christ was not always man, but became man at the time of His Incarnation.**

Q. What do you mean by the Incarnation?
A. **By the Incarnation I mean that the Son of God was made man.**

Q. How was the Son of God made man?
A. **The Son of God was conceived and made man by the power of the Holy Ghost, in the womb of the Blessed Virgin Mary.**

Q. Is the Blessed Virgin Mary truly the Mother of God?
A. **The Blessed Virgin Mary is truly the Mother of God, because the same Divine Person who is the Son of God is also the Son of the Blessed Virgin Mary.**

Q. On what day was the Son of God conceived and made man?
A. **The Son of God was conceived and made man on Annunciation day — the day on which the Angel Gabriel announced to the Blessed Virgin Mary that she was to be the Mother of God.**

Q. On what day was Christ born?
A. **Christ was born on Christmas Day in a stable at Bethlehem, over nineteen hundred years ago.**

Problem Questions

1. What extraordinary, in fact, supernatural events attended the birth of Christ?

2. What does "annunciation" mean? How many annunciations were there in fact? Why do we call the announcement to Mary, *the* Annunciation?

3. Compare the reception of the announcement to Mary and to Zachary.

PREPARE YE THE WAY

4. Was the announcement to the shepherds an announcement to you also? How did the shepherds respond? And what is your response?

5. Why did Joseph and Mary go to Bethlehem to be enrolled? Why is Christ sometimes called the Nazarene?

6. What thoughts are suggested by the fact that Joseph and Mary could find no place in an inn, and Christ was born in a stable?

7. Show how each of the Messianic prophecies are fulfilled in Christ.

8. What is the exact year of the birth of Christ?

Quotations from the Bible

For each of the following quotations:
a) Identify the speaker.
b) State the conditions under which the statement was made.
c) Give the meaning.
d) Tell its significance.

"Hail full of grace, the Lord is with thee; Blessed art thou among women" (Luke i. 28).

"I bring you good tidings of great joy, that shall be to all the people; for, this day is born to you a Savior, who is Christ the Lord, in the city of David. And this shall be a sign unto you. You shall find the infant wrapped in swaddling clothes, and laid in a manger" (Luke ii. 10–12).

"Glory to God in the highest and peace on earth to men of good will."

"Fear not, I bring you tidings of great joy."

"And she shall bring forth a son: and thou shalt call His name Jesus. For He shall save His people from their sins" (Matt. i. 21).

"The Word was made flesh, and dwelt among us (and we saw His glory, the glory as it were of the Only-Begotten of the Father) full of grace and truth" (John i. 14).

"Behold the handmaid of the Lord; be it done to me according to thy word" (Luke i. 38).

To what incident does the following description refer?
Who was present?
What is the significance of the event?

"The voice of one crying in the desert: Prepare ye the way of the Lord, make straight in the wilderness the paths of our God" (Isa. xl. 3).

Chapter XVII
THE EARLY LIFE OF CHRIST

The Birth of Christ Divides Time. Men have looked upon the birth of Jesus Christ, Savior of men, as so important that they date all time from the year in which He was born. The year of the birth of Christ is the year 1. All time before it is dated backward from it, the year just before it is the year 1 B.C., two years before is 2 B.C., and so on. Cæsar Augustus, who was Emperor of Rome during the life of Christ, was born 63 B.C.

Anno Domini. The year 1 is called the year A.D. 1, which is an abbreviation for *Anno Domini* 1. This means in the year of our Lord. A.D. 1931 means the 1931st year of our Lord. Thus every time we write the number of the year, we pay a tribute to the Lord.*

Birth of Christ. He was conceived by the Holy Ghost and born of the Virgin Mary, according to the will of God. This is according to the prophets in the Old Testament. This is the fact of history.

Angels Announce the Birth of Christ. The birth was a wonderful thing in every way. It was so important that angels were sent directly by God to earth — a rare happening. An angel came to tell Mary in advance that she had found favor with God and was to be the Mother of the Son of God. Angels appeared to the shepherds on December 25, to tell them the good tidings of great joy. And they left their sheep to visit the Shepherd of men, Jesus Christ, and adore Him.

The Presentation in the Temple. In accordance with the Jewish law, the Child Jesus was taken to Jerusalem to have offered for Him the sacrifice which was required, an offering of

---
*The actual year of the birth of our Lord was probably several years before the year A.D. 1 in our calendar. See *Catholic Encyclopedia*, Vol. III, pp. 735–736.

THE EARLY LIFE OF CHRIST

THE NATIVITY
Painting by Murillo.

a pair of turtle doves, or two young pigeons. It was while the Child was being presented in the Temple, and this sacrifice was being made, that the holy man, Simeon, made the prophecy: That this Child is set for the ruin and the resurrection of many in Israel. And to Mary he said: "Thy own soul a sword shall pierce" (see Luke ii. 34–35). It was at this time also that Anna, the prophetess, at once recognized the Christ and gave praise to the Lord "and spoke of Him to all that looked for the redemption of Israel" (Luke ii. 38).

The Wise Men. So also three Wise Men of the East, called Magi, saw the star of Christ in the heavens, and reaching Jerusalem, asked of Herod the King, where is He that is born King of the Jews? Herod was worried and sending the Wise Men to Bethlehem, told them to search out diligently for the Child, that he "may come and adore Him."

And when they had heard the king, they went their way; and behold, the star which they had seen in the East, went before them, until it came and stood over where the Child was. And seeing the star they rejoiced with exceeding great joy. And entering into the house, they found the child with Mary His Mother, and falling down, they adored Him; and opening their treasures, they offered Him gifts; gold, frankincense, and myrrh. And having received an answer in sleep that they should not return to Herod, they went back another way into their country (Matt. ii. 9–12. See also Mich. v. 2).

The Flight into Egypt. An angel of the Lord then appeared to Joseph after the Magi had gone, and told him to take the Child and Mother into Egypt, and "be there until I shall tell thee. For it will come to pass that Herod will seek the Child to destroy Him" (Matt. ii. 13). Joseph took Mary and Jesus to Egypt. This happened as prophesied. (See Osee xi. 1.)

And then came the murder of the Innocents, the first to die for Christ. This event, which the Church commemorates, the Feast of the Holy Innocents, December 28, is described by St. Matthew thus:

Then Herod perceiving that he was deluded by the Wise Men, was exceeding angry; and sending, killed all the men children that were in Bethlehem, and all the borders thereof, from two years old and under, according to the time which he had diligently inquired of the Wise Men.

Then was fulfilled that which was spoken by Jeremias the prophet, saying: A voice in Rama was heard, lamentation and great mourning; Rachel bewailing her children, and would not be comforted, because they were not (Matt. ii. 16–18).

The Return from Egypt. Herod died, and the angel appeared to Joseph, "Arise, and take the Child and His mother, and go into the land of Israel. For they are dead who sought the life of the Child" (Matt. ii. 20), and Joseph returned, but learning that the cruel son of Herod ruled in Judea, did not go to Bethlehem, but went to Nazareth in Galilee. Hence, we sometimes hear Jesus referred to as "the Nazarene."

Early Life Almost Unknown. Except for one very important thing, we know almost nothing of Christ's childhood, youth, and young manhood until the time when John baptized Jesus. Jesus was at this time 29 years old.

THE HOLY FAMILY
Painting by Giovanni Gagliardi, nineteenth century.

Jesus Twelve Years Old. The only event we do know anything about happened when Jesus was twelve years old, at the Jewish feast of the Pasch (our Easter). St. Luke tells the story in his Gospel:

And the Child grew, and waxed strong, full of wisdom; and the grace of God was in Him.

And His parents went every year to Jerusalem, at the solemn day of the Pasch.

And when He was twelve years old, they going up into Jerusalem, according to the custom of the feast,

And having fulfilled the days, when they returned, the child Jesus remained in Jerusalem; and His parents knew it not.

And thinking that He was in the company, they came a day's journey, and sought Him among their kinsfolks and acquaintance.

And not finding Him, they returned into Jerusalem, seeking Him.

And it came to pass, that, after three days, they found Him in the temple, sitting in the midst of the doctors, hearing them and asking them questions.

And all that heard Him were astonished at His wisdom and His answers.

And seeing *Him* they wondered. And His Mother said to Him: Son, why hast Thou done so to us? behold Thy father and I have sought Thee sorrowing.

And He said to them: How is it that you sought Me? Did you not know, that I must be about My Father's business?

And they understood not the word that He spoke unto them.

And He went down with them, and came to Nazareth, and was subject to them. And His Mother kept all these words in her heart.

And Jesus advanced in wisdom, and age, and grace with God and men (ii. 40–52).

The Expectation of the Child. From His twelfth year to His twenty-ninth, we know nothing of the life of Christ except that, in the words of the Scriptures "He was subject" to His parents; that is, He depended on them and obeyed them in all things. In the summer and autumn of the latter year, John the Baptist was preaching. People who were looking for the Christ, asked of John if he were the Christ. John's answer was clear and unmistakable:

I indeed baptize you with water; but there shall come One mightier than I, the latchet of whose shoes I am not worthy to loose: He shall baptize you with the Holy Ghost, and with fire: Whose fan is in His hand, and

He will purge His floor, and will gather the wheat into His barn; but the chaff He will burn with unquenchable fire (Luke iii. 16–17).

John Baptizes Christ. And Christ was baptized by John in December of His twenty-ninth year.

> Now it came to pass, when all the people were baptized, that Jesus also being baptized and praying, heaven was opened;
> And the Holy Ghost descended in a bodily shape, as a dove upon Him; and a voice came from heaven: Thou art My beloved Son; in Thee I am well pleased (Luke iii. 21–22).

The true nature of God had not been told or revealed to men until the coming of Christ. In the passage just quoted we have the three persons of God brought together before men.

There is God the Father who says, "This is My beloved Son, in whom I am well pleased."

This is God the Father's testimony that Christ is His beloved Son — God the Son.

The Holy Spirit is also God. He is sent by God the Father. He appears here descending as a dove.

God is One. We know for certain there is God the Father, God the Son, and God the Holy Ghost, and we know that God being supreme and infinite, cannot be divided, and cannot have an equal. God is one. There cannot be more than one God.

The Blessed Trinity. There is but one God, but with our limited and finite minds it is impossible to understand His nature. We call it a mystery because we do not understand it, but in the passages just quoted and in others, God has revealed to us His nature. The main points of this revelation are:

1. There is but one God.
2. There are three Divine Persons in God, so we call God the Blessed Trinity.
3. These Persons are really distinct and equal in all things — the Father, the Son, the Holy Ghost.
4. The Father is God and the First Person of the Blessed Trinity.
5. The Son is God and the Second Person of the Blessed Trinity.

6. The Holy Ghost is God and the Third Person of the Blessed Trinity.

7. The three Divine Persons
   a) are equal in all things,
   b) are one and the same God,
   c) have one and the same Divine nature and substance.

We shall learn more about the Father, the Son, and the Holy Ghost, but the Blessed Trinity will remain a mystery for our finite minds. We know it is true because it was told man by God Himself, but we do not fully understand it.

The Joyful Mysteries of the Rosary. Whenever you say your Rosary and meditate on the joyful mysteries you will recall the facts told in this and the preceding chapter about the childhood of Christ. The joyful mysteries are:

1. The Incarnation of our Lord.
2. The Visitation.
3. The Birth of our Lord.
4. The Presentation in the Temple.
5. The Finding of our Lord in the Temple.

Two of the Sorrows of Mary. Of the seven sorrows of Mary, two relate to the childhood of Christ. They are:

1. The Flight into Egypt.
2. The Losing of the Child Jesus.

Questions from the Catechism

Q. Is there but one God?
A. **Yes; there is but one God.**

Q. Why can there be but one God?
A. **There can be but one God because God, being supreme and infinite, cannot have an equal.**

Q. How many persons are there in God?
A. **In God there are three Divine persons, really distinct and equal in all things — the Father, the Son, and the Holy Ghost.**

Q. Is the Father God?
A. **The Father is God and the First Person of the Blessed Trinity.**

Q. Is the Son God?
A. **The Son is God and the Second Person of the Blessed Trinity.**

THE EARLY LIFE OF CHRIST

Q. Is the Holy Ghost God?
A. **The Holy Ghost is God and the Third Person of the Blessed Trinity.**
Q. What do you mean by the Blessed Trinity?
A. **By the Blessed Trinity I mean one God in three Divine Persons.**
Q. Are the three Divine Persons equal in all things?
A. **The three Divine Persons are equal in all things.**
Q. Are the three Divine Persons one and the same God?
A. **The three Divine Persons are one and the same God, having one and the same Divine nature and substance.**
Q. Can we fully understand how the three Divine Persons are one and the same God?
A. **We cannot fully understand how the three Divine Persons are one and the same God, because this is a mystery.**
Q. What is a mystery?
A. **A mystery is a truth which we cannot fully understand.**

Problem Questions

1. What are the principal events in the first twenty-nine years of Christ's life?

2. So far as you can find out, is there as good proof for these facts as there is for other facts (e.g., about Cæsar Augustus) of the same time?

3. Name (give artist's name) or find a great picture illustrating each of the events in the early life of Christ.

4. What does *Anno Domini* mean? What is the abbreviation for this?

5. What was the statement by Simeon when Christ was presented in the temple? What is meant by "presentation"? Who was Simeon?

6. When was Simeon's prophecy fulfilled?

7. What statement was made by Anna, the prophetess?

8. Show Heaven's guardianship of Christ during His early years.

9. Make a list of the appearances of angels in connection with the coming of Christ and His early life.

10. Describe the baptism of Christ by John in the River Jordan.

11. What significance have these facts with reference to the doctrine of the Trinity?

12. What is the doctrine of the Trinity? When was it first revealed to men?

13. What relation have the joyful mysteries of the Rosary to the childhood of Christ? What sorrows of Mary have relation to the childhood of Christ?

14. Why is Joseph called the foster father of Jesus?

Quotations from the Bible

For each of the following quotations:
a) Identify the speaker.
b) State the conditions under which the statement was made.
c) Give the meaning.
d) Tell its significance.

"Arise and take the Child and His Mother and go into the Land of Israel. For they are dead who sought the life of the Child" (Matt. ii. 20).

"Did you not know that I must be about My Father's business" (Luke ii. 49).

"I indeed baptize you with water; but there shall come one mightier than I, the latchet of whose shoes I am not worthy to loose: He shall baptize you with the Holy Ghost, and with fire" (Luke iii. 16).

"Thou art My beloved Son; in Thee I am well pleased" (Luke iii. 22).

Chapter XVIII
THE DIVINITY OF CHRIST: THE MIRACLES

The first twenty-nine years of Christ's life were not eventful, except for the striking happening in the temple during His twelfth year, when He amazed all who heard Him. For all else in His life during this period, we have only these words: "And He went down with them [Mary and Joseph], and came to Nazareth, and was subject to them. . . . And Jesus increased in wisdom and age and grace with God and man."

The Beginning of Christ's Public Life. The baptism of Christ by John is the beginning of Christ's public life. For a little more than three years He lived a public life until His death on the cross on Good Friday. In the next four chapters we shall concern ourselves only with the events of His public life up to a week before His death. This period is full of events; one follows right after the other, but they do not come so fast as in the last week before His death, which shall be treated in a later chapter.

The first and perhaps most striking fact of Christ's public life was the performance of miracles. The miracles prove without doubt that Christ is Divine for He performed them in His own name. Christ is God. No one but God, or one sent by God with power, could set aside God's laws which rule the world. Christ, merely by His word, cures a leper, a paralytic, a man sick with the palsy, or a man with a withered hand. He makes the blind see, the lame walk. He stills the storm: the winds obey Him. He walks on the water. He raises Lazarus from the dead, and the son of the widow of Naim. And so we shall see in the chapter on the Passion of Christ a series of *stupendous* miracles, the changing of the bread and wine into His own Body and Blood, His resurrection from the dead, and His ascension into heaven.

Giving the Power to Others. He, moreover, was able to give to mere men, the Apostles and others, the power to perform miracles in His name.

And they cast out many devils, and anointed with oil many that were sick and healed them (Mark vi. 13).

And heal the sick that are therein, and say to them: The kingdom of God is come nigh unto you (Luke x. 9).

And the seventy-two returned with joy, saying: Lord, the devils also are subject to us in Thy name (Luke x. 17).

Changing Water into Wine. Jesus began His miracles in Cana of Galilee, when He changed water into wine at the wedding feast. This is what happened:

And the third day, there was a marriage in Cana of Galilee: and the mother of Jesus was there.

And Jesus also was invited, and His disciples, to the marriage.

And the wine failing, the Mother of Jesus saith to Him: They have no wine.

And Jesus saith to her: Woman, what is that to Me, and to thee? My hour is not yet come.

His Mother saith to the waiters: Whatsoever He shall say to you, do ye.

Now there were set there six waterpots of stone, according to the manner of the purifying of the Jews, containing two or three measures apiece.

Jesus saith to them: Fill the waterpots with water. And they filled them up to the brim.

And Jesus saith to them: Draw out now, and carry to the chief steward of the feast. And they carried it.

And when the chief steward had tasted the water made wine, and knew not whence it was, but the waiters knew who had drawn the water; the chief steward calleth the bridegroom.

And saith to him: Every man at first setteth forth good wine, and when men have well drunk, then that which is worse. But thou hast kept the good wine until now (John ii. 1–10).

Feeding the Multitudes. His healing many and His cures have been mentioned in the first paragraph of this chapter. On two occasions He performed a remarkable miracle in feeding, amounting to four or five thousand people, with food enough for only a handful. In the case of feeding the five thousand men who had listened to Him, the story is as follows:

And when it was evening, His disciples came to Him, saying: This is a desert place, and the hour is now past: send away the multitudes, that going into the towns, they may buy themselves victuals.

THE DIVINITY OF CHRIST

But Jesus said to them: They have no need to go: give you them to eat. They answered Him: We have not here, but five loaves, and two fishes. He said to them: Bring them hither to Me.

And when He had commanded the multitudes to sit down upon the grass, He took the five loaves and the two fishes, and looking up to heaven, He blessed, and brake, and gave the loaves to His disciples, and the disciples to the multitudes.

And they did all eat, and were filled. And they took up what remained, twelve full baskets of fragments.

And the number of them that did eat, was five thousand men, besides women and children (Matt. xiv. 15–21).

The story of feeding the four thousand at another time is thus told:

And Jesus called together His disciples, and said: I have compassion on the multitudes, because they continue with Me now three days, and have not what to eat, and I will not send them away fasting, lest they faint in the way.

And the disciples say unto Him: Whence then should we have so many loaves in the desert, as to fill so great a multitude?

And Jesus said to them: How many loaves have you? But they said: Seven, and a few little fishes.

And He commanded the multitude to sit down upon the ground.

And taking the seven loaves and the fishes, and giving thanks, He brake, and gave to His disciples, and the disciples gave to the people.

And they did all eat, and had their fill. And they took up seven baskets full, of what remained of the fragments.

And they that did eat, were four thousand men, beside children and women (Matt. xv. 32–38).

He Controls Nature by His Word. As we read the story of Christ in the Gospels, we are amazed at His power. He walks on the seas: and He enables Peter to do the same:

But the boat in the midst of the sea was tossed with the waves: for the wind was contrary.

And in the fourth watch of the night, He came to them walking upon the sea.

And they seeing Him walking upon the sea, were troubled, saying: It is an apparition. And they cried out for fear.

And immediately Jesus spoke to them, saying: Be of good heart: it is I, fear ye not.

And Peter making answer, said: Lord, if it be Thou, bid me come to Thee upon the waters.

And He said: Come. And Peter going down out of the boat, walked upon the water to come to Jesus.

But seeing the wind strong, he was afraid: and when he began to sink, he cried out, saying: Lord, save me.

And immediately Jesus stretching forth His hand took hold of him, and said to him: O thou of little faith, why didst thou doubt?

And when they were come up into the boat, the wind ceased (Matt. xiv. 24–32).

He Stills the Storm

And when He entered into the boat, His disciples followed Him:

And behold a great tempest arose in the sea, so that the boat was covered with waves, but He was asleep.

And they came to Him, and awakened Him, saying: Lord, save us, we perish.

And Jesus saith to them: Why are you fearful, O ye of little faith? Then rising up He commanded the winds, and the sea, and there came a great calm (Matt. viii. 23–26).

In the face of such power, we must say, as the centurion did at the foot of the cross, "Surely this is the Son of God."

He Raises Men from the Dead. What seems to us even greater than walking on the waters or making the winds quickly cease, or stilling the storm, is raising men from the dead. Three such miracles are told of in the Gospels. Two are told here: The raising of Lazarus from the dead is told by St. John in these words:

Now there was a certain man sick, named Lazarus, of Bethania, of the town of Mary and of Martha her sister.

And Mary was she that anointed the Lord with ointment, and wiped His feet with her hair, whose brother Lazarus was sick.

His sisters therefore sent to Him, saying: Lord, behold he whom Thou lovest is sick.

And Jesus hearing it, said to them: This sickness is not unto death, but for the glory of God: that the Son of God may be glorified by it.

Now Jesus loved Martha, and her sister Mary, and Lazarus.

When He had heard therefore that he was sick, He still remained in the same place two days.

Then after that, He said to His disciples: Let us go into Judea again.

The disciples said to Him: Rabbi, the Jews but now sought to stone Thee: and goest Thou thither again?

THE DIVINITY OF CHRIST

Jesus answered: Are there not twelve hours of the day? If a man walk in the day, he stumbleth not, because he seeth the light of this world.

But if he walk in the night, he stumbleth, because the light is not in him.

These things He said; and after that He said to them: Lazarus our friend sleepeth; but I go that I may awake him out of sleep.

His disciples therefore said: Lord, if he sleep, he shall do well.

But Jesus spoke of his death; and they thought that He spoke of the repose of sleep.

Then therefore Jesus said to them plainly: Lazarus is dead.

And I am glad, for your sakes, that I was not there, that you may believe: but let us go to him.

Thomas therefore, who is called Didymus, said to his fellow disciples: Let us also go, that we may die with Him.

Jesus therefore came, and found that he had been four days already in the grave.

(Now Bethania was near Jerusalem, about fifteen furlongs off.)

And many of the Jews were come to Martha and Mary, to comfort them concerning their brother.

Martha therefore, as soon as she heard that Jesus was come, went to meet Him: but Mary sat at home.

Martha therefore said to Jesus: Lord, if Thou hadst been here, my brother had not died.

But now also I know that whatsoever Thou wilt ask of God, God will give it Thee.

Jesus saith to her: Thy brother will rise again.

Martha saith to Him: I know that he shall rise again, in the resurrection at the last day.

Jesus said to her: I am the resurrection and the life: he that believeth in Me, although he be dead, shall live.

And everyone that liveth, and believeth in Me, shall not die forever. Believest thou this?

She saith to Him: Yea, Lord, I have believed that Thou art Christ the Son of the living God, who art come into this world.

And when she had said these things, she went and called her sister Mary secretly, saying: The Master is come, and calleth for thee.

She, as soon as she heard *this*, riseth quickly, and cometh to Him.

For Jesus was not yet come into the town: but He was still in that place where Martha had met Him.

The Jews therefore, who were with her in the house, and comforted her, when they saw Mary that she rose up speedily and went out, followed her, saying: She goeth to the grave to weep there.

When Mary therefore was come where Jesus was, seeing Him, she fell down at His feet, and saith to Him: Lord, if Thou hadst been here, my brother had not died.

Jesus, therefore, when He saw her weeping, and the Jews that were come with her, weeping, groaned in the spirit, and troubled Himself,

And said: Where have you laid him? They say to Him: Lord, come and see.

And Jesus wept.

The Jews therefore said: Behold how He loved him.

But some of them said: Could not He that opened the eyes of the man born blind, have caused that this man should not die?

Jesus therefore again groaning in Himself, cometh to the sepulcher. Now it was a cave; and a stone was laid over it.

Jesus saith: Take away the stone. Martha, the sister of him that was dead, saith to Him: Lord, by this time he stinketh, for he is now of four days.

Jesus saith to her: Did not I say to thee, that if thou believe, thou shalt see the glory of God?

They took therefore the stone away. And Jesus lifting up His eyes said: Father, I give Thee thanks that Thou hast heard Me.

And I knew that Thou hearest Me always: but because of the people who stand about have I said it, that they may believe that Thou hast sent Me.

When He had said these things, He cried with a loud voice: Lazarus, come forth.

And presently he that had been dead came forth, bound feet and hands with winding bands; and his face was bound about with a napkin. Jesus said to them: Loose him, and let him go (John xi. 1–44).

Raising from the Dead, the Son of the Widow. The raising from the dead of the son of the widow of Naim is thus told by St. Luke:

And it came to pass afterwards, that He went into a city that is called Naim; and there went with Him His disciples, and a great multitude.

And when He came nigh to the gate of the city, behold a dead man was carried out, the only son of his mother; and she was a widow: and a great multitude of the city was with her.

Whom when the Lord had seen, being moved with mercy toward her, He said to her: Weep not.

And He came near and touched the bier. And they that carried it, stood still. And He said: Young man, I say to thee, arise.

And he that was dead, sat up, and began to speak. And He gave him to his mother (Luke vii. 11–15).

Christ is God. And one cannot help repeating the centurion's statement at the foot of the cross: "Indeed this was the Son of

THE DIVINITY OF CHRIST

God." For only God could raise men from the dead, could make the wind and the sea obey Him, could walk on the waters, could multiply food that would hardly feed a handful so that it was more than enough for four or five thousand. This is the power of God. This is indeed the Son of God. This is truly God.

Problem Questions

1. What is a miracle?
2. Make a list of the miracles performed by Christ according to the Gospels of St. Matthew, St. Luke, St. Mark, St. John. Describe two not given in this book.
3. Is Christ God because He performed the miracles, or did He perform the miracles because He is God?
4. When was the statement made, "Surely this is the Son of God"? By whom?
5. Is there any other explanation of Christ's power except that He is God?

Quotations from the Bible

For each of the following quotations:
a) Identify the speaker.
b) State the conditions under which the statement was made.
c) Give the meaning.
d) Tell its significance.

"I have compassion on the multitudes, because they continue with Me now three days, and have not what to eat, and I will not send them away fasting, lest they faint in the way" (Matt. xv. 32).

"Be of good heart: it is I, fear ye not" (Matt. xix. 27).

"Young man, I say to thee arise" (Luke vii. 14).

"I saw, and I gave testimony, that this is the Son of God" (John i. 34).

"This is My beloved Son, in whom I am well pleased" (Matt. iii. 17; xvii. 5).

Chapter XIX
THE PUBLIC LIFE OF CHRIST: THE PARABLES

Preaching. What is the general character of the public life of Christ? A young man of thirty years goes about from synagogue to synagogue talking to people, on mount or plain, in market place or in the wheat fields, telling them about the kingdom of God, or the kingdom of heaven, which is at hand. It is His Father's kingdom. This plainly is not the kind of kingdom most of the Jews looked for, but we shall learn more about that almost at once.

Performing Miracles. As He passed from place to place preaching this Gospel of the kingdom, He showed by His wonderful power that truly He was the Son of God. He made the blind see and the lame walk; the lepers are cleansed, the deaf hear, and the dead are raised up again. These are only some of the miracles. His first miracle was to change water into wine. He fed five thousand people on five loaves and two fishes, and there remained twelve full baskets of fragments. He made the winds obey Him. These miracles confirmed His Divine power. Truly, as the Jews said: "God has visited His people."

The Parables. Christ went about teaching the people by means of parables. These are short stories in which a certain likeness makes clear the lesson He wished to teach. These stories are about things taken from the lives of the people themselves, things they knew about. Most of Christ's hearers were what we should call country people. He went about teaching as described by St. Matthew:

The same day Jesus going out of the house, sat by the seaside.
And great multitudes were gathered together unto Him, so that He went up into a boat and sat: and all the multitude stood on the shore.
And He spoke to them many things in parables, saying: Behold the sower went forth to sow.

And whilst he soweth some fell by the wayside, and the birds of the air came and ate them up.

And other some fell upon the stony ground, where they had not much earth: and they sprung up immediately, because they had no deepness of earth.

And when the sun was up they were scorched: and because they had not root, they withered away.

And others fell among thorns: and the thorns grew up and choked them.

And others fell upon good ground: and they brought forth fruit, some an hundredfold, some sixtyfold, and some thirtyfold.

He that hath ears to hear, let him hear (Matt. xiii. 1–9).

This is one of the few parables of which Christ Himself has given us an explanation. This is what He said it means:

Hear you therefore the parable of the sower.

When anyone heareth the word of the kingdom, and understandeth it not, there cometh the wicked one, and catcheth away that which was sown in his heart: this is he that received the seed by the wayside.

And he that received the seed upon stony ground, is he that heareth the word, and immediately receiveth it with joy.

Yet hath he not root in himself, but is only for a time: and when there ariseth tribulation and persecution because of the word, he is presently scandalized.

And he that received the seed among the thorns, is he that heareth the word, and the care of this world and the deceitfulness of riches choketh up the word, and he becometh fruitless.

But he that received the seed upon good ground, is he that heareth the word, understandeth, and beareth fruit, and yieldeth the one an hundredfold, and another sixty, and another thirty (Matt. xiii. 18–23).

Perhaps it will be well to quote another parable.

Another parable He proposed to them, saying: The kingdom of heaven is likened to a man that sowed good seed in his field.

But while men were asleep, his enemy came and oversowed cockle among the wheat and went his way.

And when the blade was sprung up, and had brought forth fruit, then appeared also the cockle.

And the servants of the good man of the house coming said to him: Sir, didst thou not sow good seed in thy field? Whence then hath it cockle?

And he said to them: An enemy hath done this. And the servants said to him: Wilt thou that we go and gather it up?

And he said: No, lest perhaps gathering up the cockle, you root up the wheat also together with it.

Suffer both to grow until the harvest, and in the time of the harvest, I will say to the reapers: Gather up first the cockle, and bind it into bundles to burn, but the wheat gather ye into my barn (Matt. xiii. 24–30).

Write out an explanation of this parable like the explanation of the Sower. The teacher will then read verses of the thirteenth chapter of St. Matthew.

Building a House. But these stories from the daily life of the people to whom He was talking could easily be understood by others as well. Another famous parable appeals to an experience we will easily understand if we have the right disposition.

Everyone therefore that heareth these My words, and doth them, shall be likened to a wise man that built his house upon a rock, and the rain fell, and the floods came, and the winds blew, and they beat upon that house, and it fell not, for it was founded on a rock.

And everyone that heareth these My words, and doth them not, shall be like a foolish man that built his house upon the sand, and the rain fell, and the floods came, and the winds blew, and they beat upon that house, and it fell, and great was the fall thereof (Matt. vii. 24–27).

Purpose of the Parables. The purpose of the parables is to tell the people the real nature of the kingdom of God, that it was not an earthly kingdom as they expected. That which makes it hard to accept this kingdom is not in Christ, the Sower, nor in His doctrine, the seed, but in the soil in which it is planted, in men who fall away in time of temptation (rock), and in those who are choked with the cares, riches, and pleasures of this life. The kingdom of heaven is for those who have a good and upright heart.

Do Penance. "From that time" (the time of His baptism by John and His fast of forty days in the desert), the Gospel says, "Jesus began to preach and to say: Do penance, for the kingdom of heaven is at hand" (Matt. iv. 17). And St. Luke quotes Christ Himself: "To other cities also I must preach the kingdom of of God: for therefore am I sent" (Luke iv. 43). The glad tidings of the kingdom of God were the starting point and the center of our Lord's whole public life. He was sent to announce this kingdom, to bring men by His miracles to believe in His teachings, and to unite all in this new kingdom. This is the kingdom of the Messiah. On earth it is the Church, and in the end, it will be the kingdom of God in glory, with Christ sitting on the right hand of God.

The Nature of the Kingdom of God. The parables tell, in a way suited to man, the character of this kingdom; what must be done by members of the kingdom; and who the head of the kingdom is. The character of the kingdom of God is told in the parable of the Sower, and in the parable of the tare and cockles which have been quoted and explained. In the Gospel of St. Matthew there is given a whole series of explanations of what the kingdom of heaven is like. These are so briefly stated, that many of them may be quoted entire:

The Mustard Seed:

Another parable He proposed unto them, saying: The kingdom of heaven is like to a grain of mustard seed, which a man took and sowed in his field.

Which is the least indeed of all seeds; but when it is grown up, it is greater than all herbs, and becometh a tree, so that the birds of the air come, and dwell in the branches thereof (Matt. xiii. 31–32).

The Leaven:

Another parable He spoke to them: The kingdom of heaven is like to leaven, which a woman took and hid in three measures of meal, until the whole was leavened (Matt. xiii. 33).

The Hidden Treasure:

The kingdom of heaven is like unto a treasure hidden in a field. Which a man having found, hid it, and for joy thereof goeth, and selleth all that he hath, and buyeth that field (Matt. xiii. 44).

The Pearl of Great Price:

Again the kingdom of heaven is like to a merchant seeking good pearls. And when he had found one pearl of great price, went his way, and sold all that he had, and bought it (Matt. xiii. 45–46).

The Fishing Net:

Again the kingdom of heaven is like to a net cast into the sea, and gathering together of all kinds of fishes.

Which, when it was filled, they drew out, and sitting by the shore, they chose out the good into vessels, but the bad they cast forth.

So shall it be at the end of the world. The angels shall go out, and shall separate the wicked from among the just.

And shall cast them into the furnace of fire: there shall be weeping and gnashing of teeth (Matt. xiii. 47–50).

The Members of the Kingdom. The duties and responsibilities and the spirit and attitude of the members of God's kingdom are told also in a number of parables. Perhaps the best known of these parables and the fullest of meaning are the ones called "The Pharisee and the Publican" and the "Good Samaritan."

The Pharisee and the Publican. The parable of the Pharisee and the Publican is as follows:

Two men went up into the temple to pray: the one a Pharisee, and the other a publican.

The Pharisee standing, prayed thus with himself: O God, I give Thee thanks that I am not as the rest of men, extortioners, unjust, adulterers, as also this publican. I fast twice in a week: I give tithes of all that I possess.

And the publican, standing afar off, would not so much as lift up his eyes toward heaven: but struck his breast, saying: O God, be merciful to me a sinner (Luke xviii. 10–13).

The Good Samaritan. The story of the Good Samaritan is thus told:

A certain man went down from Jerusalem to Jericho, and fell among robbers, who also stripped him, and having wounded him went away, leaving him half dead. And it chanced, that a certain priest went down the same way: and seeing him, passed by. In like manner also a Levite, when he was near the place and saw him, passed by.

But a certain Samaritan being on his journey, came near him, and seeing him, was moved with compassion. And going up to him, bound up his wounds, pouring in oil and wine: and setting him upon his own beast, brought him to an inn, and took care of him.

And the next day he took out two pence, and gave to the host, and said: Take care of him; and whatsoever thou shalt spend over and above, I, at my return, will repay thee.

Which of these three, in thy opinion, was neighbor to him that fell among the robbers? (Luke x. 30-36.)

The Head of the Kingdom. There is a series of parables that tells us about the Head of the kingdom straight from the lips of the Messiah Himself. He is the light of the world. He is the vine. He is the physician. He is the good shepherd. He is the good father receiving the returned prodigal.

The Light of the World. St. John in his Gospel quotes Christ's words repeating this fact that He is the light of the world:

And this is the judgment: because the light is come into the world, and men loved darkness rather than the light: for their works were evil.

For everyone that doth evil hateth the light, and cometh not to the light, that his works may not be reproved.

But he that doth truth, cometh to the light, that his works may be made manifest, because they are done in God (John iii. 19–21).

Again therefore Jesus spoke to them, saying: I am the light of the world: he that followeth Me, walketh not in darkness, but shall have the light of life (John viii. 12).

As long as I am in the world, I am the light of the world (John ix. 5).

Jesus, therefore, said to them: Yet a little while the light is among you. Walk whilst you have the light, that the darkness overtake you not. And he that walketh in darkness, knoweth not whither he goeth.

Whilst you have the light, believe in the light, that you may be the children of light (John xii. 35–36).

I am come a light into the world; that whosoever believes in Me may not remain in darkness (John xii. 46).

Christ is the Vine. In the parable of the vine, the form of the other parables is followed more closely.

I am the true vine: and My Father is the husbandman. Every branch in Me that beareth not fruit He will take away: and every one that beareth fruit He will purge it, that it may bring forth more fruit.

Now you are clean by reason of the word, which I have spoken to you.

Abide in Me, and I in you. As the branch cannot bear fruit of itself, unless it abide in the vine, so neither can you, unless you abide in Me.

I am the vine; you the branches: he that abides in Me, and I in him, the same beareth much fruit: for without Me you can do nothing.

If anyone abide not in Me, he shall be cast forth as a branch, and shall wither, and they gather him up, and cast him into the fire, and he burneth.

If you abide in Me, and My words abide in you, you shall ask whatever you will, and it shall be done unto you.

In this is My Father glorified; that you bring forth very much fruit, and become My disciples (John xv. 1–8).

The Physician. And the parable of the physician is briefly told:

And Jesus answering, said to them: They that are whole, need not the physician: but they that are sick.
I came not to call the just, but sinners to penance (Luke v. 31–32).

The Good Shepherd. The parable which has impressed men in every generation and caught the imagination of artists in every age, is the parable of the Good Shepherd. This parable is as follows:

Amen, amen, I say to you: He that entereth not by the door into the sheepfold, but climbeth up another way, the same is a thief and robber.
But he that entereth in by the door is the shepherd of the sheep.
To him the porter openeth; and the sheep hear his voice: and he calleth his own sheep by name, and leadeth them out.
And when he hath let out his own sheep, he goeth before them: and the sheep followeth him, because they know his voice.
But a stranger they follow not, but fly from him, because they know not the voice of strangers.
This proverb Jesus spoke to them. But they understood not what He spoke to them.
Jesus therefore said to them again: Amen, amen I say to you, I am the door of the sheep.
All *others*, as many as have come, are thieves and robbers: and the sheep heard them not.
I am the door. By Me, if any man enter in, he shall be saved: and he shall go in, and go out, and shall find pastures.
The thief cometh not, but for to steal, and to kill, and to destroy. I am come that they may have life, and may have it more abundantly.
I am the good shepherd. The good shepherd giveth his life for his sheep.
But the hireling, and he that is not the shepherd, whose own the sheep are not, seeth the wolf coming, and leaveth the sheep and flieth: and the wolf catcheth, and scattereth the sheep.
And the hireling flieth, because he is a hireling: and he hath no care for the sheep.
I am the Good Shepherd; and I know Mine, and Mine know Me.
As the Father knoweth Me, and I know the Father: and I lay down My life for My sheep.

And other sheep I have, that are not of this fold: them also I must bring, and they shall hear My voice, and there shall be one fold and one shepherd (John x. 1–16).

The Prodigal Son. Another parable which expresses very well indeed the mercy of God, is the Prodigal Son:

And he said: A certain man had two sons:

And the younger of them said to his father: Father, give me the portion of substance that falleth to me. And he divided unto them his substance.

And not many days after, the younger son, gathering all together, went abroad into a far country: and there wasted his substance, living riotously.

And after he had spent all, there came a mighty famine in that country: and he began to be in want.

And he went and cleaved to one of the citizens of that country. And he sent him into his farm to feed swine.

And he would fain have filled his belly with the husks the swine did eat; and no man gave unto him.

And returning to himself, he said: How many hired servants in my father's house abound with bread, and I here perish with hunger?

I will arise, and will go to my father, and say to him: Father, I have sinned against heaven, and before thee:

I am not worthy to be called thy son: make me as one of thy hired servants.

And rising up he came to his father. And when he was yet a great way off, his father saw him, and was moved with compassion, and running to him fell upon his neck, and kissed him.

And the son said to him: Father, I have sinned against heaven, and before thee, I am not worthy to be called thy son.

And the father said to his servants: Bring forth quickly the first robe, and put it on him, and put a ring on his hand, and shoes on his feet:

And bring hither the fatted calf, and kill it, and let us eat and make merry:

Because this my son was dead, and is come to life again: was lost, and is found. And they began to be merry.

Now his elder son was in the field, and when he came and drew nigh to the house he heard music and dancing:

And he called one of the servants, and asked what these things meant.

And he said to him: Thy brother is come, and thy father hath killed the fatted calf, because he hath received him safe.

And he was angry, and would not go in. His father, therefore coming out began to entreat him.

And he answering, said to his father: Behold, for so many years do I serve thee, and I have never transgressed thy commandment, and yet thou hast never given me a kid to make merry with my friends:

But as soon as thy son is come, who hath devoured his substance with harlots, thou hast killed for him the fatted calf.

But he said to him: Son, thou art always with me, and all I have is thine.

But it was fit that we should make merry and be glad, for this thy brother was dead and is come to life again; he was lost and is found (Luke xv. 11-32).

The Kingdom of God. It is in these parables that Christ states in simple terms the truths about the kingdom of God.

Problem Questions

1. What is a parable?

2. Make a list of the parables given in the Gospel according to St. Matthew, St. Mark, St. Luke, St. John. Describe three parables not given in this book.

3. Classify your list of parables by marking "1" after those parables which describe the kingdom of God, "2" after those parables which tell what must be done by members of the kingdom, and "3" after those parables which describe the head of the kingdom. (The teacher will consult Fonck's *The Parables of Christ*.)

4. Rewrite your list now putting those three lists with the 1's together, the 2's together, and the 3's together. Give each list an appropriate title.

5. What is your duty, according to the parables as a member of the kingdom of God?

6. What qualities of the parables made them easy to understand?

7. Why, then, do you think more of the Jews did not become followers of Christ?

Quotations from the Bible

For each of the following quotations:
a) Identify the speaker.
b) State the conditions under which the statement was made.
c) Give the meaning.
d) Tell its significance.

"It fell not, for it was founded upon a rock" (Matt. vii. 25).

"The kingdom of heaven is like to a grain of mustard seed, which a man took and sowed in his field" (Matt. xiii. 31-32).

"O God, be merciful to me a sinner" (Luke xviii. 9-14).

"Which of these three, in thy opinion, was neighbor to him that fell among the robbers?" (Luke x. 30–37.)

"I am the light of the world: he that followeth Me, walketh not in darkness, but shall have the light of life" (John viii. 12).

"I am the vine; you the branches: he that abides in Me, and I in him, the same beareth much fruit: for without Me you can do nothing" (John xv. 5).

"I am the good Shepherd: and I know Mine, and Mine know Me" (John x. 1–16).

"As the Father knoweth Me, and I know the Father: and I lay down My life for My sheep" (John x. 15).

"I have sinned against heaven, and before thee" (Luke xv. 21).

Chapter XX
SOME MEMORABLE SAYINGS OF CHRIST

The teachings of Christ have now lived for twenty centuries. His words have entered into the writings of men in every country and every age since. Our everyday language has in it many of Christ's ideas even though we do not recognize them. The parables of the Good Samaritan, and the Prodigal Son are examples of this. Many people call a person a "good Samaritan" without recalling the story from which the title came. You might have a pleasant time in class recalling other examples.

In this chapter we shall quote a number of Christ's sayings which, because of their beauty and truth, are especially worth memorizing.

The most famous sermon ever preached is the one preached by Christ, which is called the Sermon on the Mount. It opens with a series of sentences which man has loved from that time to this. They are called the Beatitudes because they tell us the way to blessedness. They, too, are the way men must travel to gain their last home, which is in heaven. It is the opposite of the devil's way. It is opposite to what many people seem to give up their whole life for: wealth, position, pride, and the like.

The Beatitudes. Learn these Beatitudes and try to live their spirit on the road to your Father's home. They are:

Blessed are the poor in spirit: for theirs is the kingdom of heaven.
Blessed are the meek: for they shall possess the land.
Blessed are they that mourn: for they shall be comforted.
Blessed are they that hunger and thirst after justice: for they shall have their fill.
Blessed are the merciful: for they shall obtain mercy.
Blessed are the clean of heart: for they shall see God.
Blessed are the peacemakers: for they shall be called the children of God.

The Eight Beatitudes

Blessed are the poor in spirit for theirs is the kingdom of heaven.

Blessed are the meek, for they shall possess the land.

Blessed are they that mourn, for they shall be comforted.

Blessed are they that hunger and thirst after justice, for they shall be filled.

Blessed are the merciful, for they shall obtain mercy.

Blessed are the clean of heart, for they shall see God.

Blessed are the peacemakers, for they shall be called the children of God.

Blessed are they that suffer persecution for justice' sake, for theirs is the kingdom of God.

Blessed are they that suffer persecution for justice' sake: for theirs is the kingdom of heaven.

Blessed are ye when they shall revile you, and persecute you, and speak all that is evil against you, untruly, for My sake (Matt. v. 3–11).

Christ's Love of Children. Christ's spirit of meekness was often shown in His love for little children. Christ loved little children and, in fact, said, "of such is the kingdom of heaven." Some of Christ's sayings about children worth learning by heart are given in the following paragraphs.

One of the happenings which showed His great love for children, is connected with a situation in which even the disciples did not seem to understand:

Then were little children presented to Him, that He should impose hands upon them and pray. And the disciples rebuked them.

But Jesus said to them: Suffer the little children, and forbid them not to come to Me: for the kingdom of heaven is for such (Matt. xix. 13–14).

And St. Matthew has another passage on children in which the true spirit of those who will enter the kingdom of heaven is dramatically revealed:

> At that hour the disciples came to Jesus, saying: Who thinkest Thou is the greater, in the kingdom of heaven?
> And Jesus calling unto Him a little child, set him in the midst of them, and said: Amen I say to you, unless you be converted and become as little children, you shall not enter into the kingdom of heaven.
> Whosoever therefore shall humble himself as this little child, he is the greater in the kingdom of heaven. And he that shall receive one such little child in My name, receiveth Me. But he that shall scandalize one of these little ones that believe in Me, it were better for him that a millstone should be hanged about his neck, and that he should be drowned in the depth of the sea (Matt. xviii. 1–6).

And it was children who acclaimed Christ:

> And the chief priests and scribes, seeing the wonderful things that He did, and the children crying in the temple, and saying *Hosanna to the Son of David,* were moved with indignation.
> And said to Him: Hearest Thou what these say? And Jesus said to them: Yea, have you never read: *Out of the mouths of infants and of sucklings Thou hast perfected praise?* (Matt. xxi. 15–16.)

What doth it profit a man if he gain the whole world and suffer the loss of his own soul, or what exchange shall a man give for his soul? For the Son of Man shall come in the glory of His Father with His angels: and then will He render to every man according to his works. *Matt. XVI: 26-27.*

What Shall I Do to Gain Everlasting Life? There is a story we might use here in which Christ brings out strongly the fact that His followers, as the Jews of old, must keep the commandments given on Mt. Sinai.

A certain rich man asked Christ the question, "What good shall

I do that I may have everlasting life?" And Christ answered his direct question thus:

Why askest thou Me concerning good? One is good, God. But if thou wilt enter into life, keep the commandments.

He said to Him: Which? And Jesus said: *Thou shalt do no murder, Thou shalt not commit adultery, Thou shalt not steal, Thou shalt not bear false witness.*

Honor thy father and thy mother; and Thou shalt love thy neighbor as thyself.

The young man said to Him: All these have I kept from my youth, what is yet wanting to me?

Jesus saith to him: If thou wilt be perfect, go sell what thou hast, and give to the poor, and thou shalt have treasure in heaven: and come follow Me.

And when the young man had heard this word, he went away sad: for he had great possessions.

Then Jesus said to His disciples: Amen, I say to you, that a rich man shall hardly enter into the kingdom of heaven.

And again I say to you: It is easier for a camel to pass through the eye of a needle, than for a rich man to enter into the kingdom of heaven (Matt. xix. 16–24).

Which is the Greatest Commandment? And the Pharisees thought they might catch Christ — foolishly indeed. Notice how these questions are turned by Christ to enforce the lessons He wants to teach.

A lawyer, a Pharisee, wished to tempt Christ with this question:

Master, which is the great commandment in the law?

Jesus said to him: *Thou shalt love the Lord thy God with thy whole heart, and with thy whole soul, and with thy whole mind.*

This is the greatest and the first commandment.

And the second is like to this: *Thou shalt love thy neighbor as thyself* (Matt. xxii. 36–39).

It is to this same lawyer, according to St. Luke, that Christ told the story of the Good Samaritan in answer to a question by which he wished to justify himself, "And who is my neighbor?"

Render to God the Things That Are God's. Another one of the questions which the Pharisees asked of Christ that they might catch Him, or "have to accuse Him," is this: "Is it lawful to pay tribute to Cæsar?"

"Then the Pharisees going, consulted among themselves how to ensnare Him in His speech. And they sent to Him their disciples with the Herodians, saying: Master, we know that Thou art a true speaker, and teachest the way of God in truth, neither carest Thou for any man: for Thou dost not regard the person of men. Tell us therefore what dost Thou think, is it lawful to give tribute to Cæsar, or not?

But Jesus knowing their wickedness, said: Why do you tempt Me, ye hypocrites? Show Me the coin of the tribute. And they offered Him a penny.

And Jesus saith to them: Whose image and inscription is this? They say to Him: Cæsar's. Then He saith to them: Render therefore to Cæsar the things that are Cæsar's; and to God, the things that are God's (Matt. xxii. 15–21).

How foolish man is. This answer, too, helps us to guide ourselves on God's Highway to eternal life. Render to God the things that are God's; that is the clear, unmistakable way. What are the things of God? What does Cæsar stand for?

What Shall a Man Give in Exchange for His Soul? The following words of our Lord and Savior Jesus Christ, we should not only learn by heart, but bear always in mind:

For what doth it profit a man, if he gain the whole world, and suffer the loss of his own soul? Or what exchange shall a man give for his soul?

For the Son of Man shall come in the glory of His Father with His angels: and then will He render to every man according to his works (Matt. xvi. 26–27).

There is nothing in the world worth as much as a human soul. The entire world is not equal in value to a single human soul. A little money or much money, a little pleasure or much pleasure, a little or much satisfaction in the praise of men, or position or reputation, is not worth your soul. You may not prize it so high, but God does — *and you should*. Hence the question, What shall a man give in exchange for his soul?

Hence these words should always be kept in mind, and serve to guide us on God's Highway to our home with Him in heaven.

Seek ye therefore first the kingdom of God and His justice, and all these things shall be added unto you (Matt. vi. 33).

MEMORABLE SAYINGS OF CHRIST

Questions from the Catechism

Q. Which are the Beatitudes?
A. **The Beatitudes are:**
 1. Blessed are the poor in spirit, for theirs is the kingdom of heaven.
 2. Blessed are the meek, for they shall possess the land.
 3. Blessed are they that mourn, for they shall be comforted.
 4. Blessed are they that hunger and thirst after justice, for they shall be filled.
 5. Blessed are the merciful, for they shall obtain mercy.
 6. Blessed are the clean of heart, for they shall see God.
 7. Blessed are the peacemakers, for they shall be called the children of God.
 8. Blessed are they that suffer persecution for justice' sake, for theirs is the kingdom of heaven.

Q. What words should we bear always in mind?
A. **We should bear always in mind these words of our Lord and Savior Jesus Christ:** "What doth it profit a man if he gain the whole world and suffer the loss of his own soul, or what exchange shall a man give for his soul? For the Son of man shall come in the glory of His Father with His angels; and then will He render to every man according to his works."

Problem Questions

1. Quote the Beatitudes.
2. What is meant by "beatitude"?
3. What is regarded as Christ's greatest address? Can you quote any part of it besides the Beatitudes?
4. Quote any statement of Christ about children. Can you quote one not given in this book?
5. What were Christ's answers to the following questions:
 What shall I do to gain everlasting life?
 Which is the greatest commandment?
 Is it lawful to pay tribute to Cæsar (the state)?
 What shall a man give in exchange for his soul?
 Who is my neighbor?
6. What application to your own life is contained in answer to each of the foregoing questions?

Quotations from the Bible

For each of the following quotations:
a) Identify the speaker.

b) State the conditions under which the statement was made.
c) Give the meaning.
d) Tell its significance.

"Suffer the little children, and forbid them not to come to Me: for the kingdom of heaven is for such" (Matt. xix. 13-15).

"Whosoever therefore shall humble himself as this little child, he is the greater in the kingdom of heaven. And he that shall receive one such little child in My name, receiveth Me. But he that shall scandalize one of these little ones that believe in Me, it were better for him that a millstone should be hanged about his neck, and that he should be drowned in the depth of the sea" (Matt. xviii. 1-6).

"For what doth it profit a man, if he gain the whole world, and suffer the loss of his soul? Or what exchange shall a man give for his soul?" (Matt. xvi. 26.)

"Seek ye first the kingdom of God, and His justice, and all these things will be added unto you" (Matt. vi. 33).

"Blessed are the clean of heart: for they shall see God" (Matt. v. 8).

"My little children, let us not love in word, nor in tongue, but in deed, and in truth" (I John iii. 18).

Chapter XXI
CHRIST AND THE HOLY EUCHARIST

Palm Sunday. On a Sunday which gets its name from the event, Jesus rode into Jerusalem on an ass's colt, and the people took branches of palm and laid them in His path, and cried, "Hosanna to the Son of David. Blessed is He that cometh in the name of the Lord: Hosanna in the highest" (Matt. xxi. 9). This is the first Palm Sunday. And this is the way St. Mark tells us what happened:

And when they were drawing near to Jerusalem and to Bethania at Mount of Olives, He sendeth two of His disciples.

And saith to them: Go into the village that is over against you, and immediately at your coming in thither, you shall find a colt tied, upon which no man yet hath sat: loose him, and bring him.

And if any man shall say to you, What are you doing? say ye that the Lord hath need of him: and immediately he will let him come hither.

And going their way, they found the colt tied before the gate without, in the meeting of two ways: and they loose him.

And some of them that stood there said to them: What do you loosing the colt?

Who said to them as Jesus had commanded them; and they let him go with them.

And they brought the colt to Jesus; and they lay their garments on him, and He sat upon them.

And many spread their garments in the way: and others cut down boughs from the trees, and strewed them in the way.

And they that went before and they that followed, cried, saying: *Hosanna, blessed is He that cometh in the name of the Lord.*

Blessed be the kingdom of our father David that cometh: Hosanna in the highest (Mark xi. 1–10).

Driving Money Changers Out of the Temple. Christ thus enters Jerusalem triumphantly. At evening He goes with the twelve to Bethany and returns the following morning, the

JESUS DRIVING THE SELLERS FROM THE TEMPLE
Painting by Cavallino.

CHRIST AND THE EUCHARIST

Monday of Holy Week, goes to the temple, and drives out the money changers:

And Jesus went into the temple of God, and cast out all them that sold and bought in the temple, and overthrew the tables of the money changers, and the chairs of them that sold doves:

And He saith to them: It is written, *My house shall be called the house of prayer; but you have made it a den of thieves.*

And there came to Him the blind and the lame in the temple; and He healed them.

And the chief priests and scribes, seeing the wonderful things that He did, and the children crying in the temple, and saying: *Hosanna to the Son of David;* were moved with indignation.

And said to Him: Hearest Thou what these say? And Jesus said to them: Yea, have you never read: *Out of the mouths of infants and of sucklings Thou hast perfected praise?* (Matt. xxi. 12–16.)

His Daily Preaching. He preaches in the temple daily, on faith, forgiveness, the resurrection of the body, and on the commandments. He accuses the scribes and Pharisees. All the works they do to be seen of men. They love the chief seats in the synagogues. They are fools and blind hypocrites. He says to them at last:

You serpents, generation of vipers, how will you flee from the judgment of hell? (Matt. xxiii. 33.)

But Christ teaches daily in the temple, and especially He tells who He really is:

But Jesus cried, and said: He that believeth in Me, doth not believe in Me, but in Him that sent Me.

And he that seeth Me, seeth Him that sent Me.

I am come a light into the world; that whosoever believeth in Me, may not remain in darkness.

And if any man hear My words, and keep them not, I do not judge him: for I came not to judge the world, but to save the world.

He that despiseth Me, and receiveth not My words, hath one that judgeth him; the word that I have spoken, the same shall judge him in the last day.

For I have not spoken of Myself; but the Father who sent Me, He gave Me commandment what I should say, and what I should speak.

And I know that His commandment is life everlasting. The things therefore that I speak, even as the Father said unto Me, so do I speak (John xii. 44–50).

A Prophecy. He told that the temple would be destroyed and that not a stone shall be left standing on a stone. And He also told of His own second coming:

And then shall appear the sign of the Son of Man in heaven: and then shall all the tribes of the earth mourn: and they shall see the Son of Man coming in the clouds of heaven with much power and majesty.

And He shall send His angels with a trumpet, and a great voice: and they shall gather together His elect from the four winds, from the farthest parts of the heavens to the utmost bounds of them (Matt. xxiv. 30–31).

To the question when shall these things be, the answer is given by Christ:

But of that day and hour no one knoweth, no not the angels of heaven, but the Father alone (Matt. xxiv. 36).

The Feast of the Pasch. The Jewish priests plot Christ's death, and Judas plans with them to betray Him, and they promise to give Judas money. And Christ prepares for the Passover for which He is at Jerusalem. St. Mark gives us the detailed statement of the preparation.

Now on the first day of the unleavened bread, when they sacrificed the Pasch, the disciples say to Him: Whither wilt Thou that we go, and prepare for Thee to eat the Pasch?

And He sendeth two of His disciples, and saith to them: Go ye into the city; and there shall meet you a man carrying a pitcher of water, follow him:

And whithersoever he shall go in, say to the master of the house, The Master saith, Where is My refectory, where I may eat the Pasch with My disciples?

And he will show you a large dining room furnished; and there prepare ye for us.

And His disciples went their way, and came into the city; and they found as He had told them, and they prepared the Pasch.

And when evening was come, He cometh with the twelve.

And when they were at table and eating, Jesus saith: Amen I say to you, one of you that eateth with Me shall betray Me.

But they began to be sorrowful, and to say to Him one by one: Is it I?

Who saith to them: One of the twelve who dippeth with Me his hand in the dish.

And the Son of Man indeed goeth, as it is written of Him, but woe to that man by whom the Son of Man shall be betrayed. It were better for him if that man had not been born (Mark xiv. 12–21).

On the Palm Sunday of the thirty-third year of Christ's life begins that series of events which ends in His Crucifixion and Resurrection. Let us here briefly summarize what happened in the four days before the institution of the Holy Eucharist.

Monday. On Monday morning, He begins with the story of the barren fig tree on the way to Jerusalem and upon entering the temple He overthrows the tables of the money changers and the chairs of them that sold doves, and the traders He drives from the temple.

Tuesday. On Tuesday He was teaching in the Temple and preaching the Gospel. Then begins the quarrel with the chief priests, the scribes, and the ancients. They ask by what authority He teaches. They try to trap Him by the trick of the tribute money, but they fail. They try to trap Him on the doctrine of the resurrection of the dead and marriage. They fail here too. The Pharisees try also to catch Him by asking Him about the commandments, and here, too, they fail. The last encounter comes that day when Christ teaching in the temple asks them: "What think you of Christ?" Then that day He criticizes the scribes and Pharisees in strong, vigorous language:

> All their works they do to be seen of men.
> They love the first places at feasts and the first chairs in the synagogues.
> Woe to you, scribes and Pharisees, hypocrites; because you tithe mint, and anise, and cummin, and have left the weightier things of the law; judgment, and mercy, and faith.
> Woe to you, scribes and Pharisees, hypocrites; because you make clean the outside of the cup and of the dish, but within you are full of rapine and uncleanness.
> You serpents, generation of vipers, how will you flee from the judgment of hell?

Wednesday. On Wednesday, Christ again foretells His passion, and on this day Judas arranged with the Jewish high priests to betray Christ for thirty pieces of silver.

Thursday. This is the day we know as Holy Thursday — the first Holy Thursday. Christ wished to keep the feast of the Pasch. The Apostles strive for the first places but Christ rebukes them.

He shows His own spirit and ministry in His washing of the feet of the Apostles. They are gathered for the feast when Christ foretells His betrayal by Judas.

Institution of the Holy Eucharist. Christ celebrates the Jewish passover on Thursday night with the Apostles. The preparation had been made early in the day. At this celebration of the feast of the Pasch, Christ institutes the Holy Eucharist at the Last Supper, and this is indeed the greatest miracle of His earthly career.

But when it was evening, He sat down with His twelve disciples.

And whilst they were eating, He said: Amen I say to you, that one of you is about to betray Me.

And they being very much troubled, began everyone to say: Is it I, Lord?

But He answering, said: He that dippeth his hand with Me in the dish, he shall betray Me.

The Son of Man indeed goeth, as it is written of Him: but woe to that man by whom the Son of Man shall be betrayed: it were better for him if that man had never been born.

And Judas that betrayed Him, answering, said: Is it I, Rabbi? He saith to him. Thou hast said *it* (Matt. xxvi. 20–25).

And these are Jesus' words:

And whilst they were at supper, Jesus took bread, and blessed and broke: and gave to His disciples, and said: Take ye, and eat. This is My Body.

And taking the chalice He gave thanks, and gave to them, saying: Drink ye all of this.

For this is My Blood of the New Testament, which shall be shed for many unto remission of sins.

And I say to you, I will not drink from henceforth of this fruit of the vine, until that day when I shall drink it with you new in the kingdom of My Father (Matt. xxvi. 26–29).

Prophecy of Peter's Denial. And the story as told by St. Matthew thus continues:

And a hymn being said, they went out unto Mount Olivet.

Then Jesus saith to them. All you shall be scandalized in Me this night. For it is written: *I will strike the shepherd, and the sheep of the flock shall be dispersed.*

But after I shall be risen again, I will go before you into Galilee.

CHRIST AND THE EUCHARIST

And Peter answering, said to Him: Although all shall be scandalized in Thee, I will never be scandalized.

Jesus said to him: Amen, I say to thee, that in this night before the cock crow, thou wilt deny Me thrice.

Peter saith to Him: Yea, though I should die with Thee, I will not deny Thee. And in like manner said all the disciples.

Then Jesus came with them into a country place which is called Gethsemani; and He said to His disciples: Sit you here, till I go yonder and pray.

And taking with Him Peter and the two sons of Zebedee, He began to grow sorrowful and to be sad.

Then He saith to them: My Soul is sorrowful even unto death: stay you here and watch with Me.

And going a little further, He fell upon His face, praying, and saying: My Father, if it be possible, let this chalice pass from Me. Nevertheless not as I will, but as Thou wilt.

And he cometh to His disciples, and findeth them asleep, and He saith to Peter: What? Could you not watch one hour with Me?

Watch ye, and pray that ye enter not into temptation. The spirit indeed is willing, but the flesh weak.

Again the second time, He went and prayed, saying: My Father, if this chalice may not pass away, but I must drink it, Thy will be done.

And He cometh again, and findeth them sleeping: for their eyes were heavy.

And leaving them, He went again: and He prayed the third time, saying the selfsame word.

Then He cometh to His disciples, and saith to them: Sleep ye now and take your rest; behold the hour is at hand, and the Son of Man shall be betrayed into the hands of sinners.

Rise, let us go: behold he is at hand that will betray Me (Matt. xxvi. 30–46).

The Betrayal of Christ. Jesus, as is His custom, goes to Mount Olivet. His soul is sorrowful even unto death. It is here in the Garden that Judas betrays Christ with a kiss. Christ is arrested and led first to Annas. The chief priests and all the Council seek for false witnesses against Jesus that they may put Him to death, but they can find none. At night they take Him before Caiphas and the Sanhedrin or council of Jewish priests. The high priest asks Christ:

I adjure Thee by the living God, that Thou tell us if Thou be the Christ, the Son of God.

Jesus saith to Him: Thou hast said *it*. Nevertheless I say to you, hereafter you shall see the Son of Man sitting on the right hand of the power of God, and coming in the clouds of heaven.

Then the high priest rent his garments, saying: He hath blasphemed; what further need have we of witnesses? Behold now you have heard the blasphemy:

What think you? But they answering, said: He is guilty of death (Matt. xxvi. 63–66).

Christ is insulted, spit upon, buffeted, and mocked. In the morning He is again brought before Caiphas and the Sanhedrin with the same result as during the night. Jesus is then bound and led to the governor's hall.

And when morning was come, all the chief priests and ancients of the people took counsel against Jesus, that they might put Him to death.

And they brought Him bound, and delivered Him to Pontius Pilate, the governor (Matt. xxvii. 1, 2).

Peter Denies Christ Three Times

But Peter sat without in the court: and there came to him a servant maid, saying: Thou also wast with Jesus the Galilean.

But he denied before them all, saying: I know not what thou sayest.

And as he went out of the gate, another maid saw him, and she saith to them that were there: This man also was with Jesus of Nazareth.

And again he denied with an oath: I know not the man.

And after a little while they came that stood by, and said to Peter: Surely thou also art one of them; for even thy speech doth discover thee.

Then he began to curse and to swear that he knew not the man. And immediately the cock crew.

And Peter remembered the word of Jesus which He had said: Before the cock crow, thou wilt deny Me thrice. And going forth, he wept bitterly (Matt. xxvi. 69–75).

Judas Hangs Himself. And Judas, who had received thirty pieces of silver for betraying Christ, comes to the chief priests and elders with it, saying:

I have sinned in betraying innocent blood. But they said: What is that to us? Look thou to it.

And casting down the pieces of silver in the temple, he departed: and went and hanged himself with an halter (Matt. xxvii. 4, 5).

Before Pontius Pilate. The high priests go to see Pilate,

CHRIST AND THE EUCHARIST

and demand Christ as a "great malefactor be tried by the Roman law," for the Jews say, "It is not lawful for us to put a man to death," and that is what they want done. Then Pilate enters the judgment hall. Christ is first brought before Pilate. Because Christ is a Galilean He is sent to Herod, but He is sent back again to Pilate.

Pilate therefore went into the hall again, and called Jesus, and said to Him: Art Thou the king of the Jews?

Jesus answered: Sayest thou this thing of thyself, or have others told it to thee of Me?

Pilate answered: Am I a Jew? Thy own nation, and the chief priests, have delivered Thee up to me: what hast Thou done?

Jesus answered: My kingdom is not of this world. If My kingdom were of this world, My servants would certainly strive that I should not be delivered to the Jews: but now My kingdom is not from hence.

Pilate therefore said to Him: Art Thou a king then? Jesus answered: Thou sayest that I am a king. For this was I born, and for this came I into the world; that I should give testimony to the truth. Everyone that is of the truth, heareth My voice.

Pilate saith to Him: What is truth? And when he said this, he went out again to the Jews, and saith to them: I find no cause in Him.

But you have a custom that I should release one unto you at the Pasch: will you, therefore, that I release unto you the king of the Jews?

Then cried they all again, saying: Not this man, but Barabbas. Now Barabbas was a robber (John xviii. 33–40).

He Suffers Under Pontius Pilate. The other events to His condemnation to death are thus told by St. John:

Then therefore, Pilate took Jesus and scourged Him.

And the soldiers platting a crown of thorns, put it upon His head; and they put on Him a purple garment.

And they came to Him, and said: Hail, king of the Jews; and they gave Him blows.

Pilate therefore went forth again, and saith to them: Behold, I bring Him forth unto you, that you may know that I find no cause in Him.

(Jesus therefore came forth, bearing the crown of thorns and the purple garment.) And he saith to them: Behold the Man.

When the chief priests, therefore, and the servants, had seen Him, they cried out, saying: Crucify Him, crucify Him. Pilate saith to them: Take Him you, and crucify Him: for I find no cause in Him.

The Jews answered him: We have a law; and according to the law He ought to die, because He made Himself the Son of God.

When Pilate therefore had heard this saying, he feared the more.

And he entered into the hall again and said to Jesus: Whence art Thou? But Jesus gave Him no answer.

Pilate therefore saith to Him: Speakest Thou not to me? knowest Thou not that I have power to crucify Thee, and I have power to release Thee?

Jesus answered: Thou shouldst not have any power against Me, unless it were given thee from above. Therefore, he that hath delivered Me to thee, hath the greater sin.

And from henceforth Pilate sought to release Him. But the Jews cried out, saying: If thou release this man, thou art not Cæsar's friend. For whosoever maketh himself a king, speaketh against Cæsar.

Now when Pilate had heard these words, he brought Jesus forth, and sat down in the judgment seat, in the place that is called Lithostrotos, and in Hebrew Gabbatha.

And it was the parasceve of the Pasch, about the sixth hour, and he saith to the Jews: Behold your king.

But they cried out: Away with Him; away with Him; crucify Him. Pilate saith to them: Shall I crucify your king? The chief priests answered: We have no king but Cæsar.

Then therefore he delivered Him to them to be crucified. And they took Jesus and led Him forth (John xix. 1–16).

Questions from the Catechism

Q. When did Christ institute the Holy Eucharist?

A. **Christ instituted the Holy Eucharist at the Last Supper, the night before He died.**

Q. Who were present when our Lord instituted the Holy Eucharist?

A. **When our Lord instituted the Holy Eucharist the twelve Apostles were present.**

Q. How did our Lord institute the Holy Eucharist?

A. **Our Lord instituted the Holy Eucharist by taking bread, blessing, breaking, and giving to His Apostles, saying: "Take ye and eat. This is My Body"; and then by taking the cup of wine, blessing, and giving it, saying to them: "Drink ye all of this. This is My Blood which shall be shed for the remission of sins. Do this for a commemoration of Me."**

Problem Questions

1. Trace the happenings of the last week of Christ's life, day by day, up to the Crucifixion.

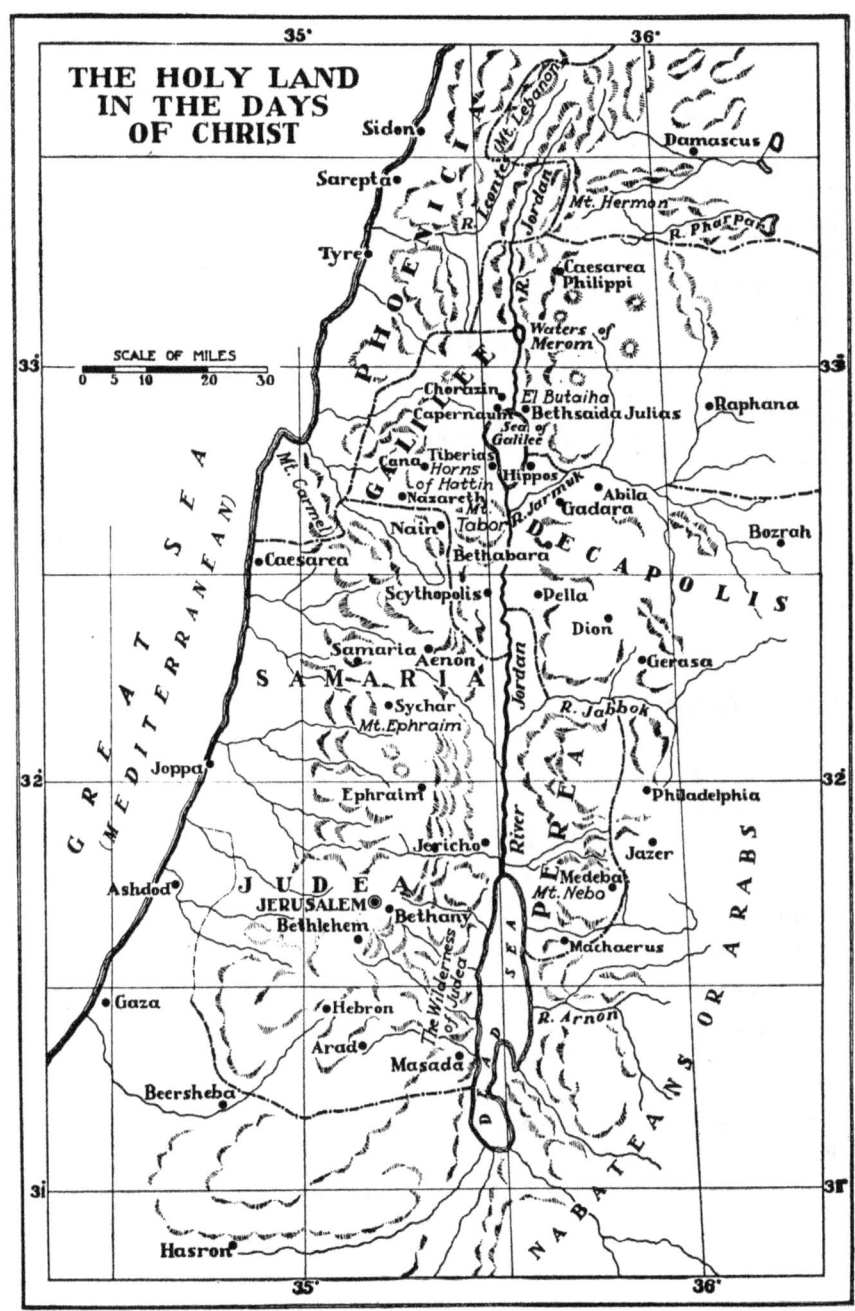

2. What was the feast of the Pasch? When was it instituted? In memory of what happenings?

3. What did Christ think of the Jewish priests?

4. Describe the events of Thursday evening.

5. What do we mean by the phrase "betrayed by a kiss"? Describe the events in Christ's life (beginning early Thursday evening) which gave rise to this expression.

6. Describe what happened in Christ's two appearances before Pontius Pilate.

Quotations from the Bible

For each of the following quotations:
a) Identify the speaker.
b) State the conditions under which the statement was made.
c) Give the meaning.
d) Tell its significance.

"Hosanna, blessed is He that cometh in the name of the Lord" (Mark xi. 1–10).

"It were better for him, if that man had not been born" (Mark xiv. 12–21).

"This is My Body" (Matt. xxvi. 20).

"For this is My Blood of the New Testament, which shall be shed for many unto remission of sins" (Matt. xxvi. 28).

"Amen I say to thee, that in this night before the cock crow, thou wilt deny Me thrice" (Matt. xxvi. 34).

"I have sinned in betraying innocent blood" (Matt. xxvii. 4).

"Behold the Man" (John xix. 5).

"This is the Bread which cometh down from heaven; that if any man eat of it, he may not die" (John vi. 50).

"I am the living Bread which came down from heaven" (John vi. 51).

"And whilst they were at supper, Jesus took bread, and blessed, and broke: and gave to His disciples, and said: Take ye, and eat. This is My Body" (Matt. xxvi. 26).

"Whosoever drinketh of this water, shall thirst again, but he that shall drink of the water that I will give him, shall not thirst forever" (John iv. 13).

Chapter XXII
THE CRUCIFIXION

The story of the Passion and the Crucifixion and Death of our Lord can be told best in the words of the Gospels:

Christ is Lead to His Death:

And after they had mocked Him, they took off the cloak from Him, and put on Him His own garments, and led Him away to crucify Him.

And going out, they found a man of Cyrene, named Simon: him they forced to take up His cross (Matt. xxvii. 31, 32).

The Women of Jerusalem:

And there followed Him a great multitude of people, and of women, who bewailed and lamented Him.

But Jesus turning to them, said: Daughters of Jerusalem, weep not over Me; but weep for yourselves, and for your children.

For behold, the days shall come, wherein they will say: Blessed are the barren, and the wombs that have not borne, and the paps that have not given suck.

Then shall they begin to say to the mountains: Fall upon us; and to the hills: Cover us.

For if in the green wood they do these things, what shall be done in the dry? (Luke xxiii. 27–31.)

On Mount Calvary:

And they came to the place that is called Golgotha, which is the place of Calvary.

And they gave Him wine to drink mingled with gall. And when He had tasted, He would not drink (Matt. xxvii. 33, 34).

He is Crucified:

And after they had crucified Him, they divided His garments, casting lots; that it might be fulfilled which was spoken by the prophet, saying: *They divided My garments among them; and upon My vesture they cast lots.* And they sat and watched Him (Matt. xxvii. 35, 36).

The King of the Jews:

And they put over His head His cause written: This is Jesus the King of Jews (Matt. xxvii. 37).

The Two Thieves:

Then were crucified with Him two thieves: one on the right hand, and one on the left (Matt. xxvii. 38).

Mary at the Foot of the Cross:

Now there stood by the cross of Jesus, His mother, and His mother's sister, Mary of Cleophas, and Mary Magdalen.

When Jesus therefore had seen His mother and the disciple standing whom He loved, He saith to His mother: Woman, behold thy son.

After that, He saith to the disciple: Behold thy mother. And from that hour, the disciple took her to his own (John xix. 25–27).

I Thirst:

Afterwards, Jesus knowing that all things were now accomplished, that the scripture might be fulfilled, said: I thirst (John xix. 28).

He is Mocked:

And they that passed by, blasphemed Him, wagging their heads,

And saying: Vah, Thou that destroyest the temple of God, and in three days doth rebuild it: save Thy own self; if Thou be the Son of God, come down from the cross.

In like manner also the chief priests, with the scribes and ancients, mocking, said:

He saved others; Himself He cannot save. If He be the King of Israel, let Him now come down from the cross, and we will believe Him.

He trusted in God; let Him now deliver Him if He will have Him; for He said: I am the Son of God.

And the selfsame thing the thieves also, that were crucified with Him, reproached Him with (Matt. xxvii. 39–44).

The Good Thief:

And one of those robbers who were hanged, blasphemed Him, saying: If Thou be Christ, save Thyself and us.

But the other answering, rebuked him, saying: Neither dost thou fear God, seeing thou art under the same condemnation?

And we indeed justly, for we receive the due reward of our deeds; but this Man hath done no evil.

And he said to Jesus: Lord, remember me when Thou shalt come into Thy kingdom.

THE VIA DOLOROSA

The street through which Christ passed on the way to Calvary. Jerusalem has been razed many times since that fateful day, but it is believed that this is the exact location of the original site. (Publisher's Photo Service, N. Y.)

And Jesus said to him: Amen I say to thee, this day thou shalt be with Me in Paradise (Luke xxiii. 39–43).

From the Sixth to the Ninth Hour:

Now from the sixth hour there was darkness over the whole earth, until the ninth hour.

And about the ninth hour Jesus cried with a loud voice, saying: Eloi, Eloi, lamma sabacthani? that is, My God, why hast Thou forsaken Me?

And some that stood there and heard, said: This Man calleth Elias.

And immediately one of them running took a sponge, and filled it with vinegar; and put it on a reed, and gave Him to drink (Matt. xxvii. 45–48).

Christ Died:

And Jesus crying with a loud voice, said: Father, into Thy hands I commend My spirit. And saying this, He gave up the ghost (Luke xxiii. 46).

Christ died on the cross on Mount Calvary on the Friday of that eventful week. He suffered and died for our sins. We call that week Holy Week, because of Christ's death and the meaning of the events for the redemption and salvation of men. We call that Friday, *Good* Friday in spite of the terrible, cruel suffering of the crucifixion, and the agonized death of Christ, because by His death He showed His great love for man, and purchased for man every blessing. In short, He redeemed man.

The Seven Last Words of Jesus on the Cross
Father forgive them: for they know not what they do.
This day shalt thou be with Me in Paradise.
Behold thy mother: Behold thy son.
My God, My God, why hast Thou forsaken Me?
I thirst.
It is consummated
Father into Thy hands I commend My spirit.

THE CRUCIFIXION
Painting by Guido Reni, in the Church of St. Lawrence in Lucina, at Rome.

Testimony of St. John:

Then the Jews (because it was the parasceve), that the bodies might not remain upon the cross on the Sabbath day (for that was a great Sabbath day), besought Pilate that their legs might be broken, and that they might be taken away.

The soldiers therefore came; and they broke the legs of the first, and of the other that was crucified with Him.

But after they were come to Jesus, when they saw that He was already dead, they did not break His legs.

But one of the soldiers with a spear opened His side, and immediately there came out blood and water.

And he that saw it hath given testimony; and His testimony is true. And he knoweth that He saith true; and you also may believe.

For these things were done, that the scripture might be fulfilled: *You shall not break a bone of Him.*

And again another scripture saith: *They shall look on Him whom they pierced* (John xix. 31-37).

The Events Immediately Following:

And behold the veil of the temple was rent in two from the top even to the bottom, and the earth quaked, and the rocks were rent.

And the graves were opened: and many bodies of the saints that had slept arose.

And coming out of the tombs after His resurrection, came into the holy city, and appeared to many.

Now the centurion and they that were with him watching Jesus, having seen the earth quake, and the things that were done, were sore afraid, saying: Indeed this was the Son of God.

And there were there many women afar off, who had followed Jesus from Galilee, ministering unto Him:

Among whom was Mary Magdalen, and Mary the mother of James and Joseph, and the mother of the sons of Zebedee.

And when it was evening, there came a certain rich man of Arimathea, named Joseph, who also himself was a disciple of Jesus.

He went to Pilate, and asked the body of Jesus. Then Pilate commanded that the body should be delivered.

And Joseph taking the body, wrapped it up in a clean linen cloth.

And laid it in his own new monument, which he had hewed out in a rock. And he rolled a great stone to the door of the monument, and went his way.

And there was there Mary Magdalen, and the other Mary sitting over against the sepulcher (Matt. xxvii. 51-61).

THE CRUCIFIXION

He Descended into Hell. The question naturally arises, when Christ died, what happened to His soul between the time of His death and the resurrection? The basis for the answer is found in a statement of St. Peter and the tradition of the Church. St. Peter said: speaking of Christ's "being put to death indeed in the flesh, but enlivened in spirit, in which also coming He preached to those spirits that were in prison." In this passage "the spirits that were in prison" meant "the place of the dead"; i.e., the place or abode called Limbo in which were the souls that had not gained the happiness of heaven. Christ visited this place to free these just souls whether they had died in Christ's lifetime before the crucifixion, or in all the ages before. This abode of the dead, this prison, is called in the Scriptures, hell. Usually when the word "hell" is used it means the bottomless pit, the place of lost souls (the damned). But the word is also used to mean purgatory. It is also used to mean a third kind of place or abode where the souls of the just were received before the coming of Christ. It is into this place called Limbo, that Christ went, while His body was still in the holy sepulcher. When we say Christ descended into hell, it is this place and not the "place of lost souls" that we mean.

Summary in the Creed. These events are briefly summarized in part of the second article of the Apostles' Creed:

I believe in Jesus Christ, His only Son, our Lord; who was conceived by the Holy Ghost, born of the Virgin Mary, suffered under Pontius Pilate, was crucified; died, and was buried. He descended into hell.

Summary in the Rosary. The events in this chapter are also summarized in the five sorrowful mysteries of the Rosary:

1. Prayer of our Lord in the Garden of Olives.
2. The scourging of our Lord.
3. The crowning of our Lord with thorns.
4. The carrying of the cross.
5. The crucifixion.

Another Summary: The Stations of the Cross. They are also summarized more fully in the fourteen stations of the cross.

1. Jesus is condemned to death.

2. Jesus is laden with the cross.
3. Jesus falls the first time under His cross.
4. Jesus meets His afflicted Mother.
5. The Cyrenian helps Jesus to carry His cross.
6. Veronica wipes the face of Jesus.
7. Jesus falls the second time.
8. Jesus speaks to the women of Jerusalem.
9. Jesus falls the third time.
10. Jesus is stripped of His garments.
11. Jesus is nailed to the cross.
12. Jesus dies on the cross.
13. Jesus is taken down from the cross.
14. Jesus is placed in the sepulcher.

Questions from the Catechism

Q. What did Jesus Christ suffer?
A. **Jesus Christ suffered a bloody sweat, a cruel scourging, was crowned with thorns, and was crucified.**

Q. On what day did Christ die?
A. **Christ died on Good Friday.**

Q. Why do you call that day "good" on which Christ died so sorrowful a death?
A. **We call the day good on which Christ died, because by His death He showed His great love for man, and purchased for him every blessing.**

Q. Where did Christ die?
A. **Christ died on Mount Calvary.**

Q. How did Christ die?
A. **Christ was nailed to the cross and died on it between two thieves.**

Q. Why did Christ suffer and die?
A. **Christ suffered and died for our sins.**

Q. What lessons do we learn from the sufferings and death of Christ?
A. **From the sufferings and death of Christ we learn the great evil of sin, the hatred God bears to it, and the necessity of satisfying for it.**

Q. Whither did Christ's soul go after His death?
A. **After Christ's death His soul descended into hell.**

Q. Did Christ's soul descend into the hell of the damned?
A. **The hell into which Christ's soul descended was not the hell of**

THE CRUCIFIXION

the damned, but a place or state of rest called Limbo, where the souls of the just were waiting for Him.

Q. Why did Christ descend into Limbo?

A. **Christ descended into Limbo to preach to the souls who were in prison** — that is, to announce to them the joyful tidings of their redemption.

Q. Where was Christ's body while His soul was in Limbo?

A. **While Christ's soul was in Limbo His body was in the holy sepulcher.**

Problem Questions

1. Describe step by step the events on Friday after the condemnation of Christ.

2. What events are omitted in the devotions of the "stations"?

3. Name the fourteen "stations."

4. What statements of Christ on that first Good Friday are the basis of the devotion called the "Tre Ore"?

5. Why was the "good thief" admitted to heaven? What application is there in the incident of the good thief to our life?

6. What pictures of the crucifixion appeal especially to you? Why? Name the artists of these pictures.

7. Has the crucifixion been treated often in literature? Why?

8. What is meant by a Passion Play? Which is the most famous of the Passion Plays? Can you find out the history of the Passion Play?

9. What basis is there for the statement that "Christ descended into hell" (Limbo)?

Quotations from the Bible

For each of the following quotations:

a) Identify the speaker.
b) State the conditions under which the statement was made.
c) Give the meaning.
d) Tell its significance.

"Woman, behold thy Son" (John xix. 26).

"I thirst" (John xix. 28).

"Lord, remember me when Thou shalt come into Thy kingdom" (Luke xxiii. 42).

"My God, My God, why hast Thou forsaken Me?" (Matt. xxvii. 46.)

"Father, into Thy hands I commend My spirit" (Luke xxiii. 46).

"Thou hast said it. Nevertheless I say to you, hereafter you shall see the Son of Man sitting on the right hand of the power of God, and coming in the clouds of heaven" (Matt. xxvi. 64–65).

"The Jews answered Him: We have a law; and according to the law He ought to die, because He made Himself the Son of God" (John xix. 7).

"And the centurion who stood over against Him, seeing that crying out in this manner He had given up the ghost, said: Indeed this Man was the Son of God" (Mark xv. 39).

"This day thou shalt be with Me in Paradise" (Luke xxiii. 43).

"Father, forgive them, for they know not what they do" (Luke xxiii. 34).

"Jesus therefore, when He had taken the vinegar, said: It is consummated" (John xix. 30).

To what incident does the following description refer?
Who was present?
What is the significance of the event?

"Christ died for all" (II Cor. v. 15).

"He is the Propitiation for our sins: and not for ours only, but also for those of the whole world" (I John ii. 2).

Chapter XXIII
HE IS RISEN

"He is risen" is the most joyful news ever told to man. It is the fulfillment of that other great announcement, "Behold, I bring you tidings of great joy." It is the announcement that He who was crucified, died, and was buried in the sepulcher, had risen from the dead.

Between Good Friday and Easter Sunday. We have seen what happened between the Crucifixion on Friday, and the announcement of the angels on Sunday that He is risen. The climax of all the events of this week, with the dark hours of the Crucifixion which seemed like an inglorious end, is the event of Easter Sunday, the Resurrection. He is risen. Christ rose from the dead, glorious and immortal, on Easter Sunday, the third day after His death. This is the story as told us in the Gospel according to St. Matthew.

And in the end of the Sabbath, when it began to dawn toward the first day of the week, came Mary Magdalen and the other Mary, to see the sepulcher.

And behold there was a great earthquake. For an angel of the Lord descended from heaven, and coming, rolled back the stone, and sat upon it.

And his countenance was as lightning, and his raiment as snow.

And for fear of him, the guards were struck with terror, and became as dead men.

And the angel answering, said to the women: Fear not you; for I know that you seek Jesus who was crucified.

He is not here, for He is risen, as He said. Come, and see the place where the Lord was laid.

And going quickly, tell ye His disciples that He is risen: and behold He will go before you into Galilee; there you shall see Him. Lo, I have foretold it to you.

And they went out quickly from the sepulcher with fear and great joy, running to tell His disciples.

And behold Jesus met them, saying: All hail. But they came up and took hold of His feet, and adored Him.

Then Jesus said to them: Fear not. Go, tell My brethren that they go into Galilee, there they shall see Me.

Who when they were departed, behold some of the guards came into the city, and told the chief priests all things that had been done.

And they being assembled together with the ancients, taking counsel, gave a great sum of money to the soldiers.

Saying: Say you, His disciples came by night, and stole Him away when we were asleep.

And if the governor shall hear of this, we will persuade him, and secure you.

So they taking the money, did as they were taught: and this word was spread abroad among the Jews, even unto this day (Matt. xxviii. 1–15).

The Forty Days on Earth. He is risen? But where? And to leave no doubt but that He was risen, He remains on earth forty days, appearing to many people alone and in groups, and many times. So one of Christ's great followers said:

But if there be no resurrection of the dead, then Christ is not risen again.

And if Christ be not risen again, then is our preaching vain, and your faith is also vain. . . .

But now Christ is risen from the dead, the first fruits of them that sleep (I Cor. xv. 13, 14, 20).

Buried with Him in baptism, in whom also you are risen again by the faith of the operation of God, who hath raised Him up from the dead (Col. ii. 12).

Therefore, if you be risen with Christ, seek the things that are above; where Christ is sitting at the right hand of God (Col. iii. 1).

This follower knew of Christ's appearances and confidently preached the Resurrection.

Appearances of Christ Between Resurrection and Ascension. Jesus appeared at least ten times between His Resurrection and His Ascension. There is a tradition in the Church that right at the time of His Resurrection Christ appeared to His Mother Mary, but this is not told in the New Testament. The appearances of Christ are as follows:

On the first day:
1. To Mary Magdalen (John xx. 14; Mark xvi. 9).

THE HOLY WOMEN AT THE TOMB
Painting by Axel Ender. (From Gramsdorff Bros.)

2. To the other women (Matt. xxviii. 9).
3. To Peter (Luke xxiv. 34; I Cor. xv. 5).
4. To the two disciples on the way to Emmaus, on Sunday evening (Mark xvi. 12, 13; Luke xxiv. 13–32).
5. To the Apostles, except Thomas, on Sunday evening (Mark xvi. 14; Luke xxiv. 36; John xx. 19–24). All these appearances occurred on the first day.

Later appearances:

6. To the Apostles, including Thomas, a week later (John xx. 24–29).
7. In Galilee near the Lake Genesareth, to seven disciples (John xxi).
8. On a mountain in Galilee to a multitude of disciples (Matt. xxviii. 16–20; I Cor. xv. 6).
9. To James (I Cor. xv. 7).
10. The final appearance closing with the Ascension (Luke xxiv. 50–51; Acts i. 9–10).

The First Appearance to the Disciples. The first appearance to the disciples as a group came on the day after the Resurrection when Thomas was not with them. For our purpose three appearances need be described in detail. They are the three appearances to the disciples as told by St. John.

Now when it was late that same day, the first of the week, and the doors were shut, where the disciples were gathered together, for fear of the Jews, Jesus came and stood in the midst, and said to them: Peace be to you.

And when He had said this, He showed them His hands and His side. The disciples therefore were glad, when they saw the Lord (John xx. 19–20).

Doubting Thomas. Thomas returns and listens to their stories of what had happened and says:

Except I shall see in His hands the print of the nails, and put my finger into the place of the nails, and put my hand into His side, I will not believe (John xx. 25).

"My Lord and My God." Then eight days later Christ shows Himself again to the disciples; this time Thomas is with them:

And after eight days again His disciples were within, and Thomas with them. Jesus cometh, the doors being shut, and stood in the midst, and said: Peace be to you.

Then He saith to Thomas: Put in thy finger hither, and see My hands; and bring hither thy hand, and put it into My side; and be not faithless, but believing.

HE IS RISEN

Thomas answered, and said to Him: My Lord, and my God.

Jesus saith to him: Because thou hast seen Me, Thomas, thou hast believed: blessed are they that have not seen, and have believed.

Many other signs also did Jesus in the sight of His disciples, which are not written in this book.

But these are written, that you may believe that Jesus is the Christ, the Son of God: and that believing, you may have life in His name (John xx. 26–31).

The Third Appearance to the Disciples.

The third appearance to the disciples was while they were fishing in the sea of Tiberias. This is how St. John tells it:

After this, Jesus showed Himself again to the disciples at the sea of Tiberias. And He showed Himself after this manner.

There were together Simon Peter, and Thomas, who is called Didymus, and Nathanael, who was of Cana of Galilee, and the sons of Zebedee, and two others of His disciples.

Simon Peter saith to them: I go a fishing. They say to him: We also come with thee. And they went forth and entered into the ship; and that night they caught nothing.

But when the morning was come, Jesus stood on the shore: yet the disciples knew not that it was Jesus.

Jesus therefore said to them: Children, have you any meat? They answered Him: No.

He saith to them: Cast the net on the right side of the ship, and you shall find. They cast therefore; and now they were not able to draw it for the multitude of fishes.

That disciple therefore whom Jesus loved, said to Peter: It is the Lord. Simon Peter, when he heard that it was the Lord, girt his coat about him (for he was naked), and cast himself into the sea.

But the other disciples came in the ship (for they were not far from the land, but as it were two hundred cubits) dragging the net with fishes.

As soon then as they came to land, they saw hot coals lying, and a fish laid thereon, and bread.

Jesus saith to them: Bring hither of the fishes which you have now caught.

Simon Peter went up, and drew the net to land, full of great fishes, one hundred and fifty-three. And although there were so many, the net was not broken (John xxi. 1–11).

The Dinner:

Jesus saith to them: Come, and dine. And none of them who were at meat, durst ask Him: Who art Thou? knowing that it was the Lord.

And Jesus cometh and taketh bread, and giveth them, and fish in like manner.

This is now the third time that Jesus was manifested to His disciples, after He was risen from the dead (John xxi. 12–15).

Feed My Lambs, Feed My Sheep:

When therefore they had dined, Jesus saith to Simon Peter: Simon, son of John, lovest thou Me more than these? He saith to Him: Yea, Lord, Thou knowest that I love Thee. He saith to him: Feed My lambs.

He saith to him again: Simon, son of John, lovest thou Me? He saith to Him: Yea, Lord, Thou knowest that I love Thee. He saith to him: Feed My lambs.

He said to him the third time: Simon, son of John, lovest thou Me? Peter was grieved, because He had said to him the third time: Lovest thou Me? And he said to Him: Lord, Thou knowest all things: Thou knowest that I love Thee. He said to him: Feed My sheep (John xxi. 15–17).

Prophecy of Peter's Crucifixion:

Amen, amen I say to thee, when thou wast younger, thou didst gird thyself, and didst walk where thou wouldst. But when thou shalt be old, thou shalt stretch forth thy hands, and another shall gird thee, and lead thee whither thou wouldst not.

And this He said, signifying by what death He should glorify God. And when He had said this, He saith to him: Follow Me (John xxi. 18–19).

The Ascension. The book in the New Testament which tells about Christ's Apostles is called the Acts of the Apostles. It begins with a statement leading up to the Ascension of our Lord. It was written by St. Luke, who wrote one of the four Gospels, and it says in its first chapter:

To whom also He showed Himself alive after His Passion, by many proofs for forty days appearing to them, and speaking of the kingdom of God.

And eating together with them, He commanded them that they should not depart from Jerusalem, but should wait for the promise of the Father, which you have heard [saith He] by My mouth.

For John indeed baptized with water, but you shall be baptized with the Holy Ghost, not many days hence.

They therefore who were come together, asked Him, saying: Lord, wilt Thou at this time restore again the kingdom of Israel?

But He said to them: It is not for you to know the times or moments, which the Father hath put in His own power.

But you shall receive the power of the Holy Ghost coming upon you, and you shall be witnesses unto Me in Jerusalem, and in all Judea, and Samaria, and even to the uttermost parts of the earth.

And when He had said these things, while they looked on, He was raised up: and a cloud received Him out of their sight.

And while they were beholding Him going up to heaven, behold two men stood by them in white garments.

Who also said: Ye men of Galilee why stand you looking up to heaven? This Jesus who is taken up from you into heaven shall so come as you have seen Him going into heaven.

Then they returned to Jerusalem from the mount that is called Olivet, which is nigh Jerusalem, within a Sabbath day's journey (Acts. i. 3-12).

Jesus Sits on the Right Hand of God. St. Mark thus briefly tells of the Ascension. "And the Lord Jesus after He had spoken to them, was taken up into heaven and sitteth on the right hand of God" (Mark xvi. 19). And St. Stephen, the martyr, just before he was stoned to death, is described by St. Luke in his story of the Acts of the Apostles, as seeing Christ standing at the right hand of God. "But he being full of the Holy Ghost looking up steadfastly to heaven, saw the glory of God, and Jesus standing on the right hand of God. And he said: Behold I see the heavens opened, and the Son of Man standing on the right hand of God." In his letter or epistle to the Ephesians, St. Paul speaks of God the Father, "raising Him [Christ] up from the dead, and setting Him on His right hand in the heavenly places" (Eph. i. 20). In his letter to the Hebrews he also says: "We have such an High Priest, who is set on the right hand of the Throne of Majesty in the heavens" (Heb. viii. 1); and a little later he adds, "This Man, offering one sacrifice for sins, forever sitteth on the right hand of God" (Heb. x. 12). And St. Peter also adds his word: "Who [Christ] is on the right hand of God, swallowing down death, that we might be made heirs of life everlasting" (II Peter iii. 22).

Judge of the Living and the Dead. Peter, at the time of receiving the Roman centurion Cornelius into the Church, preached and said:

Him God raised up the third day to the people, and to testify that it is He who was appointed by God to be judge of the living and the dead.

And how just it is that He who was unjustly judged by men, and received the utmost in the sentence of condemnation, is Himself Judge of Men, the living and the dead!

Summary. So we can understand easily the statement in the Apostles' Creed that Christ: "ascended into heaven, and sitteth at the right hand of God, the Father Almighty, from thence He shall come to judge the living and the dead." So we complete the creed statement of our belief in Jesus Christ: I believe "in Jesus Christ, His only Son our Lord: who was conceived by the Holy Ghost, born of the Virgin Mary, suffered under Pontius Pilate, was crucified, died, and was buried. He descended into hell. The third day He arose again from the dead. He ascended into heaven, sitteth at the right hand of God, the Father Almighty. From thence He shall come to judge the living and the dead."

Questions from the Catechism

Q. Who is the Redeemer?
A. **Our Blessed Lord and Savior Jesus Christ is the Redeemer of mankind.**

Q. What do you believe of Jesus Christ?
A. **I believe that Jesus Christ is the Son of God, the Second Person of the Blessed Trinity, true God and true man.**

Q. Why is Jesus Christ true God?
A. **Jesus Christ is true God because He is the true and only Son of God the Father.**

Q. On what day did Christ rise from the dead?
A. **Christ rose from the dead, glorious and immortal, on Easter Sunday, the third day after His death.**

Q. How long did Christ stay on earth after His Resurrection?
A. **Christ stayed on earth forty days after His Resurrection to show that He was truly risen from the dead, and to instruct His Apostles.**

Q. After Christ had remained forty days on earth whither did He go?
A. **After forty days Christ ascended into heaven, and the day on which He ascended into heaven is called Ascension day.**

Q. Where is Christ in heaven?
A. **In heaven Christ sits at the right hand of God, the Father Almighty.**

HE IS RISEN

Q. What do you mean by saying that Christ sits at the right hand of God?
A. **When I say that Christ sits at the right hand of God, I mean that Christ as God is equal to His Father in all things, and that as man He is in the highest place in heaven next to God.**

Problem Questions

1. Describe the Resurrection.
2. Describe the Ascension.
3. Why is the Resurrection the most important event of Christ's life on earth?
4. Make a list from the New Testament of all the appearances of Christ between the Resurrection and the Ascension.
5. Are the proofs of these appearances as clear as the proof for other historical events of the time?
6. Would not one appearance after the Resurrection to all the Apostles or most of them have been enough? What explanation do you suggest for so many appearances?
7. What is the special meaning to you of the absence of Thomas at one of the appearances and His presence later? What was Thomas's exclamation when he was present? At what time in the Mass might you use this exclamation?

Quotations from the Bible

For each of the following quotations:
a) Identify the speaker.
b) State the conditions under which the statement was made.
c) Give the meaning.
d) Tell its significance.

"He is risen."

"Except I shall see in His hands the print of the nails, and put my finger into the place of the nails, and put my hand into His side, I will not believe" (John xx. 25).

"My Lord and my God" (John xx. 28).

"Feed My lambs. Feed My sheep" (John xxi. 15–17).

"I am the Resurrection and the Life: he that believeth in Me, although he be dead, shall live" (John xi. 25).

"For I delivered unto you first of all, which I also received: how that Christ died for our sins, according to the Scriptures" (I Cor. xv. 3–8).

"So also is the resurrection of the dead. It is sown in corruption, it shall rise in incorruption. It is sown in dishonor, it shall rise in glory. It is sown in weakness, it shall rise in power. It is sown a natural body, it shall rise a spiritual body" (I Cor. xv. 42–44).

"Immediately he preached Jesus in the synagogues, that He is the Son of God" (Acts ix. 20).

"They that were in the boat came and adored Him, saying: Indeed Thou art the son of God" (Matt. xiv. 33).

"Nathanael answered Him, and said: Rabbi, Thou art the Son of God, Thou art the King of Israel" (John i. 49).

"She saith to Him: Yea, Lord, I have believed that Thou art Christ the Son of the Living God, who art come into this world" (John xi. 27).

"He, answering, said: I believe that Jesus Christ is the Son of God" (Acts viii. 37).

"The centurion who stood over against Him, seeing that crying out in this manner He had given up the ghost, said: Indeed, this man was the Son of God" (Mark xv. 39).

"Crying with a loud voice, he said: What have I to do with Thee, Jesus, the Son of the Most High God?" (Mark v. 7.)

"Jesus said to them: Amen, amen, I say to you, before Abraham was made, I am" (John viii. 58).

"He is not here, for He is risen, as He said" (Matt. xxviii. 6).

To what incident does the following description refer?
Who was present?
What is the significance of the event?

"These are written, that you may believe that Jesus is the Christ, the Son of God; and that believing you may have life in His Name" (John xx. 31).

"The Lord Jesus, after He had spoken to them, was taken up into heaven, and sitteth on the right hand of God" (Mark xvi. 19).

Chapter XXIV
MARY, FULL OF GRACE

Angel Gabriel Greets Mary. The visit of the angel Gabriel to a simple Jewish maiden in Nazareth named Mary to bring her the news of the greatest joy and hope for mankind, is told very simply by St. Luke.

And in the sixth month, the angel Gabriel was sent from God into a city of Galilee, called Nazareth.

To a virgin espoused to a man whose name was Joseph, of the house of David; and the virgin's name was Mary (Luke i. 26, 27).

You will see in the angel Gabriel's greeting the beginning of the prayer you say every day:

And the angel being come in, said unto her: Hail, full of grace, the Lord is with thee: blessed art thou among women (Luke i. 28).

Prophecy of the Birth of the Son of God. Mary understood quickly that the greeting of the angel meant a child should be born to her, but she feared because she was a virgin. But the Angel Gabriel reassured her.

Behold thou shalt conceive in thy womb, and shalt bring forth a son; and thou shalt call His name Jesus.

He shall be great, and shall be called the Son of the Most High; and the Lord God shall give unto Him the throne of David His father; and He shall reign in the house of Jacob forever.

And of His kingdom there shall be no end.

And Mary said to the angel: How shall this be done, because I know not man?

And the angel answering, said to her: The Holy Ghost shall come upon thee, and the power of the Most High shall overshadow thee. And therefore also the Holy which shall be born of thee shall be called the Son of God. . . .

Because no word shall be impossible with God (Luke i. 31–35, 37).

Be it Done to Me According to Thy Word. And with simple faith and bowing to the divine will, Mary said:

Behold the handmaid of the Lord; be it done to me according to thy word. And the angel departed from her (Luke i. 38).

The Visitation. Mary then went into a city of Juda and visited her cousin Elizabeth, who was to be soon the mother of John the Baptist. And upon seeing Mary, Elizabeth greets her thus:

And she cried out with a loud voice, and said: Blessed art thou among women, and blessed is the fruit of thy womb.

And whence is this to me, that the mother of my Lord should come to me? (Luke i. 42, 43.)

The Magnificat

My soul doth magnify the Lord.

And my spirit hath rejoiced in God my Savior.

Because He hath regarded the humility of His handmaid: for behold from henceforth all generations shall call me blessed.

Because He that is mighty, hath done great things to me; and holy is His name.

And His mercy is from generation unto generations to them that fear Him.

He hath shewed might in His arm: He hath scattered the proud in the conceit of their heart.

He hath put down the mighty from their seat, and hath exalted the humble.

He hath filled the hungry with good things: and the rich He hath sent empty away.

He hath received Israel His servant, being mindful of His mercy;

As He spoke to our fathers, to Abraham and to his seed for ever. *Luke I, 46-55.*

The Magnificat. And then Mary sings the greatest song of praise ever formed by human lips:

And Mary said: My soul doth magnify the Lord, and my spirit hath rejoiced in God my Savior.
Because He hath regarded the humility of His handmaid; for behold from henceforth all generations shall call me blessed.
Because He that is mighty, hath done great things to me; and holy is His name.
And His mercy is from generation unto generations, to them that fear Him.
He hath shewed might in His arm: He hath scattered the proud in the conceit of their heart.
He hath put down the mighty from their seat, and hath exalted the humble.
He hath filled the hungry with good things; and the rich He hath sent empty away.
He hath received Israel His servant, being mindful of His mercy:
As He spoke to our fathers, to Abraham and to his seed forever (Luke i. 46–55).

Mary, the Mother of God. The facts about the birth of Christ we have given fully in another place. We may restate them here briefly from the standpoint of Mary and Joseph. There was ordered an enrollment, or census, of all persons in the Roman Empire. Joseph being of the house of David went to Bethlehem, the city of David, to be enrolled. Because of the crowds in Bethlehem, Joseph and Mary could find no place to stay except a stable. Here the Child was born, wrapped in swaddling clothes, and placed in the manger. They were visited there by the shepherds to whom the angels appeared, and later by the Wise Men who saw Christ's star in the East. And Mary kept the words of the shepherds, and all these events, pondering them in her heart.

These facts fulfill the promise of God when Eve ate the fruit in the garden of Eden, that the seed of another woman would save mankind, and also the prophecy of Isaias.

Therefore the Lord Himself shall give you a sign. Behold a virgin shall conceive, and bear a Son, and His name shall be called Emmanuel (Isa. vii. 14).

The Presentation. In accordance with the Jewish custom the

Child was presented in the temple, at Jerusalem forty days after His birth. Here, Simeon, a just and pious man full of the Holy Ghost, acknowledges that He is the Christ. And Mary and Joseph "were wondering at those things which were spoken concerning Him." Simeon prophesies about Mary:

> And thy own soul a sword shall pierce, that out of many hearts, thoughts may be revealed (Luke ii. 35).

In Egypt. An angel appeared to Joseph after the Wise Men or Magi called on Herod, asking him about the Child who is born King of the Jews. The angel warned Joseph to take the Mother and Child and fly into Egypt, and "be there until I shall tell thee. For it will come to pass that Herod will seek the Child to destroy Him" (Matt. ii. 13). They fled into Egypt. Herod died. The angel of the Lord appeared to Joseph in sleep in Egypt and told him he could return. Jesus and Mary and Joseph returned to Nazareth.

The Holy Family went every year to Jerusalem at the solemn day of Pasch. And it was on one of these visits to Jerusalem that Christ, now twelve years old, was accidentally left behind, because Mary and Joseph thought He was with relatives. They returned to seek Him. He was found talking with the doctors in the temple who wondered at His wisdom and His answers.

> And seeing Him, they wondered. And His mother said to Him: Son, why hast Thou done so to us? Behold Thy father and I have sought Thee sorrowing.
> And He said to them: How is it that you sought Me? Did you not know, that *I must be about My Father's business?*
> And they understood not the word that He spoke unto them.
> And He went down with them, and came to Nazareth, and was subject to them. And His mother kept all these words in her heart.
> And Jesus advanced in wisdom, age, and grace with God and men (Luke ii. 48–52).

It is worth while noticing that Christ performed His first miracle because Mary asked Him to; this was the changing of the water to wine at the marriage feast at Cana.

After Cana, His mother went down with Him to Capharnaum. In another instance Mary and the disciples were standing outside

THE SISTINE MADONNA
Painting by Raphael, sixteenth century, preserved in the Dresden Gallery.

the synagogue waiting for Him. No other appearance of Mary is mentioned until we find her standing at the foot of the cross of Christ:

> Now there stood by the Cross of Jesus, His mother, and His mother's sister, Mary of Cleophas, and Mary Magdalen.
> When Jesus therefore had seen His mother and the disciple standing whom He loved, He saith to His mother: Woman, behold thy son.
> After that, He saith to the disciple: Behold thy mother. And from that hour, the disciple took her to his own (John xix. 25–27).

Mary With the Apostles. It is part of the tradition of the Church that Christ appeared to Mary first after the Resurrection, but this is not mentioned in the Gospels. Immediately after the Ascension of Christ, on Mount Olivet, the Apostles return to Jerusalem, a Sabbath day's journey from the Mount, and they go up into the upper rooms where they lived. Then we read:

> All these were persevering with one mind in prayer with the women, and Mary the mother of Jesus, and with His brethren (Acts i. 14).

These are about all the facts that are told about Mary, the Mother of Christ, in the New Testament. About what happened to her afterwards, or where she died, we do not know. In the great prophetic book of the New Testament, the Apocalypse, we read this reference to Mary in heaven.

> And a great sign appeared in heaven: A woman clothed with the sun, and the moon under her feet, and on her head a crown of twelve stars (Apoc. xii. 1).

The Immaculate Conception. Mary was the daughter of St. Joachim and St. Anne. She was from the beginning without the stain of original sin. This was a great privilege given to her through the merits of her Divine Son, Christ. This privilege had been given to no other human being, man or woman. It was true from the very time of Mary's conception. The Immaculate Conception of Mary is sometimes confused with the virgin birth of Christ.

This privilege of Mary of being born without the stain of original sin is called the Immaculate Conception of Mary, and from all that we know it is clear she never committed any sin, mortal

THE IMMACULATE CONCEPTION
Painting by Murillo, seventeenth century, preserved in the Louvre, Paris.

or venial. Rightly, then, may Mary be greeted and addressed, "Hail, full of grace." Being without sin, there was no obstacle to the flow of the grace of God. "Thou art all fair" as we read in the Canticle of Canticles, and "there is no spot in thee."

Mary, Ever Virgin. Christ was born of the Virgin Mary. Joseph was advised by the angel in His sleep: "Joseph, son of David, fear not to take unto thee Mary thy wife, for that which is conceived in her, is of the Holy Ghost" (Matt. i. 20). Joseph and Mary were espoused or married, and so Joseph was the guardian and protector of Jesus and Mary. But Mary remained ever a virgin.

The Assumption of the Blessed Virgin Mary. It is a tradition in the Church, that upon her death, Mary was assumed or taken up body and soul, to heaven. The Church celebrates this on August 15, the Feast of the Assumption.

Memorial of Mary. The Church celebrates the events of Mary's life in several ways. One is to call to mind the life of Mary and especially her sorrows. The easy way to do this is by recalling the "Seven Sorrows of Mary." These are:

1. The Prophecy of Holy Simeon.
2. The Flight into Egypt.
3. The Losing of the Child Jesus.
4. The Meeting of Jesus Carrying the Cross.
5. Witnessing the Sufferings and Death of Her Divine Son.
6. The Taking Down of Her Dead Son from the Cross.
7. The Placing of Jesus in the Sepulcher.

The Rosary. The great prayer and memorial to Mary after the "Hail Mary" is "The Rosary of the Blessed Virgin." In the prayer we are to call to mind the facts of her life and her relations to her Son, and the main facts of His life. This is done by meditating on the mysteries while saying the prayers of the Rosary. These mysteries are:

The Joyful Mysteries

1. The Incarnation of Our Lord (The Annunciation).
2. The Visitation of Mary to St. Elizabeth.
3. The Nativity of Our Lord.

4. The Presentation of Our Lord in the Temple.
5. The Finding of Our Lord in the Temple.

The Sorrowful Mysteries

1. The Agony of Our Lord in the Garden.
2. The Scourging of Our Lord at the Pillar.
3. The Crowning of Our Lord with Thorns.
4. The Carrying of the Cross.
5. The Crucifixion of Our Lord.

The Glorious Mysteries

1. The Resurrection of Our Lord.
2. The Ascension of Our Lord.
3. The Descent of the Holy Ghost.
4. The Assumption of the Blessed Virgin.
5. The Crowning of the Blessed Virgin in Heaven.

Question from the Catechism

Q. Was anyone ever preserved from original sin?
A. **The Blessed Virgin Mary, through the merits of her Divine Son, was preserved free from the guilt of original sin, and this privilege is called her Immaculate Conception.**

Problem Questions

1. Describe two Madonnas you like, and tell why.
2. Name and describe five great paintings of events of Mary's life. Name the artist.
3. Write a brief biography of Mary's life.
4. Quote the Magnificat.
5. What are the great feast days of Mary? Are any of them holydays of obligation?
6. Name the mysteries of the Holy Rosary. Are they a summary of Mary's life?
7. What are the "Sorrows of Mary"?
8. What is meant by the Immaculate Conception of Mary? by the virgin birth of Jesus?
9. Justify five of the titles given to Mary in the Litany of the Blessed Virgin Mary (or assign one or two different ones to each member of the class).

Quotations from the Bible

For each of the following quotations:
a) Identify the speaker.

b) State the conditions under which the statement was made.
c) Give the meaning.
d) Tell its significance.

"My soul doth magnify the Lord" (Luke i. 46).

"And thy own soul a sword shall pierce, that, out of many hearts, thoughts may be revealed" (Luke iii. 35).

Chapter XXV
CHRIST AND THE APOSTLES

The Life of Christ. For twenty-nine years the life of Christ was uneventful except for the incident in the temple; for three years we have events, preachings, miracles almost piling one on the other, until the Crucifixion, the Resurrection, and the Ascension. For our purpose we have separated our Lord's life before the Passion into several separate chapters, one dealing with the parables of Christ about the kingdom of God, another dealing with the miracles, and another dealing with some of the memorable sayings of Christ. We then treated the Passion of Christ, His Crucifixion, Resurrection, and Ascension. We now come to the events of Christ's life looked at from a special angle: His relations to the Apostles.

The Childhood of Christ. With a wonderful series of announcements by angels from God the good tidings of great joy were brought: Christ was born in a stable in Bethlehem, the city of David, of the Virgin Mary, who was espoused to Joseph, a carpenter. The shepherds to whom the angels brought the announcement of the Savior came to worship Him, and later came the Wise Men who saw His star in the East, who was to be King of Israel. Then followed the flight into Egypt and the return upon the death of Herod, who had ordered the slaughter of all children under two years of age. Then nothing more until Mary and Joseph returning from Jerusalem, after being on their way for a day, found that the twelve-year-old Child was not with them; they hurried back and found Christ in the temple in the midst of the doctors.

The Beginning of Public Life. Then silence for seventeen years more, and Christ was baptized by John, and the public ministry began. The events of the three years following changed the history of the world, and for twenty centuries since, they have been the greatest influence in the world.

One of the most interesting facts in the history of Christ is His relation to His Apostles. St. Luke tells, in more detail than the other evangelists, the first step in the choosing of the Apostles, particularly Peter, James, and John, who were to be the pillars of the Church, as St. Paul later called them.

Peter, James, John, and Andrew are Called. From the time of the baptism of Christ by John the Baptist, men began following Christ as His disciples, but not in the number that we might have expected. Some followed Him and then dropped away. This may surprise us when we remember the miracles that He performed before their very eyes, the wonderful character of His teaching, and His fine personality. He calls first Simon, who is also called Peter, and Andrew, the brother of Peter, and also James and John, who were the sons of Zebedee. This first calling of disciples who were later to be Apostles, is told in detail by St. Luke as follows, though he does not mention Andrew by name:

And it came to pass, that when the multitudes pressed upon Him to hear the word of God, He stood by the lake of Genesareth.

And saw two ships standing by the lake: but the fishermen were gone out of them, and were washing their nets.

And going into one of the ships that was Simon's, He desired him to draw back a little from the land. And sitting He taught the multitudes out of the ship.

Now when He had ceased to speak, He said to Simon: Launch out into the deep, and let down your nets for a draught.

And Simon answering said to Him: Master, we have labored all the night, and have taken nothing: but at Thy word I will let down the net.

And when they had done this, they inclosed a very great multitude of fishes, and their net broke.

And they beckoned to their partners that were in the other ship, that they should come and help them. And they came, and filled both the ships, so that they were almost sinking.

Which when Simon Peter saw, he fell down at Jesus' knees, saying: Depart from me, for I am a sinful man, O Lord.

For he was wholly astonished, and all that were with him, at the draught of the fishes which they had taken.

And so were also James and John the sons of Zebedee, who were Simon's partners. And Jesus saith to Simon: Fear not: from henceforth thou shalt catch men.

And having brought their ships to land, leaving all things, they followed Him (Luke v. 1-11).

Andrew is referred to on this occasion by St. Matthew and St. Mark (see Matt. iv. 19, 20; Mark i. 17, 18).

Matthew is Called. After Christ healed a man sick of the palsy, He passed on from the multitude. In the custom house, seeing Matthew sitting, He said to Him: "Follow Me," and as the Gospel says, Matthew arose and followed Him.

Selection of the Twelve Apostles. Jesus later named the twelve whom He had chosen to be in a special way His Apostles, the foreshadowing of the Church. The Gospel of St. Luke says:

And it came to pass in those days, that He went out into a mountain to pray, and He passed the whole night in the prayer of God.

And when day was come, He called unto Him His disciples, and He chose twelve of them (whom also He named Apostles):

Simon, whom He surnamed Peter, and Andrew his brother, James and John, Philip and Bartholomew,

Matthew and Thomas, James the son of Alpheus, and Simon who is called Zelotes,

And Jude, the brother of James, and Judas Iscariot, who was the traitor (Luke vi. 12-16).

Christ later commissioned them and sent them forth. He is training them as we shall see. There is need to rebuke them, even Peter, their chief. They, at times do not seem fully to understand, but we shall learn what Christ did to prepare them for the great work they were to undertake. Some of Christ's statements on His commission of them are:

And having called His twelve disciples together, He gave them power over unclean spirits, to cast them out, and to heal all manner of diseases, and all manner of infirmities.

And going, preach, saying: The kingdom of heaven is at hand.

Heal the sick, raise the dead, cleanse the lepers, cast out devils: freely have you received, freely give.

Do not possess gold, nor silver, nor money in your purses:

Nor scrip for your journey, nor two coats, nor shoes, nor a staff; for the workman is worthy of his meat.

And whosoever shall not receive you, nor hear your words: going forth out of that house or city shake off the dust from your feet.

Amen, I say to you, it shall be more tolerable for the land of Sodom and Gomorrha in the day of judgment, than for that city.

But beware of men. For they will deliver you up in councils, and they will scourge you in their synagogues.

And you shall be brought before the governors, and before kings for My sake, for a testimony to them and to the Gentiles:

But when they shall deliver you up, take no thought how or what to speak: for it shall be given you in that hour what to speak.

For it is not you that speak, but the Spirit of your Father that speaketh in you.

Everyone therefore that shall confess Me before men, I will also confess him before My Father who is in heaven.

But he that shall deny Me before men, I will also deny him before My Father who is in heaven.

And whosoever shall give to drink to one of these little ones a cup of cold water only in the name of a disciple, amen, I say to you, he shall not lose his reward (Matt. x. 1, 7, 8, 9, 10, 14, 15, 17, 18, 19, 20, 32, 33, 42).

And it came to pass, when Jesus had made an end of commanding His twelve disciples, He passed from thence, to teach and preach in their cities (Matt. xi. 1).

The Apostles were ever with Christ. They saw the multiplication of the loaves so that five thousand were fed, they saw the miraculous feeding of the four thousand. They saw Him still the storm. They saw Him walk on the waters, and what is even more, they saw Peter walk on the water. The answer that was to be brought back to John the Baptist, these Apostles knew and witnessed.

These twelve Jesus sent: commanding them, saying: Go ye not into the way of the Gentiles, and into the city of the Samaritans enter ye not (Matt. x. 5).

It seems to us no wonder, then, that Peter should recognize that Christ was God. Peter's confession of faith near the city of Cæsarea Philippi cannot be too often repeated.

And Jesus came into the quarters of Cæsarea Philippi: and He asked His disciples, saying: Whom do men say that the Son of Man is?

CHRIST AND THE APOSTLES

But they said: Some John the Baptist, and other some Elias, and others Jeremias, or one of the prophets.

Jesus saith to them: But whom do you say that I am?

Simon Peter answered and said: Thou art Christ, the Son of the living God.

And Jesus answering, said to him: Blessed art thou, Simon Bar-Jona: because flesh and blood hath not revealed it to thee, but My Father who is in heaven.

And I say to thee: That thou art Peter; and upon this rock I will build My Church, and the gates of hell shall not prevail against it.

And I will give to thee the keys of the kingdom of heaven. And whatsoever thou shalt bind upon earth, it shall be bound also in heaven: and whatsoever thou shalt loose on earth, it shall be loosed also in heaven.

Then He commanded His disciples, that they should tell no one that He was Jesus the Christ.

From that time Jesus began to show to His disciples, that He must go to Jerusalem, and suffer many things from the ancients and scribes and chief priests, and be put to death, and the third day rise again (Matt. xvi. 13–21).

The Rebuke of Peter. And in connection with the last statement Christ rebuked Peter. To the prophecy of the Crucifixion and the Resurrection, Peter says:

And Peter taking Him, began to rebuke Him, saying: Lord, be it far from Thee, this shall not be unto Thee (Matt. xvi. 22).

And to these words of protest, or of hope that they might not be true, Christ says:

Who turning, said to Peter: Go behind Me, Satan, thou art a scandal unto Me: because thou savorest not the things that are of God, but the things that are of men.

Then Jesus said to His disciples: If any man will come after Me, let him deny himself, and take up his cross, and follow Me.

For he that will save his life, shall lose it, and he that shall lose his life for My sake, shall find it.

For what doth it profit a man, if he gain the whole world, and suffer the loss of his own soul? Or what exchange shall a man give for his soul?

For the Son of Man shall come in the glory of His Father with His angels: and then will He render to every man according to his works.

Amen I say to you, there are some of them that stand here, that shall not taste death, till they see the Son of Man coming in His kingdom (Matt. xvi. 23–28).

THE TRANSFIGURATION
Painting by Raphael, sixteenth century, in the Vatican.

And at another time, after the Transfiguration when the Samaritans refused to receive Him, this happened:

And when His disciples James and John had seen this, they said: Lord, wilt Thou that we command fire to come down from heaven, and consume them?

And turning, He rebuked them, saying: You know not of what spirit you are.

The Son of Man came not to destroy souls, but to save. And they went into another town (Luke ix. 54–56).

The Transfiguration. The transfiguration is seen by three Apostles, Peter, James, and John. The story as told by St. Luke is as follows:

And it came to pass about eight days after these words, that He took Peter, and James, and John, and went up into a mountain to pray.

And whilst He prayed, the shape of His countenance was altered, and His raiment became white and glittering.

And behold two men were talking with Him. And they were Moses and Elias,

Appearing in majesty. And they spoke of His decease that He should accomplish in Jerusalem.

But Peter and they that were with Him were heavy with sleep. And waking, they saw His glory, and the two men that stood with Him.

And it came to pass, that as they were departing from Him, Peter saith to Jesus: Master, it is good for us to be here; and let us make three tabernacles, one for Thee, one for Moses, and one for Elias; not knowing what he said.

And as he spoke these things, there came a cloud, and overshadowed them: and they were afraid, when they entered into the cloud.

And a voice came out of the cloud, saying: This is My beloved Son; hear Him.

And whilst the voice was uttered, Jesus was found alone. And they held their peace, and told no man in those days of any of these things which they had seen (Luke ix. 28–36).

Teaching the Apostles. Christ taught and trained the Apostles. He taught them to pray. The instruction to the Apostles included the prayer we use today, the "Our Father," the Lord's Prayer. He told them what they might expect in the way of suffering and denial, but He promised them certainly the greatest thing of all, the pearl without price — *life everlasting*. He taught them to beware of the Pharisees and the scribes who were full of corruption and whose religion was not from the heart. He taught them humility and love. He washed the feet of the Disciples at the Last Supper in order to show His own humility. He told them that they must become as little children. This story is told at another time just after He has used the story of the Publican and Pharisee to teach them how to pray. This is the incident relating to the spirit of children.

And they brought unto Him also infants, that He might touch them. Which when the disciples saw, they rebuked them.

But Jesus, calling them together, said: Suffer children to come to Me, and forbid them not: for of such is the kingdom of God.

Amen, I say to you: Whosoever shall not receive the kingdom of God as a child, shall not enter into it (Luke xviii. 15–17).

Betrayal by Judas. But even with His loving example before them, and with the clear proof that He was God, we see from the Gospels that they did not understand what was happening around them nor did they understand Him. One of the Apostles was to sell Him for thirty pieces of silver, and betray Him with a kiss to the Jews. Christ knew this and prophesied it in advance. We know, too, the rest of the story, how Judas tried to return the money, because he did not want to be guilty of innocent blood, his later suicide by hanging, and his burial in the potter's field.

Denials by Peter. Even Peter for whom Christ prayed, and chose as the head of the Apostles, denied Him three times. Do we ever deny Him? Christ foretells these denials by Peter. "Before the cock crow twice thou shalt deny Me thrice" (Mark xiv. 30). And he did.

Apostles Misunderstand. Just after the institution of the Holy Eucharist at the Last Supper, there arose strife among the disciples as to which of them was greater. And Christ rebuked them for their lack of understanding. In His kingdom and in His church those who have power must use it for love. Power is given to serve. Pope, bishop, and priest, have their power to serve those for whom Christ died, in love, not to lord it over them as is the habit among those who know not Christ. And so after the Resurrection the Apostles asked Him when He would establish

His kingdom, as if it were to be an earthly kingdom, instead of a heavenly kingdom.

Peter Does Not Believe Mary Magdalen. And again, after the Resurrection we find some happenings that may seem strange to us. Jesus rises from the dead on Easter Sunday, the third day after His Crucifixion on Good Friday. Mary Magdalen and the other Mary went with spices to the sepulcher on the Sunday after the Crucifixion and found the stone moved. Mary Magdalen hurried to tell Peter and the other disciple whom Jesus loved They ran to the sepulcher and John outran Peter: they found what Mary told them to be true and they wondered. While Mary was standing outside of the sepulcher Christ appeared to her. But when she told it to His disciples, they did not believe, and when He appeared to the holy women later and they reported it to the disciples, they did not believe them. "And these words seemed to them as idle tales; and they did not believe them" (Luke xxiv. 11).

The Apostles Do Not Believe Peter. Christ appeared to two disciples, on the road between Jerusalem and Emmaus, and talked with them about what had happened, and how these things were the fulfillment of the prophecies of the Old Testament, and He broke bread with them in the evening and disappeared. Cleophas, which was the name of one of these disciples, hurried to the eleven Apostles; he told what had happened, and ended by saying "the Lord is risen indeed." And the Scripture says "neither did they believe them [two disciples]."

Thomas Doubts. Christ then appeared to the Apostles. But Thomas was away when this happened and he did not believe the others when they told him. This incident, with our Lord's later appearance when Thomas was present is told by St. John (see John xx. 24–29).

The Descent of the Holy Ghost. We can follow in the next chapter the remarkable effect on the Apostles of the descent of the Holy Ghost on Pentecost. All doubt and hanging back, all fear and cowardice is gone. They are strengthened by the Spirit of the Father and the Son. How they spread their work over the world is told fully in the book of the Bible called "The Acts of the Apostles." We learn from that book, too, how Matthias is chosen as one of the twelve to take the place of Judas.

St. Paul and His Conversion. There came a little later another person who is called Paul, the Apostle to the Gentiles. His original name was Saul. He was of the tribe of Benjamin, a Hebrew, born in Tarsus, the chief city of Cilicia in Asia Minor. He was a tentmaker by trade. He was brought up as a Pharisee, under the teaching at Jerusalem, and the training of the famous rabbi, Gamaliel. He persecuted the Christians and allowed the martyrdom of Stephen.

On the Road to Damascus. The most important event in his life was his conversion to Christianity on the road to Damascus. This is the story as told by St. Luke in the Acts of the Apostles.

And Saul as yet breathing out threatenings and slaughter against the disciples of the Lord, went to a high priest.

And asked of him letters to Damascus, to the synagogues: that if he found any men and women of this way, he might bring them bound to Jerusalem.

And as he went on his journey, it came to pass that he drew nigh to Damascus; and suddenly a light from heaven shined round about him.

And falling on the ground, he heard a voice saying to him: Saul, Saul, why persecutest thou Me?

Who said: Who art Thou, Lord? And He: I am Jesus whom thou persecutest. It is hard for thee to kick against the goad.

And he trembling and astonished, said: Lord, what wilt Thou have me to do?

And the Lord said to him: Arise and go into the city, and there it shall be told thee what thou must do. Now the men who went in company with him, stood amazed, hearing indeed a voice, but seeing no man.

And Saul arose from the ground; and when his eyes were opened, he saw nothing. But they leading him by the hands, brought him to Damascus.

And he was there three days, without sight, and he did neither eat nor drink.

Now there was a certain disciple at Damascus, named Ananias. And the Lord said to him in a vision: Ananias. And he said: Behold I am here, Lord.

And the Lord said to him: Arise, and go into the street that is called

Strait, and seek in the house of Judas, one named Saul of Tarsus. For behold he prayeth.

(And he saw a man named Ananias coming in, and putting his hands upon him, that he might receive his sight.)

But Ananias answered: Lord, I have heard by many of this man, how much evil he hath done to Thy saints in Jerusalem.

And here he hath authority from the chief priests to bind all that invoke Thy name.

And the Lord said to him: Go thy way; for this man is to Me a vessel of election, to carry My name before the Gentiles, and kings, and the children of Israel.

For I will show him how great things he must suffer for My name's sake.

And Ananias went his way, and entered into the house. And laying his hands upon him, he said: Brother Saul, the Lord Jesus hath sent me, He that appeared to thee in the way as thou camest; that thou mayest receive thy sight, and be filled with the Holy Ghost.

And immediately there fell from his eyes as it were scales, and he received his sight; and rising up, he was baptized.

And when he had taken meat, he was strengthened. And he was with the disciples that were at Damascus, for some days.

And immediately he preached Jesus in the synagogues, that He is the Son of God.

And all that heard him, were astonished, and said: Is not this he who persecuted in Jerusalem those that called upon this Name: and came hither for that intent, that he might carry them bound to the chief priests?

But Saul increased much more in strength, and confounded the Jews who dwelt at Damascus, affirming that this is the Christ.

And when many days were passed, the Jews consulted together to kill him.

But their laying in wait was made known to Saul. And they watched the gates also day and night, that they might kill him.

But the disciples taking him in the night, conveyed him away by the wall, letting him down in a basket.

And when he was come into Jerusalem, he essayed to join himself to the disciples; and they all were afraid of him, not believing that he was a disciple (Acts ix. 1–26).

The Apostle to the Gentiles. From that time Paul became the greatest missionary in the early Church. His strong personality, his warmth, and ardent nature were given up wholly to Christ. He visited many places in Asia Minor and in Europe. His writings which are inspired by the Holy Ghost are part of the Scriptures, and very important documents for the explanation of Christ's doctrine. We cannot follow in detail his life though we know he was in prison in Rome in 61 and later, according to the tradition of the Church, he suffered martyrdom. He has in his writings a paragraph which tells shortly of his life, warning the Corinthians against false apostles, which are among them. St. Paul states the facts about himself, just as an assurance to them.

They are Hebrews: so am I. They are Israelites: so am I. They are the seed of Abraham: so am I.

They are the ministers of Christ (I speak as one less wise): I am more; in many more labors, in prisons more frequently, in stripes above measure, in deaths often.

Of the Jews five times did I receive forty stripes, save one.

Thrice was I beaten with rods, once I was stoned, thrice I suffered shipwreck, a night and a day I was in the depth of the sea.

In journeying often, in perils of waters, in perils of robbers, in perils from my own nation, in perils from the Gentiles, in perils in the city, in perils in the wilderness, in perils in the sea, in perils from false brethren.

In labor and painfulness, in much watchings, in hunger and thirst, in fastings often, in cold and nakedness.

Besides those things which are without: my daily instance, the solicitude for all the churches.

Who is weak, and I am not weak? Who is scandalized, and I am not on fire?

If I must needs glory, I will glory of the things that concern my infirmity.

The God and Father of our Lord Jesus Christ, who is blessed forever, knoweth that I lie not.

At Damascus, the governor of the nation under Aretas the king, guarded the city of the Damascenes, to apprehend me.

And through a window in a basket was I let down by the wall, and so escaped his hands (II Cor. xi. 22–33).

Questions from the Catechism

Q. How long did Christ live on earth?
A. **Christ lived on earth about thirty-three years, and led a most holy life in poverty and suffering.**

Q. Why did Christ live so long on earth?
A. **Christ lived so long on earth to show us the way to heaven by His teachings and example.**

CHRIST AND THE APOSTLES

Problem Questions

1. Name the twelve Apostles.
2. Describe how Christ called them.
3. Write the life of Peter.
4. Describe Judas' betrayal of Christ. How was the Apostle chosen in place of Judas? What was his name?
5. Describe the Apostles in general. Were they an exceptional group of men in any way? Why do you think Christ selected such a group?
6. Keeping in mind yourself and other human beings that you know well, what do you think of the denials of Christ, the betrayal of Christ, and the misunderstandings of Christ's kingdom among the Apostles?
7. Describe the conversion of Paul.
8. Write the life of Paul.
9. Draw a map of the missionary journeys of Paul.
10. Make a collection of pictures in which the Apostles are portrayed. List them, give name of author, and write a sentence telling what you think is the most striking thing in the picture.

Quotations from the Bible

For each of the following quotations:
a) Identify the speaker.
b) State the conditions under which the statement was made.
c) Give the meaning.
d) Tell its significance.

"Depart from me, for I am a sinful man, O Lord" (Luke v. 8).

"And going, preach, saying: The kingdom of heaven is at hand.

"Heal the sick, raise the dead, cleanse the lepers, cast out devils: freely have you received, freely give.

"Do not possess gold, nor silver, nor money in your purses:

"Nor scrip for your journey, nor two coats, nor shoes, nor a staff; for the workman is worthy of his meat" (Matt. x. 7-10).

"Thou art Christ, the Son of the living God" (Matt. xvi. 16).

"Thou art Peter; and upon this rock I will build My Church, and the gates of hell shall not prevail against it" (Matt. xvi. 18).

"This is My beloved Son; hear Him" (Luke ix. 28, 36).

"Behold I am here, Lord" (Acts ix. 10).

"Because thou hast seen Me, Thomas, thou hast believed: blessed are they that have not seen, and have believed" (John xx. 29).

"Lord what wilt Thou have me to do?" (Acts ix. 6.)

"You have not chosen Me: but I have chosen you; and have appointed you, that you should go, and should bring forth fruit; and your fruit should remain: that whatsoever you shall ask of the Father in My name, He may give it to you" (John xv. 16).

"Come ye after Me, and I will make you to be fishers of men" (Matt. iv. 19).

"Going therefore, teach ye all nations" (Matt. xxviii. 19).

"He that heareth you, heareth Me" (Luke x. 16).

Chapter XXVI
THE HOLY GHOST ON PENTECOST

Promise of the Holy Ghost at the Last Supper. In that remarkable discourse of Christ after the Last Supper, as told in the Gospel of St. John, we learn of the nature of the Blessed Trinity and especially the promise of the Holy Ghost.

> And I will ask the Father, and He shall give you another Paraclete, that He may abide with you forever.
> The Spirit of Truth, whom the world cannot receive, because it seeth Him not, nor knoweth Him: but you shall know Him; because He shall abide with you, and shall be in you (John xiv. 16, 17).

The Names of the Holy Ghost. This promise, as you may recall, was made to the Apostles. In it the Holy Ghost is called the Spirit of Truth, and it is said that He shall remain with the Apostles and shall be in them. The names which the Holy Ghost is given here and elsewhere should be noted. He is called in the Old Testament, the Giver of Life, though just what He is, was not fully revealed until Christ came. He is called by Peter the Spirit of Christ, and He is called by St. Paul in one place the Spirit of God, and in another place the Sanctifier.

The Holy Ghost Will Come. Later in this same address our Lord made a definite promise to send the Holy Ghost upon the Apostles:

> But the Paraclete, the Holy Ghost, whom the Father will send in My name, He will teach you all things, and bring all things to your mind, whatsoever I shall have said to you (John xiv. 26).

And another time in this same discourse Christ repeats the idea, and makes clear the nature of the Holy Trinity. He says:

> But when the Paraclete cometh, whom I will send you from the Father, the Spirit of Truth, who proceedeth from the Father, He shall give testimony of Me (John xv. 26).

It is Christ Himself who will send the Paraclete, and as He says a little later:

THE LAST SUPPER

Painting by Leonardo da Vinci, fifteenth century, preserved at Milan.

THE HOLY GHOST ON PENTECOST 219

... It is expedient to you that I go: for if I go not, the Paraclete will not come to you; but if I go, I will send Him to you (John xvi. 7).

The Descent of the Holy Ghost on the Apostles. So the Holy Ghost, the Spirit of Truth, the Sanctifier, the Third Person of the Blessed Trinity, is promised and will be sent by Christ when He goes. Christ ascended into heaven, forty days after the Resurrection. Ten days after the Ascension, Christ sent the Holy Ghost to the Apostles. This was the fiftieth day after the Resurrection — the Pentecost, which in Greek means fiftieth.[1] Here is the full account of the descent of the Holy Ghost on the Apostles in the form of parted tongues as it were of fire, and here is recorded also the gift of tongues to the Apostles.

And when the days of the Pentecost were accomplished, they were all together in one place;

And suddenly there came a sound from heaven, as of a mighty wind coming, and it filled the whole house where they were sitting.

And there appeared to them parted tongues as it were of fire, and it sat upon every one of them.

And they were all filled with the Holy Ghost, and they began to speak with divers tongues, according as the Holy Ghost gave them to speak.

Now there were dwelling at Jerusalem, Jews, devout men, out of every nation under heaven.

And when this was noised abroad, the multitude came together, and were confounded in mind, because that every man heard them speak in his own tongue.

And they were all amazed, and wondered, saying: Behold, are not all these, that speak, Galileans?

And how have we heard, every man our own tongue wherein we were born?

Parthians, and Medes, and Elamites, and inhabitants of Mesopotamia, Judea, and Cappadocia, Pontus and Asia,

Phrygia, and Pamphylia, Egypt, and the parts of Lybia about Cyrene, and strangers of Rome.

Jews also and proselytes, Cretes, and Arabians: we have heard them speak in our own tongues the wonderful works of God.

---

[1]Pentecost came to be called Whitsunday (i.e., White Sunday) in England from about the twelfth century. It was called White Sunday because of the white coifs that children wore who were baptized at that time.

And they were all astonished, and wondered, saying one to another: What meaneth this?

But others mocking, said: These men are full of new wine (Acts ii. 1-13).

The Fulfillment of Prophecy. And Peter, with the new strength of the Holy Ghost, spoke out explaining the wonderful recent events as the fulfillment of the prophecies of the Old Testament:

But Peter standing up with the eleven, lifted up his voice, and spoke to them: Ye men of Judea, and all you that dwell in Jerusalem, be this known to you, and with your ears receive my words.

For these are not drunk, as you suppose, seeing it is but the third hour of the day:

But this is that which was spoken of by the prophet Joel:

And it shall come to pass in the last days (saith the Lord), I will pour out of My Spirit upon all flesh: and your sons and your daughters shall prophesy, and your young men shall see visions, and your old men shall dream dreams.

And upon My servants indeed, and upon My handmaids will I pour out in those days of My Spirit, and they shall prophesy.

And I will show wonders in the heaven above, and signs on the earth beneath: blood and fire, and vapor of smoke.

The sun shall be turned into darkness, and the moon into blood, before the great and manifest day of the Lord come.

And it shall come to pass that whosoever shall call upon the Name of the Lord, shall be saved.

Ye men of Israel, hear these words: Jesus of Nazareth, a man approved of God among you, by miracles, and wonders, and signs, which God did by Him, in the midst of you, as you also know:

This same being delivered up, by the determinate counsel and foreknowledge of God, you by the hands of wicked men have crucified and slain.

Whom God hath raised up, having loosed the sorrows of hell, as it was impossible that He should be holden by it.

For David saith concerning Him: *I foresaw the Lord before my face: because He is at my right hand, that I may not be moved.*

For this my heart hath been glad, and my tongue hath rejoiced: moreover my flesh also shall rest in hope.

Because Thou wilt not leave my soul in hell, nor suffer Thy Holy One to see corruption.

Thou hast made known to me the ways of life: Thou shalt make me full of joy with Thy countenance.

THE HOLY GHOST ON PENTECOST

Ye men, brethren, let me freely speak to you of the patriarch David: that he died, and was buried; and his sepulcher is with us to this present day.

Whereas therefore he was a prophet, and knew that *God hath sworn to him with an oath, that of the fruit of his loins one should sit upon his throne.*

Foreseeing this, he spoke of the resurrection of Christ. For neither was he left in hell, neither did his flesh see corruption.

This Jesus hath God raised again, whereof all we are witnesses.

Being exalted therefore by the right hand of God, and having received of the Father the promise of the Holy Ghost, He hath poured forth this which you see and hear.

For David ascended not into heaven: but he himself said: *The Lord said to my Lord, sit Thou on My right hand,*

Until I make Thy enemies Thy footstool.

Therefore let all the house of Israel know most certainly, that God hath made both Lord and Christ, this same Jesus, whom you have crucified (Acts ii. 14–36).

The Results of the New Spirit on the People. And the results on the people of the new spirit of the Apostles, the signs and wonders that were done, the conversions that are made are told briefly:

Now when they had heard these things, they had compunction in their heart, and said to Peter, and to the rest of the Apostles: What shall we do, men and brethren?

But Peter *said* to them: Do penance, and be baptized every one of you in the name of Jesus Christ, for the remission of your sins: and you shall receive the gift of the Holy Ghost.

For the promise is to you, and to your children, and to all that are far off, whomsoever the Lord our God shall call.

And with very many other words did he testify and exhort them, saying: Save yourselves from this perverse generation.

They therefore that received his word, were baptized; and there were added in that day about three thousand souls.

And they were persevering in the doctrine of the Apostles, and in the communication of the breaking of bread, and in prayers.

And fear came upon every soul: many wonders also and signs were done by the Apostles in Jerusalem, and there was great fear in all.

And all they that believed, were together, and had all things common.

Their possessions and goods they sold, and divided them to all, according as every one had need.

And continuing daily with one accord in the temple, and breaking

THE SUPPER AT EMMAUS
Painting by Caravaggio, sixteenth century.

THE HOLY GHOST ON PENTECOST

bread from house to house, they took their meat with gladness and simplicity of heart;

Praising God, and having favor with all the people. And the Lord increased daily together such as should be saved (Acts ii. 37–47).

Effect on Apostles. The effect of the descent of the Holy Ghost on the Apostles was immediate. Before the Passion they had been timid, weak, and fearful; they now became brave, strong, and unafraid. They were made strong in their faith. They boldly taught the Gospel of Christ. Doubt, ignorance, misgivings, were replaced by faith, knowledge, and understanding. They became strong enough even to bear martyrdom for Christ. The Holy Ghost abiding with them and in them must have sanctified them, giving them the gifts and fruits of the Holy Ghost.

Questions from the Catechism

Q. Who is the Holy Ghost?
A. **The Holy Ghost is the Third Person of the Blessed Trinity.**

Q. From whom does the Holy Ghost proceed?
A. **The Holy Ghost proceeds from the Father and the Son.**

Q. Is the Holy Ghost equal to the Father and the Son?
A. **The Holy Ghost is equal to the Father and the Son, being the same Lord and God as they are.**

Q. On what day did the Holy Ghost come down upon the Apostles?
A. **The Holy Ghost came down upon the Apostles ten days after the Ascension of our Lord; and the day on which He came down upon the Apostles is called Whitsunday, or Pentecost.**

Q. How did the Holy Ghost come down upon the Apostles?
A. **The Holy Ghost came down upon the Apostles in the form of tongues of fire.**

Q. Who sent the Holy Ghost upon the Apostles?
A. **Our Lord Jesus Christ sent the Holy Ghost upon the Apostles.**

Q. Why did Christ send the Holy Ghost?
A. **Christ sent the Holy Ghost to sanctify His Church, to enlighten and strengthen the Apostles, and to enable them to preach the Gospel.**

Q. Will the Holy Ghost abide with the Church forever?
A. **The Holy Ghost will abide with the Church forever, and guide it in the way of holiness and truth.**

Problem Questions

1. What promises were made in advance that the Holy Ghost would come?
2. Describe the descent of the Holy Ghost on the Apostles.
3. Select the picture of the Descent of the Holy Ghost on the Apostles which you like best, and tell why.
4. What happened to the Apostles as a result of the descent of the Holy Ghost?
5. Go back now and read your answers to the question (Chap. XXV) keeping in mind yourself and other human beings you know well, what do you think of the denials of Christ, the betrayal of Christ, and the misunderstandings of Christ's kingdom among the Apostles?

Quotations from the Bible

For each of the following quotations:
a) Identify the speaker.
b) State the conditions under which the statement was made.
c) Give the meaning.
d) Tell its significance.

"Then they laid their hands upon them and they received the Holy Ghost" (Acts viii. 17).

"And they were filled with the Holy Ghost, and they began to speak with divers tongues, according as the Holy Ghost gave them to speak" (Acts ii. 4).

Chapter XXVII
THE ROMAN CATHOLIC CHURCH

The Roman Catholic Church. Christ clearly did not come only for the people of the time in which He lived. He did not die on the cross on Calvary for only His generation. He died for the salvation of all men in all time. He told the Apostles to go into the world and teach all nations, Jews and Gentiles. The promise was given to Peter that the gates of hell would not prevail against the Church which would be established with him as its head; the promise was given to Peter that whatever he bound on earth would be bound in heaven, and whatever he loosed on earth would be loosed in heaven. And in the Church has echoed through the ages Christ's words to Peter: Feed My lambs; feed My lambs; feed My sheep.

The Promise of the Holy Ghost. But perhaps even more important was the promise that Christ would send the Holy Ghost to abide with the Church forever. These were His promises to the Church about the Holy Ghost.

The first statement is from St. John, which is as follows:

And I will ask the Father, and He shall give you another Paraclete, that He may abide with you forever.

The Spirit of Truth, whom the world cannot receive, because it seeth Him not, nor knoweth Him: but you shall know Him; because He shall abide with you, and shall be in you. . . .

But the Paraclete, the Holy Ghost, whom the Father will send in My name, He will teach you all things, and bring all things to your mind, and whatsoever I shall have said to you (John xiv. 16, 17, 26).

In the next chapter St. John says further:

But when the Paraclete cometh, whom I will send you from the Father, the Spirit of Truth, who proceedeth from the Father, He shall give testimony of Me.

And you shall give testimony because you are with Me from the beginning (John xv. 26, 27).

And once more St. John says:

These things have I spoken to you, that you may not be scandalized.

They will put you out of the synagogues: yea, the hour cometh, that whosoever killeth you, will think that he doth a service to God.

And these things will they do to you; because they have not known the Father, nor Me.

But these things I have told you, that when the hour shall come, you may remember that I told you of them.

But I told you not these things from the beginning, because I was with you. And now I go to Him that sent Me, and none of you asketh Me: Whither goest Thou?

But because I have spoken these things to you, sorrow hath filled your heart.

But I tell you the truth: it is expedient to you that I go: for if I go not, the Paraclete will not come to you; but if I go, I will send Him to you.

And when He is come, He will convince the world of sin, and of justice, and of judgment.

Of sin: because they believed not in Me.

And of justice: because I go to the Father; and you shall see Me no longer.

And of judgment: because the Prince of this world is already judged.

I have yet many things to say to you: but you cannot bear them now.

But when He, the Spirit of Truth, is come, He will teach you all truth. For He shall not speak of Himself; but what things soever He shall hear, He shall speak; and the things that are to come, He shall show you.

He shall glorify Me; because He shall receive of Mine, and shall show it to you.

All things whatsoever the Father hath, are Mine. Therefore I said, that He shall receive of Mine, and show it to you.

A little while, and now you shall not see Me; and again a little while, and you shall see Me: because I go to the Father (John xvi. 1–16).

The Holy Ghost on Pentecost. And in the passage quoted from the Acts of the Apostles we have the promise fulfilled when the Holy Ghost descended on the Apostles on Pentecost in the shape of tongues of fire. It is from the Holy Ghost, the Spirit of Truth, sent by Christ, that the Church receives its undying life and infallible authority. He is the Spirit of love and holiness, who unites and sanctifies its members throughout the world, for He remains with the Church forever.

THE ROMAN CATHOLIC CHURCH 227

Christ Abides With the Church Forever. It is quite clear from this that the society represented in Christ's time by His Apostles was to last forever for the Spirit of Truth would abide with it forever and guide it in the way of holiness and truth. Did not Christ Himself say "I am with you all days even to the consummation of the world"?

The organization which Christ established was to be a teaching organization. He said to the Apostles:

Going therefore, teach ye all nations; baptizing them in the name of the Father, and of the Son, and of the Holy Ghost.

Teaching them to observe all things whatsoever I have commanded you: and behold I am with you all days, even to the consummation of the world (Matt. xxviii. 19, 20).

What is the nature of this organization? Christ said, "I am come that you may have life, and have it more abundantly." This life which Christ was to give us is grace. It makes our soul more like God. It wipes sin out of the soul and ennobles it. It makes us one with Christ. He said: "I am the vine and you are the branches." But a figure used by St. Paul said Christ is the head, and we are the body. The Church is the mystical body of Christ.

The Head Contributes Life or Grace to the Body. When we have grace we are united to Christ in His body. So the membership of the Church is the Body of Christ. It is by reception into this Body by baptism, that we can live the life of Christ. Christ is the real though the invisible head of the Church.

But This Body of Christ is Organized. Christ is its invisible Head. He made in His own day Peter the head of the Apostles. He gave to Peter the "power of the keys." He commanded Peter to "feed My lambs," "feed My lambs," "feed My sheep." He was the head of the Apostles. When Christ ascended to heaven forty days after the Resurrection, Peter was the visible head of the Body or Church of Christ, though Christ remains its invisible Head and always the source of its life or grace and all its riches.

Jesus saith to them: But whom do you say that I am?

Simon Peter answered and said: Thou art Christ, the Son of the living God.

And Jesus answering said to him: Blessed art thou, Simon Bar-Jona: because flesh and blood hath not revealed it to thee, but My Father who is in heaven.

And I say to thee: That thou art Peter: and upon this rock I will build My Church, and the gates of hell shall not prevail against it.

And I will give to thee the keys of the kingdom of heaven. And whatsoever thou shalt bind upon earth, it shall be bound also in heaven: And whatsoever thou shalt loose on earth, it shall be loosed also in heaven (Matt. xvi. 15–19).

Peter was the first bishop of Rome, where he suffered martyrdom. He was the first pope. The Church was not established only for the years of the life of the Apostles. The special right as chief of the Apostles given to Peter goes to the popes, the bishops of Rome; they became the vicars of Christ on earth. "I am with you all days, even to the consummation of the world" (Matt. xxviii. 20). The powers given to the Apostles went to their successors, the bishops and archbishops of the Roman Catholic Church. Thus we have the Body of Christ, His visible organization, the Roman Catholic Church. We shall see later by His own institution how Christ provided to give to His mystical Body, the Church, the grace which is its life, through the seven sacraments. In this way we share in the fruits of Redemption. It is from the Church, through which God speaks to us, that we shall know the things in which we are to believe. By the Church we mean here not a building, but the Body of Christ, an organization or congregation of all who profess the faith of Christ, partake of the same sacraments, and are governed by the visible head of the Church, the pope, and the lawful pastors.

The Church of Christ is One. The qualities of the Church of Christ must be clear from the fact that Christ is the Head and the members are His Body. It must have unity. It must be *one*. This is so because Christ is the Head of it and the source of its life. Beside this inner unity; it has an outward visible unity. It is under one head, the pope, the bishop of Rome, the vicar of Christ on earth. It is all joined together in *one* communion, and all profess *one* faith. There is, as St. Paul says, One Lord, One Faith, One Baptism.

The Church of Christ is Holy. Having unity because of its source in Christ, it must also be holy, because Christ its founder is holy. The doctrine it teaches, which is Christ's doctrine, is holy. It invites all to imitate Christ and thus lead a holy life. That it is holy is plain from the very great holiness of its members in the beginning when it included the Apostles, and particularly Mary, the Mother of Christ, and many of the canonized saints in the following ages, and of many thousands of its saintly children in every age. So truly may we say it is holy.

The Church of Christ is Catholic or Universal. If Christ's doctrine is to be taught to every rational creature in all times, even to the end of the world, the institution that teaches this doctrine must be universal or Catholic. It must exist in all ages, and it must teach all nations, for that is the reason why Christ established it, according to His own words. The doctrine or truth which it teaches must be all God's truth; necessary for man's salvation, so it upholds all truth. In these senses the Church of Christ is Catholic or universal.

The Church of Christ is Apostolic. The Church of Christ traces its beginning to Christ and His Apostles. Christ chose the Apostles. He trained them. They were the first teachers and priests in Christ's Church. So we say it is Apostolic. It continues to be Apostolic because it continues to be taught and ministered to by the lawful successors of the Apostles, the bishops of the Roman Catholic Church. It has never ceased to teach the doctrine which the Apostles taught, and judging by two thousand years of history and the promises of Christ, it will never cease to teach them. The chief truths which the Church teaches are found in the Apostles' Creed.

The Marks of the Church. The marks of the Church of Christ are four. The Church of Christ must be One, Holy, Catholic, and Apostolic. It is in the Roman Catholic Church alone that these marks are found. Being established by Christ, and receiving from Him as its head, its life which raises it from the natural to the supernatural, it is and must be One, Holy, Catholic, and Apostolic. The promise of Christ to send the Holy

Ghost, the Spirit of Love and Holiness, to stay with the Church forever has made and kept it One, Holy, and Catholic as it was in the times of the Apostles, and unites and sanctifies its members wherever they are throughout the world. So, too, the Holy Ghost, the Spirit of Truth as well as of love and holiness, dwelling in the Church, gives to it its undying life and infallible authority which we shall explain more fully later.

Indefectibility of the Church. The organization which Christ founded which we know as the Church, was intended by Christ to be His means for the redemption and salvation of men. We know it must last till the end of time, because that was Christ's promise, that He would be with it always. This attribute we call indefectibility. It is similar to one of the marks of the Church in that it is universal or Catholic. If Christ died for all men, then the means He established for their salvation must exist as long as men exist; i.e., until the end of time. The Church of Christ will last till the end of time.

Authority of the Church. The Church will, as the Body of Christ, teach "all things whatsoever I have commanded you." The authority to teach the members of the Church, i.e., the faithful, and to govern them was given by Christ to Peter and the Apostles. Naturally, in a Church carrying on Christ's mission on earth there must have been authority, the right and the power to teach and govern the faithful. Naturally that authority is given to the lawful successors of Peter and the Apostles. In other words, the pope and bishops of the Church tracing their power in every case directly to Peter and the Apostles, have the right and power to teach and govern the faithful. The Church of Christ will not only have this authority, but will know that it has it.

Infallibility of the Church. The Church was set up by Christ as a means of opening up to all men, in every age, the benefits of the Redemption, which He gained through His death upon the cross. Since Christ set up authority in this Church until the end of time, it is certain that such a teaching authority, established by Christ Himself, must be saved from error when it teaches those things which are necessary for man's salvation —

teachings of faith or morals. This attribute of infallibility would seem to be absolutely necessary in such a church as Christ founded. It is, as a matter of fact, the power He gave. To safeguard this power, He promised to the Church the Holy Ghost, the Paraclete, the Spirit of Truth.

But the Paraclete, the Holy Ghost, whom the Father will send in My name, He will teach you all things, and bring all things to your mind, whatsoever I shall have said to you (John xiv. 26).

And again,

I have yet many things to say to you: but you cannot bear them now.
But when He, the Spirit of Truth, is come, He will teach you all truth. For He shall not speak of Himself; but what things soever He shall hear, He shall speak; and the things that are to come, He shall show you (John xvi. 12, 13).

Popes and Councils. This power naturally is had only in matters of faith and morals; i.e., things relating to man's salvation. It would naturally be exercised by the head of the Church, the pope, the vicar of Christ on earth, or by the pope and the bishops of the Church who are the successors of the Apostles. This second method is in the form of a general council of the Church, made up of the pope and the bishops united in council. This great power of teaching infallibly, that is without being able to make mistakes, is limited to matters of faith and morals. The Church thus teaches only when it speaks through the pope and bishops united in general council, or through the pope alone when he proclaims to all the faithful a doctrine of faith or morals. In the history of the Church there have been only twenty general councils as follows:

1. Nicaea Council (I), 325,
2. Constantinople Council (I), 381,
3. Ephesus Council, 431,
4. Chalcedon, 451,
5. Constantinople Council (II), 553,
6. Constantinople Council (III), 680–1,
7. Nicaea Council (II), 787,
8. Constantinople Council (IV), 869,
9. Lateran Council (I), 1123,

10. Lateran Council (II), 1139,
11. Lateran Council (III), 1179,
12. Lateran Council (IV), 1215,
13. Lyons Council (I), 1245,
14. Lyons Council (II), 1274,
15. Vienne Council, 1311–13,
16. Constance Council, 1414–18 (in part only),
17. Basle-Ferrara-Florence Council, 1431–43,
18. Lateran Council (V), 1512–17,
19. Trent Council, 1545–1563,
20. Vatican Council, 1869, adjourned 1870.

So the infallible authority of the pope and council has not been used often, and doctrines have been defined rarely. Any statement or declaration of pope, or pope and bishops in general council, other than on faith or morals, is not infallible.

Full Power in Pope. The three attributes of authority, indefectibility, and infallibility of the Church of Christ are found in their fullness in the pope, the visible head of the Church whose infallible authority to teach bishops, priests, and people in matters of faith or morals will last to the end of time.

The Body and the Soul of the Church. Christ instituted the means of salvation. He is the Head of the Church, the source of power and grace. It is His doctrine that it teaches. So we understand the statement that there is no salvation outside of the Church, the means instituted by Christ. But we must distinguish between the body and the soul of the Church. All members of the Catholic Church in communion with it are members of the body of the Church. They know the means in the Church for grace and life everlasting. Being a member of the Body of Christ in itself is not enough for salvation; we must live a Christian life. But there are large numbers of people who are not in communion with the Catholic Church, but who follow the truth as they see it. They are members of the soul of the Church. There is salvation for them through their membership in the soul of the Church if they lead a good life and have the love of God in their heart. This is the condition of all Christians. Those who are baptized are members of the body of the Church, unless they

ST. PETER'S, IN ROME

renounce their faith. They are called, too, the visible members of the Church; others of good disposition and with the love of God are members of the Church, too — the soul of the Church. Whether a person is a member of the body or soul of the Church, he must live up to the faith that is in him. "In every nation," as St. Peter says, "he that feareth God and worketh justice is acceptable to Him."

Church Militant, Suffering, and Triumphant. The description which we just gave of the Church is the Church on earth. It is called the Church Militant or fighting. Its *live* members are those who are in a state of grace. Its *dead* members, but still in a true sense, members, are those who are in sin. All are members of the Church Militant. There are people who died, and who were members of the Church Militant, either of its body or soul, who had in their heart the love of God and tried to serve Him on earth, and who had true sorrow for their sins. These go to heaven and are members of the Church Triumphant. Others who die without deserving the punishment of hell go to the middle state called purgatory and are members of the Church Suffering who when they have fully satisfied for their sins, will be admitted into heaven. The Church consists of these three branches: the Church Militant, the Church Suffering, and the Church Triumphant.

The Communion of Saints. The membership in the Church Militant, the Church Suffering, and the Church Triumphant forms the communion of saints. *Saints* is here used, as it is used by St. Paul, as a general name for Christians. It is not used, in the other sense in which we use the word *saint* as a person of special holiness.

All these parts of the Church are joined together in communion. The graces of the saints in heaven can be used by all of us here on earth as we shall see in detail in the discussion of indulgences. We honor and glorify the saints in heaven and ask for their help. The souls in purgatory we may help by our prayers and good works. "It is a holy and wholesome thought to pray for the dead." We may help each other too, on earth, by our prayers, good works, and good will. All are in communion in the Church under the headship of Christ. "As in one body we have many members . . . so we being many, are one body in Christ" (Rom. xii. 4, 5).

The benefits gained from the communion of saints are, (1) the faithful on earth assist one another by their prayers and good works, and (2) they are aided by the intercession of the saints in heaven, while both the saints in heaven and the faithful on earth help the souls in purgatory.

Questions from the Catechism

Q. How shall we know the things which we are to believe?
A. **We shall know the things which we are to believe from the Catholic Church, through which God speaks to us.**

Q. Where shall we find the chief truths which the Church teaches?
A. **We shall find the chief truths which the Church teaches in the Apostles' Creed.**

Q. What is the Church?
A. **The Church is the congregation of all those who profess the faith of Christ, partake of the same sacraments, and are governed by their lawful pastors under one visible head.**

Q. Who is the invisible head of the Church?
A. **Jesus Christ is the invisible head of the Church.**

Q. Who is the visible head of the Church?
A. **Our Holy Father the Pope, the Bishop of Rome, is the vicar of Christ on earth and the visible head of the Church.**

Q. Why is the Pope, the Bishop of Rome, the visible head of the Church?
A. **The Pope, the Bishop of Rome, is the visible head of the Church because he is the successor of St. Peter, whom Christ made the chief of the Apostles and the visible head of the Church.**

Q. Who are the successors of the other Apostles?
A. **The successors of the other Apostles are the bishops of the Holy Catholic Church.**

Q. Why did Christ found the Church?
A. **Christ founded the Church to teach, govern, sanctify, and save all men.**

Q. Are all bound to belong to the Church?
A. **All are bound to belong to the Church, and he who knows the Church to be the true Church and remains out of it cannot be saved.**

Q. Which are the attributes of the Church?

A. The attributes of the Church are three: authority, infallibility, and indefectibility.

Q. What do you mean by the authority of the Church?
A. By the authority of the Church I mean the right and power which the Pope and the bishops, as the successors of the Apostles, have to teach and to govern the faithful.

Q. What do you mean by the infallibility of the Church?
A. By the infallibility of the Church I mean that the Church cannot err when it teaches a doctrine of faith or morals.

Q. When does the Church teach infallibly?
A. The Church teaches infallibly when it speaks through the Pope and bishops united in general council, or through the Pope alone when he proclaims to all the faithful a doctrine of faith or morals.

Q. What do you mean by the indefectibility of the Church?
A. By the indefectibility of the Church I mean that the Church, as Christ founded it, will last till the end of time.

Q. In whom are these attributes found in their fullness?
A. These attributes are found in their fullness in the Pope, the visible head of the Church, whose infallible authority to teach bishops, priests, and people in matters of faith or morals will last to the end of the world.

Q. Has the Church any marks by which it may be known?
A. The Church has four marks by which it may be known: it is One; it is Holy; it is Catholic; it is Apostolic.

Q. How is the Church One?
A. The Church is One because all its members agree in one faith, are all in one communion, and are all under one head.

Q. How is the Church Holy?
A. The Church is Holy because its founder, Jesus Christ, is holy; because it teaches a holy doctrine; invites all to a holy life; and because of the eminent holiness of so many thousands of its children.

Q. How is the Church Catholic or universal?
A. The Church is Catholic or universal because it subsists in all ages, teaches all nations, and maintains all truth.

Q. How is the Church Apostolic?
A. The Church is Apostolic because it was founded by Christ on His Apostles, and is governed by their lawful successors, and because it has never ceased, and never will cease, to teach their doctrine.

THE ROMAN CATHOLIC CHURCH

Q. In which Church are these attributes and marks found?
A. **These attributes and marks are found in the Holy Roman Catholic Church alone.**

Q. From whom does the Church derive its undying life and infallible authority?
A. **The Church derives its undying life and infallible authority from the Holy Ghost, the spirit of truth, who abides with it forever.**

Q. By whom is the Church made and kept One, Holy, and Catholic?
A. **The Church is made and kept One, Holy, and Catholic by the Holy Ghost, the spirit of love and holiness, who unites and sanctifies its members throughout the world.**

Q. Is it enough to belong to God's Church in order to be saved?
A. **It is not enough to belong to the Church in order to be saved, but we must also keep the Commandments of God and of the Church.**

Q. Who are they who neglect to profess their belief in what God has taught?
A. **They who neglect to profess their belief in what God has taught are all those who fail to acknowledge the true Church in which they really believe.**

Q. Can they who fail to profess their faith in the true Church in which they believe expect to be saved while in that state?
A. **They who fail to profess their faith in the true Church in which they believe cannot expect to be saved while in that state, for Christ has said: "Whoever shall deny Me before men, I will also deny him before My Father who is in heaven."**

Q. Are we obliged to make open profession of our faith?
A. **We are obliged to make open profession of our faith as often as God's honor, our neighbor's spiritual good, or our own requires it. "Whosoever," says Christ, "shall confess Me before men, I shall also confess him before My Father who is in heaven."**

Problem Questions

1. What was the purpose of Christ, the Son of God, in becoming man?
2. How does the fulfillment of such a purpose require the establishment of an institution to carry on the work of the Redemption?
3. What is the name of the institution which Christ established to continue, or through which He might act after the Ascension?
4. When was the Roman Catholic Church established?

5. What promise was made to the Church regarding the Holy Ghost? regarding Christ Himself?

6. What is meant by Paraclete?

7. What is the relation of the Church to Christ? If it were possible to conceive it, what meaning would the Church have without Christ?

8. What do you mean by the statement that the Church is the Body of Christ?

9. Why must the Church of Christ be One? Holy? Catholic? Apostolic?

10. What church has these four marks of the true Church of Christ?

11. What is meant by the words "indefectibility," "authority," "infallibility"?

12. In what ways are the attributes of the Church, indefectibility, authority, and infallibility, directly traceable to Christ?

13. Through what instruments does the infallibility of the Church of Christ express itself?

14. What is a general council of the Church? How many have been held?

15. What is meant by the body of the Church?

16. What is meant by the soul of the Church?

17. Who are members of the soul but not of the body of the Church?

18. What is meant by the Church Militant, the Church Suffering, and the Church Triumphant?

19. Of what part of the Church are you a member? Of what part is St. Francis of Assisi? Of what part are the souls in purgatory?

20. What is meant by the Communion of Saints? What does saints in this connection mean? Are you a saint?

Quotations from the Bible

For each of the following quotations:

a) Identify the speaker.

b) State the conditions under which the statement was made.

c) Give the meaning.

d) Tell its significance.

"I am the Way, and the Truth, and the Life. No man cometh to the Father but by Me" (John xiv. 6).

"Thou art Peter: and upon this rock I will build My Church, and the gates of hell shall not prevail against it" (Matt. xvi. 18).

"These twelve Jesus sent: commanding them, saying: Go ye not into the way of the Gentiles, and into the city of the Samaritans enter ye not. But go ye rather to the lost sheep of the House of Israel. And going, preach, saying: The kingdom of heaven is at hand. Heal the sick, raise the dead, cleanse the lepers, cast out devils: freely have you received, freely give. Do not possess gold, nor silver, nor money in your purses:

THE ROMAN CATHOLIC CHURCH 239

Nor scrip for your journey, nor two coats, nor shoes, nor a staff: for the workman is worthy of his meat" (Matt. x. 5-10).

"Jesus coming spoke to them, saying: All power is given to Me in heaven and in earth. Going therefore, teach ye all nations; baptizing them in the name of the Father, and of the Son, and of the Holy Ghost. Teaching them to observe all things whatsoever I have commanded you: and behold I am with you all days, even to the consummation of the world" (Matt. xxviii. 18-20).

"He said therefore to them again: Peace be to you. As the Father hath sent Me, I also send you. When He had said this, He breathed on them; and He said to them: Receive ye the Holy Ghost. Whose sins you shall forgive, they are forgiven them; and whose sins you shall retain they are retained" (John xx. 21-23).

"Jesus saith to Simon Peter: Simon, son of John, lovest thou Me more than these? He saith to Him: Yea, Lord, Thou knowest that I love Thee. He saith to him: Feed My lambs. He saith to him again: Simon, son of John, lovest thou Me? He saith to Him: Yea, Lord, Thou knowest that I love Thee. He saith to him: Feed My lambs. He said to him the third time: Simon, son of John, lovest thou Me? Peter was grieved, because He said to Him the third time, Lovest thou Me? And he said to Him: Lord, Thou knowest all things; Thou knowest that I love Thee. He said to him: Feed My sheep" (John xxi. 15-17).

"Beware of false prophets, who come to you in the clothing of sheep, but inwardly they are ravening wolves" (Matt. vii. 15).

"But the Paraclete, the Holy Ghost, whom the Father will send in My Name, He will teach you all things, and bring all things to your mind, whatsoever I shall have said to you" (John xiv. 26).

"I am with you all days even to the consummation of the world."

"Thou art Christ, the Son of the living God."

To what incident does the following description refer?
Who was present?
What is the significance of the event?

"Other foundation no man can lay, but that which is laid; which is Christ Jesus" (I Cor. iii. 11).

"The stone which the builders rejected; the same is become the head of the corner" (Ps. cxvii. 22).

"I am the vine, you the branches" (John xv. 5).

"One body and one Spirit; as you are called in one hope of your calling. One Lord, one faith, one baptism. One God and Father of all" (Eph. iv. 4-6).

Chapter XXVIII
GRACE AND THE SACRAMENTS

The disobedience of Adam in the Garden of Eden has a serious effect on human nature. The children of Adam, because of their disobedience, ceased to be the children of God. They lost grace. They lost the beauty of holiness which they had. They are born in the state of original sin.

God's Love of Man. In this fallen state, as we have seen, God did not leave man to himself but gave him as a first guide the Ten Commandments to help him on the Highway of Life to his heavenly home. He promised, too, that He would send the Messiah, who would redeem man and would be the means of the salvation of all men. With the coming of Christ, the Redeemer, we learned what God's love for man really was. How infinite! How divine! How much greater than anything man could have expected or even thought.

The Redeemer or Savior of Men. God sent His only-begotten Son as the Messiah. God became man, and had to undergo all things that other men have to undergo except sin, even to the death on the cross. He became the propitiation or satisfaction for the sins of mankind. He thus became the Redeemer of mankind.

In order that the fruits of Redemption might be open to men, our Lord established an organization through which man certainly would know the way, and could make use of the means for his eternal salvation. This organization is the Roman Catholic Church. It provides for men a knowledge of the way they can travel the Highway to Eternal Life, with the aids which Christ Himself instituted to guide men on the way.

The Sacraments. These aids, given to man by Christ through His Church, are the sacraments. They are outward signs of the grace of God which flows from His Passion and death. It was another sign of God's tender kindness and thoughtfulness for man that His power and love, and the means Christ instituted to aid man to gain eternal life should be easily seen by him in clear and unmistakable sensible signs.

Essentials of a Sacrament. Because of our weakness, and because we need outward, visible, or sensible signs to understand, we have these signs which we call sacraments. They are the outward and visible signs of the invisible grace which they confer on our soul, for our salvation. Only God could give this grace to the soul. Christ Himself instituted these sacraments when He was on earth. We have the authority of Scriptures and the Church for this. These sources of our spiritual life, this spiritual food and spiritual medicine, the sacraments, all have three special marks:

1. They were instituted by Christ Himself.
2. There is an outward or visible sign.
3. There accompanies this sign an inward grace.

We shall see these marks in each of the sacraments as we study each separately.

Signs in Old and New Law. "In the Old Law, God ordained that every important promise should be confirmed by certain signs, so in the New Law, Christ, the Savior, when He promised pardon for sin, divine grace, the communication of the Holy Spirit, instituted certain visible and sensible signs by which He might oblige Himself, as it were, by pledges, and make it impossible to doubt that He would be true to His promises" (*Catechism of the Council of Trent,* p. 149). In the Old Law, for the most part, the signs reminded the people what God had done for them, stirred up their faith, and aroused other good dispositions, which prepared their souls to win from God the gift of sanctifying grace.

What Are the Sensible Signs? When we study each of the sacraments we will mention in more detail the sensible signs which are the outward part of the sacraments. These include, for example, in baptism not only the water, but the words, "I baptize thee in the name of the Father, and of the Son, and of the Holy Ghost." So in confirmation it includes not only the chrism, but the words of the bishop; and in extreme unction, it includes not only the oil, but the words of the priest.

Sensible Sign of the Sacrament. Except by the power of God no merely sensible sign could reach man's soul, impress it, or aid it to gain its final ends. Because they are instituted by Christ, who is God, and in fulfillment of His purpose as the Savior of man, these words or sensible signs have in themselves the power to produce the grace which is the spiritual life of the soul. These signs are different from others used in religion, and because of their institution by Christ, they are not only a sign of holiness and grace, but also are able to give holiness and righteousness.

Matter and Form of Sacraments. The sensible, outward, or visible sign of a sacrament can always be divided into two parts:

1. The things used or done, which is called the *matter* of the sacrament.

2. The words spoken, which is called the *form* of the sacrament.

The matter and form of the sacrament are the essence. The sacrament is not a sacrament without them. But to show great reverence for these acts of God, and to keep in the minds of the faithful how holy the sacraments are, and to enable the faithful to understand and appreciate the goodness of God, the Church has added a third point:

3. Certain ceremonies.

These ceremonies cannot be left out without sin unless there is necessity.

Channels of Grace. "For, through the sacraments, as through a channel, must flow into the soul the efficacy of the Passion of Christ, that is, the grace which He merited for us on the altar of the cross, and without which we cannot hope for salvation. Hence, our most merciful Lord has bequeathed to His Church sacraments stamped with the sanction of His word and promise, through which, provided we make pious and devout use of these remedies, we firmly believe that the fruit of His passion is really communicated to us" (*Catechism of the Council of Trent*, p. 149).

The Natural and Spiritual Life. If we think of our natural life, we can, perhaps, get some idea of the spiritual life of the soul. We can think then of God's grace as the food and medicine of the soul. "In order to exist, to preserve existence, and to contribute to his own and to the public good, seven things seem necessary to man: to be born, to grow, to be nurtured, to be cured when sick, when weak to be strengthened; as far as regards the public welfare, to have magistrates invested with authority to govern, and to perpetuate himself and his species by legitimate offspring" (*Catechism of the Council of Trent,* p. 153).

These things are enough like the life by which the soul lives to God for us to see in them a reason why there are seven sacraments, no more or no less.

The Seven Sacraments. First comes baptism, which is the gate to the Church and to all the other sacraments. By this we are born again unto Christ — our second birth. The next is confirmation, by which we grow up and are made strong in the grace of God: for, as St. Augustine observes, to the Apostles who had already received baptism, the Redeemer said: "Stay you in the city till you be endued with power from on high." The third is the Eucharist, that true Bread from heaven which nourishes and sustains our souls to eternal life, according to these words of the Savior: "My Flesh is meat indeed, and My Blood is drink indeed." The fourth is penance through which lost health is recovered after we have been wounded by sin. Next is extreme unction which wipes out the remains of sin and puts life into the powers of the soul; for speaking of this sacrament St. James says: "If he be in sins, they shall be forgiven him." Then follows holy orders by which power is given to exercise forever in the Church the public administration of the sacraments and to perform all the sacred duties. The last is matrimony, instituted to the end that, by means of the lawful and holy union of man and woman, children may be procreated and religiously educated for the service of God, and for the preservation of the human race (*Catechism of the Council of Trent,* p. 153).

Sacraments Effective Through Power of Christ. The outward signs of the sacraments not only indicate, but they actually give grace to the soul that receives them worthily. This is so, because being instituted or established by Christ, they are the means through which His power acts. Water, oil, bread, have no such power in themselves as we know, but Christ has that power; namely, to convey grace to the soul.

Sanctifying Grace. All the sacraments give the soul sanctifying grace or increase it when it is already present. If they are worthily received, we become, by adoption, children of God. By good intentions and good works for the love of God, we increase God's grace more and more in our souls and we gain in Christ perfection. We become more and more like unto God, in whose image we are made. We become Christlike, the highest thing that can be said about a human being. This grace is placed within our reach by the merits of Jesus Christ through His Crucifixion. The Crucifixion was the expiation for all human sins and insults to God. It was an infinite sacrifice. This grace remains in the soul and increases so long as we do not commit a mortal sin; for that reason it is sometimes called *habitual* grace.

Faith, Hope, and Charity. With sanctifying grace there are certain gifts that are infused, that is, added to the soul. They are gifts like sanctifying grace itself freely given. These gifts or Divine virtues are:

1. The virtue by which we believe the truths which God has revealed. This is the divine virtue of Faith.

2. The virtue by which we firmly trust that God will give us eternal life and the means to obtain it. This is the divine virtue of Hope.

3. The virtue by which we love God above all things for His own sake, and our neighbor as ourselves for the love of God. This is the divine virtue of Charity.

These virtues are called "divine" or "supernatural" because they are a gift of God through Christ. We may develop the virtues of Faith, Hope, and Charity from our own experience. We then call these virtues natural. These natural virtues are not enough for salvation. The gifts or virtues that are infused or given with sanctifying grace are the freely bestowed divine virtues of Faith, Hope, and Charity.

Actual Grace. Sanctifying grace is a permanent quality of the soul, that is, it remains in the soul until it is driven out by mortal sin. It is the life of the soul. It makes the soul holy and pleasing to God. Because of its permanent character, it is also called *habitual* grace. There is another kind of grace. It comes now and then, in flashes, as it were, in time of need. This kind of grace is called *actual* grace. It gives us the light to do the right thing. It enlightens our mind, and moves our will to shun evil and do good. It was actual grace that St. Paul responded to in his conversion to Christ on the road to Damascus. "And," as the Scripture says, "he trembling and astonished, said: 'Lord, what wilt Thou have me to do?'" (Acts ix. 6.)

Perseverance. To our efforts to keep on God's Highway by keeping the grace of God in our soul, there is also given us a special gift of God, the gift, or as it is sometimes called the grace, of perseverance. This is an actual grace. This gift of perseverance helps us or makes us able to remain in a state of grace until death. It is better to use the word *gift* here, rather than *grace* because we should use grace in the sense which we have defined in the foregoing as "a supernatural gift of God bestowed on us through the merits of Jesus Christ for our salvation." Our hope in securing this gift is founded in St. Peter's word, that the Lord is "not willing that any should perish" (II Peter iii. 9).

Sacramental Grace. We receive also in the sacraments the grace which enables us to gain the specific thing for which the sacrament was instituted. This is an actual grace, to which the person who receives the sacrament is entitled in connection with the object of the sacrament, as he needs it in his life. This is called *sacramental* grace, and is, of course, different for each sacrament. If each sacrament did not give some special actual or sacramental graces, there would be no need of more than one sacrament. The sacrament of baptism gives us the grace to renounce the devil with all his works and pomps; *penance* gives us the grace to bear and guard against sin; *confirmation* gives us the grace to be brave in the service of God, and if necessary, to die for the faith, besides giving us the seven gifts of the Holy Ghost; holy orders gives the grace to perform the duties and to have the *power and the authority* of the priesthood of God; Holy Communion gives us the grace to desire to nourish the soul with the food that came down from heaven; matrimony gives to husband and wife the grace to live a blessed married life, and to bring up their children in the *love of God;* extreme unction gives us the grace not to fear death, or strengthens us for recovery, or makes us resigned to God's will.

The Sacraments of the Dead. Some of the sacraments give sanctifying grace to the soul and some increase it. Baptism is the first sacrament we receive, and it restores our fallen nature to a life of grace. This is the absolutely necessary first step to the Christian life. If after baptism we fall into sin, the sacrament of penance restores life to the soul by its sanctifying grace. These two sacraments, baptism and penance, are called the sacraments of the dead because they take away sin, which is the death of the soul, and give grace, which is its life. They are called so because they may be received by those who are spiritually dead. Spiritually speaking, we are dead when we are in the state of mortal sin. Baptism restores us to spiritual life, the life of the soul, from the death due to original sin and other sins that we may have committed before baptism. Penance restores the soul to spiritual life through the pardon of sins we may have committed since baptism or since our last confession. We were dead to Christ, now we live in Him.

The Sacraments of the Living. The other five sacraments — confirmation, Holy Eucharist, extreme unction, holy orders, and matrimony — increase the sanctifying grace in the soul, and are called sacraments of the living. To receive these sacraments the soul must be free from mortal sin, must be alive. Through baptism and penance the soul has received sanctifying grace and is alive, before the sacraments of the living may be received. They are, therefore, called sacraments of the living, because those who receive them worthily are already living the life of grace. To receive the sacraments of the living in a state of mortal sin is a sacrilege, which is great sin, because it is an abuse of a sacred thing.

The Spiritual Mark on the Soul. The sacraments of baptism, confirmation, and holy orders can be received but once; the others may be received more often, as will be shown later. The Holy Eucharist must be received at least once a year at Easter time, and the habit of monthly, weekly, and even daily Communion is growing. The three sacraments of baptism, confirmation, and holy orders imprint a character on our soul, which is a spiritual mark and which remains forever, even after death, for the honor and glory of those who are saved; for the shame and punishment of those who are lost.

The Power of the Sacraments. The sacraments always, of their own power, because of their institution by Christ, confer grace if received worthily. The power of these signs to actually cause the effect in the human soul is solely because of the merits of Jesus Christ: Christ said about the Holy Eucharist, "He that eateth My Flesh, and drinketh My Blood, hath everlasting life" (John vi. 55). In connection with the sacrament of penance, He gave a promise to the Church, "Whose sins you shall forgive, they are forgiven them; and whose sins you shall retain, they are retained" (John xx. 23).

Receive Sacraments Worthily. The sacraments always confer grace on those who receive them worthily. While the flow of grace can be gained by all, the person who attempts to receive it unworthily, stops it, and commits a sacrilege. *An unrepented mortal sin* is, of course, an obstacle to the flow of grace from the sacraments. On the other hand, persons of better dispositions are given more graces than the spiritually weak or negligent.

Sacramentals. There are used in the Church other outward signs or ceremonies that, in themselves, have no power to give grace. This is an important difference between these signs called sacramentals and the sacraments. The sacraments were instituted by Christ; the sacramentals were instituted by the Church. They are means instituted by the Church to help us spiritually. They call to our minds the great facts of religion, they promote piety within us, they move our hearts, they help form our wills, and in this way are effective as our dispositions are good. These signs or ceremonies or devotions are called *sacramentals* as distinguished from sacraments. Some examples of sacramentals are:

1. The sign of the cross is the chief sacramental of the Church. It is the sign of the Christian. It reminds us of the Incarnation and the Crucifixion of our Lord by its form, and of the Unity and Trinity of God by its words. Every time we make the sign of the cross we profess our faith in these things.

2. The stations of the cross, which keep before us the Passion and Crucifixion.

3. The rosary of Our Lady, reminding us of the life of Christ and His Mother's devotion through the sorrowful, joyful, and glorious mysteries.

4. The Benediction of the Blessed Sacrament, reminding us of the Last Supper and Christ's love for men.

5. Holy water is a sacramental very often used. It is in the founts at the doors of our churches and it can be had for home use from your pastor. Holy water is water blessed by the priest with the solemn prayer of the Church to beg God's blessing on those who use it, and protection from the power of darkness.

6. Crucifixes, scapulars, palms, blessed candles, and medals, images of the Blessed Virgin and of the saints, and rosaries, all cause holy thoughts and thus move the will.

These are our aids to move us to the right disposition, to contrition, to penitence, to love of God, and thus receive the fullness of God's grace according to our own readiness or preparation, or willingness to receive it.

Questions from the Catechism

Q. Which are the chief effects of the Redemption?
A. **The chief effects of the Redemption are two: The satisfaction of God's justice by Christ's sufferings and death, and the gaining of grace for men.**

Q. What do you mean by grace?

GRACE AND THE SACRAMENTS

A. By grace I mean the supernatural gift of God bestowed on us, through the merits of Jesus Christ, for our salvation.

Q. How many kinds of grace are there?
A. There are two kinds of grace, sanctifying grace and actual grace.

Q. What is sanctifying grace?
A. Sanctifying grace is that grace which makes the soul holy and pleasing to God.

Q. What do you call those graces or gifts of God by which we believe in Him, hope in Him, and love Him?
A. Those graces or gifts of God by which we believe in Him, hope in Him, and love Him, are called the divine virtues of Faith, Hope, and Charity.

Q. What is Faith?
A. Faith is a divine virtue by which we firmly believe the truths which God has revealed.

Q. What is Hope?
A. Hope is a divine virtue by which we firmly trust that God will give us eternal life and the means to obtain it.

Q. What is Charity?
A. Charity is a divine virtue by which we love God above all things for His own sake, and our neighbor as ourselves for the love of God.

Q. What is actual grace?
A. Actual grace is that help of God which enlightens our mind and moves our will to shun evil and do good.

Q. Is grace necessary to salvation?
A. Grace is necessary to salvation, because without grace we can do nothing to merit heaven.

Q. Can we resist the grace of God?
A. We can, and unfortunately often do, resist the grace of God.

Q. What is the grace of perseverance?
A. The grace of perseverance is a particular gift of God which enables us to continue in the state of grace till death.

Q. Which are the means instituted by our Lord to enable men at all times to share in the fruits of the Redemption?
A. The means instituted by our Lord to enable men at all times to share in the fruits of the Redemption are the Church and the sacraments.

Q. What is a Sacrament?
A. **A Sacrament is an outward sign instituted by Christ to give grace.**

Q. How many sacraments are there?
A. **There are seven sacraments: baptism, confirmation, Holy Eucharist, penance, extreme unction, holy orders, and matrimony.**

Q. Whence have the sacraments the power of giving grace?
A. **The sacraments have the power of giving grace from the merits of Jesus Christ.**

Q. What grace do the sacraments give?
A. **Some of the sacraments "give" sanctifying grace, and others "increase" it in our souls (notice limited meaning of give).**

Q. Which are the sacraments that give sanctifying grace?
A. **The sacraments that give sanctifying grace are baptism and penance; and they are called "sacraments of the dead."**

Q. Why are baptism and penance called "sacraments of the dead"?
A. **Baptism and penance are called "sacraments of the dead," because they take away sin, which is the death of the soul, and give grace, which is its life.**

Q. Which are the sacraments that increase sanctifying grace in our soul?
A. **The sacraments that increase sanctifying grace in our soul are: confirmation, Holy Eucharist, extreme unction, holy orders, and matrimony; and they are called "sacraments of the living."**

Q. Why are confirmation, Holy Eucharist, extreme unction, holy orders, and matrimony called "sacraments of the living"?
A. **Confirmation, Holy Eucharist, extreme unction, holy orders, and matrimony, are called "sacraments of the living," because those who receive them worthily are already living the life of grace.**

Q. What sin does he commit who receives the sacraments of the living in mortal sin?
A. **He who receives the sacraments of the living in mortal sin commits a sacrilege, which is a great sin, because it is an abuse of a sacred thing.**

Q. Besides sanctifying grace do the sacraments give any other grace?
A. **Besides sanctifying grace the sacraments give another grace called sacramental grace.**

Q. What is sacramental grace?
A. Sacramental grace is a special help which God gives, to attain the end for which He instituted each sacrament. (It might be well to point out here this is an actual grace. This is in addition to sanctifying grace which all sacraments give.)

Q. Do the sacraments always give grace?
A. The sacraments always give grace, if we receive them with the right dispositions.

Q. Can we receive the sacraments more than once?
A. We can receive the sacraments more than once, except baptism, confirmation, and holy orders.

Q. Why can we not receive baptism, confirmation, and holy orders more than once?
A. We cannot receive baptism, confirmation, and holy orders more than once, because they imprint a character in the soul.

Q. What is the character which these sacraments imprint in the soul?
A. The character which these sacraments imprint in the soul is a spiritual mark which remains forever.

Q. Does this character remain in the soul even after death?
A. This character remains in the soul even after death; for the honor and glory of those who are saved; for the shame and punishment of those who are lost.

Q. What is a sacramental?
A. A sacramental is anything set apart or blessed by the Church to excite good thoughts, and to increase devotion, and through these movements of the heart to remit venial sin.

Q. What is the difference between the sacraments and the sacramentals?
A. The difference between the sacraments and the sacramentals is: First, the sacraments were instituted by Jesus Christ and the sacramentals were instituted by the Church; Second, the sacraments give grace of themselves when we place no obstacle in the way; the sacramentals excite in us pious dispositions, by means of which we may obtain grace.

Q. Which is the chief sacramental used in the Church?
A. The chief sacramental used in the Church is the sign of the cross.

Q. How do we make the sign of the cross?
A. We make the sign of the cross by putting the right hand to the forehead, then on the breast, and then to the left and right shoulders, saying, "In the name of the Father, and of the Son, and of the Holy Ghost. Amen."

Q. Why do we make the sign of the cross?
A. **We make the sign of the cross to show that we are Christians and to profess our belief in the chief mysteries of our religion.**

Q. How is the sign of the cross a profession of faith in the chief mysteries of our religion?
A. **The sign of the cross is a profession of faith in the chief mysteries of our religion because it expresses the mysteries of the Unity and Trinity of God and of the Incarnation and death of our Lord.**

Q. How does the sign of the cross express the mystery of the Unity and Trinity of God?
A. **The words, In the name, express the Unity of God; the words that follow, of the Father, and of the Son, and of the Holy Ghost, express the mystery of the Trinity.**

Q. How does the sign of the cross express the mystery of the Incarnation and death of our Lord?
A. **The sign of the cross expresses the mystery of the Incarnation and death of our Lord by reminding us that the Son of God, having become man, suffered death on the cross.**

Q. What other sacramental is in very frequent use?
A. **Another sacramental in very frequent use is holy water.**

Q. What is holy water?
A. **Holy water is water blessed by the priest with solemn prayer to beg God's blessing on those who use it, and protection from the powers of darkness.**

Q. Are there other sacramentals besides the sign of the cross and holy water?
A. **Besides the sign of the cross and holy water there are many other sacramentals, such as blessed candles, ashes, palms, crucifixes, images of the Blessed Virgin and of the saints, rosaries, and scapulars.**

Problem Questions

1. What is grace? Why is it called the "life of the soul"?
2. What relation is there between the doctrine of grace and Adam?
3. Who is the single source of grace?
4. What is the meaning of "sacrament"?
5. What are the three necessary marks of a sacrament?
6. Make a list of the "outward signs" of each sacrament.
7. Discuss the sacraments as channels of grace.

GRACE AND THE SACRAMENTS

8. Do the outward signs of each sacrament actually give the grace, or are they only outward signs or symbols of it?

9. What is sanctifying grace?

10. What is actual grace?

11. If the sacraments gave only one grace, show that there would be need but for a single sacrament.

12. Who is the sole source of the power of the sacrament?

13. Does each sacrament give sanctifying grace?

14. What is meant by the divine virtues of Faith, Hope, and Charity? Are these also natural virtues?

15. What is the difference between the sacraments of the living and the sacraments of the dead?

16. Show the usefulness of having only the sacraments of baptism, confirmation, and holy orders leave a mark (charisma) on the soul.

17. What is the effect of the unworthy reception of the sacraments?

18. What are sacramentals? How do they operate? Name five sacramentals.

Quotations from the Bible

For each of the following quotations:

a) Identify the speaker.

b) State the conditions under which the statement was made.

c) Give the meaning.

d) Tell its significance.

"If any man love Me, he will keep My word, and My Father will love him, and We will come to him, and will make Our abode with him" (John xiv. 23).

"Come to Me, all you that labor and are burdened, and I will refresh you" (Matt. xi. 28).

"Without Me you can do nothing" (John xv. 5).

"The Lord is not willing that any should perish" (II Peter iii. 9).

Chapter XXIX
BAPTISM

"Unless a man be born again of water and of the Holy Ghost, he cannot enter into the Kingdom of God" (John iii. 5).

Restoration of Human Nature. Our first parents as they lived in the Garden of Eden, coming straight from the hand of God, had a human nature full of grace. Because of Adam's disobedience, this life of grace was taken from them. Through the infinite merits of Jesus Christ, our Lord, this life of grace could be given back to man in the way He pointed out. This is by the sacraments, and it is brought about in the first place, by the sacrament of baptism. By it we are made Christians, children of God, and heirs of heaven. Without it we cannot enter the kingdom of heaven.

Christ Speaks to Nicodemus. The record is clear and unmistakable that this way is pointed out by Christ and established by Him. One of the Pharisees, Nicodemus, came to Christ by night, and said to Him:

Rabbi, we know that Thou art come a teacher from God; for no man can do these signs which Thou dost, unless God be with him (John iii. 2).

And Jesus' answer, as given by St. John, contained the instruction on baptism.

Jesus answered, and said to him: Amen, amen I say to thee, unless a man be born again, he cannot see the kingdom of God.

Nicodemus saith to Him: How can a man be born when he is old? Can he enter a second time into his mother's womb, and be born again?

Jesus answered: Amen, amen, I say to thee, unless a man be born again of water and the Holy Ghost, he cannot enter into the kingdom of God (John iii. 3–5).

So are we born into the new life, the supernatural life, the life of grace. We become sons of God, as St. Paul says.

Water. Christ has here pointed out the outward sign that is to be used in the sacrament of baptism; that is, water. And how suitable that seems. Just as water is necessary to the life of our body, so is baptism necessary, in the spiritual life, for every person. And how suitable it is, too, to use something which is found everywhere and is so closely joined with the idea of cleansing. How we are cleansed by baptism. The old life is washed away, and we live the new, clean life in Christ. We put on the white garment of Christ. It is clear that this sacrament should be received at the earliest possible time in a person's life. Infants, as soon as they can be brought safely to the Church should be baptized. "Since children have no other means of salvation, except baptism, we may easily understand how grievously those persons sin who permit them to remain without the grace of the Sacrament longer than necessity may require, particularly at an age so tender as to be exposed to numberless dangers of death" (*Catechism of the Council of Trent*, p. 178).

Christ Prescribes Words for Baptism. But there must go with the water the words which Christ ordered. After Christ was raised from the dead, He met the disciples on the road, and told them to go into Galilee before Him. He said to them, "Going therefore, teach ye all nations; baptizing them in the name of the Father, and of the Son, and of the Holy Ghost" (Matt. xxviii. 19, 20). And so with the water must go the words, "I baptize thee in the name of the Father, and of the Son, and of the Holy Ghost," for so Christ commanded. When these words were uttered by Christ, we are taught, it became necessary for everyone to be baptized.

Form of Administration. The usual way to administer the sacrament today is to pour water on the head of the infant or person to be baptized and while doing this to say: "I baptize thee in the name of the Father, and of the Son, and of the Holy Ghost." These are the necessary things. The ordinary ministers of the sacraments are priests, but in cases of necessity anyone may administer the sacrament of baptism, even a non-Catholic, who intends to do what the Church does and what Christ ordered.

The Sponsors. According to a most ancient practice of the

Church, there are other persons who assist at the baptismal font. They are the persons whom we call the godfather and godmother of the child, or as they used to be called, the sponsors, a term which is often used today. The need for sponsors is seen if we recall Christ's words that in baptism we are born again, born in the spiritual life. "As then everyone after his birth, requires a nurse and instructor by whose assistance and attention he is brought up and formed to learning and useful knowledge, so those, who, by the waters of baptism, begin to live a spiritual life should be intrusted to the fidelity and prudence of someone from whom they may imbibe the precepts of the Christian religion and may be brought up in all holiness, and thus grow gradually in Christ, until, with the Lord's help, they at length arrive at perfect manhood." The sponsors are given in baptism, in order that they may promise, in the name of the child, what the child itself would promise if it had the use of reason. In this sacrament the sponsors for the child renounce the devil, and all his works and pomps. The works of the devil are sins, and the pomps of the devil are the sources or occasions of sin.

The Duties of Sponsors. The sponsors are, in the eyes of the Church, the spiritual father and mother — the godfather and godmother — of the baptized child, and should see to it that he is properly brought up in the spiritual and religious life. This is an especial duty if the parents die or if they neglect the duty of religious and spiritual instruction. Besides the word *sponsor*, the word *surety* was used in former times, and the godfather and godmother become surety before God, as the great St. Augustine said, for their godchildren. Therefore only good Catholics who know and understand their religion, and have the zeal to teach it, can act as sponsors in baptism.

Baptism of Desire. Baptism being so necessary for salvation, it is most important that it should be simply and easily administered. Water is generally easy to get. The formula is simple and generally known, and any person, having the right intention, may administer it. But even where the actual baptism of water is not possible, the grace of baptism may be had where it is desired and where there is sorrow for one's sins. Where there is real love of God in the soul, it is secured. "Every one that loveth is born of God" (I John iv. 7). This is the baptism of desire. It is the ardent wish of an unbaptized person to receive baptism of water, and to do all that God has ordained or prescribed for salvation. This has the effects of baptism of water, if it is not possible to receive baptism in the usual way. Baptism of desire makes us children of God and heirs of heaven.

Baptism of Blood. As to the martyr, or any person who sheds his blood for Christ, it is part of our faith that he, if unbaptized, will receive the grace of baptism. We see in this all the conditions of the baptism of desire, but with more than desire, a real sacrifice for the love of God. "Greater love hath no man than this that he lay down his life for his friend." This shedding of one's blood for the faith of Christ is for the unbaptized a baptism of blood. "He that shall lose his life for Me," said Christ, "shall find it" (Matt. x. 39).

Baptism of Adults. As we have seen, children should be baptized as soon as possible, and always in case of danger of death, at once. In the early Church, pagans and Jews who accepted Christianity were usually given some further instruction, but within a few months were received into the Church, generally at Easter time and Pentecost. There was not the same danger with them as with infants; their intention and determination to receive baptism and their sorrow for their sins would avail them. This is the baptism of desire. The baptism of water, in the case of adults, or children who have come to the use of reason, not only blots out the stain of original sin, but also cleanses the soul of all actual sins. Baptism of desire would have the same effects, if baptism of water could not be received.

Ceremonies of Baptism. Baptism may be private, when it is necessarily performed; for example, as when one is in danger of death, and it may be solemn, performed with the ceremonies of the Church. Solemn baptism is baptism performed with the full ceremonies of the Church; private baptism is baptism performed without these ceremonies. Classify the ceremonies of baptism under the following heads:

1. Ceremonies observed before coming to the font.
2. Ceremonies observed after coming to the font.
3. Ceremonies that follow baptism.

The ceremonies in baptism are as follows:

1. The consecration of baptismal water (on Holy Saturday and the vigil of Pentecost).
2. The person to be baptized stands at the church door.
3. Catechetical instruction.
4. The exorcism.
5. The salt is put on mouth of person to be baptized.
6. The sign of the cross is made on forehead, nostrils, breast, shoulders, and ears.
7. Nostrils and ears are touched with saliva.
8. The renunciation of Satan.
9. The profession of faith.
10. The wish to be baptized.
11. Pouring of water.
12. "In the name of the Father, and of the Son, and of the Holy Ghost."
13. Chrism is placed on crown of head.
14. The white garment or white cloth is placed on the baptized.
15. The lighted candle is placed in the hand of the baptized.
16. The name is given.

Conditional Baptism. A conditional baptism is performed when there is doubt whether baptism given before was valid or not, or no certain knowledge that there has ever been a baptism. This is done just to make sure that the person is really baptized. It is not a second baptism. If the person has been really baptized before, the conditional baptism is, of course, without effect on the soul.

Baptism Necessary for Salvation. The first effect of the Redemption gained for us by the infinite sacrifice of Christ on the cross for the sins of mankind, comes to us in baptism. Baptism restores to us the grace of God. It gives us again a right to heaven. We are heirs of heaven because we are again children of God. We gain this new state by baptism, a baptism of water, a baptism of desire, or a baptism of blood. Baptism in one of these forms is

The Form of Lay Baptism

Pour common water on the forehead or face of the person to be baptized, and say while pouring it:

I baptize thee in the name of the Father, and of the Son, and of the Holy Ghost.

necessary for salvation; without it we cannot enter into the kingdom of heaven. Much has been said as to what happens to children who have died without baptism. This has not been revealed, but though they may not enjoy the beatific vision, they may enjoy a natural happiness forever far greater than any happiness this world can offer.

Questions from the Catechism

Q. What is baptism?
A. **Baptism is a sacrament which cleanses us from original sin, makes us Christians, children of God, and heirs of heaven.**

Q. Are actual sins ever remitted by baptism?
A. **Actual sins and all the punishment due to them are remitted by baptism, if the person baptized be guilty of any.**

Q. Is baptism necessary to salvation?
A. **Baptism is necessary to salvation, because without it we cannot enter into the kingdom of heaven.**

Q. Who can administer baptism?
A. **The priest is the ordinary minister of baptism; but in case of necessity anyone who has the use of reason may baptize.**

Q. How is baptism given?
A. **Whoever baptizes should pour water on the head of the person to be baptized; and say, while pouring the water, I baptize thee in the name of the Father, and of the Son, and of the Holy Ghost.**

Q. How many kinds of baptism are there?
A. **There are three kinds of baptism: baptism of water, baptism of desire, and baptism of blood.**

Q. What is baptism of water?
A. Baptism of water is that which is given by pouring water on the head of the person to be baptized, and saying at the same time, I baptize thee, in the name of the Father, and of the Son, and of the Holy Ghost.
Q. What is baptism of desire?
A. Baptism of desire is an ardent wish to receive baptism, and to do all that God has ordained for our salvation.
Q. What is baptism of blood?
A. Baptism of blood is the shedding of one's blood for the faith of Christ.
Q. Is baptism of desire or of blood sufficient to produce the effects of baptism of water?
A. Baptism of desire or of blood is sufficient to produce the effects of the baptism of water, if it is impossible to receive the baptism of water.
Q. What do we promise in baptism?
A. In baptism we promise to renounce the devil with all his works and pomps.
Q. Why is the name of a saint given in baptism?
A. The name of a saint is given in baptism in order that the person baptized may imitate his virtues and have him for a protector.
Q. Why are godfathers and godmothers given in baptism?
A. Godfathers and godmothers are given in baptism in order that they may promise, in the name of the child, what the child itself would promise if it had the use of reason.
Q. What is the obligation of a godfather and a godmother?
A. The obligation of a godfather and a godmother is to instruct the child in its religious duties, if the parents neglect to do so or die.

Problem Questions

1. Baptism is an initiation ceremony. Into what society does baptism admit one? May one, after joining, leave it at will?

2. Before going "over the top," Shocky Roder, who had been given that nickname on account of a heavy head of hair, said to his Catholic friend: "Jerry, I have never been baptized; I want to be a Catholic. Won't you baptize me since there is no priest around?" Jerry, a devout Catholic, eager for the opportunity, obtained some fresh water, poured it directly over the top of Shocky's head, saying at the same time, "I baptize thee in the name of the Father, and of the Son, and of the Holy

BAPTISM 261

Ghost." Did Shocky receive the sacrament of baptism? Explain. If not actually, was Shocky's desire for baptism enough should he have been killed? Discuss.

3. The story is told of a certain man who on the day after his confirmation learned that he had been baptized with milk. Why was the man's baptism not valid? What would have to be done in a case of this kind?

4. A man, alone in the woods, accidentally shot himself. He had never been baptized but had often thought of taking the final step and had learned the essentials of baptism. Knowing that he would never be able to leave the woods alive, he succeeded in getting his canteen open and with the words: "I baptize thee in the name of the Father, and of the Son, and of the Holy Ghost," poured water over his head. Was the man baptized? Discuss.

5. In a certain grade school which a few Protestant children attended, the teacher had been explaining the sacrament of baptism. At the noon recess, two of the girls had succeeded, as they said, "in baptizing" one of their Protestant friends in spite of violent protests. Had they succeeded? Discuss.

6. Mr. Solberg, a baptized Lutheran, joined the Catholic Church and received conditional baptism. Why did Mr. Solberg receive conditional baptism? Are his sins forgiven by this conditional baptism? Explain.

7. Mrs. Kelly, whose father is a devout Catholic but whose mother is a Protestant, earnestly desires her parents to be sponsors for her infant daughter in baptism. May Mrs. Kelly's parents be sponsors? Discuss.

8. John, a fourteen-year-old boy and a close friend of the Ross family, had been asked to be sponsor in baptism for Mary Anne. After a period of twenty years, a friendship so close had grown up between John and Mary Anne that they wished to marry. What must John and Mary Anne do? Why?

Review Questions

1. Is baptism a sacrament?
2. What are the three important marks of a sacrament?
3. Who is the ordinary minister of the sacrament?
4. May anyone else administer this sacrament? If so, under what conditions?
5. What is the necessary act done by the person administering this sacrament?
6. Is this part of a longer ceremony? What other acts are part of the ceremony?
7. What are the necessary words used in administering this sacrament?
8. Name now the two parts of the "outward sign" of this sacrament.
9. May this sacrament be received more than once? Can it?

10. Is this one of the sacraments that leaves a distinct mark on the soul?

11. Besides sanctifying grace what is the grace peculiar to this sacrament?

12. What is ordinarily the condition of the soul when one receives baptism?

13. Justify calling baptism a sacrament of the dead.

Quotations from the Bible

For each of the following quotations:

a) Identify the speaker.
b) State the conditions under which the statement was made.
c) Give the meaning.
d) Tell its significance.

"Amen, amen, I say to thee, unless a man be born again, he cannot see the kingdom of God" (John iii. 3).

"Going therefore, teach ye all nations; baptizing them in the name of the Father, and of the Son, and of the Holy Ghost" (Matt. xxviii. 19).

"He that shall lose his life for Me, shall find it" (Matt. x. 39).

"Unless a man be born again of water and the Holy Ghost, he cannot enter into the kingdom of God" (John iii. 5).

Chapter XXX
THE FORGIVENESS OF SINS

"As the Father hath sent Me, I also sent you. When he had said this, He breathed on them, and He said to them: Receive ye the Holy Ghost: Whose sins you shall forgive they are forgiven them, and whose sins you shall retain they are retained" (*John xx. 21–23*).

The Children of God by Baptism. We became Christians in baptism. The supernatural life of the soul was begun. The soul regained the grace which had been withheld from it because of Adam's sin, and which is now granted because of Christ's sacrifice. We were made ready to start on God's Highway with a new strength and power through Christ. We became again the children of God, the sons of God.

God's Mercy and Man's Sins After Baptism. It would be glorious for man and for the world if he could keep his state of soul after baptism. But man has the power of free will; he may choose to do a thing or he may not do it. He may be obedient to God's commandments and laws, or he may be disobedient. He may forget and drift into sin. He is often weak and does not keep the laws of God. He may willfully break God's laws and refuse God's grace. By a mortal sin he loses baptismal innocence and kills the life of the soul. Man later is sorry for his sins, and desires to do penance, but of himself he has no power to satisfy God's justice. By Christ's Crucifixion and because of the purpose of the Incarnation man was not left to his own power or his own devices. It was made possible for him to gain the grace of God to restore him to God in the sacrament of penance. It is this sacrament, a second chance for man, that we are to study in this and some following chapters.

The Sacrament of Penance and God's Love of Man. Sometimes we lose our baptismal innocence. We have at the age of seven some real understanding of what God's law is, and the evil of willfully breaking God's law and refusing God's grace. Yet how often people do this! We find it hard always to keep God's law. Therefore we need a source of help that will be always with us, and can be used often. The sacrament of penance is just such a help. Let us see how well suited it is to do this wonderful good to men.

The Forgiveness of Sins. The sins of man must be forgiven if he is to be restored to God's friendship, and keep on God's main highway to his home with God. But only God can forgive sins. Christ forgave sins when He was on earth. But it was not in the divine plan that Christ should remain on earth forever, but during only a brief human life of thirty-three years, so this great need of man for forgiveness of sin had to be provided for. Let us see what Christ did.

The Power of the Keys to Peter: Promise. When Peter made his simple but profound profession of faith in the divinity of Christ: "Thou art Christ, the Son of the Living God," Christ gave Peter the "power of the keys." Christ's answer to Peter's confession of faith was:

Blessed art thou, Simon Bar-Jona; because flesh and blood hath not revealed it to thee, but My Father who is in heaven.
And I say to thee: That thou art Peter: and upon this rock I will build My Church, and the gates of hell shall not prevail against it.
And I will give to thee the keys of the kingdom of heaven. And whatsoever thou shalt bind upon earth, it shall be bound also in heaven: and whatsoever thou shalt loose on earth, it shall be loosed also in heaven (Matt. xvi. 17, 18, 19).

And the power was given also to the Apostles for Christ said to them:

"Amen I say to you, whatsoever you shall bind upon earth, shall be bound also in heaven; and whatsoever you shall loose on earth, shall be loosed also in heaven" (Matt. xviii. 18).

Fulfillment. This promise of giving to the Apostles the power for the forgiveness of sins is fulfilled when Christ appears to them after the Resurrection at the time when Thomas was absent.

He said therefore to them again: Peace be to you. As the Father hath sent Me, I also send you.
When He had said this, He breathed on them; and He said to them: Receive ye the Holy Ghost.

Whose sins you shall forgive, they are forgiven them; and whose sins you shall retain, they are retained (John xx. 21–23).

The Need for Penance. But how shall the sins of an individual be forgiven? Was such power given so that those to whom it was given might use it for the benefit of one and not for another? Might a person be refused forgiveness because of conditions over which he had no control? Surely not, for Christ died for all men. We can be lost only if we do no penance. "Unless," Christ said, "you shall do penance, you shall all perish" (see Luke xiii. 3). In penance is our hope for the forgiveness of our sins. In the Old Testament we read in the prophet Ezechial:

> But if the wicked do penance for all his sins which he hath committed, and keep all My commandments, and do judgment, and justice, living he shall live, and shall not die (Ezech. xviii. 21).

If we have sinned, no matter how great our sins, if we are truly sorry, they shall be forgiven. "If your sins be as scarlet, they shall be made as white as snow." We must always have hope in God, no matter how far we may have strayed from God's Highway.

The Conditions of Forgiveness. How shall the sins of man be forgiven? The power to forgive sins, or retain them was given to Peter and the Apostles, and to their successors, the Pope, bishops, and priests of the Roman Catholic Church. They are Christ's ministers or representatives in the forgiveness of sins. What shall an individual do to have his sins forgiven? He must go to the persons who can forgive sins. But what is necessary on his part? "Penance" you answer very properly. But what does that include as used by Christ? Can we believe that man would sin, go to the priest for forgiveness, and feel free to go and sin again? Most certainly not. Having broken God's law and lost His friendship, more than that should be necessary. Even among men we expect certain things. Of a person who has done wrong to another who is his equal or even his subordinate or inferior, we expect certain things:

1. An acknowledgment of the wrong and its greatness and if committed more than once, an acknowledgment of each wrong.

2. A genuine feeling of sorrow for the wrong done.

3. A promise of resolution and expectation that it will never happen again, deliberately, and

4. An act, or some acts in reparation for the wrongs to the person.

The Opportunity to Secure Forgiveness. Why should we do less for God? To Him we owe our life, to Him we owe everything we have. He is truly in the language of Christ, "Our Father." We owe Him love. If we have a pure love of God and act from it, we have fulfilled our purpose as creatures. But we sin against God time after time. In His infinite goodness, through His Crucifixion, God has given us a means, a tribunal for forgiveness called the sacrament of penance. It demands exactly the steps we outlined above. To any man, however great his sin, the way for forgiveness is always open, if he will confess his sin, show true sorrow for it, and make a resolution to sin no more with the aid of God's grace.

The Steps in Securing Forgiveness and God's Grace. The steps in this process as followed in the Church are simple and effective means of restoring one to God's friendship. These steps are:

1. **Examination of Conscience.** A looking into one's past to learn how often or how greatly through forgetfulness, or weakness, or malice, we have broken God's commandments or the commandments of the Church, or been unjust in any way to God or our neighbor, especially in important matters. This is a preparatory step called "examination of conscience."

2. **Sorrow or Contrition.** The examination, when seriously made, shows us the number and kinds of our offenses against God. It would do no good if it remained at that. If we knew we sinned and felt no sorrow for it, it would be of no use and it would stop there. But if our souls are moved and we feel a real sorrow for our sins because we really love God with all our strength, or even because we "dread the loss of heaven and the pains of hell," then we have hope. This is *sorrow* or *contrition* for sin.

3. **Resolution to Sin no More.** If, besides this calling of our sins to mind, acknowledging them as sins, and feeling a real

sorrow or contrition for them, we make up our minds or resolve firmly to do everything in our power not to sin again, we have all that is necessary to permit us to go to the priest to confess and gain forgiveness.

4. Confession. We, therefore, go to the priest, in the confessional, and we tell our sins, their kind and their number, and receive the absolution through the power of Christ. This is the *confession*.

5. Penance. At the end of the confession the priest gives the penitent a penance to do; it may be only to say some prayers to show his sorrow and his resolution to sin no more. This is called the *penance* or satisfaction for our sins. It too, is a part of the sacrament.

Summary. To receive the sacrament of penance worthily it is necessary that these five steps be taken:

1. A careful examination of conscience.
2. A genuine sorrow or contrition for one's sins.
3. A firm resolution to amend one's life.
4. Confession of sins to a priest in confession.
5. Acceptance of the penance imposed.

A True Sacrament. Before considering these in more detail, it may be well to see if the sacrament of penance has the marks necessary for any sacrament. These are: (1) institution by Christ, (2) an outward sign, (3) a source of grace.

Instituted by Christ. The sacrament of penance was, as we have seen, first promised by Christ and definitely established when He appeared to the Apostles after the Resurrection and said to them: "Whose sins you shall forgive they are forgiven them, whose sins you shall retain, they are retained."

Outward Sign. The matter of the outward sign is in this sacrament different from that of the other sacraments. The matters are: the acts of the penitent — the contrition, confession, and satisfaction of the person asking forgiveness. The form of the sacrament is the words of the priest, "I absolve thee from thy sins, in the name of the Father, and of the Son, and of the Holy Ghost. Amen."

Inward Grace. The immediate effect of the sacrament of penance is the forgiveness of the sins committed since baptism or since the last confession, and thus restoring sanctifying grace to the soul, if lost by mortal sin, or increasing it if not lost. It gives us also sacramental grace to avoid evil and do good, to foresee and overcome temptation: it gives us right to actual graces in special times of our life.

Penance, a True Sacrament. So penance is a true sacrament. It was instituted by Christ. It has certain outward signs which actually produce an inward grace in the soul. It is the sacrament in which the sins committed after baptism or since the last confession are forgiven. The sins are forgiven by the absolution of the priest as a minister of God and in His name. The sins are forgiven and we are restored to the friendship of God.

Questions from the Catechism

Q. What is the sacrament of penance?
A. **Penance is a sacrament in which the sins committed after baptism are forgiven.**

Q. How does the sacrament of penance remit sin, and restore to the soul the friendship of God?
A. **The sacrament of penance remits sin and restores the friendship of God to the soul by means of the absolution of the priest.**

Q. How do you know that the priest has the power of absolving from the sins committed after Baptism?
A. I know that the priest has the power of absolving from the sins committed after baptism, because Jesus Christ granted that power to the priests of His Church when He said: "Receive ye the Holy Ghost. Whose sins you shall forgive, they are forgiven them; whose sins you shall retain, they are retained."

Q. How do the priests of the Church exercise the power of forgiving sins?
A. **The priests of the Church exercise the power of forgiving sins by hearing the confession of sins, and granting pardon for them as ministers of God and in His name.**

Q. What must we do to receive the sacrament of penance worthily?
A. **To receive the sacrament of penance worthily we must do five things:**
   1. We must examine our conscience.

2. We must have sorrow for our sins.
3. We must make a firm resolution never more to offend God.
4. We must confess our sins to the priest.
5. We must accept the penance which the priest gives us.

Quotations from the Bible

For each of the following quotations:
  a) Identify the speaker.
  b) State the conditions under which the statement was made.
  c) Give the meaning.
  d) Tell its significance.

"And I will give to thee the keys of the kingdom of heaven. And whatsoever thou shalt bind upon earth, it shall be bound also in heaven: And whatsoever thou shalt loose on earth, it shall be loosed also in heaven" (Matt. xvi. 19).

"He said therefore to them again: Peace be to you. As the Father hath sent Me, I also send you.

"When He had said this, He breathed on them; and He said to them: Receive ye the Holy Ghost.

"Whose sins you shall forgive, they are forgiven them; and whose sins you shall retain, they are retained" (John xx. 21–23).

"O God, be merciful to me a sinner. I say to you, this man went down into his house justified rather than the other; because everyone that exalteth himself, shall be humbled: and he that humbleth himself, shall be exalted" (Luke xviii. 13–14).

Chapter XXXI
THE CONFESSION OF SINS

Making a Confession. The way of making a confession is known to us:

I. Usually we go to church and kneel down in the pew and prepare ourselves for the confession. In this preparation:

1. We pray to God:
2. We ask light to know all our sins.
3. We ask grace to detest them.
4. We examine our conscience systematically to recall our sins.

II. We wait our turn and enter the confessional.

III. The priest then shows that he is ready to hear our confession. Then the steps are as follows:

1. We ask the blessing of the priest. "Bless me, Father. I confess to Almighty God and to you, Father, that I have sinned."
2. We tell how long it has been since our last confession. "It has been one week since my last confession" (or the length of time).
3. Then we tell the name and number of our mortal sins, and any other things which may make them a different kind of sin.
4. We may tell any venial sins.
5. We should end the confession of our sins by saying, "I also accuse myself of all the sins of my past life" (adding, if we choose, one or more of our past sins).
6. We answer truthfully any questions the priest asks.
7. We listen closely to his advice.
8. Pay attention to the penance given by the priest.
9. While the priest absolves us, we say an act of contrition, "O my God, I am heartily sorry," etc.

IV. Right after leaving the confessional, we usually go to a place in a pew and say our penance. In any case, we must say it before our next confession.

Although this process of making a confession is well known to us, it will be well to look a little more deeply into the meaning of the steps in the process, or to find ways to do them better.

A Method of Examination of Conscience. We should enter the Church early enough so that we will have plenty of time to make the examination of our past to recall the sins we have committed. We first pray to God for light to know our sins and grace to detest them. There is something in the soul of man, which is called the conscience, which makes him feel guilty when he does a wrong or bad or evil thing. This examination of our past for our sins we call the examination of conscience. A habit of examination, daily or weekly, even when we are not going to confession is very helpful. This we should do especially before a spiritual Communion at Mass when, for any reason, we cannot receive Holy Communion sacramentally.

The certain way of making a good examination of conscience is to go about it systematically, asking ourselves whether we have sinned against each of the Ten Commandments, the six precepts of the Church, etc. The first series of tests will be on the Ten Commandments of God.

The Ten Commandments of God. We will think carefully about those commandments which we have broken in the past, or against which our life offers us temptation. A second series of tests for us is to go systematically, one after the other, over the six commandments of the Church.

Other Tests. These are the main points, but we could add for a more complete examination: *The Seven Capital Sins,* and the *Duties of Our State of Life.*

While the violation of the duties of our state of life which are seen will be included under the Ten Commandments of God, it might be well to meditate upon this especially, for it will help us much in the effort to amend our life.

Perfect Contrition Forgives Sin. The second main topic is contrition or sorrow for sin. We should feel sorry for our sins because being an offense against God our Creator, our Preserver, and our Redeemer, it is the greatest of evils. And if we should die without sorrow for our mortal sins, they shut us out of heaven, and condemn us to the eternal pains of hell. We should feel sorry for our sins because we realize what an ingratitude to God, what an injustice, what an offense against Him, a mortal sin is. In this state of mind we hate sin and have a true grief for having offended God. Sometimes this sorrow comes because we realize how infinitely good God is in Himself and worthy of all love. This is the pure love of God. This is the perfect contrition. It is the highest and best motive for our sorrow. Perfect contrition is so pleasing to God, that because of it our sins are forgiven even before we confess them, but we must confess our sins as soon as possible. The sins are forgiven because a perfect love of God and sin could not be in the soul at the same time. We must confess our sins even in this case, if possible, because we are so human that we cannot always be sure that our contrition is perfect, and moreover we receive the benefits of the sacrament. Besides, if we know that we have committed a mortal sin, we are not allowed to receive Holy Communion till we have confessed it, even though we have made an act of perfect contrition. Naturally, with a pure love of God, we should want to go to His tribunal to receive from the lips of His priest the words of pardon.

Imperfect Contrition. But for the most part our contrition is imperfect; it does not reach the perfection of a pure love of God. It is a hatred of sin, an offense against God, because we fear the loss of heaven and the pains of hell, or because sin is so hateful in itself. When we understand that we have before us for all eternity the joys of heaven or the pains of hell, we might well hate sin, the thing that causes us to lose the friendship of God and suffer forever in hell.

Imperfect Contrition Sufficient for Confession. But sorrow based on the fear of the loss of heaven and the pains of hell; i.e., imperfect contrition, is all that is necessary for pardon in confession. Naturally, in all of us there is some love of God and our prayer is for greater love of God, but perfect love need not be had for pardon of our sins in confession, though we should try to

THE CONFESSION OF SINS

have perfect contrition. This is only one of many things in our religion showing how God loves sinners and wants to do everything to bring them back to His service, and to make it easy for them to return if they stray from the right path.

True Contrition is Interior. If there is real contrition, it will come from the heart, which is also the source of sins. It will not be merely a memorized act of contrition, which is good in itself. It must not be only words on the lips, but it must really come from the heart. It is interior; that is, it is in the heart and not merely on the lips. Christ felt this among the people of His own day: "This people," He says, "honoreth Me with their lips; but their heart is far from Me" (Matt. xv. 8).

True Contrition is Supernatural. This interior sorrow should come from our love of God, or from some motive or reason connected with faith such as the love or fear of God, the loss of heaven, because of Christ's sufferings and crucifixion. It should be of this supernatural kind. While merely natural motives, such as loss of position or good name may be helpful in starting true contrition, such motives in themselves are not enough. Contrition must be supernatural and not merely natural.

True Contrition is Sovereign. True contrition will arise from our knowing that the loss of God's love is a greater sacrifice and a greater loss than any merely human loss such as loss of friends, money, or position, loss of property, or loss of any merely human or natural thing. When we recognize that the loss of God's friendship or love is our greatest loss, and are sorry because of it, then our contrition is said to be supreme or sovereign, because it puts God above all creatures and all things.

True Contrition is Universal. There is one other quality of true contrition. It extends to every last one of our mortal sins. It detests all of them without exception. It realizes that man can lose his soul for one mortal sin unrepented of. The contrition is more perfect when it extends to every venial sin. When we are sorry for every mortal sin committed without exception, our sorrow is universal.

Qualities of True Contrition. True contrition or sorrow for our sins has therefore four qualities: It is interior; It is supernatural; It is sovereign; It is universal.

Fixed Purpose of Sinning no More. It is not enough to have a true sorrow or contrition for our sins. There must go along with it a firm resolution or purpose to sin no more. With true contrition in our heart, with the realization of the great evil of sin, and with a love of God in greater or less degree filling us, we make a fixed resolve or resolution not only to avoid sin, but also to avoid the near occasions of sins. In the "Our Father" we pray that we may not be led into temptation. Certainly we should not seek it or dally with it. The near occasions are those persons, places, or things that may easily lead us into sin. We know these from our past experience. What is for one person an occasion of sin is not necessarily so for another. If our contrition is really sovereign, we will gladly keep away from these persons, places, or things. "He that loveth danger shall perish in it."

Confession is Even Humanly Helpful. The central fact in the sacrament of penance is the confession of sins to a duly authorized priest for the purpose of obtaining forgiveness. Even if confession were no sacrament, still it would be a very wise thing. With our merely human burdens and troubles it is always helpful to be able to go to tell some sympathetic person about our problems, even if they cannot help us. How very much more helpful to be able to take our greater burdens of sin to our changeless Friend, knowing He has wanted us to come, and being sure He can help us, is ready to help us, and will help us. "Come to Me all ye that are burdened and I will refresh you." What heavier burden is there than sin, and in what condition is there greater need for refreshment?

Qualities of a Good Confession. We go, therefore, to the confessional and in the presence of Christ's representative, the priest, we unburden ourselves. We tell or confess all our mortal sins, and we may include our venial sins, too. We go without pride, and we accuse ourselves of our sins because we have a deep shame and sorrow for having offended God, for whom we have a real love, even though at times we are weak enough to sin. This makes our confession *humble*. In this spirit of humility we tell the number and kind of our sins, and any circumstances which change their nature. We tell *all* our mortal sins. This makes our confession *entire*. Knowing it is to Christ we are really speaking, we tell these sins honestly and truthfully, neither exaggerating nor excusing them. This makes our confession *sincere*. We make our confession humbly, sincerely, entirely, because it is to God we speak and from Him we shall have help.

Remembering the Number of Our Sins. There are some difficulties that people have in trying to make a good confession humble, sincere, and entire. One of these is the trouble sometimes of remembering the number of our sins. In that case, we should tell the number as nearly as possible. To help us in that it would be well to say how often we have sinned in a day, a week, or a month, which ever we remember best or can recall, and to add how long the habit or practice has lasted. Sometimes, we may forget to confess a mortal sin, without our fault. When this comes to mind some days later we wonder whether our confession is worthy. If, after careful examination, without our own fault, we forget to confess a mortal sin, our confession is worthy, and the sin is forgiven, but it must be told in the next confession if it comes to our mind.

Concealing Sins in Confession, a Sacrilege. But it is entirely different, and very grievous indeed, if we willfully conceal a mortal sin in confession. Nothing would seem to be more foolish and absurd. It is mocking God. It is, as it were, telling a lie to the Holy Ghost. It is a serious offense indeed, and makes our confession worthless. It makes our confession worthless, our contrition hypocritical. To the sins told in the confession which are not forgiven for the matter of the outward sign of the sacrament is not there, there is added the very great sin of sacrilege. A person who willfully conceals a mortal sin in confession must not only confess it in his next confession, but must repeat the sins confessed in his unworthy confession, and those which were committed later.

The necessary means for the forgiveness of sin is the confession of sins to a duly authorized priest as the representative of God.

The necessary steps in a worthy confession, as we have seen, are:

1. Examination of conscience.
2. Genuine sorrow or contrition for our sins.
3. The confession proper, of our sins.
4. A firm resolution to sin no more.
5. A willing acceptance of a penance.

Questions from the Catechism

Q. What is the examination of conscience?

A. **The examination of conscience is an earnest effort to recall to mind all the sins we have committed since our last worthy confession.**

Q. How can we make a good examination of conscience?

A. **We can make a good examination of conscience by calling to memory the commandments of God, the precepts of the Church, the seven capital sins, and the particular duties of our state of life, to find out the sins we have committed.**

Q. What should we do before beginning the examination of conscience?

A. **Before beginning the examination of conscience we should pray to God to give us light to know our sins and grace to detest them.**

Q. What is contrition, or sorrow for sin?

A. **Contrition, or sorrow for sin, is a hatred of sin and a true grief of the soul for having offended God, with a firm purpose of sinning no more.**

Q. What kind of sorrow should we have for our sins?

A. **The sorrow we should have for our sins should be interior, supernatural, universal, and sovereign.**

Q. What do you mean by saying that our sorrow should be interior?

A. **When I say that our sorrow should be interior, I mean that it should come from the heart, and not merely from the lips.**

Q. What do you mean by saying that our sorrow should be supernatural?

A. **When I say that our sorrow should be supernatural, I mean that it should be prompted by the grace of God, and excited by motives which spring from faith, and not by merely natural motives.**

Q. What do you mean by saying that our sorrow should be universal?

THE CONFESSION OF SINS

A. When I say that our sorrow should be universal, I mean that we should be sorry for all our mortal sins without exception.

Q. What do you mean when you say that our sorrow should be sovereign?

A. When I say that our sorrow should be sovereign, I mean that we should grieve more for having offended God than for any other evil that can befall us.

Q. Why should we be sorry for our sins?

A. We should be sorry for our sins, because sin is the greatest of evils and an offense against God our Creator, Preserver, and Redeemer, and because it shuts us out of heaven and condemns us to the eternal pains of hell.

Q. How many kinds of contrition are there?

A. There are two kinds of contrition; perfect contrition and imperfect contrition.

Q. What is perfect contrition?

A. Perfect contrition is that which fills us with sorrow and hatred for sin, because it offends God, who is infinitely good in Himself and worthy of all love.

Q. What is imperfect contrition?

A. Imperfect contrition is that by which we hate what offends God, because by it we lose heaven and deserve hell; or because sin is so hateful in itself.

Q. Is imperfect contrition sufficient for a worthy confession?

A. Imperfect contrition is sufficient for a worthy confession, but we should endeavor to have perfect contrition.

Q. What do you mean by a firm purpose of sinning no more?

A. By a firm purpose of sinning no more, I mean a fixed resolve not only to avoid all mortal sin, but also its near occasions.

Q. What do you mean by the near occasions of sin?

A. By the near occasions of sin I mean all the persons, places, and things that may easily lead us into sin.

Q. What is confession?

A. Confession is the telling of our sins to a duly authorized priest, for the purpose of obtaining forgiveness.

Q. What sins are we bound to confess?

A. We are bound to confess all our mortal sins, but it is well also to confess our venial sins.

Q. Which are the chief qualities of a good confession?

A. The chief qualities of a good confession are three; it must be humble, sincere, and entire.

Q. When is our confession humble?
A. Our confession is humble, when we accuse ourselves of our sins, with a deep sense of shame and sorrow for having offended God.

Q. When is our confession sincere?
A. Our confession is sincere, when we tell our sins honestly and truthfully, neither exaggerating nor excusing them.

Q. When is our confession entire?
A. Our confession is entire when we tell the number and kinds of our sins and the circumstances which change their nature.

Q. What should we do if we cannot remember the number of our sins?
A. If we cannot remember the number of our sins, we should tell the number as nearly as possible, and say how often we may have sinned in a day, a week, or a month, and how long the habit or practice has lasted.

Q. Is our confession worthy if, without our fault, we forget to confess a mortal sin?
A. If without our fault we forget to confess a mortal sin, our confession is worthy, and the sin is forgiven; but it must be told in confession if it again comes to our mind.

Q. Is it a grievous offense willfully to conceal a mortal sin in confession?
A. It is a grievous offense willfully to conceal a mortal sin in confession, because we thereby tell a lie to the Holy Ghost, and make our confession worthless.

Q. What must he do who has willfully concealed a mortal sin in confession?
A. He who has willfully concealed a mortal sin in confession must not only confess it, but must also repeat all the sins he has committed since his last worthy confession.

Q. What should we do on entering the confessional?
A. On entering the confessional we should kneel, make the sign of the cross, and say to the priest: Bless me, father; then add, I confess to Almighty God and to you, father, that I have sinned.

Q. Which are the first things we should tell the priest in confession?
A. The first things we should tell the priest in confession are the

time of our last confession, and whether we said the penance and went to Holy Communion.

Q. After telling the time of our last confession and Communion what should we do?
A. **After telling the time of our last confession and Communion we should confess all the mortal sins we have since committed, and all the venial sins we may wish to mention.**

Q. What must we do when the confessor asks us questions?
A. **When the confessor asks us questions we must answer them truthfully and clearly.**

Q. What should we do after telling our sins?
A. **After telling our sins we should listen with attention to the advice which the confessor may think proper to give.**

Q. How should we end our confession?
A. **We should end our confession by saying, I also accuse myself of all the sins of my past life, telling, if we choose, one or several of our past sins.**

Q. What should we do while the priest is giving us absolution?
A. **While the priest is giving us absolution we should from our heart renew the act of contrition.**

Problem Questions

1. Mrs. Seidel admits the necessity of everyone to have a trustworthy friend yet she says, "Confession is an invention of priests." What can we say to her?

2. Ned Black was caught in the act of stealing a large sum of money He was arrested and sentenced. Ned was sorry he stole the money because he was caught. Ned has contrition. Is this contrition enough for the reception of the Sacrament of Penance? Why? How must contrition be? Why must contrition precede the confession of sins?

3. One penitent accuses himself by saying, "I missed Sunday Mass five or ten times"; another, "I sinned against the First Commandment, the Second Commandment, the Fourth Commandment," etc.; a third, "I sinned in thought, word, and deed"; a fourth, "I stole"; and a fifth, "I spoke improper words." What is wrong with all these statements? How must one's confession be made? How might each one of these statements be made in the right way so as to eliminate the necessity of the priest's asking questions?

4. Francis McDougall has been a daily communicant for some time and now very rarely falls into serious sin. He goes to confession weekly and

has again and again been requested by his confessor to include a sin from his past life. Why does the confessor request this? What is a good way to end all confessions?

5. Discuss the words of St. Augustine: "Accuse thyself, and God will excuse thee; excuse thyself and God will accuse thee."

Quotations from the Bible

For each of the following quotations:
a) Identify the speaker.
b) State the conditions under which the statement was made.
c) Give the meaning.
d) Tell its significance.

"Father, I have sinned against heaven, and before thee, I am not now worthy to be called thy son" (Luke xv. 21).

"The publican, standing afar off, would not so much as lift up his eyes toward heaven; but struck his breast, saying: O God, be merciful to me a sinner" (Luke xviii. 13).

Chapter XXXII
THE PUNISHMENT OF SIN

The Eternal Punishment of Sin Wiped Out by the Sacrament of Penance. Just as in human offense there is a judging of guilt and a giving of punishment, so with the offenses against God, of which we accuse ourselves in confession. The guilt of our sins is forgiven in confession, and we willingly accept the punishment that may be imposed. The eternal punishment of sin is remitted or wiped out by the sacrament or by perfect contrition.

The Temporal Punishment of Sin. But because our contrition is often so imperfect, the reparation to God for our sins is not absolute, and there is due a temporal punishment to be suffered either here on earth or in purgatory. It seems to us also just, that there should be some atonement for the great evil of sin against an infinitely merciful God. When our sorrow for our sins is very great the punishment of sin may be wiped out, both temporal and eternal. But we can never be sure whether the entire temporal punishment of sin is wiped out. This is not known to man, only to God who determines it.

Penance After Confession. To make some satisfaction to God for our sins, and to remind us of the great evil of sin, and to prevent, if possible, our falling into sin again, the priest at the end of a confession gives us a "penance." Of course, if we have stolen we must restore the property to the rightful owner. If we have done any injustice, we are ordered to remedy it, if it is within our power. We must repair, as far as we can, the evil we have done. Besides we are bound to say the prayers or to do the good works of fasting or almsgiving that the priest gives us for penance. Even the greatest penance does not make up fully for the evil of a single sin, but our sorrow and good disposition is the effective basis of the working of Christ's merits and mercy in us. If the priest states a time for doing the penance, then we must do it at that time; otherwise any time before our next confession will do. It is a good rule to perform the penance before we leave the church after confession, so that we will not forget it. To neglect our penance willfully is to commit a new sin. To perform it is to diminish the temporal punishment for our sins.

The Spiritual Works of Mercy. We can also make some satisfaction for our sins by showing our love of our neighbor for the love of God, by doing the corporal and spiritual works of mercy. In the spiritual works of mercy we minister to our neighbor's mind and soul. We must realize how deep are hurts to people's feelings, and how deep their pain of mind may be. Because the need for these spiritual works of mercy is not as clear to us as that of the corporal works, we are likely to neglect to do them. The spiritual works of mercy are seven: (1) to admonish the sinner; (2) to instruct the ignorant; (3) to counsel the doubtful; (4) to comfort the sorrowful; (5) to bear wrongs patiently; (6) to forgive all injuries; (7) to pray for the living and the dead.

The Corporal Works of Mercy. We can likewise satisfy in some degree the temporal punishment due to sin by performing the corporal works of mercy. These are works done for the body of our neighbor, or his physical welfare. They all appeal to us directly and unless we are hard-hearted and selfish, we quickly do what we can in our neighbor's need, because we are fellow men and God's creatures. Moreover, the help that is needed is clear and readily performed. The corporal works of mercy are seven, too: (1) to feed the hungry; (2) to give drink to the thirsty; (3) to clothe the naked; (4) to ransom the captive; (5) to harbor the harborless; (6) to visit the sick; (7) to bury the dead.

Offering Our Trials as Satisfaction for Sins. If it is our part in life to have trials, to suffer the ills of life, to be a victim of injustice, we shall bear our sufferings patiently for the love of God. We shall remember that Christ suffered for love of us, and we should offer up our sufferings for our own sins, and the temporal punishment due to them, and for all the sins of human beings against their Creator.

Indulgences as Satisfaction for Sin. Still another way to satisfy the temporal punishment that may be due to sin, is to gain indulgences. This is a much misunderstood, if not misrepresented, topic. Many high-school history books, are, to put it mildly, inaccurate when they discuss indulgences in connection with the Protestant Reformation in European history. You should be on your guard when you come to read them.

A Spiritual Treasury. The forgiving of sins and the remission of the eternal or temporal punishment due to them must come from God. The basis of it all is the infinite merits of our Lord's Passion and Crucifixion. In the Church at all times, there have lived, holy men and women who have made satisfaction for their own sins far beyond any punishment that God may have imposed upon them. This is so because of their pure love of God. The Blessed Virgin Mary, who never committed sin herself, patiently and gladly accepted great sufferings from the hand of God. We call her the Queen of Martyrs. We recognize an overabundance of satisfaction, in a lesser degree, in the saints of the Church, and in unnamed good men and women in every age. The Church teaches that these merits, because of the brotherhood of man and the communion of saints, are a sort of spiritual treasury which we may draw upon.

State of Grace Needed to Gain Indulgence. Indulgences may not be bought, as no spiritual thing or service may be bought without sin, and surely there can be no permission to commit sin. The first condition for gaining indulgences is that we must be in the state of grace. To a person in mortal sin there can be no remission of the temporal punishment due to sin through indulgences. We must also intend to gain the indulgence, and say the prayers or do the good works to which the indulgence may be attached.

Plenary and Partial Indulgences. Indulgences are of two kinds, plenary and partial. Plenary indulgence is a blotting out or remission of all the punishment due to our sins up to that time. A partial indulgence is remission of part of the temporal punishment due to sin. This is expressed in a certain number of days or years which does not mean shortening one's time in purgatory by that number of days or years. "To say that an indulgence of so many days or years is granted means that it cancels an amount of purgatorial punishment equivalent to that which would have been remitted, in the sight of God, by the performance of so many days or years of the ancient canonical penance. . . . God alone knows what penalty remains to be paid and what its precise amount is in severity and duration" (*Catholic Encyclopedia,* pp. 783–784). To gain a plenary indulgence, besides the conditions stated above, it is required always that the person should be free from all mortal sin. For the most part, too, the person must go to confession, receive Communion, and pray for the intention of the Pope. And sometimes it is necessary that fasting or almsgiving or visiting a church or other good works be done. Some indulgences can be gained only for oneself, while others may be gained for the souls in purgatory.

Brief Summary. The eternal punishment due to sin is wiped out by the sacrament of penance, but there may remain a temporal punishment of sin to satisfy the justice of God. This will be wiped out in whole or part, too, by perfect contrition, by prayer, fasting, almsgiving, the patient suffering of the ills of life, by doing the corporal or spiritual works of mercy, and from that great spiritual treasury available to all members of the Church from the infinite merits of Jesus and from the good works of the saints and holy men and women of all ages.

Questions from the Catechism

Q. Why does the priest give us a penance after confession?
A. **The priest gives us a penance after confession that we may satisfy God for the temporal punishment due to our sins.**

Q. Does not the sacrament of penance remit all punishment due to sin?
A. **The sacrament of penance remits the eternal punishment due to sin, but it does not always remit the temporal punishment which God requires as satisfaction for our sins.**

Q. Why does God require a temporal punishment as a satisfaction for sin?
A. **God requires a temporal punishment as a satisfaction for sin,**

THE PUNISHMENT OF SIN

to teach us the great evil of sin, and to prevent us from falling again.

Q. Which are the chief means by which we satisfy God for the temporal punishment due to sin?

A. The chief means by which we satisfy God for the temporal punishment due to sin are prayer, fasting, almsgiving, all spiritual and corporal works of mercy, and the patient suffering of the ills of life.

Q. Which are the chief spiritual works of mercy?

A. The chief spiritual works of mercy are seven: To admonish the sinner, to instruct the ignorant, to counsel the doubtful, to comfort the sorrowful, to bear wrongs patiently, to forgive all injuries, and to pray for the living and the dead.

Q. Which are the chief corporal works of mercy?

A. The chief corporal works of mercy are seven: To feed the hungry, to give drink to the thirsty, to clothe the naked, to ransom the captive, to harbor the harborless, to visit the sick, and to bury the dead.

Q. What is an indulgence?

A. An indulgence is the remission in whole or in part of the temporal punishment due to sin.

Q. Is an indulgence a pardon of sin, or a license to commit sin?

A. An indulgence is not a pardon of sin, nor a license to commit sin, and one who is in a state of mortal sin cannot gain an indulgence.

Q. How many kinds of indulgences are there?

A. There are two kinds of indulgences — plenary and partial.

Q. What is a plenary indulgence?

A. A plenary indulgence is the full remission of the temporal punishment due to sin.

Q. What is a partial indulgence?

A. A partial indulgence is the remission of a part of the temporal punishment due to sin.

Q. How does the Church by means of indulgences remit the temporal punishment due to sins?

A. The Church by means of indulgences remits the temporal punishment due to sin by applying to us the merits of Jesus Christ, and the superabundant satisfactions of the Blessed Virgin Mary and of the saints; which merits and satisfactions are its spiritual treasury.

Q. What must we do to gain an indulgence?
A. **To gain an indulgence we must be in the state of grace and perform the works enjoined.**

Review Questions

1. Is penance a sacrament?
2. What are the three essentials of a sacrament?
3. Who is the ordinary minister of the sacrament?
4. May anyone else administer this sacrament?
5. What is the essential act done by the person administering this sacrament?
6. Is this part of a longer ceremony? What other acts are part of the ceremony?
7. What are the essential words used in administering this sacrament?
8. Name now the two parts of the "outward sign" of this sacrament.
9. May this sacrament be received more than once?
10. Is this one of the sacraments that leaves a distinct mark on the soul?
11. Besides sanctifying grace what is the grace peculiar to this sacrament?
12. What is ordinarily the condition of the soul when one receives penance?
13. Justify calling penance a sacrament of the dead.

Quotations from the Bible

For each of the following quotations:
a) Identify the speaker.
b) State the conditions under which the statement was made.
c) Give the meaning.
d) Tell its significance.

"Jesus began to preach, and to say: Do penance" (Matt. iv. 17).

"Unless you shall do penance, you shall all likewise perish" (Luke xiii. 3).

"Let him do penance for his sin" (Lev. v. 5).

Chapter XXXIII
THE SACRAMENT OF THE HOLY EUCHARIST

"Whilst they were at supper, Jesus took bread, and blessed, and broke: and gave to His disciples, and said: Take ye and eat: THIS IS MY BODY. *And taking the chalice He gave thanks: and gave to them, saying: Drink ye all of this.* FOR THIS IS MY BLOOD *of the New Testament which shall be shed for many unto remission of sins (Matt. xxvi. 26–28).*

The Life of the Soul. Those on God's Highway know that there is a life of the soul as there is a life of the body. We have all known when our body was in good health, keen, eager for every activity, and when it was weak, without energy, and almost lifeless. We have known, too, when our soul's health was not so good if we have sinned, and when we were happy and fit after a good confession. The real life of the soul began with baptism. Our soul overcome by original sin was restored to the grace of God by the waters of baptism. The life thus begun in baptism is preserved during the early years of a child's life until he can be said to really know and understand the nature of sin. This is called "the age of reason" and for most of us begins at about the seventh year of our life.

The Age of Reason. Then the child begins really to know what sin is and its evil. Of course, such a child could not understand fully what sin is and its evil. That will come to him as he grows with the experience of life, with his reading, and with his thinking. But at about seven his responsibility begins within the range of his understanding. He understands in his simple way God the Father, the Creator of heaven and earth, and why we must love Him and Christ our Lord. He knows he is on the Highway to God. He understands that sin is our enemy and destroys our love of God. Thus his *responsible* supernatural life, or his responsibility for the life of his soul begins.

Nourishment for the Soul. The body needs nourishment, food and drink. The child knows that. He can see that the soul too will need nourishment, food and drink. The life of the soul being a spiritual life will need spiritual nourishment, spiritual food and spiritual drink. And the question must have come into our minds when that idea first struck us: Where shall we get this food and drink? Our feeling must be somewhat like that of the woman of Samaria whom Christ met at Jacob's well in Sichar:

> There cometh a woman of Samaria, to draw water. Jesus saith to her: Give Me to drink.
> For His disciples were gone into the City to buy meats.
> Then that Samaritan woman saith to Him: How dost Thou, being a Jew, ask of me to drink, who am a Samaritan woman? For the Jews do not communicate with the Samaritans.
> Jesus answered, and said to her: If thou didst know the gift of God, and who He is that saith to thee, Give Me to drink, thou perhaps wouldst have asked of Him, and He would have given thee living water.
> The woman saith to Him: Sir, Thou hast nothing wherein to draw, and the well is deep; from whence then hast Thou living water?
> Art Thou greater than our father Jacob, who gave us the well, and drank thereof himself, and his children, and his cattle?
> Jesus answered, and said to her: Whosoever drinketh of this water, shall thirst again, but he that shall drink of the water that I will give him, shall not thirst forever:
> But the water that I will give him, shall become in him a fountain of water, springing up into life everlasting.
> The woman saith to Him: Sir, give me this water, that I may not thirst, nor come hither to draw (John iv. 7–15).

What the soul needs is exactly this: a fountain of water springing up into life everlasting. And to deserve it, perhaps we need to be reminded of what Christ told this woman just before His disciples returned. These are Christ's words:

> But the hour cometh, and now is, when the true adorers shall adore the Father in spirit and in truth. For the Father also seeketh such to adore Him.
> God is a spirit; and they that adore Him, must adore Him in spirit and in truth (John iv. 23–24).

The Paschal Lamb. The question, Where shall this spiritual

THE HOLY EUCHARIST

food come from?, was answered by the One Person who could answer it. It was answered by Christ Himself. The day was the day for the celebration of the feast of the unleavened bread, the feast of the Paschal Lamb, or simply as stated in the Gospel, the Pasch or Passover. In the book of Exodus we read about the establishment of this feast:

And the Lord said to Moses and Aaron in the land of Egypt:

This month shall be to you the beginning of months: it shall be the first in the months of the year.

Speak ye to the whole assembly of the children of Israel, and say to them: On the tenth day of this month let every man take a lamb by their families and houses.

But if the number be less than may suffice to eat the lamb, he shall take unto him his neighbor that joineth to his house, according to the number of souls which may be enough to eat the lamb.

And it shall be a lamb without blemish, a male, of one year: according to which rite also you shall take a kid.

And you shall keep it until the fourteenth day of this month: and the whole multitude of the children of Israel shall sacrifice it in the evening.

And they shall take of the blood thereof, and put it upon both the side posts, and on the upper door posts of the houses, wherein they shall eat it.

And they shall eat the flesh that night roasted at the fire, and unleavened bread with wild lettuce (Exod. xii. 1–9).

And I will pass through the land of Egypt that night, and will kill every first-born in the land of Egypt both man and beast: and against all the gods of Egypt I will execute judgments: I *am* the Lord.

And the blood shall be unto you for a sign in the houses where you shall be: and I shall see the blood, and shall pass over you: and the plague shall not be upon you to destroy you, when I shall strike the land of Egypt.

And this day shall be for a memorial to you: and you shall keep it a feast to the Lord in your generations with an everlasting observance.

Seven days shall you eat unleavened bread: in the first day there shall be no leaven in your houses: Whosoever shall eat anything leavened, from the first day until the seventh day, that soul shall perish out of Israel (Exod. xii. 12, 13, 14, 15).

The first month, the fourteenth day of the month in the evening, you shall eat unleavened bread, until the one and twentieth day of the same month in the evening.

Seven days there shall not be found any leaven in your houses: he that shall eat leavened bread, his soul shall perish out of the assembly of Israel, whether he be a stranger or born in the land (Exod. xii. 18, 19).

Christ Institutes the Holy Eucharist. It was on this feast of the Lord that Christ revealed to man the nature of the spiritual food for his soul, that was ordered by God. The twelve Apostles were gathered together with Christ to celebrate the feast of the Pasch. In the presence of the twelve Apostles the following events took place:

And whilst they were at supper, Jesus took bread, and blessed, and broke: and gave to His disciples, and said: Take ye, and eat. This is My Body. And taking the chalice He gave thanks, and gave to them, saying: Drink ye all of this. For this is My Blood of the New Testament, which shall be shed for many unto remission of sins (Matt. xxvi. 26–28).

And whilst they were eating, Jesus took bread; and blessing, broke, and gave to them, and said: Take ye; This is My Body. And having taken the chalice, giving thanks, He gave it to them. And they all drank of it. And He said to them: This is My Blood of the New Testament, which shall be shed for many (Mark xiv. 22–24).

And taking bread, He gave thanks, and brake it; and gave to them saying: This is My Body, which is given for you. Do this for a commemoration of Me. In like manner the chalice also, after He had supped, saying: This is the chalice, the New Testament in My Blood, which shall be shed for you (Luke xxii. 19–20). (See also I Cor. xi. 23–29.)

The next day, Good Friday, He was crucified and died on the cross.

The Canon of the Mass. In the Canon of the Mass every Sunday and holyday, and as often as we go to Mass, we see this last supper kept in its exact sense and in Christ's words. After some other prayers, the priest comes to the Consecration, thus:

Which oblation do Thou, O God, vouchsafe in all things to bless, approve, ratify, make worthy and acceptable: that it may become for us the Body and Blood of Thy most beloved Son our Lord Jesus Christ.

Who the day before He suffered took bread into His holy and venerable hands, and with His eyes lifted up toward heaven, unto Thee, God, His almighty Father, giving thanks to Thee, blessed, broke, and gave to His disciples, saying: Take and eat ye all of this, FOR THIS IS MY BODY.

In like manner, after He had supped, taking also this excellent chalice into His holy and venerable hands, and giving thanks to Thee, He blessed and gave to His disciples, saying: Take and drink ye all of this, FOR THIS IS THE CHALICE OF MY BLOOD, OF THE NEW AND ETERNAL TESTAMENT: THE MYSTERY OF FAITH: WHICH SHALL BE SHED FOR YOU AND FOR MANY UNTO THE REMISSION OF SINS.

As often as ye shall do these things, ye shall do them in remembrance of Me.

It should be noted that the words *eternal* and *the mystery of faith* are not in the Gospel account, but have been kept in the Church from apostolic tradition.

Various Names of the Sacrament. It is called the *Eucharist* which may be translated "good grace" and "thanksgiving." Both are very fitting. The grace of God, the Apostle tells us, is eternal life, and, of course, that is just what it is, good grace to life eternal.

In the Gospel account we read:

And taking bread, He gave thanks, and brake; and gave to them, saying, This is My Body, which is given for you. Do this for a commemoration of Me (Luke xxii. 19).

For taking bread He brake it *and gave thanks*. So, to the Jews of Old, to Christ, and to ourselves the original feast of the Old Law and the spiritual feast of the New Law is truly a thanksgiving. "I will give thanks to the Lord, His praise shall ever be in my mouth" should be our continuous prayer for this feast.

It is often called the *Communion* following, no doubt, a passage in St. Paul:

The chalice of Benediction, which we bless, is it not the Communion of the Blood of Christ.
And the bread, which we break, is it not the partaking of the Body of the Lord? (I Cor. x. 16.)

That it is rightly called the Sacrament of Peace and Love is easy to understand, and also what it requires of us.

Perhaps one of the most significant names of this sacrament from the standpoint of this book is the *Viaticum*. How fitting on the Highway to God. We read:

It is also frequently called the Viaticum by sacred writers, both because it is spiritual food by which we are sustained in our pilgrimage through this life, and also because it paves our way to eternal glory and happiness. Wherefore, according to an ancient usage of the Catholic Church, we see that none of the faithful are permitted to die without this Sacrament (*Catechism of the Council of Trent*, p. 215).

Essentials of the Sacrament. Christ established the sacrament as told in the four Gospels. The exact words we know, but which may be regarded as necessary for the sacrament we know from the practice of the Church. These words are:

> THIS IS MY BODY
> THIS IS MY BLOOD

These words are important because they are not only the very words He said, but they also reveal the wonderful thing He had done, changed the unleavened bread and the wine into His own Body and Blood.

This points out the material of the sacrament, the unleavened bread and the wine. From the practice of the Jews we know that the bread served on the first day of the Feast of Unleavened Bread was unleavened bread, for the Jews were allowed to have no other in their houses. And this is the practice of the Church, though the sacrament can be had without unleavened bread. Bread is the essential. The other matter and element of the sacrament is wine and a little water. With the wine the Church of God has always mingled a small amount of water: First because Christ did so; second, because by this mixture we are reminded of the blood and the water that flowed from His side; and third in the Apocalypse, water is a sign of the people, and hence, water mixed with wine was a sign of the union of the faithful with Christ, their Head.

We have now to consider the aptitude of these two symbols of bread and wine to represent those things of which we believe and confess they are the sensible signs.

In the first place, then, they signify to us Christ, as the true life of men; for our Lord Himself says: My Flesh is meat indeed, and My Blood is drink indeed. As, then, the Body of Christ the Lord furnishes nourishment into eternal life to those who receive this Sacrament with purity and holiness, rightly is the matter composed chiefly of those elements by which our present life is sustained, in order that the faithful may easily understand that the mind and soul are satiated by the Communion of the precious Body and Blood of Christ.

These very elements serve also somewhat to suggest to men the truth of the Real Presence of the Body and Blood of the Lord in the Sacrament. Observing, as we do, that bread and wine are every day changed by the power of nature into human flesh and blood, we are led the more easily by this analogy to believe that the substance of the bread and wine is changed, by the heavenly benediction, into the real Flesh and real Blood of Christ.

This admirable change of the elements also helps to shadow forth what takes place in the soul. Although no change of the bread and wine appears externally, yet their substance is truly changed into the Flesh and Blood of Christ; so, in like manner, although in us nothing appears changed, yet we are renewed inwardly unto life, when we receive in the Sacrament of the Eucharist the true life (*Catechism of the Council of Trent,* pp. 222-23).

A True Sacrament. The Sacrament of the Holy Eucharist is the Sacrament which contains the Body and Blood, Soul and Divinity, of our Lord Jesus Christ, under the appearances of bread and wine. It signifies three things: It recalls to us the Passion of Christ, our Lord. The Apostle Paul reminds the Corinthians of this. In his Epistle to them he reminds them: "As often as you shall eat this Bread, and drink the Chalice, you shall show the death of the Lord, until He come" (I Cor. xi. 26). It directs our attention in the past to the source of the sacrament in the events following its institution by Christ. It calls to our mind in the present the effect of the sacrament in giving divine grace to nourish, support, and preserve the soul, and it directs our attention to the future, the eternal inheritance of joy and glory which is the reason Christ became man, and died on the cross. So in a true sense it is a sacrament. It was instituted by Christ. It has outward signs which are truly a source, a fountain of spiritual life, the grace of God.

Questions from the Catechism

Q. What is the Holy Eucharist?
A. **The Holy Eucharist is the sacrament which contains the Body and Blood, Soul and Divinity, of our Lord Jesus Christ, under the appearances of bread and wine.**
Q. When did Christ institute the Holy Eucharist?

A. Christ instituted the Holy Eucharist at the Last Supper, the night before He died.

Q. Who were present when our Lord instituted the Holy Eucharist?
A. When our Lord instituted the Holy Eucharist the twelve Apostles were present.

Q. How did our Lord institute the Holy Eucharist?
A. Our Lord instituted the Holy Eucharist by taking bread, blessing, breaking, and giving to His Apostles, saying: "Take ye and eat. This is My Body"; and then by taking the cup of wine, blessing and giving it, saying to them: "Drink ye all of this. This is My Blood which shall be shed for the remission of sins. Do this for a commemoration of Me."

Q. What happened when our Lord said, "This is My Body; this is My Blood"?
A. When our Lord said, "This is My Body," the substance of the bread was changed into the substance of His body; when He said, "This is My Blood," the substance of the wine was changed into the substance of His Blood.

Q. Is Jesus Christ whole and entire both under the form of bread and under the form of wine?
A. Jesus Christ is whole and entire both under the form of bread and under the form of wine.

Q. Did anything remain of the bread and wine after their substance had been changed into the substance of the Body and Blood of our Lord?
A. After the substance of the bread and wine had been changed into the substance of the Body and Blood of our Lord there remained only the appearances of bread and wine.

Q. What do you mean by the appearances of bread and wine?
A. By the appearances of bread and wine I mean the figure, the color, the taste, and whatever appear to the senses.

Q. What is this change of the bread and wine into the Body and Blood of our Lord called?
A. This change of the bread and wine into the Body and Blood of our Lord is called Transubstantiation.

Q. How was the substance of the bread and wine changed into the substance of the Body and Blood of Christ?
A. The substance of the bread and wine was changed into the substance of the Body and Blood of Christ by His almighty power.

THE HOLY EUCHARIST 295

Q. Does this change of bread and wine into the Body and Blood of Christ continue to be made in the Church?
A. **This change of bread and wine into the Body and Blood of Christ continues to be made in the Church by Jesus Christ through the ministry of His priests.**
Q. When did Christ give His priests the power to change bread and wine into His Body and Blood?
A. **Christ gave His priests the power to change bread and wine into His Body and Blood when He said to the Apostles, "Do this in commemoration of Me."**
Q. How do the priests exercise this power of changing bread and wine into the Body and Blood of Christ?
A. **The priests exercise this power of changing bread and wine into the Body and Blood of Christ through the words of consecration in the Mass, which are the words of Christ: "This is My Body; this is My Blood."**

Problem Questions

1. Protestant religions in general teach that our Lord is present in the Holy Eucharist only spiritually, and is only spiritually received, and that the words of our Lord, "This is My Body," are to be understood as meaning, "This is a symbol of My Body; partake in memory of Me." What is the correct meaning of our Lord's words? What is the Sacrament of the Eucharist? How do we know that Christ is present in this sacrament?

2. Steve Ross, one day talking about the Real Presence with an intimate Catholic friend, Jim Nevon, put the question: "If you believe that Christ is really present in that tiny wafer, tell me how He got there." Answer for Jim. Name the principal parts of the Mass. What is the best way to take part in the Mass? Why?

3. Jack Ertman forgot to mention a serious sin in confession. He thought of it immediately after he had left the confessional. He is a Knight of Columbus and very much desires to receive Holy Communion on the morrow with the other members of the organization. Is Jack in the state of grace? Discuss. If without great inconvenience he could go back to the confessional should he do so? Explain.

4. About two weeks ago a certain engineer had the misfortune of falling into serious sin. On a Sunday morning he got into the city just in time to attend an eight o'clock Mass. At Communion time of the Mass he very much desired to receive yet hesitated because of the consciousness of serious sin. Upon second thought, he made an act of perfect contrition and approached the Holy Table. Was he in the state of grace? Discuss. Why may he not receive Holy Communion? Is he guilty of sin? Explain.

5. Mrs. Thein has a very annoying cough. On Saturday she made a good

confession with the intention of receiving Holy Communion the next day. Sunday morning her cough was particularly annoying, so she took a dose of cough medicine. May she receive Holy Communion? Discuss. Under what condition may one receive Holy Communion when not fasting?

6. Miriam Steele understands as far as is possible to the human mind, the greatness of the Holy Eucharist; for this reason she feels unworthy to approach the Holy Table and remains away. Why is Miriam wrong? What words of Holy Scripture impress upon us the necessity of receiving the Body and Blood of Christ often? Why does the Church oblige the faithful to receive Holy Communion, at least once a year, during the Easter season?

7. Dick Steven would very much like to begin the practice of receiving Holy Communion daily. However, he hesitates because of the many venial sins he commits day after day. Should this keep Dick from receiving Holy Communion daily? Discuss. How can Dick greatly overcome these defects?

8. On a questionnaire of a certain men's college, they were asked "to please state frankly your own experience with frequent Communion." Here are some of the frank statements:

"I seldom if ever commit a mortal sin on the days on which I receive Holy Communion. If I stay away from the sacraments for several days I usually fall into many and grievous sins."

"When I am receiving frequently, I am a soldier; when I am not, I am a moral traitor."

"I cannot do without it now, I actually feel a physical difference when I neglect it for a morning. Yet all the time I am battling rotten desires."

"I have received so many favors and such consolation from the practice that I feel that the old saying is true: 'God can get along without you, but you cannot get along without God.'"

Would it not be possible for you to go to Holy Communion weekly? Daily?

Quotations from the Bible

For each of the following quotations:
a) Identify the speaker.
b) State the conditions under which the statement was made.
c) Give the meaning.
d) Tell its significance.

"Come to Me, all you that labor, and are burdened, and I will refresh you" (Matt. xi. 28).

"I am the Living Bread which came down from heaven" (John vi. 51).

"He that eateth My Flesh, and drinketh My Blood, hath everlasting life" (John vi. 55).

THE HOLY EUCHARIST

"Whilst they were at supper, Jesus took bread, and blessed, and broke: and gave to His disciples, and said: Take ye, and eat: This is My Body. And taking the chalice He gave thanks, and gave to them, saying: Drink ye all of this. For this is My Blood of the New Testament, which shall be shed for many unto remission of sins" (Matt. xxvi. 26–28).

"Amen, amen I say unto you: He that believeth in Me, hath everlasting life. I am the Bread of Life. Your fathers did eat manna in the desert, and are dead. This is the Bread which cometh down from heaven; that if any man eat of It, he may not die. I am the Living Bread, which came down from heaven. If any man eat of this Bread, he shall live forever: and the Bread that I will give, is My Flesh, for the life of the world. The Jews therefore strove among themselves, saying: How can this man give us His Flesh to eat?" (John vi. 47–53.)

"Whosoever drinketh of this water, shall thirst again, but he that shall drink of the water that I will give him, shall not thirst forever: But the water that I will give him, shall become in him a fountain of water, springing up into life everlasting" (John iv. 13, 14).

"This is My Body."
"This is My Blood."
"I am the bread of life: he that cometh to Me shall not hunger: and he that believeth in Me shall never thirst" (John vi. 35).

"He that eateth My Flesh, and drinketh My Blood, hath everlasting life: and I will raise him up in the last day.

"For My Flesh is meat indeed: and My Blood is drink indeed."
"He that eateth My Flesh, and drinketh My Blood, abideth in Me, and I in him" (John vi. 55–57).

To what incident does the following description refer?
Who was present?
What is the significance of the event?

"Whosoever shall eat this Bread, or drink the Chalice of the Lord unworthily, shall be guilty of the Body and of the Blood of the Lord" (I Cor. xi. 27).

Chapter XXXIV
THE REAL PRESENCE

The Mystery of the Real Presence. We believe that by virtue of Christ's Divine power and the simple direct words that He used when He said at the Last Supper, "This is My Body" and "This is My Blood," the substance of the bread was really changed into the substance of His Body, and the substance of the wine was changed into the substance of His Blood. And when in answer to the command, "Do this in commemoration of Me," the priests of the Catholic Church commemorate the occasion, using the words and the materials which Christ used, the same mysterious change occurs and the bread and wine become the Body and Blood of Christ. It is the teaching of the Church that in the Blessed Eucharist, Christ Himself, His Body and Blood, His Soul and Divinity, are really, truly, and substantially present under the species or appearances of bread and wine. By the appearances of bread and wine we mean that they appear so to the senses, in figure, or form, in color, in taste, or other appearances to the sense. In substance they are the Body and Blood of Christ. Such is the doctrine of the Real Presence.

Anticipation of the Mystery of the Real Presence. Such a miracle of miracles, more wonderful even than walking on the waters, or raising the dead to life, may be understood a little better if we make note of the promises of Christ concerning this mystery. From this we can see that He had in mind no figure of speech, no mere symbol or sign, but the overpowering fact.

I am the Bread of Life. When, as told in the sixth chapter of St. John, Christ crossed the Sea of Galilee, and the Pasch of the Jews, the festival day, was near at hand, a great crowd followed Him. He went up to a mountain, and the very great crowd, numbering five thousand, was seated. And Christ fed them

THE REAL PRESENCE

by the miraculous multiplication of the five barley loaves and two fishes, and gathered up twelve baskets of the fragments which remained over and above to them that had eaten. How the people wanted to take Him by force, make Him King, His escape from them, His walking on the waters, and their finding Him at Capharnaum is told in the Gospel. But His speech to them, then, is of special interest. He said:

> Amen, amen I say to you, you seek Me, not because you have seen miracles, but because you did eat of the loaves, and were filled.
>
> Labor not for the meat which perisheth, but for that which endureth unto life everlasting, which the Son of Man will give you. For Him hath God, the Father, sealed.
>
> They said therefore unto Him: What shall we do, that we may work the works of God?
>
> Jesus answered, and said to them: This is the work of God, that you believe in Him whom He hath sent.
>
> They said therefore to Him: What sign therefore dost Thou show, that we may see, and may believe Thee? What dost Thou work?
>
> Our fathers did eat manna in the desert, as it is written: *He gave them bread from heaven to eat.*
>
> Then Jesus said to them: Amen, amen I say to you; Moses gave you not bread from heaven, but My Father giveth you the true bread from heaven.
>
> For the bread of God is that which cometh down from heaven, and giveth life to the world.
>
> They said therefore unto Him: Lord, give us always this bread.
>
> And Jesus said to them: I am the bread of life: he that cometh to Me shall not hunger: and he that believeth in Me shall never thirst (John vi. 26–36).
>
> The Jews therefore murmured at Him, because He had said: I am the living bread which came down from heaven.
>
> And they said: Is not this Jesus, the son of Joseph, whose father and mother we know? How then saith He, I came down from heaven? (John vi. 41–43.)
>
> I am the bread of life.
>
> Your fathers did eat manna in the desert, and are dead.
>
> This is the bread which cometh down from heaven; that if any man eat of it, he may not die.
>
> I am the living bread which came down from heaven.
>
> If any man eat of this bread, he shall live forever; and the bread that I will give, is My Flesh, for the life of the world.

The Jews therefore strove among themselves, saying: How can this Man give us His flesh to eat?

Then Jesus said to them: Amen, amen I say unto you; Except you eat the Flesh of the Son of Man, and drink His Blood, you shall not have life in you.

He that eateth My Flesh, and drinketh My Blood, hath everlasting life: and I will raise him up in the last day.

For My Flesh is meat indeed: and My Blood is drink indeed.

He that eateth My Flesh, and drinketh My Blood, abideth in Me, and I in him.

As the living Father hath sent Me, and I live by the Father; so he that eateth Me, the same also shall live by Me.

This is the bread that came down from heaven. Not as you fathers did eat manna, and are dead. He that eateth this bread, shall live forever.

These things He said, teaching in the synagogue, in Capharnaum (John vi. 48–61).

The Fulfillment. Even those men who had seen the multiplication of loaves, the walking on the waters, and other miracles would not believe Him. It was a hard saying. They walked with Him no more. How full of meaning are these statements of Christ to us who can view them in the light of the later events. This anticipation is fulfilled in the words of the actual institution of the sacrament at a later feast of the Pasch. Thus the promise was made at the time of the Pasch and was fulfilled at a later feast of the Pasch.

The words of the institution of the sacrament could not be simpler or more direct.

THIS IS MY BODY.

THIS IS MY BLOOD.

St. Paul and the Holy Eucharist. Moreover this is the meaning of the rite in the early Church. St. Paul's words could hardly be more specific:

For I have received of the Lord that which also I delivered unto you, that the Lord Jesus, the same night in which He was betrayed, took bread. And giving thanks, broke, and said: Take ye, and eat; this is My Body, which shall be delivered for you: this do for the commemoration of Me. In like manner also the chalice, after He had supped, saying: This chalice is the New Testament in My Blood: this do ye, as often as you shall drink, for the commemoration of Me. For as often as you shall eat this Bread, and drink the Chalice, you shall show the death of the Lord, until He come. Therefore whosoever shall eat this Bread, or drink the Chalice of the Lord unworthily, shall be guilty of the Body and of the Blood of the Lord. But let a man prove himself: and so let him eat of that Bread, and drink of the Chalice. For he that eateth and drinketh unworthily, eateth and drinketh judgment to himself, not discerning the Body of the Lord (I Cor. xi. 23–29).

The Doctrine in the Church Always. So the saints testify in the early Church and for a thousand years almost no question is raised about it, and then only weakly. The doctrine coming directly from Christ, understood in its literal sense among the Apostles, and taught always by the Church, is the truth — and what a joyous and consoling doctrine it is for men on the Highway to God.

Christ Entirely Present Under Either Species and in Each Part. Since it is a living Christ who is present in the sacrament, uniting Body and Blood, Soul and Divinity, it must be clear that Christ must be present entirely in each particle. For at the *moment of consecration* the wonderful change takes place, and the bread and wine while keeping the form of the bread and wine, are in every particle the Body and Blood, Soul and Divinity of Christ entire. So when the faithful receive the Eucharist under the one species of bread they receive Christ entire, Body and Blood, Soul and Divinity. Such is the power of God and such His love for men.

Transubstantiation. By transubstantiation we mean the change of the bread and wine into the Body and Blood of Christ, so that nothing remains of the bread and wine but what we know by the senses. While the form is the same, the substance is changed. It is not bread, it is Christ. It is not wine, it is Christ. How can this be? we ask — if we think in merely human terms about human things. But the moment we recall that Christ is God, and that nothing is impossible to Him, there is no need to wonder about it. *It is.* The great wonder is that God in His divine way should be so kind to man. He comes down to us that we may be lifted up to Him. It is a pledge of everlasting life.

Effects of the Sacrament. We receive Christ in the Holy Eucharist.

He that eateth My Flesh, and drinketh My Blood abideth in Me and I in him (John vi. 57).

And in the next verse, Christ says:

He that eateth Me, the same shall also live by Me (John vi. 58).

When we possess Christ, the source of all grace, how the soul is strengthened, sustained, and gladdened by this priceless treasure. In this life if we are worthy to receive Him and do receive Him, we shall through His grace be kept from sin and made strong against temptation, while our evil inclinations shall be weakened and many spiritual diseases be warded off by His abiding presence.

He that eateth My Flesh and drinketh My Blood abideth in Me and I in him.

He that eateth Me, the same shall also live by Me (John vi. 57–58).

Fast Necessary for Holy Communion. To receive Communion worthily we must be in a state of sanctifying grace, and, ordinarily, have fasted from midnight. The fast demanded is to abstain from everything which is taken as food or drink from midnight until the time of receiving Communion. The only time Communion may be received without fasting is in the case of persons in danger of death. Such persons are permitted to receive Holy Communion, if in a state of sanctifying grace, even though they are not fasting.

Holy Communion and Grace. We prepare ourselves for Holy Communion first by putting ourselves in a state of grace by means of the Sacrament of Penance. Naturally, we do not have to go to confession every time we want to receive Holy Communion if we are in a state of grace; i.e., if we have committed no mortal sin since our last confession. If we should receive Holy Communion in the state of mortal sin, we should not receive God's grace, even though we receive the Body and Blood of Christ. And we should be guilty of a sacrilege. "For," as St. Paul says, "he that eateth and drinketh unworthily, eateth and drinketh judgment to himself, not discerning the Body of the Lord" (I Cor. xi. 23-29). The graces we receive will depend, too, on ourselves. It is enough to be free from mortal sin to receive Holy Communion, but to receive God's grace plentifully, it is not enough merely to be free from mortal sin, but we should be free from all affection for venial sin, and should make acts of lively faith, of firm hope, and of ardent love. Naturally, too, we should receive Holy Communion often, for in receiving Jesus Christ, the Author of all grace and the Source of all good, we have the greatest possible aid to a holy life. For so great a gift from God we should be thankful indeed. It is well to receive Holy Communion at a Mass, and we should spend some time after receiving so great a gift in adoring the Giver of it, our Lord, in thanking Him for the grace we have received, and in asking Him for the blessings we need.

Questions from the Catechism

Q. Why did Christ institute the Holy Eucharist?
A. **Christ instituted the Holy Eucharist:**
   1. To unite us to Himself and to nourish our soul with His divine life.
   2. To increase sanctifying grace and all virtues in our soul.
   3. To lessen our evil inclinations.
   4. To be a pledge of everlasting life.
   5. To fit our bodies for a glorious resurrection.
   6. To continue the Sacrifice of the Cross in His Church.

Q. How are we united to Jesus Christ in the Holy Eucharist?
A. **We are united to Jesus Christ in the Holy Eucharist by means of Holy Communion.**

Q. What is Holy Communion?
A. **Holy Communion is the receiving of the Body and Blood of Christ.**

Q. What is necessary to make a good Communion?

A. To make a good Communion it is necessary to be in the state of sanctifying grace and to be fasting from midnight.

Q. Does he who receives Communion in mortal sin receive the Body and Blood of Christ?

A. He who receives Communion in mortal sin receives the Body and Blood of Christ, but does not receive His grace, and he commits a great sacrilege.

Q. Is it enough to be free from mortal sin to receive plentifully the graces of Holy Communion?

A. To receive plentifully the graces of Holy Communion it is not enough to be free from mortal sin, but we should be free from all affection to venial sin, and should make acts of lively faith, of firm hope, and ardent love.

Q. What is the fast necessary for Holy Communion?

A. The fast necessary for Holy Communion is the abstaining from midnight from everything which is taken as food or drink.

Q. Is anyone ever allowed to receive Holy Communion when not fasting?

A. Anyone in danger of death is allowed to receive Holy Communion when not fasting.

Q. When are we bound to receive Holy Communion?

A. We are bound to receive Holy Communion, under pain of mortal sin, during the Easter time and when in danger of death.

Q. Is it well to receive Holy Communion often?

A. It is well to receive Holy Communion often, as nothing is a greater aid to a holy life than often to receive the Author of all grace and the Source of all good.

Q. What should we do after Holy Communion?

A. After Holy Communion we should spend some time in adoring our Lord, in thanking Him for the grace we have received, and in asking Him for the blessings we need.

Quotations from the Bible

For each of the following quotations:
a) Identify the speaker.
b) State the conditions under which the statement was made.
c) Give the meaning.
d) Tell its significance.

"I am the bread of life: he that cometh to Me shall not hunger: and he that believeth in Me shall never thirst" (John vi. 26–36).

THE REAL PRESENCE

"Amen, amen I say unto you: Except you eat the Flesh of the Son of Man, and drink His Blood, you shall not have life in you.

"He that eateth My Flesh, and drinketh My Blood, hath everlasting life: And I will raise him up in the last day.

"For My Flesh is meat indeed: and My Blood is drink indeed.

"He that eateth My Flesh, and drinketh My Blood, abideth in Me, and I in him.

"As the living Father hath sent Me, and I live by the Father; so he that eateth Me, the same also shall live by Me.

"This is the Bread that came down from heaven. Not as your fathers did eat manna, and are dead. He that eateth this Bread, shall live forever" (John vi. 54–59).

"Whosoever shall eat this Bread, or drink the Chalice of the Lord unworthily, shall be guilty of the Body and of the Blood of the Lord" (I Cor. xi. 26–29).

"And taking bread, He gave thanks, and brake: and gave to them, saying: This is My Body, which is given for you. Do this for a commemoration of Me.

"In like manner the chalice also, after He had supped, saying: 'This is the Chalice, the New Testament in My Blood, which shall be shed for you'" (Luke xxii. 19, 20).

"Behold, I am with you all days, even to the consummation of the world" (Matt. xxviii. 20).

Chapter XXXV
THE EUCHARIST AS A SACRIFICE: THE HOLY MASS

The New and the Old Sacrifice. We have spoken of the Holy Eucharist as a sacrament; now we will study it as a sacrifice, something entirely different. Christ, in anticipation of the crucifixion the next day, celebrated the feast of the Pasch, and at this typical sacrifice of the Old Law, instituted the great sacrifice of the New Law.

The Sacrifices of the Old Law. By way of introduction, a word may be said about sacrifices under the Old Law. God commanded the Jews to worship Him by sacrifices. These sacrifices are described in the Books of Exodus, Leviticus, Numbers, and Deuteronomy. He ordered that they should be offered in the Tabernacle alone and by a special priesthood. The sacrifices offered were the bloody sacrifices of animals, or the unbloody sacrifices or clean offerings of wine, bread, or other food.

Of the bloody sacrifices, the chief was the Holocaust, offered on the altar of Holocausts which stood outside the Tabernacle but within the inclosure; it was the great public act of Divine worship, and was offered up every day, morning and evening; after the blood had been poured out beside the altar the entire victim was burnt, to signify the supreme dominion of God over creatures. Bloody sacrifices were also offered to obtain forgiveness of sin (sacrifices for sin or trespass) or to praise and thank God and beg His blessings (sacrifices of peace). (Sheehan, p. 141.)

By offering sacrifices at the command of God, the Jews confessed that the creature is subject to his Creator, the one true God. The Jew joined himself with the victim, and made the offering of the blood, the seal of life of the animal, as the symbol of his own soul. The Lord said:

Because the life of the flesh is in the blood: and I have given it to you, that you may make atonement with it upon the altar for your souls, and the blood may be for an expiation of the soul (Lev. xvii. 11).

THE HOLY MASS

These sacrifices of the Old Law were types (figures, or images) of the sacrifice of Christ on the cross for our sins. When they were sincerely offered, they touched the heart of the individual and his will by his acknowledgment of his dependence on God, his own destiny, and his need for the forgiveness of sins, which under the Old Law he received when he made an act of perfect love or perfect contrition, even as we do now.

The Nature of Sacrifice. If we examine the sacrifices of the Old Law, the great public acts of divine worship, we can see several necessary parts in them. There was first a victim, a host, or oblation that was offered to God. It was offered visibly and outwardly by a priest at an altar. The sacrifice was made chiefly to acknowledge God's supreme dominion or ownership of man, that he is God's creature, or that he desired to be united to God in love or thanksgiving or praise, as the Source of his happiness. There are always victim, priest, altar, and sacrifice. By the sacrifice here we mean the offering of the victim to God in adoration and atonement. While confessing our complete subjection to God, and God's complete lordship over us, we may also wish to praise Him, to thank Him, to ask Him for something, or to satisfy Him for our sins. Hence, we have sacrifices of praise, thanksgiving, petition, and expiation or atonement.

The Sacrifice of the Cross. Christ was offered up, a sacrifice on the cross, a redemption for many. "He hath delivered Himself an oblation and a sacrifice to God," says St. Paul; and elsewhere he says "in whom we have redemption through His Blood, the remission of sins." So likewise St. Peter says, "Christ . . . died for our sins . . . swallowing down death, that we might be made heirs of life everlasting" (I Peter iii. 18–22). And so St. Paul, teaching that the sacrifices of the Old Law had given place to the sacrifice of the New Law, says: "If the blood of goats and of oxen . . . sanctify such as are defiled . . . how much more shall the Blood of Christ, who by the Holy Ghost offered Himself unspotted unto God, cleanse our conscience" (Heb. ix. 13–14).

A Perfect Sacrifice. As we think of the growth of religion, it must strike us what a great difference there is between the great sacrifice of the New Testament, and the sacrifices of the Old Testament. The sacrifice of the New Testament is a perfect sacrifice. It is pointed out clearly in the following passage:

> In the Sacrifice of the Cross, Christ was at once the priest and the victim, divinely chosen and appointed for each of these offices. He offered and surrendered His life to God, (1) to show that God was the Master of that most perfect life, and therefore, much more, of the lives of all other creatures; (2) to make atonement for sin; (3) to restore the lost gift of sanctifying grace; (4) to praise, thank, and glorify God. As a Priest, He offered His life to God; as a victim, He gave it. He was perfect as a Priest, because with His human and His Divine nature He was perfectly fitted to act as Mediator between God and man: from the perfection of His understanding and His Will, and from the infinite value of His acts, He, as Man, was able to offer to God on our behalf an adoration and an atonement so perfect that God forgot His anger, and placed once more within our reach the privileges of Divine sonship. He was perfect as a victim, not only because of His dignity as God and Man, but because He was a living, conscious victim, permitting His executioners to put Him to death, accepting to His last breath freely, fully, and with infinite love, every suffering inflicted on Him: "He was offered because it was His own will" (I lay down My life. . . . I lay it down of Myself, and I have power to lay it down). (Sheehan, p. 146.)

Institution of Sacrifice of the Mass. The Sacrifice of the Mass was instituted at the Last Supper; "This do in commemoration of Me." There were at the Last Supper the necessary elements of sacrifice as there was most clearly on Calvary and as there is in the Sacrifice of the Mass.

Last Supper, Calvary, and the Mass. The victim in all three cases is Christ, the Lord — at the Last Supper, on Calvary, in the Sacrifice of the Mass. At the Last Supper just as at the consecration of the Mass, the victim present is Christ, when the words are uttered:

>> THIS IS MY BODY.
>> THIS IS THE CHALICE OF MY BLOOD.

On Calvary the victim is the Crucified Christ.

There was present on all three occasions the same priest, Christ, the High Priest. He was in all three cases at the same time Priest and Victim. On Calvary and at the Last Supper He offered His life to God and as Victim He gave it. In the Mass, He is mystically present as the Priest, acting through an earthly priest, because the Mass is not a new sacrifice; it is the sacrifice of the cross. It is a display of divine power.

The Victim, Christ, is offered up to God by the High Priest, Christ, at the Last Supper, on Calvary, and in the Mass, for the same purposes: for the [eternal] life of the world and "for the remission of sin." The words used in the Canon of the Mass are full of meaning here. "We [the priest and the people] . . . offer unto Thy most excellent Majesty . . . a pure Victim, a holy Victim, an unspotted Victim, the Holy Bread of Eternal Life and the Chalice of Everlasting Salvation." On the cross, Christ was offered up in a bloody manner, and at the Last Supper and in the Mass, He is offered in an unbloody manner. The sacrifice is made to God in satisfaction for our sins and for our redemption. The Priest and Victim is the Son of God in whom God was well pleased.

The Sacrifice of the Mass and the Sacrifice on Calvary. In the Mass, through the consecration of the priest, a power given by Christ, the bread and the wine are changed into the Body and Blood of Christ. Transubstantiation takes place. The Mass is essentially this fact and the offering of the Body and Blood of Christ. It is the unbloody sacrifice of the Body and Blood of Christ. The Mass is the same sacrifice as that of the cross. This is so because as we have seen, the offering or Victim and the Priest are the same, Christ, our Blessed Lord; and the ends for which the sacrifice of the Mass are offered are the same as the ends for which the sacrifice of the cross was made. These are:

1. To honor and glorify God.
2. To thank Him for all the graces bestowed on the whole world.
3. To satisfy God's justice for the sins of men.
4. To obtain all graces and blessings.

The manner in which the sacrifice is offered is different as, of course, it must be. On the cross Christ really shed His Blood and was really killed; in the Mass there is no real shedding of blood

THE HIGHWAY TO GOD

| GOSPEL SIDE | ALTAR CENTER | EPISTLE SIDE |

ORDER OF MASS

I. Introductory Service

(Mass of Catechumens)
A. PRAYER PART (Giving)

	Center	Epistle Side
	1. Prayers at foot of altar	2. *Introit*
	3. Kyrie	5. *Collect(s)*
	4. <u>Gloria</u>	
4. *Gospel*	B. INSTRUCTION PART (Receiving)	1. *Epistle*
5. *Sermon*	3. Prayer before Gospel	2. *Gradual* / *Alleluia* / *Tract* / *Sequence*
	6. <u>Nicene Creed</u>	

II. Eucharistic SACRIFICE
(Mass of Faithful)
A. OBLATION (Giving)

1. *Offertory verse*
2. Offering of bread
4. Offering of wine
6. Pray brethren
7. *Secret(s)*
8. Preface
9. Holy, Holy, Holy
   (bell rings three times)
10. (Canon) Memento for Church, living, saints
11. Oblation prayer (bell)
12. Consecration
    (bell rings six times)
13. Oblation prayer
14. Memento for dead, us sinners, all nature
15. Doxology and Amen

3. {Wine and water
5. Lavabo

B. BANQUET (Receiving)
1. Our Father
2. The Peace of the Lord
3. Lamb of God
4. Priest's Communion
   (bell rings three times)
5. Communion of people
6. First ablution
10. <u>Dismissal</u>
11. <u>Blessing</u>

7. 2nd ablution
8. *Comm. verse*
9. *Post-Comm.(s)*

12. Last Gospel

Parts in Italic vary. Parts underlined are sometimes left out. (Taken from the *St. Andrew's Missal*, courtesy of E. M. Lohmann Co.)

THE HOLY MASS

nor real death, because Christ can die no more; but the Sacrifice of the Mass, through the separate consecration of the bread and of the wine, represents His death on the cross.

The Mass of the Catechumens and the Mass of the Faithful. The Mass is made up of two essential parts: An introductory part called the Mass of the Catechumens, and the Mass proper, called the Mass of the Faithful. The first part of the Mass was the part which was attended by those who wished to be Christians and were being instructed. They were called "catechumens." They left the Church after the *Credo*. Only Christians, i.e., the faithful, could attend the Mass proper, the offering of the bread and wine, the consecration, and the Communion. The parts of the Mass classified under these two headings are:

A. Mass of the Catechumens

First Part: PREPARATION, from the Asperges to the Collect. Acts of Contrition, or the Purification of Love.

1. The Sprinkling of Holy Water.
2. The Sign of the Cross.
3. The Psalm Judica Me.
4. Public Confession.
5. The Priest ascends the Altar.
6. The Introit.
7. The Kyrie.
8. The Gloria.

Second Part: INSTRUCTION, from the Collect to the Credo. Acts of Faith, or the Enlightenment of Love.

1. The Collect or Prayers.
2. The Epistle, or sayings of the Prophets and Apostles.
3. The Gradual and Alleluia.
4. The Gospel, or sayings of our Lord.
5. The Sermon.
6. The Credo.

B. Mass of the Faithful

Third Part: OFFERTORY, from the Offering to the Preface. Acts of Self-Surrender, or the Oblation of Love.

1. The Offering of Bread and Wine.
2. The Incensing of the Offerings and of the Faithful.
3. Washing of the Hands.
4. Prayer to the Most Holy Trinity.
5. The Orate Fratres and Secret, with the Amen ratifying the Offertory.

Fourth Part: CONSECRATION, from the Preface to the Lord's Prayer. Acts of Hope, or the Sacrifice of Love.

1. The Preface to the Canon.
2. The Canon or Rite of Consecration.
3. Reading of the Diptychs.
4. Prayers preparatory to the Consecration.
5. The Transubstantiation and major Elevation.
6. Oblation of the Victim to God.
7. Reading of the Diptychs.
8. End of the Canon and Minor Elevation, with the Amen ratifying the prayers of the Canon.

Fifth Part: COMMUNION, from the Lord's Prayer to the Ablutions. Acts of Love. Participation of Love in the Sacrifice by receiving Christ immolated.

1. The Lord's Prayer and Libera Nos.
2. Breaking of the Host.
3. The Agnus Dei.
4. Prayers preparatory to the Communion.
5. Receiving of the Body and Blood of Our Lord, with the Amen of association — formerly uttered by the Congregation.

Sixth Part: THANKSGIVING, from the Communion to the end. Acts of Gratitude, or the Thanksgiving of Love.

1. Prayers during the Ablutions.
2. The Communion Antiphon, and Post-Communion.
3. The Ite Missa Est and Blessing.
4. The last Gospel.
5. Prayers at the foot of the Altar.
6. Canticle of the three Children.

Cardinal Newman on the Mass. One who understands does not wonder at Cardinal Newman's ecstasies regarding the Mass. When we really understand in our hearts and realize fully what the Mass is, we may say with Cardinal Newman:

To me nothing is so consoling, so piercing, so thrilling, so overcoming, as the Mass. . . . It is not a mere form of words — it is a great action, the greatest action that can be on earth. . . . Words are necessary, but as means, not as ends; they are not mere addresses to the throne of grace; they are instruments of what is far higher, of consecration, of sacrifice. They hurry on as if impatient to fulfill their mission. . . . Quickly they pass; because as the lightning which shineth from one part of heaven unto the other, so is the coming of the Son of Man. . . . And as Moses on the mountain, so we too "make haste and bow our heads to the earth, and adore." So we, all around, each in his place, look out for the great Advent. . . . Each in his place, with his own heart, with his own wants, with his own thoughts, with his own intention, with his own prayers, separate but concordant, watching what is going on, watching its progress, uniting in

DIVISION OF THE ECCLESIASTICAL YEAR

(A) CHRISTMAS CYCLE—MYSTERY OF THE INCARNATION

PREPARATION . . . . (*Purple vestments*)	I. **Advent** (4 Sundays) . . . . (*From 1st Sunday of Advent to Dec. 24.*)	4
CELEBRATION . . . . {CHRISTMAS {EPIPHANY (*White vestments*)	II. **Christmastide** (2 to 3 Sundays) . (*Dec. 24 to Jan. 14.*)	2
PROLONGATION . . . . . . (*Green vestments*)	III. **Time after the Epiphany** (6 Sundays) (*Jan. 14 to Septuagesima Sunday.*)	6

(B) EASTER CYCLE—MYSTERY OF THE REDEMPTION

PREPARATION (*Purple vest.*) {remote {near {immediate	I. **Septuagesima** (3 Sundays) . . . (*Septuagesima to Ash Wednesday.*) II. **Lent** (4 Sundays) . . . . (*Ash Wednesday to Passion Sunday.*) III. **Passiontide** (2 Sundays) . . . . (*Passion Sunday to Easter.*)	3 4 2
CELEBRATION . . . {EASTER {PENTECOST (*White and red vest.*)	IV. **Eastertide** (7 Sundays) . . . . (*Easter Sunday to Trinity Sunday.*)	7
PROLONGATION . . . . . . (*Green vest.*)	V. **Time after Pentecost** (24 Sundays) (*Trinity Sunday to Advent.*)	24
	Sundays = 52	

(Taken from *St. Andrew's Missal,* courtesy of E. M. Lohmann Co.)

its consummation; not painfully and hopelessly following a hard form of prayer from beginning to end, but, like a concert of musical instruments, each different, but concurring in a sweet harmony, we take our part with God's priest, supporting him, yet guided by him. There are little children there, and old men, and simple laborers, and students from seminaries, priests preparing for Mass, priests making their thanksgiving; there are innocent maidens, and there are penitent sinners; but out of these many minds rises one eucharistic hymn and the great Action is the measure and scope of it.

Assisting at Mass. If we understood what the Mass really is, if we could have Cardinal Newman's love for it, we would understand that we should assist at it with great interior recollection and piety and with every mark of respect and devotion. We should have the same feeling of solemnity and awe we would have had if we were at the foot of the cross on Calvary hill, when Christ hung upon it. We should offer the Mass to God for the same purpose for which it was said. During the Mass, with the help of the Missal, we should meditate on Christ's sufferings and death. We should as often as possible — every day if we can — go to Holy Communion.

Holy Eucharist as Sacrifice and Sacrament. There is a point that may escape us if we do not call special attention to it; that is, the Holy Eucharist as a Sacrament and the Holy Eucharist as a Sacrifice. The presence of Christ in the Holy Eucharist is certainly a great human consolation and a source of infinite graces. We know, too, that unless we eat of the Body and Blood of the Son of Man we have no life (grace) in us.

But the excellence of the Mass comes from the fact that it *is* the sacrifice of Calvary. We are at the foot of the cross with Mary. We are joined with Christ in His Offering of Himself and He works with us. He takes up our acts of adoration, thanksgiving, praise, petition, satisfaction, and atonement, and gives them infinite value through His mediation as the High Priest of the Sacrifice. "No work," says the *Catechism of the Council of Trent,* "can be performed by the faithful, so holy, so Divine as this tremendous mystery." The Mass, therefore, can never be done away with, and it seems right that the Church should command us, as it does, to join in the Sacrifice of the Mass at least on Sundays and holydays of obligation. The finest way of showing our Christian life is to combine the Holy Eucharist as Sacrament, and the Holy Eucharist as Sacrifice by receiving Communion at Mass. Do not get into the habit of receiving Communion without attending Mass, and above all do not think you can get along without Mass because you receive Holy Communion.

Reasons for Instituting the Holy Eucharist. If we were asked why Christ instituted the Holy Eucharist as sacrifice and as sacrament, we might answer from what we have said in the three chapters on the Holy Eucharist as follows:

1. To unite us to Himself and to nourish our souls with divine life.
2. To increase sanctifying grace, and all virtues in our soul.
3. To lessen our evil inclinations.
4. To be a pledge of everlasting life.
5. To fit our bodies for a glorious resurrection.
6. To continue the sacrifice of the cross in His Church.

Questions from the Catechism

Q. How do the priests exercise this power of changing bread and wine into the Body and Blood of Christ?
A. **The priests exercise this power of changing bread and wine into the Body and Blood of Christ through the words of consecration in the Mass, which are the words of Christ: This is My Body; this is My Blood.**

Q. When and where are the bread and wine changed into the Body and Blood of Christ?
A. **The bread and wine are changed into the Body and Blood of Christ at the consecration in the Mass.**

Q. What is the Mass?
A. **The Mass is the unbloody sacrifice of the Body and Blood of Christ.**

Q. What is a sacrifice?
A. **A sacrifice is the offering of an object by a priest to God alone, and the consuming of it to acknowledge that He is the Creator and Lord of all things.**

Q. Is the Mass the same sacrifice as that of the cross?
A. **The Mass is the same sacrifice as that of the cross.**

Q. How is the Mass the same sacrifice as that of the cross?
A. **The Mass is the same sacrifice as that of the cross because the offering and the priest are the same — Christ our Blessed Lord; and the ends for which the sacrifice of the Mass is offered are the same as those of the sacrifice of the cross.**

Q. What were the ends for which the sacrifice of the cross was offered?
A. **The ends for which the sacrifice of the cross was offered were: First, to honor and glorify God; second, to thank Him for all the graces bestowed on the whole world; third, to satisfy God's justice for the sins of men; fourth, to obtain all graces and blessings.**

Q. Is there any difference between the sacrifice of the cross and the sacrifice of the Mass?
A. **Yes; the manner in which the sacrifice is offered is different. On the cross Christ really shed His Blood and was really slain; in the Mass there is no real shedding of blood nor real death, because Christ can die no more; but the sacrifice of the Mass, through the separate consecration of the bread and the wine, represents His death on the cross.**

Q. How should we assist at Mass?
A. **We should assist at Mass with great interior recollection and piety and with every outward mark of respect and devotion.**

Q. Which is the best manner of hearing Mass?
A. **The best manner of hearing Mass is to offer it to God with the priest for the same purpose for which it is said, to meditate on Christ's sufferings and death, and to go to Holy Communion.**

Review Questions

1. Is the Holy Eucharist a sacrament?
2. What are the three necessary marks of a sacrament?
3. Who is the ordinary minister of the sacrament?
4. May anyone else administer this sacrament?
5. What is the necessary act done by the person administering this sacrament?
6. Is this part of a longer ceremony? What other acts are part of the ceremony?
7. What are the necessary words used in administering this sacrament?
8. Name now the two parts of the "outward sign" of this sacrament.

THE HOLY MASS

9. May this sacrament be received more than once?
10. Is this one of the sacraments that leaves a distinct mark on the soul?
11. Besides sanctifying grace what is the special grace of this sacrament?
12. What is ordinarily the condition of the soul when one receives the Holy Eucharist?
13. Justify calling the Holy Eucharist a sacrament of the living.

Quotation from the Bible

For the following quotation:
a) Identify the speaker.
b) State the conditions under which the statement was made.
c) Give the meaning.
d) Tell its significance.

"Do this for a commemoration of Me" (Luke xxii. 19).

Chapter XXXVI
CONFIRMATION

"Who when they were come, prayed for them that they might receive the Holy Ghost. For He was not yet come upon any of them: but they were only baptized in the name of the Lord Jesus. Then they laid their hands upon them, and they received the Holy Ghost" (Acts viii. 15–17).

Beginnings of Christian Life. Baptism enrolls each of us in the Church of Christ. We become Christians by baptism. To receive baptism is necessary to salvation. "Unless a man be born again of water and the Holy Ghost, he cannot enter into the kingdom of God" (John iii. 5). The progress of our lives as Christians began when we were baptized; afterwards we were nourished by Holy Communion for which we prepared by confession. We are now ready for a further growth in our spiritual life.

Soldiers of Christ. Then there came a time when the pastor thought we were ready to be further strengthened in our faith, and to receive new graces, and to be confirmed in the faith we received at baptism. We were to be confirmed; i.e., to receive the sacrament of confirmation. We were told we were to become, in a real sense, soldiers of Christ, ready to confess our Catholic faith without any fear of pain, torture, or even death. Confirmation makes us ready for battle, whereas in baptism we were enlisted in the service of Christ. It perfects and strengthens the grace we received in baptism. It makes us strong for combats. It strengthens us. It arms us and makes us ready for conflict. It will help make us perfect Christians.

A Memorable Day. We remember generally the day we were confirmed almost as well as the day upon which we first received Holy Communion. Sometimes these two sacraments are received the same day. The bishop was coming. We had been often and

CONFIRMATION

carefully examined on Christian doctrine by the pastor, especially on the chief mysteries of our faith, on our duties as Christians, and on the nature and the effect of confirmation. The pastor was satisfied. We were told we were ready. How excited we became. We looked forward to the coming of the bishop to confirm us, for a bishop is the ordinary minister of confirmation, not a priest, who may baptize, but not confirm. The day arrived.

Communion Before Confirmation. We went to confession Saturday afternoon and to Communion on that Sunday morning, because to receive confirmation worthily one must be in a state of grace. We were all dressed up for the occasion, which was to be held on Sunday afternoon.[1] We formed in our classroom to march in procession to the Church.

The Sponsor. Back of each person to be confirmed was a friend of his who had himself been confirmed, who was to act as his sponsor, a godfather for boys, a godmother for girls.

Everybody in the church sang the hymn *Veni Creator*, which translated into English is as follows:

> Come, O Creator, Spirit blest!
> And in our souls take up Thy rest;
> Come with Thy grace and heav'nly aid,
> To fill the hearts which Thou hast made.
>
> Great Paraclete, to Thee we cry:
> O highest gift of God most high!
> O fount of life, O fire of love!
> And solemn Unction from above.
>
> The sacred sev'nfold grace is thine
> Dread finger of the hand divine!
> The promise of the Father Thou!
> Who dost the tongue with pow'r endow.
>
> Our senses touch with light and fire;
> Our hearts with charity inspire;
> And with endurance from on high
> The weakness of our flesh supply.

---

[1] This sacrament may, of course, be conferred on any day of the week.

Far back our enemy repel,
And let Thy peace within us dwell,
So may we, having Thee for guide,
Turn from each hurtful thing aside.

Oh, but Thy grace on us bestow
The Father and the Son to know,
And evermore to hold confessed
Thyself of each the Spirit blest.

To God the Father praise be paid,
Praise to the Son, Who from the dead
Arose, and perfect praise to Thee,
O Holy Ghost eternally.

The Bishop's Sermon. Before the confirmation the bishop gave a very clear sermon in which he made plain that:

1. Everyone should be confirmed.
2. Confirmation is a source of many graces for the soul.
3. It makes us soldiers of Christ as baptism made us children of Christ.
4. Sponsors have a grave duty to help the confirmed live a good life and assist them in their spiritual struggles.
5. The persons confirmed should be very sorry for all their past sins and be filled with pure love of God. This will make richer graces flow to the confirmed.
6. The sacrament will help each of us as it helped the Apostles.
7. It is a sin to neglect confirmation, especially in these days when faith and morals are exposed to so many and such violent temptations.
8. The person confirmed, strengthened as he will be by the grace of God, will joyfully and openly practice his faith which is the best way of professing or declaring it. He will never be ashamed of it as he would never be ashamed of Christ. He would rather die than deny Him.

The Confirmation Ceremony. The bishop spread his hands over all who were to be confirmed, begging the Holy Ghost to descend on them and prayed that they may receive the seven gifts of the Holy Ghost. Then we marched up to the altar with our sponsor, and went, each of us, and knelt before the bishop, with the sponsor touching our right shoulder. Then the bishop laid his hands on us and made the sign of the cross with chrism on the forehead at the same time saying:

> I sign thee with the sign of the cross, and I confirm thee with the chrism of salvation; in the name of the Father, and of the Son, and of the Holy Ghost. Amen.

The holy chrism used in the confirmation ceremony is a mixture of olive oil and balsam consecrated by the bishop on Holy Thursday. Then the bishop struck us a gentle blow on the cheek, to remind us we were soldiers of Christ, and that we must be ready to receive blows or other trials for Him. His last words were *Pax tecum* (peace be with you).

The Effect on the Apostles. What may be expected from the graces of confirmation may be learned from what happened to the Apostles when they received the Holy Ghost. The effect on the Apostles of their receiving the Holy Ghost is thus told in the *Catechism of the Council of Trent*:

> So weak and timid were they before, and even at the very time of the Passion, that no sooner was our Lord apprehended, then they instantly fled, and Peter, who had been designated the rock and foundation of the Church, and who had displayed unshaken constancy and exalted magnanimity, terrified at the voice of one weak woman, denied, not once nor twice only, but a third time, that he was a disciple of Jesus Christ, and after the Resurrection they all remained shut up at home for fear of the Jews. But, on the day of Pentecost, so great was the power of the Holy Ghost with which they were all filled that, while they boldly and freshly disseminated the Gospel confided to them, not only through Judea, but throughout the world, they thought no greater happiness could await them than that of being accounted worthy to suffer contumely, chains, torments, and crucifixion, for the name of Christ (*Catechism of the Council of Trent*, p. 210).

Their strength is shown in the incident told in the New Testament. They were tried in prison. Gamaliel, a Pharisee, a doctor of the law, pleaded for them. As a result of Gamaliel's plea, this is what happened and this is what the Apostles did:

> And calling in the Apostles, after they had scourged them, they charged

them that they should not speak at all in the name of Jesus; and they dismissed them.

And they indeed went from the presence of the council, rejoicing that they were accounted worthy to suffer reproach for the name of Jesus.

And every day they ceased not in the temple, and from house to house, to teach and preach Christ Jesus (Acts. v. 40–42).

Christ Instituted Confirmation. Christ instituted the sacrament of confirmation, though the time and place is not told in the New Testament. It was practiced from the very beginning by the Apostles. It fulfilled the promises which Christ made that He would send the Holy Ghost. This shows that the New Testament is not a complete history of what Christ did on earth, as the Gospel according to St. Luke says. Find the passage. We read in the New Testament, for example, that Peter and John confirmed the Samarians:

Now when the Apostles, who were in Jerusalem, and heard that Samaria had received the word of God, they sent unto them Peter and John.

Who, when they were come, prayed for them, that they might receive the Holy Ghost.

For He was not as yet come upon any of them: but they were only baptized in the name of the Lord Jesus.

Then they laid their hands upon them, and they received the Holy Ghost (Acts viii. 14–17).

It is thought that during the forty days after the Resurrection Christ taught the Apostles the object of the sacrament and instituted it. It is to this sacrament that Christ refers, when speaking to the Apostles in the Gospel according to St. Luke, He said, "Stay you in the city, till you be endued with power from on high" (Luke xxiv. 49).

The Outward Sign. If we look back over the ceremonies performed at confirmation we see that confirmation has all the other marks of a sacrament in addition to institution by Christ.

1. There is an outward sign.
    a) Matter. The laying on of hands, and signing the forehead with chrism with the cross.
    b) Form. I sign thee with the sign of the cross and I confirm thee with the chrism of salvation; in the name

of the Father, and of the Son, and of the Holy Ghost. Amen.

Chrism. Chrism is a mixture of oil and balsam consecrated by the bishop at another time. This mixture is a sign of the blessings of the sacrament. It strengthens as oil does, and it heals and preserves as balsam. We may say of the confirmed with the Apostle: They "are unto God, the good odor of Christ."

The Form of the Sacrament. The form of the sacrament of confirmation is significant for three things. First, for the divine power which operates in the sacrament, indicated by the words at the end of the form, *"in the name of the Father, and of the Son, and of the Holy Ghost. Amen."* Second, for the strength of soul even unto salvation, as shown in the middle group of words: *"I confirm thee with the chrism of salvation."* Third and finally, for the sign which is made on his forehead by the bishop and in his soul by Christ, as becomes a soldier of Christ, as shown in the opening words of the form: *"I sign thee with the sign of the cross."*

The Mark in the Soul. This sacrament is one of three sacraments that leave a mark in the soul; the seal of your Master and King, Christ. This mark is indelible. It cannot be wiped out. It marks you as a soldier of Christ. If you live up to that high honor, it will be well with you, here in the things worth while, and hereafter, in eternal things. This mark in confirmation is given us, once for all, and hence this sacrament is not repeated.

Inward Grace. Confirmation confers grace. It increases sanctifying grace, purifying and perfecting the life of the soul. It gives sacramental graces, the special spiritual strength and courage to profess the faith and die for it if necessary. It gives us a right to actual graces in time of need. It generally makes us strong and guides us on the Highway to God. If we study the lives of the Apostles, it will be clear what we may expect from this sacrament if we receive it worthily, and with the right disposition. We receive the gifts and the fruits of the Holy Ghost.

Gifts of the Holy Ghost. The gifts of the Holy Ghost are seven in number as listed by the prophet Isaiah; four tend to take away ignorance from the soul, and three tend to heal the wounds of sin in the soul.

Gift of Wisdom. We receive the gift of Wisdom to give us a liking for the things of God, and to direct our whole life and all our actions to His honor and glory.

Gift of Understanding. We receive the gift of Understanding to make us able to know more clearly the mysteries of faith.

Gift of Counsel. We receive the gift of Counsel to warn us of the deceits of the devil and of the dangers to salvation.

Gift of Fortitude. We receive the gift of Fortitude to strengthen us to do the will of God in all things.

Gift of Knowledge. We receive the gift of Knowledge to make us able to discover the will of God in all things.

Gift of Piety. We receive the gift of Piety to make us love God as a Father and obey Him because we love Him.

Gift of Fear of the Lord. We receive the gift of Fear of the Lord to fill us with a dread of sin.

Fruits of the Holy Ghost. The fruits of the Holy Ghost are twelve in number.

Three relate specifically to God:
  Charity, the perfect love of God;
  Joy, the joy in doing good for love of God;
  Peace, the peace of God, which surpasseth all understanding.
Six relate to our neighbor:
  Patience, bearing with others, including resignation;
  Benignity, sweetness of temper and disposition, gentleness, compassion;
  Goodness, willingness to serve, readiness to sacrifice;
  Longanimity, calmness in trial, perseverance in well-doing;
  Faith, truthfulness, trustfulness, candor, fidelity;
  Mildness, "A soft answer turneth away wrath."
Three relate especially to ourselves:
  Modesty, reserve, unassuming demeanor, sympathy;
  Continency, self-control, repression of anger, impatience, and sensuality;
  Chastity, purity of soul.

Questions from the Catechism

Q. What is confirmation?
A. **Confirmation is a sacrament through which we receive the Holy**

CONFIRMATION

Ghost to make us strong and perfect Christians and soldiers of Jesus Christ.

Q. Who administers confirmation?
A. The bishop is the ordinary minister of confirmation.

Q. How does the bishop give confirmation?
A. The bishop extends his hands over those who are to be confirmed, prays that they may receive the Holy Ghost, and anoints the forehead of each with holy chrism in the form of a cross.

Q. What is holy chrism?
A. Holy chrism is a mixture of olive oil and balsam consecrated by the bishop.

Q. What does the bishop say in anointing the person he confirms?
A. In anointing the person he confirms the bishop says: I sign thee with the sign of the cross, and I confirm thee with the chrism of salvation, in the name of the Father, and of the Son, and of the Holy Ghost.

Q. What is meant by anointing the forehead with chrism in the form of a cross?
A. By anointing the forehead with chrism in the form of a cross is meant, that the Christian who is confirmed must openly profess and practice his faith, never be ashamed of it, and rather die than deny it.

Q. Why does the bishop give the person he confirms a slight blow on the cheek?
A. The bishop gives the person he confirms a slight blow on the cheek, to put him in mind that he must be ready to suffer everything, even death, for the sake of Christ.

Q. To receive confirmation worthily is it necessary to be in the state of grace?
A. To receive confirmation worthily it is necessary to be in the state of grace.

Q. What special preparation should be made to receive confirmation?
A. Persons of an age to learn should know the chief mysteries of faith and the duties of a Christian, and be instructed in the nature and effects of this sacrament.

Q. What are the effects of confirmation?
A. The effects of confirmation are an increase of sanctifying grace, the strengthening of our faith, and the gifts of the Holy Ghost.

Q. Which are the gifts of the Holy Ghost?
A. **The gifts of the Holy Ghost are Wisdom, Understanding, Counsel, Fortitude, Knowledge, Piety, and Fear of the Lord.**

Q. Why do we receive the gift of Fear of the Lord?
A. **We receive the gift of Fear of the Lord to fill us with the dread of sin.**

Q. Why do we receive the gift of Piety?
A. **We receive the gift of Piety to make us love God as a Father and obey Him because we love Him.**

Q. Why do we receive the gift of Knowledge?
A. **We receive the gift of Knowledge to enable us to discover the will of God in all things.**

Q. Why do we receive the gift of Fortitude?
A. **We receive the gift of Fortitude to strengthen us to do the will of God in all things.**

Q. Why do we receive the gift of Counsel?
A. **We receive the gift of Counsel to warn us of the deceits of the devil, and of the dangers to salvation.**

Q. Why do we receive the gift of Understanding?
A. **We receive the gift of Understanding to enable us to know more clearly the mysteries of faith.**

Q. Why do we receive the gift of Wisdom?
A. **We receive the gift of Wisdom to give us a relish for the things of God, and to direct our whole life and all our actions to His honor and glory.**

Q. Which are the twelve fruits of the Holy Ghost?
A. **The twelve fruits of the Holy Ghost are Charity, Joy, Peace, Patience, Benignity, Goodness, Long-Suffering, Mildness, Faith, Modesty, Continency, and Chastity.**

Problem Questions

1. Mr. Smith is a convert. He cannot understand why confirmation is necessary, and therefore, constantly puts it off until next year. Is he guilty of sin? Why is he especially in need of the sacrament of confirmation?

2. John Williams was to be confirmed Pentecost afternoon. He went to confession the day before and intended to receive Holy Communion the next morning. Sunday morning, however, John thoughtlessly took a drink of water. May John be confirmed? Why?

3. Bill Fox was confirmed last Tuesday afternoon but he had not heeded

the priest's advice to go to confession the day before. Now, two Sundays ago, Bill went fishing and had deliberately not attended Mass. Did Bill receive the sacrament of confirmation? Explain. Of what sins is he guilty? Why?

4. Ray Crowley was confirmed because his friends urged him to be, but before the ceremonies Ray said to himself, "I'll just go through with it for their sakes." Did he receive the sacrament of confirmation? Explain.

5. Shirley Bolley had been given three names in baptism and refused to take another in confirmation. Discuss.

6. On Albert Barton's confirmation day the street car was delayed by a snowstorm and so he was late. He came into Church just after the bishop's first prayer and imposition of hands. Did he receive the sacrament of confirmation? Explain.

7. Mary Lee fainted just after the priest had wiped the chrism from her forehead. She was carried out of church and was unable to return for the last solemn blessing. Has she received the sacrament of confirmation? Explain.

8. In China, Father Henry confers the sacrament of confirmation. Why can he administer this sacrament?

9. In the bishop's sermon on William's confirmation day, the bishop said to those who were confirmed: "Now you are soldiers of Christ." What did he mean?

Review Questions

1. Is confirmation a sacrament?
2. What are the three necessary marks of a sacrament?
3. Who is the ordinary minister of the sacrament?
4. May anyone else administer this sacrament? If so, under what conditions?
5. What is the necessary act done by the person administering this sacrament?
6. Is this part of a longer ceremony? What other acts are part of the ceremony?
7. What are the necessary words used in administering this sacrament?
8. Name now the two parts of the "outward sign" of this sacrament.
9. May this sacrament be received more than once? Can it?
10. Is this one of the sacraments that leaves a distinct mark on the soul?
11. Besides sanctifying grace what is the grace peculiar to this sacrament?
12. What is ordinarily the condition of the soul when one receives confirmation?
13. Justify calling confirmation a sacrament of the living.

Quotations from the Bible

To what incident does the following description refer?
Who was present?
What is the significance of the event?

"And when the days of the Pentecost were accomplished, they were all together in one place:

"And suddenly there came a sound from heaven, as of a mighty wind coming, and it filled the whole house where they were sitting.

"And there appeared to them parted tongues as it were of fire, and it sat upon every one of them.

"And they were all filled with the Holy Ghost, and they began to speak with divers tongues, according as the Holy Ghost gave them to speak" (Acts ii. 1–4).

"When the Apostles, who were in Jerusalem, had heard that Samaria had received the Word of God; they sent unto them Peter and John. Who, when they were come, prayed for them, that they might receive the Holy Ghost. For He was not as yet come upon any of them; but they were only baptized in the name of the Lord Jesus. Then they laid their hands upon them, and they received the Holy Ghost" (Acts viii. 14–17).

Chapter XXXVII
MATRIMONY

"From the beginning of the creation, God made them male and female. For this cause a man shall leave his father and mother; and shall cleave to his wife. And they two shall be in one flesh. Therefore now they are not two, but one flesh. What therefore God hath joined together, let not man put asunder" (Mark x. 6–9).

A Christian Family. One of the finest pictures of human life is a Christian family in which there is love; father and mother living in perfect harmony, tenderly caring for children, and guiding them through life until perhaps they have families of their own: children, on the other hand, returning this love of parents by faithful obedience to them, and by doing little services for them out of love. Such a happy family with God's grace has its beginning in the sacrament of matrimony.

The Sacrament of Matrimony. The sacrament of matrimony is the sacrament of marriage; it is the sacrament in which a Christian man and woman become husband and wife.

Marriage in Old and New Testament. Marriage between man and woman was instituted by God Himself in the Garden of Eden. In the first book of the Bible, Genesis, will be found the account of it.

And the Lord God built the rib which He took from Adam into a woman: and brought her to Adam.
And Adam said: This now is bone of my bones, and flesh of my flesh; she shall be called woman, because she was taken out of man.
Wherefore a man shall leave father and mother and shall cleave to his wife: and they shall be two in one flesh (Gen. ii. 22–24).

Christ spoke of this passage in answer to a question from the Pharisees, as follows, as told in the Gospel according to St. Matthew.

And there came to Him the Pharisees tempting Him, and saying: Is it lawful for a man to put away his wife for every cause?

Who answering, said to them: Have ye not read, that He who made man from the beginning, made them male and female? And He said:

For this cause shall a man leave father and mother, and shall cleave to his wife, and they two shall be in one flesh.

Therefore now they are not two, but one flesh. What therefore God hath joined together, let no man put asunder.

They say to Him: Why then did Moses command to give a bill of divorce, and to put away?

He saith to them: Because Moses by reason of the hardness of your heart permitted you to put away your wives; but from the beginning it was not so.

And I say to you, that whosoever shall put away his wife, except it be for fornication, and shall marry another, committeth adultery: and he that shall marry her that is put away, committeth adultery (Matt. xix. 3-9).

So in this chapter we will study marriage and the sacrament of matrimony. For you this is not an immediate problem though it is an important one. You should understand the main points about this problem, so that if it comes to you in later years, you will understand its importance, its seriousness, and will pray for guidance in your choice of a husband or a wife, and realize the very great responsibility that is undertaken.

God Instituted Marriage. After the Fall of Man, marriage became changed. Among pagans, woman was brought down to a state of degradation. Christ restored marriage to its first condition and raised it to the dignity of a sacrament. St. Paul, in his letter to the Ephesians, says it is a great sacrament. Thus, in the first years of the Church it was taught and tradition teaches that Christ established marriage as a sacrament. Some think it was when He said, "What God hath joined, let no man put asunder," and some think it was during the forty days after the resurrection when He appeared to His disciples "speaking of the kingdom of God."

The Ministers of the Sacrament. In the sacrament of matrimony, by a very happy and beautiful provision, the persons about to be married are the ministers of the sacrament. The Church requires a priest present as an official witness, for the validity of the contract and of the sacrament. It takes the extra care too of requiring two other witnesses.

The Outward Sign. The two persons ready and consenting to the contract of marriage are the matter of the outward sign of the sacrament. The words of consent, "I do," are the form of the outward sign of the sacrament.

> Do you take this woman to be your lawful wife?
> I do.
> Do you take this man to be your lawful husband?
> I do.

This outward sign of the true sacrament increases in the soul sanctifying grace and gives besides the sacramental grace of this sacrament.

Matrimony a Sacrament of the Living. Matrimony is one of the sacraments of the living. To receive it worthily one must be in a state of grace. This, of course, means practically a worthy confession and Holy Communion. The commandments of the Church about matrimony are stated in the chapter on the Commandments of the Church.

Actual Graces of Matrimony. Where the sacrament has been received worthily, and no impediment exists and no disposition of the person prevents, there comes to the married couple the special graces of this sacrament. The first of these is to bear the weaknesses of each other and the troubles of this state of life; the difference of temper and disposition, ill health, and sickness should it come, poverty if need be, and the everyday duties of husband and wife. A second grace is to sanctify the love of the husband and wife, to help them to love and be faithful to each other, and to overcome jealousies, sin, or misery in the family. A third grace, in the most difficult duty of married life, though with the richest reward in loving children, if successful, is the grace to have the love, patience, and skill to bring up the children "the way they should go." This will include the duties of instructing them, correcting bad habits or evil manners, of watching over their company, their reading, and their other activities that no evil thing or sin befall them. The children must understand that it is the duty of the parents to do this, and it is their duty not only to help them but to do so willingly, because in the creation of the family God put this duty on parents for which He will hold them responsible.

Marriage is Indissoluble. Christ raised the marriage contract to the great dignity of a sacrament. He made it *the* way a Christian man and woman should be joined in marriage. The state may make laws for the civil effects of marriage, but it is only in the sacrament of matrimony that a Christian man and woman can be joined in lawful marriage. Christ not only raised the marriage relationship to the dignity of a sacrament, but He made it indissoluble by any human power.

"What God hath joined together, let no man put asunder."

Questions from the Catechism

Q. What is the sacrament of matrimony?
A. **The sacrament of matrimony is the sacrament which unites a Christian man and woman in lawful marriage.**

Q. Can a Christian man or woman be united in lawful marriage in any other way than by the sacrament of matrimony?
A. **A Christian man and woman cannot be united in lawful marriage in any other way than by the sacrament of matrimony, because Christ raised marriage to the dignity of a sacrament.**

Q. Can the bond of Christian marriage be dissolved by any human power?
A. **The bond of Christian marriage cannot be dissolved by any human power.**

Q. Which are the effects of the sacrament of matrimony?
A. **The effects of the sacrament of matrimony are: First, to sanctify the love of husband and wife; second, to give them grace to bear with each other's weaknesses; third, to enable them to bring up their children in the fear and love of God.**

Q. To receive the sacrament of matrimony worthily is it necessary to be in the state of grace?
A. **To receive the sacrament of matrimony worthily it is necessary to be in the state of grace, and it is necessary also to comply with the laws of the Church.**

Q. Why do many marriages prove unhappy?

MATRIMONY

A. Many marriages prove unhappy because they are entered into hastily and without worthy motives.

Q. How should Christians prepare for a holy and happy marriage?

A. **Christians should prepare for a holy and happy marriage by receiving the sacraments of penance and Holy Eucharist, by begging God to grant them a pure intention and to direct their choice; and by seeking the advice of their parents and the blessing of their pastor.**

Problem Questions

1. When fourteen years of age, Marie Carron was very ill with a lingering illness. After a long deliberation and prayer she vowed to enter a religious order should she recover. Marie got well and later felt sorry for having made the vow because she wished to marry. What should Marie do? Discuss Marie's vow.

2. From childhood Joe Segers said when it came for him to marry he would not have the banns of matrimony published because he disliked the publicity. Why does the Church insist upon the publication of the banns? If necessary, how may one be excused from the publication of the banns?

3. After careful consideration and much prayer, Louise Koch and Leonard Neil present themselves before the priest to take each other, "to have and to hold, from this day forward, for better, for worse, for richer, for poorer, in sickness, and in health" until death doth them part. Who administers the sacrament of matrimony? Explain. For how long do Louise and Leonard promise to be faithful to each other?

4. Mr. and Mrs. Borden had been married ten years when suddenly Mr. Borden became a raving maniac. Mrs. Borden had four children for whom it was very difficult to provide. A very favorable opportunity for a second marriage offered itself to Mrs. Borden and she desired to marry since there was no hope for her husband's recovery. May Mrs. Borden obtain a divorce and remarry? Discuss. When does the Church permit separation? Under what conditions may a Catholic be married a second time?

Review Questions

1. Is matrimony a sacrament?
2. What are the three necessary marks of a sacrament?
3. Who is the ordinary minister of the sacrament?
4. May anyone else administer this sacrament?
5. What is the necessary act done by the person administering this sacrament?
6. Is this part of a longer ceremony? What other acts are part of the ceremony?

7. What are the necessary words used in administering this sacrament?

8. Name now the two parts of the "outward sign" of this sacrament.

9. May this sacrament be received more than once? Under what conditions?

10. Is this one of the sacraments that leaves a distinct mark on the soul?

11. Besides sanctifying grace, what is the special grace of this sacrament?

12. What is ordinarily the condition of the soul when one receives the sacrament of matrimony?

13. Justify calling matrimony a sacrament of the living.

Quotations from the Bible

For each of the following quotations:

a) Identify the speaker.

b) State the conditions under which the statement was made.

c) Give the meaning.

d) Tell its significance.

"This now is bone of my bones, and flesh of my flesh; she shall be called woman, because she was taken out of man.

"Wherefore a man shall leave father and mother and shall cleave to his wife: and they shall be two in one flesh" (Gen. ii. 22–24).

"What therefore God hath joined together, let no man put asunder" (Matt. xix. 6).

To what incident does the following description refer?

Who was present?

What is the significance of the event?

"From the beginning of the Creation, God made them male and female. For this cause a man shall leave his father and mother; and shall cleave to his wife. And they two shall be in one flesh. Therefore now they are not two, but one flesh. What, therefore, God hath joined together, let no man put asunder" (Mark x. 6–9).

Chapter XXXVIII
EXTREME UNCTION

"Is any man sick among you? Let him bring in the priests of the Church, and let them pray over him, anointing him with oil in the name of the Lord. And the prayer of faith shall save the sick man: and the Lord shall raise him up: and if he be in sins, they shall be forgiven him" (James v. 14–15).

Statement in St. Mark. When Christ sent His disciples, two and two, before Him, He clearly indicated this sacrament which St. James later states more fully. In the Gospel of St. Mark we are told about these disciples whom Christ sent before Him that "Going forth they preached that men should do penance. And they cast out many devils, and anointed with oil many that were sick, and healed them" (Mark vi. 12–13).

St. James's Statement. The specific statement of the sacrament of extreme unction is made by St. James, the Apostle:

Is any man sick among you? Let him bring in the priests of the Church, and let them pray over him anointing him with oil in the name of the Lord. And the prayer of faith shall save the sick man: and the Lord shall raise him up: and if he be in sins, they shall be forgiven him (James v. 14).

Here, we have all the necessary facts about the sacrament, and a clear statement of its divine power in the forgiveness of sin.

The Sacrament of Extreme Unction. This sacrament has also been called the "Sacrament of the Anointing of the Sick," as well as the "Sacrament of the Dying," which indicate its general character. Extreme unction is the sacrament which, through the anointing and prayer of the priest, gives health and strength to the soul, and sometimes to the body, when we are in danger of death from sickness or other causes such as wounds or accidents.

If we understand the meaning of *unction,* i.e., the act of anointing as with oil, we see that this sacrament is truly the extreme, the last or final anointing to be given. This is true because only persons who are sick may receive the sacrament, and they must be in danger of death.

There Should be no Delay. It should under no circumstances be delayed until all hope of recovery is lost, or life begins to ebb, but should be administered while the person is conscious and has his reason. For the sacrament was instituted not only as a cure for the diseases of the soul, but also for those of the body. If administered in this way the more active coöperation of the sick person may be expected, and the more abundant graces be received, and the bodily as well as the spiritual effects of the sacrament be gained. If the person recovers as he often does, the sacrament may be received again when the person is again in danger of death.

The Essentials of the Sacrament. The priest is the minister of the sacrament of extreme unction. In the anointing he uses olive oil and no other kind. The oil has been blessed by the bishop on Holy Thursday. This he applies to the organs of sense — eyes (sight), ears (hearing), nostrils (smell), mouth (taste and speech), hands (touch), and to the feet, by which we move from place to place. This is the *matter* of the sacrament. He says a prayer when anointing: "Through this holy unction and His own most tender mercy, may the Lord pardon thee whatever sins or faults thou hast committed by sight" (and so on, for other senses). This is the *form* of the sacrament. It increases sanctifying grace in the soul, and takes away sin. In the administration of the sacrament, special prayers are also offered for the recovery of the sick person. "All who are present, and especially the pastor, should pour out their fervent aspirations to God and earnestly commend to His mercy the life and salvation of the sufferer."

Confession and Communion as Preparation. The most terrifying thing that could possibly take hold of a man in danger of death is the knowledge that he has mortal sin on his soul. One who is in the state of mortal sin must confess his sins and

EXTREME UNCTION

receive the sacrament of penance before receiving extreme unction, if it is possible for him to do so. If he cannot confess his sins, he should try to make an act of perfect contrition. However, extreme unction takes away even mortal sins for which one has at least imperfect contrition, when he is not able to confess them. When possible, after confession, the priest gives Holy Communion to the sick person before he administers the sacrament of extreme unction. This is, of course, an excellent thing for both body and soul. Why for soul? Why for body? But here, as always in life, the salvation of the soul should be the first thought of the sick man, and after that the health of the body, if it be for the good of the soul.

Use of Oil in the Sacrament. The use of oil is full of meaning because of the natural effects of oil. "Oil is very efficacious in soothing bodily pain, and the power of the sacrament lessens the pain and anguish of the soul. Oil restores health, brings joy, feeds light, and is very efficacious in refreshing bodily fatigue. All these effects signify what the divine power accomplishes in the sick man through the administration of the sacrament" (*Catechism of the Council of Trent,* p. 309).

This Sacrament in the Form of a Prayer. It should be noted that the other sacraments signify what they express and are pronounced by way of prayer. In baptism, the form is definite, "I baptize thee"; and so in confirmation, "I sign thee with the sign of the cross"; in holy orders, the form is, "Receive power." In extreme unction the form is the prayers for the spiritual grace and the recovery of health which is often granted.

Helps Remove Fear of Death. This sacrament has a number of noteworthy effects. It increases sanctifying grace, takes away venial sins and sometimes also mortal sins, and strengthens the soul to overcome the temptations of the devil at the hour of death. *It helps remove the dread of the fear of death.* One cannot help but note even the strength that comes to the body in a sick person after the administration of the sacrament of extreme unction after confession and Holy Communion. Spirits are higher, and true spiritual peace comes, and if death comes in its course, the assurance is: "Blessed are the dead who die in the Lord."

Other Effects. The purposes of the sacrament of extreme unction have been summarized as follows:

1. To comfort us in the pains of sickness and to strengthen us against temptation.

2. To remit sins and to cleanse our soul from the remains of sin; i.e., from the inclination to evil and the weakness of the will which are the result of sin and which remain after our sins have been forgiven.

3. To restore us to health when God sees fit.

Questions from the Catechism

Q. What is the sacrament of extreme unction?
A. **Extreme unction is the sacrament which through the anointing and prayer of the priest gives health and strength to the soul, and sometimes to the body, when we are in danger of death from sickness.**

Q. When should we receive extreme unction?
A. **We should receive extreme unction when we are in danger of death from sickness, or from a wound or accident.**

Q. Should we wait until we are in extreme danger before we receive extreme unction?
A. **We should not wait until we are in extreme danger before we receive extreme unction, but if possible we should receive it while we have the use of our senses.**

Q. Which are the effects of the sacrament of extreme unction?
A. **The effects of extreme unction are: First, to comfort us in the pains of sickness and to strengthen us against temptations; second, to remit venial sins and to cleanse our soul from the remains of sin; third, to restore us to health, when God sees fit.**

Q. What do you mean by the remains of sin?
A. **By the remains of sin I mean the inclination to evil and the weakness of the will which are the result of our sins, and which remain after our sins have been forgiven.**

Q. How should we receive the sacrament of extreme unction?
A. **We should receive the sacrament of extreme unction in the**

EXTREME UNCTION

state of grace, and with lively faith and resignation to the will of God.

Q. Who is the minister of the sacrament of extreme unction?
A. **The priest is the minister of the sacrament of extreme unction.**

Problem Questions

1. Arleen Kelly's father died some years ago. Her father was very ill and no hope of recovery was entertained. She notified their pastor and her brother went to bring him. While waiting for the priest she covered a small table with a white linen cloth, placed a crucifix between two candles, and arranged a glass of water, a bottle of holy water, a napkin, a tablespoon, five little balls of cotton, and a little piece of bread neatly on the table. When the priest came, Arleen met him at the door with a lighted candle, for she knew her father was to receive Viaticum also. For a little while they left their father alone with the priest while he made his last confession. Her father then received the Holy Viaticum. After a few prayers and a few words of consolation, the priest took the oils he had brought with him and made the sign of the cross on the dying man's eyes, ears, nose, lips, hands, and feet while he repeated the prayer, "Through this Holy Unction and His most tender mercy may the Lord forgive thee whatever sins thou hast committed by sight, hearing," etc.

What is the purpose of each article Arleen placed upon the table? What is the meaning of the oil used in administering the sacrament of extreme unction? Why does the priest anoint the five sense organs? What is the meaning of the prayer the priest says while anointing each member? Why should one, if possible, go to bring the priest?

2. Some people have a false notion about the reception of extreme unction. They think that when one has received the sacrament of extreme unction he is sure to die, or that the priest is called when death is certain. What is the purpose of the sacrament?

3. A person feels great peace and joy after receiving the sacrament of extreme unction. This is clear to every member of his family. What is one of the effects of the sacrament of extreme unction? Why is a holy person sometimes filled with anxiety on his deathbed.

4. All hope for the recovery of Roger Stanton had been lost. The priest was called, and immediately after the administration of the sacrament of extreme unction a decided change in the patient was noticeable. Roger did not die, but a change for the better took place and it was a matter of only a few weeks before Roger was around again. What is another effect of the sacrament of extreme unction? Why is it foolish to think that death is absolutely imminent when the sacrament of extreme unction is administered?

Review Questions

1. Is extreme unction a sacrament?
2. What are the three necessary marks of a sacrament?
3. Who is the ordinary minister of the sacrament?
4. May anyone else administer this sacrament?
5. What is the necessary act done by the person administering this sacrament?
6. Is this part of a longer ceremony? What other acts are part of the ceremony?
7. What are the necessary words used in administering this sacrament?
8. Name now the two parts of the "outward sign" of this sacrament.
9. May this sacrament be received more than once?
10. Is this one of the sacraments that leaves a distinct mark on the soul?
11. Besides sanctifying grace what is the special grace of this sacrament?
12. What is ordinarily the condition of the soul when one receives extreme unction?
13. Justify calling extreme unction a sacrament of the living.

Quotations from the Bible

For each of the following quotations:
a) Identify the speaker.
b) State the conditions under which the statement was made.
c) Give the meaning.
d) Tell its significance.

"Is any man sick among you? Let him bring in the priests of the Church, and let them pray over him, anointing him with oil in the name of the Lord. And the prayer of faith shall save the sick man: and the Lord shall raise him up: and if he be in sins, they shall be forgiven him" (James v. 14–15).

"Going forth they preached that men should do penance: And they cast out many devils, and anointed with oil many that were sick, and healed them" (Mark vi. 12–13).

Chapter XXXIX
HOLY ORDERS

"Do this for a commemoration of Me" (*Luke xxii. 19*).

Why Christ Came. "I am come in the name of the Father," said Christ. He came as He says elsewhere, not to do His own will, but the will of the Father. And as St. John has it, "Now this is eternal life: that they may know Thee, the only true God, and Jesus Christ, whom Thou hast sent" (John xvii. 3).

Christ Carrying on His Work. So Christ, after living thirty years in the bosom of the Holy Family in Nazareth, starts His public life of three years. He went about, as we have seen, and chose twelve men called Apostles. They were not great men of the earth, but He chose them to carry on His work. A little later He took seventy-two others. To the Father in heaven, He said of these men: "As Thou hast sent Me into the world, I also have sent them into the world" (John xvii. 18). He told them: "He that receiveth you, receiveth Me, and he that receiveth Me, receiveth Him that sent Me" (Matt. x. 40).

The Church. The society which Christ established to carry on His work we know as the Roman Catholic Church. There had to be someone to take the place of the Apostles. The grace which came through the Church had to have someone to pass it on. Every society must have persons to carry on its work, perform its services, so as to reach its purpose. The persons who carry on the principal work of the Church are priests and bishops.

Persons to Administer Church. It is, of course, very important that the persons who are to perform the services of the Church should be of the highest character and possess special knowledge. The highest and best human beings, as indeed all human beings, should serve God, but it is of special importance that they should be enlisted in the special service of God in the administration of the Church. They should be men of holiness of life, of knowledge, of prudence, of faith.

Qualities of Priesthood. We say that a person must have a divine call to enter the priesthood. He must feel a desire and have the purpose to enter the priesthood in order to serve God, and his fellow men for God, and to save his own soul. He must be accepted by the bishop. Though the priest must be supported by the Church, his support is, of course, no part of his reason for becoming a priest. To become a priest for the sake of gain or money is one of the greatest of sins, which we call a sacrilege. Ambition, or love of honor, or riches, or love of power must not enter into the priest's intention, only the service of God, and Him alone. If the faithful, i.e., all Catholics, must love God with their whole heart, their whole soul, and with all their strength, this is surely true of those who in a special sense are ministers of God. All Christians will naturally respect such men and look upon them as the messengers of God and the dispensers of His mysteries.

The Services of the Priest. The special services of the priest are (1) to offer the Holy Sacrifice of the Mass, for himself and for all the people, (2) to explain God's law, (3) to urge the people and to show them the way to observe it promptly and cheerfully, and (4) to administer the sacraments of Christ our Lord by means of which all grace is given and increased. To perform these duties it can be understood that the priest must live up to the highest ideals and morals of Christian life. He must be an example of a holy and innocent life. To perform these sacred duties, the priests and bishops receive the power and grace in the sacrament of holy orders. If in the Old Law persons with bodily defects were not allowed in the priesthood, so too in the New Law. But if persons of bodily defects are excluded, how much more should persons of moral defect or of mental weakness.

Special Training of Priests. It must be true also that only men of special training can enter this special service. Besides knowing how to administer the sacraments, a priest must be well informed, widely read, and have the most accurate knowledge of the Sacred Scriptures and other religious writings, so that he can inform the people from a full knowledge about the mysteries of the Christian faith, and the commands of the divine law, lead them to piety and virtue, and reclaim them from sin. He must be trained for the many other duties which he must perform besides his main duties.

The Ordination of the Priest. The duties which the priest must perform are brought out in the act of making, or, as we say, ordaining a priest. At the ceremony of ordination:

The bishop first of all imposes hands on him, as do all the other priests who are present. Then he puts a stole on his shoulders and arranges it over his breast in the form of a cross, declaring thereby that the priest is clothed with power from on high, enabling him to carry the cross of Christ our Lord and the sweet yoke of God's law, and to inculcate this law not only by words, but also by the example of a most holy and virtuous life.

He next anoints his hands with holy oil, and then gives him the chalice with wine and the paten with a host, saying at the same time: Receive the power to offer sacrifice to God, and to celebrate Masses, both for the living and for the dead. By these words and ceremonies the priest is constituted an interpreter and mediator between God and man, which indeed must be regarded as the principal function of the priesthood.

Lastly, placing his hands a second time on the head [of the person ordained], the bishop says: "Receive the Holy Ghost; whose sins you shall forgive they are forgiven them, and whose sins you shall retain they are retained," thus communicating to him that divine power of forgiving and retaining sin which was given by our Lord to His disciples. Such, then, are the special and principal functions of the sacerdotal order (*Catechism of the Council of Trent*, pp. 331–32).

Steps to Priesthood. Before the person becomes a priest, he has to go through certain stages of preparation. Sometimes these steps are combined.

Tonsure. A man who is preparing to be a priest, receives the "tonsure." His hair is cut in the form of a cross in memory of Christ's crowning of thorns. He becomes a cleric as distinct from a layman and in the Middle Ages this gave him certain privileges.

Minor Orders. Then certain offices or powers are given the future priest, which are not sacred, called minor orders: porter, reader, exorcist, and acolyte. The porter is to guard the keys and door of the church and to allow no one to enter there to whom entrance is forbidden. The reader is allowed to read from the Bible at certain services. The exorcist is given power to impose hands on those who are possessed by the devil and to drive out the devil. The acolyte helps those in major orders at the Sacrifice of the Altar, and carries and attends to the lights from which fact they are called candle bearers.

Major Orders. The candidate for the priesthood enters upon the sacred character (sacerdotal) of the priesthood in the next steps which are called major orders. These major or sacred orders are three in number, subdeaconship, deaconship, and priesthood. In general the subdeacon assists the deacon at the Sacrifice of the Mass, and the deacon is in immediate attendance on the bishop or priest saying the Mass. The priest is the one who actually offers the Sacrifice of the Mass and performs the other duties of the priesthood which we have described.

The Sacrament of Holy Orders. The person who is to become a priest and be associated in the service of the Church and to administer the sacraments should himself be given grace along with his power. He should especially have in his soul the grace of sanctification, filling and qualifying him for the performance of his functions and for the administration of the sacraments. It is, therefore, the most natural thing that the reception of holy orders is the reception of a sacrament. The power to perform the general duties of a priest, and to change bread and wine into the Body and Blood of Christ are conferred by the sacrament of holy orders.

Essentials of the Sacrament. In the sacrament of holy orders, for the priesthood itself, as distinct from the minor and major orders, the matter of the sacrament, is the laying on of hands by the bishop.

The form of the outward sign is the words of the bishop, first, when he anoints with oil the hands of the person being ordained and gives to him the chalice with wine and the paten with a host, and says:

> Receive the power to offer the Sacrifice to God, and to celebrate Masses both for the living and the dead.

and second, when the bishop lays his hand a second time on the head of the person being ordained, and says:

> Receive the Holy Ghost; whose sins you shall forgive they are forgiven them, and whose sins you shall retain they are retained.

The Mark on the Soul. This sacrament, like baptism and confirmation, confers on the person that receives it a special mark impressed on the soul which the more learned books call a *charisma*. This marks the person who especially dedicates himself to divine worship. This means a lifetime dedication on the part of the priest. The mark can never be erased. "Once a priest, forever a priest."

The Organization of the Church. Though the priesthood is one, there are degrees of dignity and power. The priest we know ordinarily is the parish priest or his assistant. We have seen how Christ chose His Apostles and the seventy-two disciples. The lawful successors of the Apostles are the bishops of the Church, the archbishops, and the pope.

The Bishop. The bishop is a priest especially consecrated to take up the apostolic work of ruling and governing the affairs of the Church in a certain area called a diocese. What diocese do you live in? Note that the name of the diocese is taken from the city in which the bishop lives. Its size varies somewhat according to the population. In this country it includes a single state (e.g., diocese of Tucson, Arizona) or a part of a state (e.g., diocese of Green Bay, Wisconsin).

The Archbishop. Of special dignity among bishops are archbishops. They are bishops with some added rights and duties. The archbishop has the right to call the bishops of his province to a council. Archbishops are located in the larger and principal cities of their area. From the fact that this city is looked upon as the metropolis (or principal city) of the region, the archbishop is called also the metropolitan. The Archbishop of Milwaukee, for example, performs the usual functions of the bishop in the Milwaukee archdiocese, which is the southeastern part of Wisconsin, but he is the metropolitan of the bishops of Green Bay (Wis.), Superior (Wis.), La Crosse (Wis.), and Marquette (Mich.). These dioceses are said to be part of the Milwaukee province. Though the archbishop enjoys greater dignity and somewhat more power, his ordination is the same as the bishops. The chief archbishop of a country is called the Primate.

Cardinals. The pope appoints certain priests or bishops or archbishops as cardinals or princes of the Church. Together they make up the College of Cardinals and elect the pope. They are otherwise advisers to the pope. The College of Cardinals is made up of seventy members.

The Pope. The Bishop of Rome, the vicar of Christ on earth, the successor of St. Peter, is the Chief Bishop, Father, and Patriarch of the world. We know him simply as the pope. He continues the authority and lawgiving power which God Himself gave to St. Peter. He is the leader of the faithful everywhere. He is the guide and teacher of bishops and of all prelates as well. He is the ruler of the Universal Church. He is, as one of his titles has it, the Servant of the Servants of God.

Questions from the Catechism

Q. What is necessary to receive holy orders worthily?
A. **To receive holy orders worthily it is necessary to be in the state of grace, to have the necessary knowledge and a divine call to this sacred office.**

Q. How should Christians look upon the priests of the Church?
A. **Christians should look upon the priests of the Church as the messengers of God and the dispensers of His mysteries.**

Q. Who can confer the sacrament of holy orders?
A. **Bishops can confer the sacrament of holy orders.**

Q. What is the sacrament of holy orders?
A. **Holy orders is a sacrament by which bishops, priests, and other**

HOLY ORDERS

ministers of the Church are ordained and receive the power and grace to perform their sacred duties.

Problem Questions

1. In the Old Testament God chose the Levites to carry on the priestly duties among His people. At the Last Supper, Christ established the priesthood when He consecrated the Apostles to their work in the words: "Do this for a commemoration of Me"; and after His Resurrection: "Receive ye the Holy Ghost, whose sins you shall forgive they are forgiven them, whose sins you shall retain they are retained." Who has the power to ordain? Discuss the Apostolic succession. What is the sacrament of holy orders?

2. Charles Coele had heard of the coming ordination of John McMahoney and out of mere curiosity made arrangements to attend. During the ceremony the bishop and the priests first imposed hands upon John. Then the bishop anointed the young man's hands with holy oils and gave him the chalice with wine and the paten with a host saying at the same time: "Receive the power to offer sacrifice to God and to celebrate Mass." Lastly, the bishop placed his hands a second time on John's head and said: "Receive the Holy Ghost, whose sins you shall forgive they are forgiven them, and whose sins you shall retain they are retained." What is the meaning of each step in the process of ordination? Why is holy orders called the sacrament of the Holy Ghost? What is the preparation for the sacrament of holy orders?

Review Questions

1. Is holy orders a sacrament?
2. What are the three essentials of a sacrament?
3. Who is the ordinary minister of the sacrament?
4. May anyone else administer this sacrament?
5. What is the essential act done by the person administering this sacrament?
6. Is this part of a longer ceremony? What other acts are part of the ceremony?
7. What are the essential words used in administering this sacrament?
8. Name now the two parts of the "outward sign" of this sacrament.
9. May this sacrament be received more than once?
10. Is this one of the sacraments that leaves a distinct mark on the soul?
11. Besides sanctifying grace what is the grace peculiar to this sacrament?
12. What is ordinarily the condition of the soul when one receives holy orders?
13. Justify calling holy orders a sacrament of the living.

THE HIGHWAY TO GOD

Quotations from the Bible

For each of the following quotations:
a) Identify the speaker.
b) State the conditions under which the statement was made.
c) Give the meaning.
d) Tell its significance.

"Do this for a commemoration of Me" (Luke xxii. 19).

"Thou art a priest forever" (Heb. v. 6).

Chapter XL
PRAYER

Prayer and Grace. To reach the true end of our life's journey on God's Highway to our home in heaven, we must have the grace of God. We have just reviewed the wonderful system of the sacraments instituted by Christ and which through the divine power of Christ gives grace to the individual soul. There is another means of gaining God's grace; namely, prayer.

Sursum Corda. The opening of the third part of the Mass can teach us much about prayer. It is:

> The Lord be with you
> And with thy spirit.
> Lift up your hearts.
> We have lifted them up to the Lord.
> Let us give thanks to the Lord, our God.
> It is meet and just.

And then the "common preface" begins:

> It is truly meet and just, right and availing unto salvation that we should at all times and in all places give thanks to Thee, O holy Lord, Father Almighty, everlasting God, through Christ, our Lord.

Sursum Corda (as the priest says it in Latin) — "Lift up your hearts." We should lift up our hearts to the Lord at all times in all places. This lifting up of our minds and hearts, whether we do it with words (vocal prayer) or without words (mental prayer) is the essence of prayer. We do it because we love God and we feel our dependence on Him. We do it because He is the Giver of all good gifts. We lift up our hearts to adore God whom we love, to thank Him for the many benefits we have received as well as for the many evils we have been protected from. We lift up our minds and hearts to God in prayer to ask Him to forgive our sins and to secure from Him all the graces whether for soul or body, which we need to keep us on God's Highway, and help us get to our home with God.

Prayer is needed for us who have the use of reason. It is our means of expressing our faith, our hope, our love for God. It is our means of asking God's help in our efforts to go to Him. It is necessary for human salvation. That our prayer will be answered and that there is need for prayer our Lord Himself tells us in the following words in the Gospel of St. Luke:

And He spoke also a parable to them, that we ought always to pray, and not to faint,
Saying: There was a judge in a certain city, who feared not God, nor regarded man.
And there was a certain widow in that city, and she came to him, saying: Avenge me of my adversary.
And he would not for a long time. But afterwards he said within himself: Although I fear not God, nor regard man,
Yet because this widow is troublesome to me, I will avenge her, lest continually coming she weary me.
And the Lord said: Hear what the unjust judge saith.
And will not God revenge His elect who cry to Him day and night: and will He have patience in their regard?
I say to you, that He will quickly revenge them. But yet the Son of Man, when He cometh, shall He find, think you, faith on earth? (Luke xviii. 1–8.)

What Prayer Is. Prayer is the lifting up of our minds and hearts to God (1) to adore Him, (2) to thank Him for His blessings (3) to ask His forgiveness, and (4) to beg of Him all the graces we need whether for soul or body. Prayer is a raising of our mind and our hearts toward God and away from merely earthly things and affections. It is putting first things first. It is one way of telling God that we depend on Him, love Him, adore Him, thank Him, and hope in Him for help in the future.

The Obligation to Pray. Prayer is not only a means which we are advised to use but it is commanded as a duty. It is necessary for salvation, and must be used by all who have reached the age of reason if they wish to be saved. Christ said: "We ought always to pray" (Luke xviii. 1), and by His example He carried out His words. He prayed often. He went apart into mountain or desert to pray. Many times He prayed the whole night through.

Christ Urges Us to Pray. Christ urges us to ask the Father anything in His name, and it will be granted. "Ask and you shall receive, that your joy may be full" (John xvi. 24), Christ says in one place. In another place He says, "If you abide in Me, and My words abide in you, you shall ask whatever you will, and it shall be done unto you" (John xv. 7). And in still another place Christ says, "All things whatsoever you shall ask in prayer, believing, you shall receive" (Matt. xxi. 22).

How to Pray: Our Father. We might very well make the request one of the disciples made of Christ: "Lord, teach us to pray." And we might remember always Christ's answer. He told them that they were to pray after this manner:

> Our Father, who art in heaven, hallowed be Thy name, Thy kingdom come, Thy will be done on earth as it is in heaven. Give us this day our daily bread and forgive us our trespasses as we forgive those who trespass against us, and lead us not into temptation, but deliver us from evil. Amen.

It is a very simple prayer. It is short. It is simple. It is complete. It opens in its address to our Father, confessing thereby that we are His children. This is followed by seven petitions followed by the word *Amen*. This may be shown graphically:

I. The Address to God.
   Our Father, who art in heaven.
II. The Seven Petitions,
   1. Hallowed be Thy name.
   2. Thy Kingdom come.
   3. Thy will be done on earth as it is in heaven.
   4. Give us this day our daily bread.
   5. And forgive us our trespasses as we forgive those who trespass against us.
   6. And lead us not into temptation.
   7. But deliver us from evil.
III. The Seal of the Lord's Prayer is Amen.

If we would meditate on the opening of the prayer and each of the petitions separately, we would begin to understand the richness and the perfection of this prayer. A word may be added here about "Amen." It was a word often used by Christ. Its meaning may be said to be: "Know that thy prayers are heard." It has the force of a response, as if God answers the one praying and kindly dismisses him, after having favorably heard his prayers. This prayer composed by Christ Himself, is perfect not only in its content, but in its authorship.

To Whom We Should Pray. It is, naturally, to God that we should pray — the three persons of the Blessed Trinity. It is of Him we should ask for the things we desire. What things these are we shall see later. It is He who invites us to "Come to Me all you that labor and are burdened, and I will refresh you" (Matt. xi. 28). We should also pray to the saints, asking them to take our prayers to God. A difference between the way we pray to God and the way we pray to the saints may be noted:

1. To God we say, "Have mercy on us, Hear us."
2. To the saints we say, "Pray for us."

The function of the saints in the divine plan is to interpret or intercede for us. Only God can grant the prayer, and it is to Him we give thanks.

What We Should Pray For. We should pray especially for the love of God, and for all things that will draw us closer to Him or unite us to Him. We should pray for any good — spiritual, bodily, or external, or mental — if it can serve to promote the glory of God, help our neighbor, and help our own salvation.

During His agony in the garden of Gethsemane, our Lord told the Apostles to pray that they enter not into temptation. We should pray constantly for grace to keep all the commandments so as never to commit a mortal sin; and that we may have the light to know and the grace to do God's will in all things. And we should pray daily for the grace of a happy death.

If we pray for temporal favors such as health, strength, an improvement of our condition in life, etc., we should always be fully resigned to God's will in these matters. God may not wish to give us just what we ask because it may not be good for our souls. Solomon prayed: "Give me neither beggary nor riches:

give me only the necessaries of life" (Prov. xxx. 8). If more is given, we must remember that we must answer to God for it, and our duty to help our neighbor. Let us keep in mind Christ's words at the end of the Sermon on the Mount:

> Be not solicitous therefore, saying, What shall we eat: or what shall we drink, or wherewith shall we be clothed?
> For after all these things do the heathens seek. For your Father knoweth that you have need of all these things.
> Seek ye therefore first the kingdom of God, and His justice, and all these things shall be added unto you (Matt. vi. 31-33).

How to Pray Well. We should pray to God in spirit and in truth. We may pray with our voice or our mind. In both of these forms of prayer it is not the words on the lips, but the intention in the heart that is most important. What are some of the things that make prayers good? They are:

1. Attention.

Prayers said with willful distractions are of no use. We must have faith and trust in our prayers, and this requires our whole attention. Our attention must be directed to God, and be on the substance of the prayer. If not we may be told: "This people honoreth Me with their lips: but their heart is far from Me" (Matt. xv. 8).

2. A sense of helplessness and dependence upon God.

The spirit of true prayer is best shown by Christ's prayer at the beginning of the Passion: "Not My will, but Thine be done" (Luke xxii. 42). It is shown too in the centurion's prayer:

> And saying, Lord, my servant lieth at home sick of the palsy, and is grievously tormented.
> And Jesus saith to him: I will come and heal him.
> And the centurion making answer, said: Lord, I am not worthy that Thou shouldst enter under my roof; but only say the word, and my servant shall be healed.
> For I also am a man subject to authority, having under me soldiers; and I say to this, Go, and he goeth, and to another, Come, and he cometh, and to my servant, Do this, and he doeth it.
> And Jesus hearing this, marveled; and said to them that followed Him: Amen I say to you, I have not found so great faith in Israel (Matt. viii. 6-10).

3. A great desire for the graces we beg of God.

If we have the faith and the desire of the woman of Canaan, we shall probably gain her reward.

> Then Jesus answering, said to her: O woman, great is thy faith: be it done to thee as thou wilt: and her daughter was cured from that hour (Matt. xv. 28).

4. Trust in God's goodness.

The prayer of the centurion, or the prayer of the prodigal son at his return, might be used to show this, but we chose the prayer of the penitent robber on the cross:

> And one of those robbers who were hanged, blasphemed Him, saying: If Thou be Christ, save Thyself and us.
>
> But the other answering, rebuked him, saying: Neither dost thou fear God, seeing thou art under the same condemnation?
>
> And we indeed justly, for we receive the due reward of our deeds; but this Man hath done no evil.
>
> And he said to Jesus: Lord, remember me when Thou shalt come into Thy kingdom.
>
> And Jesus said to him: Amen I say to thee, this day thou shalt be with Me in paradise (Luke xxiii. 39–43).

5. Perseverance.

When our Lord was teaching the disciples how to pray, to bring out the value of perseverance in prayer, He gave as an example, the case of a man who should go to his neighbor at night to borrow bread. If the neighbor and his children were in bed, he might refuse the request. But if the man continued to knock, the neighbor would get out of bed and give him as much bread as he wanted. Then Jesus promised:

> And I say to you, Ask, and it shall be given you: seek, and you shall find: knock, and it shall be opened to you (Luke xi. 9).

In the Old Testament we read, "Let nothing hinder thee from praying always" (Ecclus. xviii. 22). So in the New Testament we read, "We ought always to pray, and not to faint" (Luke xviii. 1); and again, "Pray without ceasing" (I Thess. v. 17).

6. The Name of Jesus.

We know that Christ will intercede for us in heaven. His own words may be recalled to us.

PRAYER

Amen, amen, I say to you: if you ask the Father anything in My name He will give it you. Hitherto you have not asked anything in My name. Ask and you shall receive; that your joy may be full (John xvi. 23–24).

Whatsoever you shall ask the Father in My name, that will I do (John xiv. 13).

Recommended Prayers and Time of Prayer. The prayers most recommended to us are:

1. The Lord's Prayer,
2. The Hail Mary,
3. The Apostles' Creed,
4. The Confiteor,
5. Act of Faith,
6. Act of Hope,
7. Act of Love,
8. Act of Contrition.

Besides these we will all have special prayers for our devotion, and everyone will want to pray the Mass with the priest by the use of the Missal. These prayers of our own, should be used at every appropriate occasion. Sundays and holydays are clearly appropriate times. Naturally, too, we should want to begin and end the day well, morning and night. And it is in time of danger, of temptation, and of trouble that we naturally turn to God for help. It should be no less natural to turn to Him in time of prosperity, of peace, and of progress to render to Him thanksgiving, and to confess our dependence, and to express our love.

Questions from the Catechism

Q. Is there any other means of obtaining God's grace than the sacraments?
A. **There is another means of obtaining God's grace, and it is prayer.**

Q. What is prayer?
A. **Prayer is the lifting up of our minds and hearts to God to adore Him, to thank Him for His benefits, to ask His forgiveness, and to beg of Him all the graces we need whether for soul or body.**

Q. Is prayer necessary to salvation?
A. **Prayer is necessary to salvation, and without it no one having the use of reason can be saved.**

Q. At what particular time should we pray?
A. **We should pray particularly on Sundays and holydays, every morning and night, in all dangers, temptations, and afflictions.**

Q. How should we pray?
A. **We should pray: First, with attention; second, with a sense of our own helplessness and dependence upon God; third, with a great desire for the graces we beg of God; fourth, with trust in God's goodness; fifth, with perseverance.**

Q. Which are the prayers most recommended to us?
A. **The prayers most recommended to us are the Lord's Prayer, the Hail Mary, the Apostles' Creed, the Confiteor, and the Acts of Faith, Hope, Love, and Contrition.**

Problem Questions

1. Is prayer a source of grace? What is the other principal source of grace?
2. To whom should we pray?
3. To whom should we pray for intercession?
4. Why is the "Our Father" a perfect prayer?
5. Tell the parable of the Pharisee and the Publican. What does it suggest to us about our own prayer?
6. What is mental prayer?
7. Name the characteristics of prayer.
8. Write a prayer to God for your spiritual welfare.
9. Write a prayer for your mother. Your father.
10. Write a prayer for the welfare of the United States.
11. Write a prayer that you may find in life its joyousness as St. Francis of Assisi did.
12. Write a morning prayer. An evening prayer.
13. Find a liturgical morning prayer. A liturgical evening prayer.
14. What is meant by matins, etc.?
15. Are there spiritual exercises for the soul just as there are physical exercises for the body? If so, name them.
16. Find out what you can about the life of St. Ignatius of Loyola at Manresa.
17. Find out what you can about the Spiritual Exercises of St. Ignatius of Loyola.
18. What is a retreat?

Quotations from the Bible

For each of the following quotations:
a) Identify the speaker.

PRAYER

b) State the conditions under which the statement was made.
c) Give the meaning.
d) Tell its significance.

"All things whatsoever you shall ask in prayer, believing, you shall receive" (Matt. xxi. 22).

"Lord teach us to pray" (Luke xi. 1).

"Our Father who art in heaven, hallowed be Thy name" (Matt. vi. 9).

"Come to Me, all you that labor, and are burdened, and I will refresh you" (Matt. xi. 28).

"He spoke also a parable to them, that we ought always to pray, and not to faint. Saying: . . ." (Luke xviii. 1–2).

"He passed the whole night in the prayer of God" (Luke vi. 12).

To what incident does the following description refer?
Who was present?
What is the significance of the event?

"All things whatsoever you shall ask in prayer, believing, you shall receive" (Matt. xxi. 22).

Chapter XLI
THE COMMANDMENTS OF THE CHURCH

1. The Commandments of the Church in General

Christ on Earth. Christ came to earth, became man, lived the life of a human being for thirty-three years, was crucified, died and was buried, and ascended into heaven. He did not come to serve the people of only a small area in Judea where He spent the three years of His public life. He did not come just to the people who lived in the places He visited, nor for the Jews only, but for all men in all time in every country.

Continuing the Work of Christ. We have seen His way of doing what He came to earth for, carrying on the fruits of His Incarnation, Crucifixion, Resurrection, and Ascension, by setting up the Roman Catholic Church. We may recall the promises He made to Peter:

> And I say to thee: That thou art Peter; and upon this rock I will build My Church, and the gates of hell shall not prevail against it.
> And I will give to thee the keys of the kingdom of heaven. And whatsoever thou shalt bind upon earth, it shall be bound also in heaven: And whatsoever thou shalt loose on earth, it shall be loosed in heaven (Matt. xvi. 18–19).

The Guardians of the Church. And to make strong this extraordinary power given to the Church, Christ made two promises: one, that He Himself would be with the Church all days, and second that He would send the Paraclete, the Holy Ghost, who would "abide with you forever," and "shall be in you."

Christ and the Church. After Christ had named the twelve Apostles to carry on the work, He approved the other seventy-two, "And He sent them two by two before His face into every city and place where He Himself was to come." In instructing them and in the promises He made to them He spoke to His Church. He told them, strengthening the promises mentioned in the last paragraph:

The Commandments of the Church

1. To hear Mass on Sundays and holydays of obligation.
2. To fast and abstain on the days appointed.
3. To confess at least once a year.
4. To receive the Holy Eucharist during the Easter time.
5. To contribute to the support of our pastors.
6. Not to marry persons who are not Catholics or who are related to us within the third degree of kindred, nor privately without witnesses, nor to solemnize marriage at forbidden times.

"He that heareth you, heareth Me; and He that despiseth you, despiseth Me; and He that despiseth Me, despiseth Him that sent Me" (Luke x. 16).

Christ's Desire for Our Spiritual Welfare. Remembering how Jesus organized His Church, how He taught His Apostles and sent them out to teach in His Name, commanding us to hear them as we would hear Him, and sending the Holy Ghost to remain with us to the end of the world — remembering all this, we can easily understand the power of the Church and its great desire to guide us on the path that leads to God, and we can see too why our hearts willingly follow the teaching of the Church. The Church, in its desire to keep us on the great highways leading to God, gives us directions a little more specific, as indeed Christ promised it would to "keep the road." These new signposts keep us away from dangerous side roads and crossroads, and especially from the broad road to hell.

The Canon Law. The Church, by virtue of its power, has made a great many laws. An organization so large and affecting so many people must have rules, regulations, and laws. Some relate only to the officers of the Church, bishops, priests, and religious; some relate to special conditions in certain countries, and some relate to the faithful everywhere. All these laws effective at a particular time are brought together (codified we call it) and printed. The law of the Church we call canon law as distinct from civil law, which is the law of the State. The codification of the canon law we call the Code of the Canon Law. The most recent codification, begun in 1904, was published in 1918. Of course, as lay persons, it is not necessary for us to know all the canon law. We can readily find out any special information we want by going to the parish priest. But there are certain provisions that we should all know, which apply to all the faithful and to which we must conform our actions. The very important ones we will study in this chapter as other guideposts on the Highway to our Home in Heaven.

The Six Commandments of the Church. These signposts, helping us better to follow the commandments of God, and to lead a worthy human life on earth, and as a preparation for the life to come, are known as the Commandments of the Church. Failure to obey any of these commands of the Church as the representative of Christ, is a mortal sin. They are six in number:

1. To hear Mass on Sundays and holydays of obligation.
2. To fast and abstain on the days appointed.
3. To confess at least once a year.
4. To receive the Holy Eucharist during the Easter time.
5. To contribute to the support of our pastors.
6. Not to marry persons who are not Catholics, or who are related to us within the third degree of kindred, nor privately without witnesses, nor to solemnize marriage at forbidden times.

2. The First Commandment of the Church

The first commandment of the Church is: *To hear Mass on Sundays and holydays of obligation.*

Worship on Sunday. The first commandment of the Church relates to the worship of God and tells us how to carry out the Third Commandment of God. We have seen that the important point of the Third Commandment is that man should pay worship and homage to his Creator. The commandment strengthens this sense of creatureship in the hearts of men. The law, we said at that time, of keeping holy the Sabbath was part of the ceremonial law. It was pointed out that the Apostles made Sunday the Lord's Day because it was on that day Christ had risen from the dead, and thus the regular public worship of God would remind us of the Resurrection, the central fact of our religion.

If Christ be not risen again, then is our preaching vain, and your faith is also vain (I Cor. xv. 14).

It was also on Sunday that the Holy Ghost came upon the Apostles.

Third Commandment of God. For our purpose it will be well to recall the main points of the Third Commandment of God. We are to keep holy the Lord's Day and other holydays by giving our time to the service and worship of God. We do this by attending religious services on time; i.e., by hearing Mass, by prayers, and by other good works. We are also forbidden to do certain things. These are servile works and whatever also may hinder the due observance of the Lord's Day. If, however, the honor of God, the good of our neighbor, or necessity requires it, servile works are permitted or lawful on Sunday.

The Mass in the Early Church. The saying of Mass, or the "Breaking of Bread" as it was called, on Sunday was the practice of the Church even from the earliest times. In the "Acts of the Apostles," which is the book in the New Testament of the Bible which tells what the Apostles did after the Resurrection, St. Paul is mentioned as speaking "on the first day of the week, when we were assembled to break bread" (Acts xx. 7). St. John also speaks of Sunday as the "Lord's Day" in the Apocalypse (i. 10). So from the beginning of the Church, the Apostles themselves associated their Lord and Master, Christ, with Sunday and made it the day of regular worship.

The Mass. We have seen what an infinitely higher form of sacrifice the Sacrifice of the Mass is than the sacrifices of the Old Law. We have seen that it was instituted by Christ Himself.

We see how it was part of the providence of God. We know from our own experience that it always reminds us of Christ when He made the supreme sacrifice of Calvary. For these and for many other reasons it is but natural that this particular form of worship of God through the merits of His Divine Son, in whom He said "I am well pleased," should be the central form of worship in the Catholic Church, and that we should keep the Lord's Day holy by taking part in the Mass.

The Two Changes. It was natural, therefore, that the practice of the worship of God which had been the custom among the Jews should be continued by the Apostles with the changes (1) of the form of worship to the Mass and (2) of the time of worship to the Lord's Day, the first day of the week. It was natural, too, that the Church should formally confirm the change by making attendance at Mass on Sundays the first commandment of the Church.

Attendance on Sundays and Holydays of Obligation. The first commandment of the Church requires attendance at the great act of worship of God, the Christian act of worship, the Mass, on Sunday and certain other days too. From the fact that attendance is commanded, or required, by the Church and is thus an obligation or duty for the individual, these days besides Sunday on which we must hear Mass are called days of obligation. Because of the special holy and religious character of the days, these are called holydays of obligation.

The Church, in the first commandment, requires all of us who have reached the age of reason to attend Mass on Sundays and holydays of obligation under pain of mortal sin, unless excused for a serious reason. They also commit a sin who prevent or hinder a person under their charge from attending Mass on such days. This would apply to a parent with reference to a child, a mistress of a household with reference to a servant, an employer with reference to an employee, unless there were serious reasons for the act.

Following Mass with the Missal. On Sundays, if we follow the Mass as we should by reading in the Missal with the priest the prayers of the Mass of that Sunday, we will learn much about our Holy Religion in that way, and will better aid in making, as the priest says, "Your sacrifice and mine acceptable to the Lord." Just examine the names of the Sundays from this standpoint.

Besides the facts thus brought out in the Sunday Masses, the Church wishes to direct attention in the United States especially to five other great events, and to all the saints of the Church together. These call to mind the great mysteries of religion and the virtues and rewards of saints:

1. The Birth of Christ, December 25.
2. The Circumcision of Christ, January 1.
3. The Ascension (forty days after Easter).
4. The Assumption of the Blessed Virgin Mary into Heaven, August 15.
5. All Saints' Day, November 1.
6. The Immaculate Conception, December 8.

It should be carefully borne in mind that the command to attend Mass on holydays of obligation is just as binding as the command to hear Mass on Sundays.

Questions from the Catechism

Q. What are we commanded by the Third Commandment of God?
A. **By the Third Commandment of God we are commanded to keep holy the Lord's Day and the holydays of obligation, on which we are to give our time to the service and worship of God.**

Q. How are we to worship God on Sundays and holydays of obligation?
A. **We are to worship God on Sundays and holydays of obligation by hearing Mass, by prayer, and by other good works.**

Q. Are the Sabbath day and the Sunday the same?
A. **The Sabbath day and the Sunday are not the same. The Sabbath is the seventh day of the week, and is the day which was kept holy in the Old Law; the Sunday is the first day of the week, and is the day which is kept holy in the New Law.**

Q. Why does the Church command us to keep the Sunday holy instead of the Sabbath?
A. **The Church commands us to keep the Sunday holy instead of the Sabbath because on Sunday Christ rose from the dead, and on Sunday He sent the Holy Ghost upon the Apostles.**

Q. What is forbidden by the Third Commandment?
A. **The Third Commandment forbids all unnecessary servile work and whatever else may hinder the due observance of the Lord's Day.**

Q. Are servile works on Sunday lawful?
A. **Servile works are lawful on Sunday when the honor of God, the good of our neighbor, or necessity requires them.**

Q. Is it a mortal sin not to hear Mass on Sunday or a holyday of obligation?
A. **It is a mortal sin not to hear Mass on a Sunday or a holyday of obligation, unless we are excused for a serious reason. They also commit a mortal sin who, having others under their charge, hinder them from hearing Mass, without a sufficient reason.**

Q. Why were holydays instituted by the Church?
A. **Holydays were instituted by the Church to recall to our minds the great mysteries of religion and the virtues and rewards of the saints.**

Q. How should we keep the holydays of obligation?
A. **We should keep the holydays of obligation as we should keep the Sunday.**

Q. Which are the chief commandments of the Church?
A. **The chief commandments of the Church are six:**
  1. **To hear Mass on Sundays and holydays of obligation.**
  2. **To fast and abstain on the days appointed.**
  3. **To confess at least once a year.**
  4. **To receive the Holy Eucharist during the Easter time.**
  5. **To contribute to the support of our pastors.**
  6. **Not to marry persons who are not Catholics, or who are related to us within the third degree of kindred, nor privately without witnesses, nor to solemnize marriage at forbidden times.**

Questions for the Pupil

1. Where does the Church get the power to make commandments or precepts or laws binding on you?
2. Could the Church make a law binding on us in everything?
3. What is the special field in which the Church has authority?
4. Does the first commandment of the Church come within this authority?
5. What is the first commandment of the Church?

COMMANDMENTS OF THE CHURCH

6. Is the requirement of the commandment all we should do? or the least that we should do?

7. What are the holydays of obligation in the United States?

Problem Questions

1. Roy Chanders, a Protestant friend of yours, says, "The Catholic Church has no right to command you under pain of mortal sin to attend Mass on Sundays and holydays of obligation." From whence does the Catholic Church get its authority? Why does the Church command one to attend Mass on these days? Summarize the arguments to clear up Roy's objections.

2. "I am going to Church today, Mother, just to hear the music and to hear Father Smith speak," said Rita Bailey as she left home one Sunday morning. Does Rita Bailey fulfill her duty of hearing Mass? Explain. Why is bodily presence not enough to fulfill the obligation of hearing Mass? How would the situation differ if Rita went to Church for the purpose of hearing Mass but read a storybook during the entire service?

3. Bernard Quinn went to Church on a Sunday morning with the intention of hearing Mass. He was out late the evening before, and so fell asleep soon after Mass had begun and did not wake up until the Communion of the Mass. Did Bernard fulfill his duty? Discuss. Why does the Church exhort the faithful not to attend late Saturday night functions? When may a person be excused from hearing Mass?

4. One Sunday morning Betty's mother was ready to go to Mass, when she heard that a neighbor was very ill and needed help. Instead of going to church she went to help the neighbor. Did she do right?

5. Marie was out to a dance all Saturday night. She was very tired on Sunday morning, but decided to go to Mass before returning home. She slept all during the services. Did she fulfill her obligation to hear a Mass?

6. There was no school on the Feast of Corpus Christi and John and William decided to go fishing. John thought that the feast was a holyday of obligation, but he did not attend Mass. Afterwards he heard from William that he was not obliged to hear a Mass on that day, as it was not a holyday of obligation. John said he was glad to hear that, for now he did not commit a mortal sin by not attending Mass. William said it would be a sin for John anyway, because he had thought that it was a sin when he decided to stay away. Who was right, and why?

7. Mr. Peale is a Catholic. He goes to Mass on All Saints' Day but refuses to let his servants go as they are being paid for their work. Has he a right to keep them from hearing a Mass?

8. On Sunday afternoon you get a big tear in your coat. You need your coat on Monday morning. May mother mend it for you?

9. Mr. Mack works in an office and cannot get to Mass on the Feast of the Assumption unless he rises at 4:30. Is he obliged to hear Mass?

10. May you stay away from Mass on Sunday because you have a slight headache? a toothache? because you cannot find your Sunday hat?

Quotations from the Bible

For each of the following quotations:
a) Identify the speaker.
b) State the conditions under which the statement was made.
c) Give the meaning.
d) Tell its significance.

"Keep holy the Sabbath day."

"And when you fast, be not as the hypocrites, sad. For they disfigure their faces, that they may appear unto men to fast. Amen I say to you, they have received their reward" (Matt. vi. 16).

3. The Second Commandment of the Church

To Fast and Abstain on the Days Appointed. The second commandment of the Church is: *To Fast and Abstain on the Days Appointed.* By acts of self-denial the Church wishes to remind us of Christ and keep always before us our path on God's Highway to be with Him forever. In this way we may weaken our passions by self-denial, and also make satisfaction in whole or part for our sins.

Fasting. This commandment requires us to fast on certain days and to abstain from meat on certain other days. In fasting we deny ourselves the amount of food we have been used to and eat only one full meal during a day, with a very light breakfast and a light supper, though, if more convenient, the full meal may be eaten in the evening, and a light lunch taken at noon. The custom and instructions of the bishop generally allow a cup of coffee, tea, or weak chocolate and a small piece of bread (not more than two ounces) in the morning, and not more than eight ounces or a fourth of a meal for the luncheon. The fasting days are:

1. The week days of Lent.
2. The ember days— Wednesday, Friday, and Saturday at the

beginning of each of the four seasons; there are spring, summer, autumn, and winter ember days.

3. Vigils; i.e., the day before the feasts of Pentecost, Assumption, All Saints' Day, and Christmas.

Lent. Lent is the season of penance set aside in honor of the passion and death of our Lord Jesus Christ; it is a season of penance in preparation for Easter. It begins on Ash Wednesday and ends at noon on Easter Saturday. It extends over forty-six days, but only the week days are days of fasting, forty days. This is a period often mentioned in the Scriptures. The rain fell forty days at the Deluge. Moses fasted forty days. Our Lord fasted forty days, and He remained on earth for forty days after the Resurrection.

The Church, by fasting and prayer and sorrow, wishes to remind us of the passion and death of Christ. From Ash Wednesday, when it places ashes on our forehead, to the *Tre Ore* (Three Hour) Service on Good Friday and until the resurrection on Easter Sunday it wishes to remind us of Christ's love for us, and His sacrifice for us. Fasting helps us to understand the Passion of our Lord, and to be in a mood to appreciate it.

The Ember Days. The ember days are twelve in number: they are the Wednesday, Friday, and Saturday in one week in each of the quarters or seasons of the year. In the winter season they occur in the third week of Advent; in the spring quarter in the second week of Lent; in summer in Whitsunweek; and in autumn in the third week of September. This may be presented thus:

Ember days are the Wednesdays, Fridays, and Saturdays after:
1. The first Sunday of Lent.
2. Pentecost.
3. September 14, the Feast of the Exaltation of the Holy Cross.
4. December 13, the Feast of St. Lucy.

In olden times these were the appointed seasons for ordination to the priesthood. The ember days are opportunities to thank God for the benefits of the season, and to remember we are God's creatures. It would be well, too, following the tradition of the Church, to pray God that He send us good priests.

Vigils. The vigils formerly kept in Church are days of preparation for a feast day. Fasting is a fitting preparation for a feast day. It is a reminder requiring a change from our ordinary way of life. It requires at least a little sacrifice. At the present time it is only for four of the greater feasts that the fasting is required. These are the vigils: the day before Pentecost, Assumption, All Saints' Day, and Christmas.

Dispensation from Fasting. The Church does not, however, require these fasts for every person under all conditions. Any person who might be injured in health by them, e.g., the sick, a mother nursing a baby, or a person of laborious or "nerve-wracking" occupation, does not have to keep these fasts. These rules being made by the Church, she grants dispensation from them when they might injure a person. Such dispensations should be sought from the pastor or confessor. Other self-denial or prayer may be substituted.

Abstinence. On the days of abstinence, Catholics are not allowed to eat flesh meat but may have three full meals unless a day of abstinence is also a day of fasting. The days of abstinence are:

1. All Fridays of the year.
2. Wednesdays of Lent.
3. Forenoon of Holy Saturday.
4. The ember days as for fasting.
5. The vigils as for fasting.

Dispensation from Abstinence. Here, too, certain people are excused who are sick or are just getting well. As a special privilege, the workingmen of the United States and their families are permitted to have meat at the main meal on all days of abstinence except: (1) Fridays, (2) Ash Wednesday, (3) Wednesday of Holy Week, (4) Morning of Holy Saturday, (5) Christmas Eve (vigil of Christmas).

The Ideal of Self-Denial. In asking us to fast and to abstain from flesh meat, the Church holds before us always the ideal of self-denial and self-mortification and calls our attention to our relationship to Christ and to our true end.

1. We are required to abstain from meat on Friday to remind us of the Crucifixion, for it was on Friday that this supreme and infinite act of self-denial and self-mortification took place.

2. Lent, the time of penance, is brought to our attention by making every day a fast day and the Wednesday and the morning of Holy Saturday days of abstinence also and the permitting of meat only once on the other days. This, of course, reminds us of the passion and suffering of Christ and prepares us for Good Friday and Easter Sunday.

3. The ember days, twelve in number, give us special time to thank God for His graces during the season and to ask Him pardon for our sins. Tradition tells us that on these days it is also well to pray that God's grace will be richly given to new priests and all priests.

4. Besides commanding us to keep the great feast days just as we do Sunday, the Church calls especial attention to four of them by making the vigils of these days, days of fasting and abstinence. What better way to call attention to them and to prepare for them than that.

Questions from the Catechism

Q. What do you mean by fast days?
A. **By fast days I mean days on which we are allowed but one full meal.**

Q. What do you mean by days of abstinence?
A. **By days of abstinence I mean days on which we are forbidden to eat flesh meat, but are allowed the usual number of meals.**

Q. Why does the Church command us to fast and abstain?
A. **The Church commands us to fast and abstain, in order that we may mortify our passions and satisfy for our sins.**

Q. Why does the Church command us to abstain from flesh meat on Fridays?
A. **The Church commands us to abstain from flesh meat on Fridays, in honor of the day on which our Savior died.**

Q. What is meant by the command of confessing at least once a year?

A. By the command of confessing at least once a year is meant that we are obliged, under pain of mortal sin, to go to confession within the year.

Q. Should we confess only once a year?
A. **We should confess frequently, if we wish to lead a good life.**

Q. Should children go to confession?
A. **Children should go to confession when they are old enough to commit sin, which is commonly about the age of seven years.**

Q. What sin does he commit who neglects to receive Communion during the Easter time?
A. **He who neglects to receive Communion during the Easter time commits a mortal sin.**

Q. What is the Easter time?
A. **The Easter time is, in this country, the time between the first Sunday of Lent and Trinity Sunday.**

Questions for the Pupil

1. Where does the Church get the power to make commandments or precepts or laws binding on you?

2. Could the Church make a law binding on us in everything?

3. What is the special field in which the Church has authority?

4. Does the second commandment of the Church come within this authority?

5. What is the second commandment of the Church?

6. Is the requirement of the commandment all we should do? or the least that we should do?

7. What are the days of fast?

8. What are the days of abstinence?

9. What are the usual Lenten regulations in your diocese?

10. What are the ember days?

11. What is a vigil? Why are the vigils of certain feasts included in the days of fast and abstinence?

Problem Questions

1. Harvey Hennepin spent his vacation working on the boats. Every Friday meat was served by the steward. Harvey was a practical Catholic and refused to take meat and gravy. Rene Bedard, another Catholic, ate the meat when served. One day the steward said to Harvey: "Any time you want fish you can get a can from the shelf."

"Rene's a Catholic too, so we can have it between us," remarked Harvey.

COMMANDMENTS OF THE CHURCH 371

"Oh, no," said the steward, "Let him go. He eats the meat."

What effect did the Catholic attitude of these two boys have upon the steward? Who do you think has the better chance for promotion? Why? Would the boys be obliged to refrain from eating meat aboard the boat? Discuss.

2. Mr. Kendall, a Catholic, was looking for work in a large city. He did not have a penny left and was obliged to beg for food. On a Friday he was given a meat sandwich. May Mr. Kendall eat the meat sandwich? How would the situation differ if he were not in great need of food? When you are traveling may you eat meat on Friday? Discuss.

3. Bertha Haley is not excused from fasting because of her duties. She, however, feels unable to fast. What should she do? When should this be done? What obligation still rests on those excused from fasting during Lent? Mention three other ways of doing penance. Name six classes of persons who are excused from fasting during Lent.

4. John Cannon refuses to observe the fast and abstinence regulations during the ember weeks because he claims that the Friday abstinence and the Lenten fast are sufficient. Why is John, nevertheless, guilty of sin? Why have the ember weeks been instituted? At what time of the year do the ember weeks occur?

4. The Third and Fourth Commandments of the Church

The third and fourth commandments of the Church were made as further signposts to keep us on God's Highway. The third commandment is: *To Confess Your Sins at Least Once a Year.* The fourth commandment is: *To Receive the Holy Eucharist during the Easter Time.* The fulfillment of the commandment of receiving the Holy Eucharist during the Easter time; i.e., in the United States from the first Sunday in Lent to Trinity Sunday, inclusive, will satisfy the third commandment because, as we know, we must go to confession before receiving the Holy Eucharist if we have committed a mortal sin since our last worthy confession. Not to obey this commandment or precept of the Church is a mortal sin. But, of course, the third commandment of the Church, as such, may be fulfilled at any time during the year. It is not limited to the Easter time, when it is a duty in connection with making what we call our "Easter Duty," receiving the Holy Eucharist during the Easter time. To fail to do this is a mortal sin also. Children should go to confession when they are old enough to realize what it is to commit a sin; i.e., usually about seven years of age.

The Minimum. To do less than the Church commands regarding confession and Communion would show such a neglect or indifference to the means offered by Christ through the Church as to be serious for the soul's welfare. This is the least we may do. This is so little that ordinarily it is not enough. It is to be stingy in our service to God. It is to neglect our soul. Frequent Communion should be our habit. Once a month should be our minimum. Weekly Communions are fortunately increasing; and though there was a time when people thought daily Communion was only for priests and other religious, now it is a habit with many lay people. Communion is best received during the Mass. While it is allowed to receive the Holy Eucharist before or after the Mass, the best practice is to receive It during the Mass.

Problem Questions

1. Mr. Rits, careless Catholic, wishes to fulfill his Easter duty of receiving the sacraments of penance and of the Holy Eucharist mostly because he is a member of the Catholic Order of Foresters. He knows that if he goes to confession to his pastor he will be severely scolded. Must he confess to his pastor? Discuss. What obligation has he of fulfilling these duties in his parish? What is the penalty of the Catholic Church for those who do not receive these sacraments during the Easter season?

2. In a certain parish, it is very rarely that the penitent has a chance to go to confession to any other priest than the regular pastor. While fulfilling his Easter duty, a certain young man deliberately concealed a mortal sin. On the following morning he received Holy Communion. Discuss from the Easter duty point of view. Why is such conduct the height of folly?

3. After a good confession and before receiving Holy Communion,
Jack smoked a cigarette;
Mary chewed gum;
Mr. Jenden took a headache tablet;
Some snowflakes blew into Jane's mouth. Discuss each one's case. May they receive? How does the law of fast oblige the sick?

Questions for the Pupil

1. Where does the Church get the power to make commandments or precepts or laws binding on you?

COMMANDMENTS OF THE CHURCH

2. Could the Church make a law binding on us in everything?
3. What is the special field in which the Church has authority?
4. Does the third commandment of the Church come within this authority?
5. What is the third commandment of the Church?
6. Is the requirement of the commandment all we should do? Or the least that we should do?
7. Where does the Church get the power to make commandments or precepts or laws binding on you?
8. Could the Church make a law binding on us in everything?
9. What is the special field in which the Church has authority?
10. Does the fourth commandment of the Church come within this authority?
11. What is the fourth commandment of the Church?
12. Is the requirement of the commandment all we should do? Or the least we should do?

Problem Questions

1. Thirty years ago there were no "Stop" and "Go" signals on busy street corners. Can you explain why? What would happen if there were none now? What happens to people who do not obey these signals? Do you think it will ever be necessary to make traffic laws for airplanes? When?

2. The early Christians received Holy Communion every time they went to Mass. Do you think that under those circumstances it was necessary to make a law which obliged them to go to Holy Communion at least once a year? Why not? Why do you suppose the Church had to make such a law later?

3. Mr. Goodwin says that there is nothing in the Bible about going to confession or Holy Communion at least once a year. In fact, he points out to you that this law of the Church was made in 1215 and therefore could not have come directly from Christ. What do you say? Look up the Fourth Lateran Council and tell the class what the Church decreed. (The teacher will guide you.)

4. Mr. Blake goes to confession and Holy Communion once a year at Christmas time. Does he fulfill his obligation in regard to the third commandment of the Church? To the fourth?

5. Suppose that Jack, a good friend of yours, became very ill. You advise him to see a doctor right away, but he says that just lately he has had an examination by a good doctor and that it is his practice to undergo a physical examination just once a year. What would you think of him? Which is more dangerous, to be seriously ill in body or in soul? How can

one be seriously ill in soul? Do you think it well to remain away from confession after one has sinned seriously? Why not? How soon should one go to confession after one has sinned seriously? What does confession do for the soul?

6. Mary Webb says she sees no reason why she should go to confession and Holy Communion more than once a year. She never cheats or steals, she does others no wrong and she goes to church every Sunday. What would you tell her?

7. A prominent business man of your parish, Mr. Dean, is refused Catholic burial by the pastor. For what reasons could the pastor refuse Catholic burial to a person? Mary Dean, one of the children of the family, tells you that the whole family is very angry because the pastor refused to bury her father from the Church and that they do not intend to belong to the Catholic Church any longer. Could you say anything to Mary to show her the priest was right? What about the family giving up their religion?

8. Mrs. Delaney is supposed to be a Catholic, but you never see her in Church. Later you learn that she goes to Mass and the sacraments in a Catholic church to which she does not belong. Has she a right to go where she pleases? Suppose all the members of a parish did as Mrs. Delaney, what would be the result? May she make her Easter Communion at another Church? Ought she to do so? Why?

9. James Lane was very ill at Easter time and could not make his Easter duty. He says that he need not receive the sacraments now for another year. Do you agree with him? When should he go to the sacraments?

10. Mrs. Cade says that she does not think her little girl ought to make her First Holy Communion until she knows what she is about, say at the age of twelve. Mrs. Cade herself was not allowed to go to First Communion until she was that old, and she sees no reason why the Church should have changed her views since. What would you tell her? What does Holy Communion do for the soul? At what age should children go to First Holy Communion? What pope wished to have children receive Holy Communion at an early age? What name has he therefore received?

11. James Martin went to confession and Holy Communion on Ash Wednesday. Has he made his Easter duty? During what period of time should he have gone in order to fulfill his obligation?

12. John's uncle has just lately come over from Europe. He says in his country Easter time lasts from Palm Sunday to Low Sunday. How can that be? Can you learn more about this for your class?

13. Edna says that she is not good enough to go to Holy Communion often. What would you answer her?

14. If a man received Holy Communion unworthily at Easter time, would he have fulfilled the law of the Church?

5. The Fifth Commandment of the Church

The fifth commandment of the Church is: To contribute to the support of our pastors. We owe loyalty and obedience to prelates, as St. Paul says, and we should be subject to them, of course, in spiritual matters. To do their own duty well in the service of God for their people; i.e., for you and me, they must give themselves up with their whole mind and heart to their work as pastors; nothing should distract them; there should be no divided interest or loyalty. "They that serve the altar, partake with the altar. . . . So also the Lord ordained that they who preach the Gospel, should live by the Gospel" (I Cor. ix. 13–14).

To do this they must be supported, priest, bishop or archbishop, and pope. It is our duty to support the Church and its priesthood by bearing our share of its expenses. This support of the Church takes in also the support of the Catholic school. We should give as generously as is within our power. We should give regularly and according to our means.

The whole system of the Catholic Church depends upon the support by its members. To let the other fellow do it, is to violate this commandment. Children from their earliest years should give to the Sunday collection and to special collections, as much as they can. To save a penny, or a nickle or a dime during the week from your spending money, and deny yourself candy, or some other thing you might like to have, in order to put your own money in the Sunday collection instead of asking mother or father, is a good thing for you, and shows a fine attitude, and will help you to grow in the spiritual life.

Question from the Catechism

Q. Are we obliged to contribute to the support of our pastors?

A. **We are obliged to contribute to the support of our pastors, and to bear our share in the expenses of the Church and school.**

Questions for the Pupil

1. Where does the Church get the power to make commandments or precepts or laws binding on you?

2. Could the Church make a law binding on us in everything?
3. What is the special field in which the Church has authority?
4. Does the fifth commandment of the Church come within this authority?
5. What is the fifth commandment of the church?
6. Is the priest required to give his whole time to his duties? What relation has this to his support?
7. Are the gifts of money to priests at the time of administering the sacrament of baptism and matrimony in payment of services? or when he says a Mass for an intention? or for the dead?

Problem Questions

1. Donald Brunner, twenty-one years of age, has a permanent position, is drawing a good salary, and has no one to support but himself. He feels that he is not obliged to contribute to the church because his parents are regular contributors. Why is Donald obliged to contribute? How could Donald be led to understand his duty?

6. The Sixth Commandment of the Church

The sixth commandment of the Church is: *Not to Marry Persons Who Are Not Catholics, or Who are Related to Us Within the Third Degree of Kindred, nor Privately without Witnesses, nor to Solemnize Marriage at Forbidden Times.*

The Sacrament of Matrimony and the Preparation for It. The marriage of Christians is a great event in the providence of God. It has been raised by Christ to the dignity of a sacrament. The Church requires that an announcement be made for three successive Sundays in the parish church of each of the persons to be married, in order to discover if there are any impediments, or if for any reason the marriage should not take place. This is called "publication of the banns." Besides, the Church desires that such an important step in the life of the person, a step that will last all his life and can never be undone, should not be made in a hurry or without worthy motives. It is, further, the desire of the Church that persons about to be married should prepare for a holy and happy marriage by begging God to grant them a pure intention and to direct their choice, by seeking the advice of their parents and the blessing of their pastors, and on the marriage day by receiving the sacraments of penance and Holy Communion.

COMMANDMENTS OF THE CHURCH

Four Prohibitions of the Sixth Commandment of the Church. The sixth commandment of the Church is a further guide to human beings in perhaps the most important single human relationship on the Highway of Life. This relationship between Christians; i.e., marriage, has been raised to the very great dignity of a sacrament as we have seen. The Church as a result of its experience and its insight, guided by the Holy Ghost, and in keeping with the spirit of the sacrament of matrimony has made some laws regarding marriages. There are four parts to this commandment of the Church.

1. Not to marry persons who are not Catholics.
2. Not to marry persons related to us within the third degree of kindred.
3. Not to marry privately without witnesses.
4. Not to solemnize marriage at forbidden times.

Why Both Parties Should have the Same Spiritual View of Marriage. The Catholic Church holds marriage as something very important and sacred. It is used by the Apostles as a symbol of the close and indissoluble union of Christ and the Church. It is a sacrament, and a source of graces. If one of the parties does not look upon the marriage as an indissoluble union during the life of both parties, if he or she does not look upon it as a sacrament, then it does not fulfill the ideal conditions of a sacramental union. If persons look upon marriage as a contract to be broken when they wish or as a merely human relationship, not as sacred and supernatural, then there is at the very heart of the relationship the seeds of its destruction. A marriage between a Catholic and a non-Catholic is called a mixed marriage.

Why the Church Forbids Mixed Marriages. The Church has learned, too, from experience that too often the Catholic member of a mixed marriage grows careless about his religion, becomes indifferent, and at last neglects it completely or loses his faith. Besides being an injury in this way to the greatest interest of man, the salvation of his soul, it often does great harm to the souls of the children, because such parents are likely to forget their duty to give or to see that the children receive a Catholic education. In this way, what ought to be one of the happiest of human relations results in misery or tragedy, or, in any case, always in some danger to the spiritual welfare of the Catholic member and the children.

The Conditions of Mixed Marriages. But such marriages between Catholics and non-Catholics called mixed marriages, forbidden generally, are allowed under certain conditions which aim to guard against the dangers that are found in such mixed marriages. These conditions are:

1. That the Catholic be allowed the free exercise of religion.
2. That *all* children be brought up in the Catholic religion.
3. That the non-Catholic member receive instructions in the Catholic religion, so as to understand its general ideas, particularly its teaching on marriage as a sacrament and all that doctrine implies.

A mixed marriage is not allowed by way of exception in any case unless these conditions be fulfilled and a promise made in writing that *all* the children of the marriage be brought up in the Catholic faith.

Solemnizing Marriage. Marriage may be contracted at any time of the year, and ordinarily it is solemnized; i.e., performed with special ceremony. The Church, by a solemn blessing and a special Mass shows us the beauty, the dignity, the holiness, and the supernatural character of the Christian marriage, and brings richer blessings on the people to be married and on their wedded life. The Church wishes that marriage should always be solemnized with a nuptial Mass when such solemnity does not conflict with the time of the spiritual or liturgical year. Catholics should be married at a nuptial Mass. Moreover, people about to be married look forward to the event with great joy and eagerness and express it often by great pomp. In this way, too, they show greater reverence for the holy sacrament of matrimony. But the Church, with a nice sense of what is fitting, feels that it would not be right to celebrate a marriage with the joyous nuptial Mass and with pomp during the season of Lent and in the season of

Advent. Both seasons are seasons of penance, though both end in an infinitely joyous event, the Incarnation and the Resurrection of Christ. Marriages may be contracted during these seasons, but the people must refrain from too much pomp, and except with the permission of the bishop (local ordinary) the solemn nuptial blessing cannot be given and solemn nuptial Mass cannot be said.

The Forbidden Times. These forbidden seasons for the solemnizing of marriages extends from the first Sunday in Advent to Christmas Day, inclusive; and from Ash Wednesday to Easter Sunday, inclusive. These seasons are forbidden for the solemnizing of marriage because they are times of penance, and so it would not be proper to have such celebrations. Marriage, let it be repeated, is not forbidden during these times, but its performance with great ceremony, show, or pomp, or with the nuptial Mass, is forbidden.

Marriages Held Before Priests and Two Witnesses. The Church, by its demand for the publication of marriage banns, and its desire that except in forbidden seasons it should be solemnized with a solemn nuptial blessing and a solemn nuptial Mass, would naturally make marriage a public event. Making a lifelong contract carrying such responsibilities should not be a private event, and certainly should not be performed without witnesses. The presence of witnesses is a safeguard both for the persons being married, and for all who in any way may be affected by the marriage. The Church does not recognize a marriage that is not contracted before a priest and two witnesses. The marriage may be contracted when in danger of death without the presence of a local priest or bishop, or a representative of either. But the presence of the pastor is ordinarily required.

Marriages Between Close Relatives Forbidden. The Church has learned that marriages between close relatives often have bad effects. It has bad effects on children born of such marriages and it has bad effects on those who are married. Often, too, no children are born of such marriages. This is true of close blood relationship. The rule of the Church forbids the marriage of

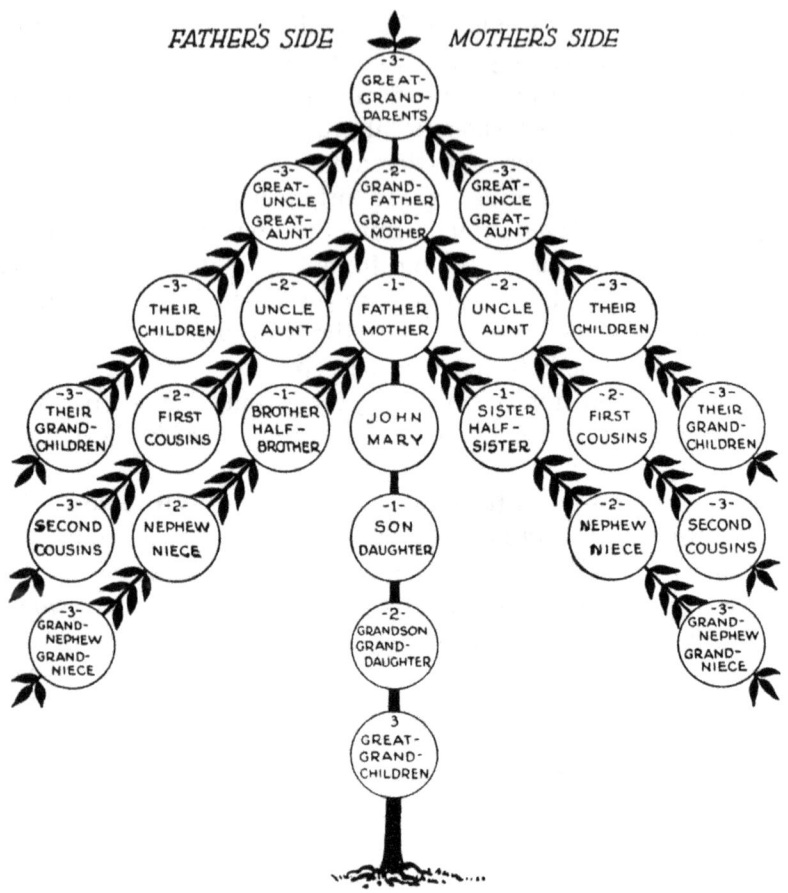

RELATIONSHIP CHART
This figure shows the method of figuring blood relationship.

brothers and sisters, of first and second cousins; i.e., within the third degree of blood relationship. The degree of kindred or blood relationship may be shown in the accompanying chart.

The Church, also forbids, through its power to make rules and regulations, the marriage of a sponsor of a child at baptism, and the child. (It also forbids marriages with certain relatives of a husband or a wife in case of the death of one of the parties.) This requirement that marriage go beyond the close family or other close relationship extends social relationships and unites wider groups of people in the bonds of Christian charity and love.

Questions from the Catechism

Q. What is the meaning of the commandment not to marry within the third degree of kindred?
A. **The meaning of the commandment not to marry within the third degree of kindred is that no one is allowed to marry another within the third degree of blood relationship.**

Q. What is the meaning of the command not to marry privately?
A. **The command not to marry privately means that none should marry without the blessing of God's priests or without witnesses.**

Q. What is the meaning of the precept not to solemnize marriage at forbidden times?
A. **The meaning of the precept not to solemnize marriage at forbidden times is that during Lent and Advent the marriage ceremony should not be performed with pomp or a nuptial Mass.**

Q. What is the nuptial Mass?
A. **The nuptial Mass is a Mass appointed by the Church to invoke a special blessing upon the married couple.**

Q. Should Catholics be married at a nuptial Mass?
A. **Catholics should be married at a nuptial Mass, because they thereby show greater reverence for the holy sacrament and bring richer blessings upon their wedded life.**

Q. Does the Church forbid the marriage of Catholics with persons who have a different religion or no religion at all?
A. **The Church does forbid the marriage of Catholics with persons who have a different religion or no religion at all.**

Q. Why does the Church forbid the marriage of Catholics with persons who have a different religion or no religion at all?
A. **The Church forbids the marriage of Catholics with persons who have a different religion or no religion at all, because such marriages generally lead to indifference, loss of faith, and to the neglect of the religious education of the children.**

Q. Why do many marriages prove unhappy?
A. **Many marriages prove unhappy because they are entered into hastily and without worthy motives.**

Q. How should Christians prepare for a holy and happy marriage?
A. **Christians should prepare for a holy and happy marriage by receiving the sacraments of penance and Holy Eucharist, by begging God to grant them a pure intention and to direct their choice; and by seeking the advice of their parents and the blessing of their pastors.**

Q. Who has the right to make laws concerning the sacrament of marriage?
A. **The Church alone has the right to make laws concerning the sacrament of marriage, though the state also has the right to make laws concerning the civil effects of the marriage contract.**

Problem Questions

1. Jim Michaels and Olive Clancy, second cousins, wish to marry. Jim's mother was a Catholic but Jim was never baptized. Olive insists upon a Catholic marriage. What must be done? Name the various impediments to this union.

2. Jane Dugan and Frank Sullivan had set their wedding date for March the seventeenth. For some weeks arrangements had been under way. About a month before the ceremony took place, they went to see the pastor about the publication of the banns. They were sorely disappointed when they could not have a nuptial Mass except by special dispensation from the bishop and even then, they could not have a dancing party afterwards. Why does the Church forbid solemnization of marriage during Lent? Does this mean no one can be married during Lent without the bishop's dispensation? Discuss.

Chapter XLII
THE SAINTS

Holiness of Church and Saints. The holiness of the Church is based in the first instance on the holiness of its Founder, our Lord Jesus Christ. It is strengthened in that long line of holy men and women throughout the ages, who have given up everything for Christ, and have reached a holiness and sanctity of life which makes them Christlike.

Saints in Every Age. Whatever the age or the time, there have appeared these holy souls. Men in all ages have called them saints in the strictest sense of the word, and the Church has raised them to the altars of God. There are many souls among us who are living holy lives of the highest kind who are, in fact, saints, but their holiness has not been seen in such unmistakable and extraordinary ways as the sanctity of those who have been canonized nor have they given proof of final perseverance.

Scripture Saints. We should naturally expect a great number of saints in the very beginning of the Church. First, of course, is the Blessed Virgin Mary, the Mother of Christ, St. Joseph, the foster father of Jesus, and the twelve Apostles, substituting Matthias for Judas Iscariot. There are, too, the writers of the Holy Scriptures, St. Matthew, St. Mark, St. Luke, St. John, of whom Matthew and John were also Apostles, the authors of the Gospels, and especially St. Paul, the Apostle to the Gentiles. Among others of the many scripture saints are St. John the Baptist; St. Timothy, and St. Titus, assistants of St. Paul, and St. Mary Magdalen, and St. Stephen, the martyr.

Other Saints. Among the greater saints may be listed: St. Augustine, St. Monica, St. Benedict, St. Francis of Assisi, St. Patrick, St. Clare, St. Dominic, St. Thomas Aquinas, St. Teresa of Avila, St. Ignatius Loyola, St. Francis Xavier, St. Stanislaus Kostka, St. Aloysius, St. John Baptist de la Salle, St. Térèse or the Little Flower, etc.

As we examine this list of saints we must be impressed by the fact that there is not just one type of saint. There are hundreds of saints, and almost as many kinds of saintliness. The servants of Christ serve in many ways.

The Life of the Saint. We cannot tell here the very interesting and instructive lives of these saints. If each member of the class will look up one of these saints and his patron saints, the result will be a very interesting class period. If you will read the Litany of the Saints you will find the praises of the saints as follows:

Who have left all things and followed Christ (see Matt. iv. 20).

Who were hated by all men for the name of Christ (see Matt. x. 22).

Who rejoiced that they were counted worthy to suffer reproach for the name of Jesus (see Acts v. 41).

Who, when endued with power from on High, and strengthened by the Holy Ghost, boldly confessed Christ (see Luke xxiv. 49).

Who obeyed God rather than men (see Acts v. 29).

Who suffered persecution for living holy in the world (see II Tim. iii. 12).

Who gloried in the cross of our Lord (see Gal. vi. 14).

Who in their patience possessed their souls (see Luke xxi. 19).

Who had trials of mockeries and stripes, bands and prisons, were stoned, cut asunder, and variously tempted (see Heb. xi. 36–37).

Who have suffered persecution for justice' sake, and now safely possess the kingdom of heaven (see Matt. v. 10).

Who, like good shepherds, laid down their lives for their sheep (see John x. 11).

Who faithfully fed, not themselves, but the Lord's flock (see Ezech. xxxiv. 2).

Who became all things to men, that they might gain all men to God (see I Cor. ix. 19).

THE SAINTS

Who put on the armor of God, and bravely stood against the deceits of the devil (see Eph. vi. 11).

Who counted all things to be but loss, that they might gain Christ (see Phil. iii. 8).

Who minded the things that are above, not those that are upon the earth (see Col. iii. 2).

Who received not the grace of God in vain (see II Cor. vi. 1).

Who loved their enemies, and did good to them that hated them (see Matt. v. 44).

Who laid up to yourselves treasures, not on earth, but in heaven (see Matt. vi. 20).

Who sought first the kingdom of God, and His justice (see Matt. vi. 33).

Who strove to enter in at the narrow gate, and the strait way, that leadeth to life (see Matt. vii. 13–14).

Who by the love of their pure hearts advanced to the sight of God (see Matt. v. 8).

Who through many tribulations are entered into the kingdom of God (see Acts xiv. 21).

Who, for hungering and thirsting after justice, are now filled with the joys of heaven (see Matt. v. 6).

Canonization. After a very careful study is made of the life, writings, and reported miracles of a dead person, and the results of the investigation is approved by the pope, the person may be beatified. He is then called Blessed, and permission is given to pay him public honor and veneration. Beatification generally, but not always, leads to canonization. Canonization is the process of making a public and official declaration of the heroic virtue or sanctity of a person, and the inclusion of his or her name in the canon or register of saints. It is simply the formal declaration by the pope that the person is a saint. The same very careful investigations are carried on as in beatification, and often go on for years.

Miracles due to the saint's intercession reported after beatification must be looked into thoroughly and proved before a person can be canonized. For a canonized saint, a day is appointed for his feast and a liturgical office prepared, his relics are publicly honored, churches and altars may be dedicated in his honor, statues and pictures used in churches, and public prayers said to him.

We must not think that all the saints, persons of extraordinary virtue or sanctity, have been formally declared saints, i.e., canonized.

Church Triumphant. Men and women such as these and countless others have gone to the just reward with God in heaven for their holy life on earth, for their service to their neighbors, and their love of neighbor and of God. These people are the Church Triumphant. They have gained the life of glory which is so much greater and richer than the life of grace. They see not through a glass darkly, but directly the vision of God. They live in the radiation from Almighty God, where there is all power, all beauty, all peace, all blessedness, and all love. There are gathered all the holy men and women, all the saints of God, both those canonized and the uncanonized. There is gathered, the "great multitude, which no man can number, of all nations, and tribes, and peoples, and tongues, standing before the throne, and in sight of the Lamb, clothed with white robes, and palms in their hands" (Apoc. vii. 9).

Saints, Living Members of the Church. We, as Catholics, think of these saints in heaven as members of the Church, of which we, too, are members. We do not think of the saints merely as persons dead and gone, whose examples we might imitate; we think of them as living members of the Church, as joined forever in love with Christ, in whom, in a final sense, they live, move, and have their being. They are the chosen friends of God. They have become active coworkers with Christ. They form part of the communion of saints — a very consoling doctrine of the Church.

The Communion of Saints. It is this study of the saints that makes us realize more deeply than ever that the Church is the mystical body of Christ, and He is its head. The saints in heaven are members of the Church of Christ just as we are. It is this communion or union of the saints in heaven, the suffering souls in purgatory, and ourselves that we mean when we speak of the Church, not the church building in our parish. The Church in heaven, and the Church on earth, and the Church in purgatory are one and the same Church and all its members are in communion with one another. This communion of the members of the Church is called communion of saints. "Saint" in this sense means simply Christian or member of the Church, not the blessed or glorified members of the Church. The word "communion" brings out the union and the coöperation which exists among the members of the Church on earth with members of the Church in heaven, and with the suffering souls in purgatory. From this communion and coöperation of the saints or members of the Church certain benefits are derived:

1. The faithful on earth assist one another by their prayers and good works.

2. The faithful on earth are helped by the prayers of the saints in heaven.

3. The souls in purgatory are helped both by the saints in heaven and the faithful on earth.

Honor and Devotion to Saints. To honor the saints in heaven, to respect them, and to recall to mind their lives and the memorials to them are acts of devotion that we owe to them because of their great holiness and their love and devotion to God. To honor relics of the saints, their bodies or other things connected with them, is also a mark of respect which we should gladly offer to holiness and to love of God. To use images, or pictures, or relics of these friends of God, to put us in mind of them, and of their love of God, is a great help in our religious life.

Honor and Respect to Images and Relics. The First Commandment of God forbids us to worship, or adore, or serve, or bow down before any graven image or other thing. We shall worship God only. But this commandment does not forbid us to *honor* relics whether these relics are the bodies of saints, or objects directly connected with the saints or with our Lord. It does not forbid us making images to put us in mind of Jesus Christ,

His Blessed Mother, and the saints. We show respect to any pictures or images of Christ and His saints, because they are representations and memorials which call them to mind more vividly.

We Do Not Worship Images. We are forbidden to make any images of Christ, His Mother, or the saints, if these images are to be adored as gods. We are forbidden to adore or to pray to the crucifix, or relics of the saints as well as images. These things have no life, nor power to help us, nor sense to hear us. We do not pray *to* them; we may, however, pray *before* them because they may help us, in two ways:

1. They enliven our devotion by exciting pious affections and desires, and

2. They remind us of Christ and of His saints in order that we may imitate their virtues.

Prayers to the Saints. We pray to the saints themselves in order to gain their help and prayers. They have not power as we have seen, to grant our prayers. Only God can do that, but we are taught by the Church that they may intercede for us. They hear us; for being with God, God makes our prayers known to them.

Questions from the Catechism

Q. Does the First Commandment forbid the honoring of saints?
A. **The First Commandment does not forbid the honoring of the saints, but rather approves of it; because by honoring the saints who are the chosen friends of God, we honor God Himself.**

Q. Does the First Commandment forbid us to pray to the saints?
A. **The First Commandment does not forbid us to pray to the saints.**

Q. What do you mean by praying to the saints?
A. **By praying to the saints we mean the asking of their help and prayers.**

Q. How do we know that the saints hear us?
A. **We know that the saints hear us; because they are with God, who makes our prayers known to them.**

Q. Why do we believe that the saints will help us?

THE SAINTS

A. We believe that the saints will help us, because both they and we are members of the same Church, and they love us as their brethren.

Q. How are the saints and we members of the same Church?
A. The saints and we are members of the same Church, because the Church in heaven and the Church on earth are one and the same Church, and all its members are in communion with one another.

Q. What is the communion of the members of the Church called?
A. The communion of the members of the Church is called the communion of saints.

Q. What does the communion of saints mean?
A. The communion of saints means the union which exists between the members of the Church on earth with one another, and with the blessed in heaven, and with the suffering souls in purgatory.

Q. What benefits are derived from the communion of saints?
A. The following benefits are derived from the communion of saints: the faithful on earth assist one another by their prayers and good works, and they are aided by the intercession of the saints in heaven, while both the saints in heaven and the faithful on earth help the souls in purgatory.

Q. Does the First Commandment forbid us to honor relics?
A. The First Commandment does not forbid us to honor relics, because relics are the bodies of the saints or objects directly connected with them or with our Lord.

Q. Does the First Commandment forbid the making of images?
A. The First Commandment does forbid the making of images if they are made to be adored as gods, but it does not forbid the making of them to put us in mind of Jesus Christ, His Blessed Mother, and the saints.

Q. Is it right to show respect to the pictures and images of Christ and His saints?
A. It is right to show respect to the pictures and images of Christ and His saints, because they are the representations and memorials of them.

Q. Is it allowed to pray to the crucifix or to the images and relics of the saints?

A. It is not allowed to pray to the crucifix or images and relics of the saints, for they have no life, nor power to help us, nor sense to hear us.

Q. Why do we pray before the crucifix and the images and relics of the saints?

A. **We pray before the crucifix and the images and relics of the saints because they enliven our devotion by exciting pious affections and desires, and by reminding us of Christ and of the saints, that we may imitate their virtues.**

Problem Questions

1. What is a saint?
2. Name your patron saints. What is his (her) feast day?
3. Write a biography of a saint you like.
4. Are there any saints today?
5. Were there any saints in the nineteenth century?
6. Are there any American saints?
7. Read the Litany of the Saints. Are the lives of the saints any evidence of the holiness of the Church?
8. What is meant by beatification?
9. What is meant by canonization?
10. What honor and devotion is shown to saints?
11. Discuss the honor and devotion to the saints in the light of the First Commandment of God.
12. Are the saints (as used in this chapter) the only members of the Church Triumphant?
13. Are there any uncanonized saints?
14. Why is the communion of saints a consoling doctrine?
15. How may the Church Militant help the Church Suffering?
16. How may the Church Triumphant help the Church Suffering and the Church Militant?
17. Why may we pray to the saints?
18. How does this differ from prayers to God?

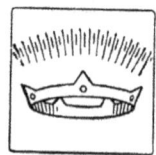

Chapter XLIII
THE ANGELS

Angels in Christ's Life. In the life of Christ as told in the Gospels angels are spoken of several times. Some of them appear alone, and some in numbers singing the praise of God, and Christ refers to the angels of God in His discourses or speeches. Let us recall some of these instances now.

1. There appeared to Zachary in the temple an angel of the Lord standing at the right side of the altar of incense who told Zachary that Elizabeth, his wife, would bear a son whom he should call John. This is John the Baptist. And Zachary, doubtful, asked how he would know this. And the angel answering, said:

> I am Gabriel, who stand before God; and am sent to speak to thee, and to bring thee these good tidings.
>
> And behold, thou shalt be dumb, and shalt not be able to speak until the day wherein these things shall come to pass, because thou hast not believed my words, which shall be fulfilled in their time (Luke i. 19–20).

2. And six months later "the Angel Gabriel was sent from God into a city of Galilee called Nazareth" to announce the birth of Christ.

3. The angel of the Lord appeared to Joseph in his sleep when he found that a child was to be born to Mary, and said, "Joseph, son of David, fear not to take unto thee Mary thy wife, for that which is conceived in her is of the Holy Ghost. And she shall bring forth a son; and thou shalt call His name Jesus. For He shall save His people from their sins" (Matt. i. 20–21).

4. We read next of an angel of the Lord standing by the shepherds in the field bringing them the good tidings of great joy: "For this day is born to you a Savior, who is Christ the Lord, in the city of David" (Luke ii. 11).

5. The angel of the Lord appeared again to Joseph in sleep, warning him to take the Child and His mother, and fly into Egypt. . . . "Herod will seek the Child to destroy Him" (Matt. ii. 13).

6. Upon Herod's death, an angel of the Lord appeared to Joseph in sleep, to tell him it was now safe to bring back to Israel, the mother and Child (Matt. ii. 20).

7. In the Garden of Gethsemane an angel appeared to Christ.

And there appeared to Him an angel from heaven strengthening Him (Luke xxii. 43).

8. And so at the end we read of the appearance of the angel of the Lord at the sepulcher.

And behold there was a great earthquake. For an angel of the Lord descended from heaven, and coming, rolled back the stone, and sat upon it.
And his countenance was as lightning, and his raiment as snow.
And for fear of him, the guards were struck with terror, and became as dead men.
And the angel answering, said to the women: Fear not you; for I know that you seek Jesus who was crucified (Matt. xxviii. 2–5).

9. And St. John tells of the appearance to Mary Magdalen of "two angels in white, sitting, one at the head, and one at the feet where the body of Jesus had been laid" (John xx. 12).

10. And at the Ascension two angels appeared to the disciples who are thus described:

And while they were beholding Him going up to Heaven, behold two men stood by them in white garments (Acts i. 10).

So much for a brief statement of the appearance of single angels in connection with the birth and death of Christ. We read of appearances of angels to Peter in the Acts of the Apostles.

The Vision of Isaias. There is added also the vision of Isaias, which contains the story referred to in the Mass:

In the year that King Ozias died, I saw the Lord sitting upon a throne high and elevated: and His train filled the temple.
Upon it stood the seraphims: the one had six wings, and the other had six wings: with two they covered His face, and with two they covered His feet, and with two they flew.

THE ANGELS

And they cried one to another, and said: Holy, holy, holy, the Lord God of Hosts, all the earth is full of His glory.

And the lintels of the doors were moved at the voice of him that cried, and the house was filled with smoke.

And I said: Woe is me, because I have held my peace; because I am a man of unclean lips, and I dwell in the midst of a people that hath unclean lips, and I have seen with my eyes the King the Lord of Hosts.

And one of the seraphims flew to me, and in his hand was a live coal, which he had taken with the tongs off the altar.

And he touched my mouth, and said: Behold this hath touched thy lips, and thy iniquities shall be taken away, and thy sin shall be cleansed.

And I heard the voice of the Lord, saying: Whom shall I send? and who shall go for us? And I said: Lo, here am I, send me (Isa. vi. 1–8).

Other Angels in the Old Testament. In the Old Testament there are records too, of the angelic visiting of human beings. Some of the more noteworthy cases are:

1. The first instance is the one where an angel of the Lord visits Abraham to prevent him from offering his son Isaac as a sacrifice to God:

And he put forth his hand and took the sword, to sacrifice his son.

And behold an angel of the Lord from heaven called to him, saying: Abraham, Abraham. And he answered: Here I am.

And he said to him: Lay not thy hand upon the boy, neither do thou any thing to him: now I know that thou fearest God, and hast not spared thy only-begotten son for My sake (Gen. xxii. 10–12).

2. Another instance is the visit to Jacob of the angel in the form of a young man who wrestled with Jacob to show him that neither Esau nor any other man should have power to hurt him.

He remained alone: and behold a man wrestled with him till morning.

And when he saw that he could not overcome him, he touched the sinew of his thigh, and forthwith it shrank.

And he said to him: Let me go, for it is break of day. He answered: I will not let thee go except thou bless me.

And he said: What is thy name? He answered: Jacob.

But he said: Thy name shall not be called Jacob, but Israel: for if thou hast been strong against God, how much more shalt thou prevail against men? (Gen. xxxii. 24–28.)

3. The Angel Raphael appeared in the form of a young man, took the name of Azarias, and guided Tobias on his journey to and from Medea. At the end he reveals himself as follows:

For I am the Angel Raphael, one of the seven, who stand before the Lord.
And when they had heard these things, they were troubled, and being seized with fear they fell upon the ground on their face.
And the angel said to them: Peace be to you, fear not.
For when I was with you, I was there by the will of God: bless ye Him, and sing praise to Him.
I seemed indeed to eat and to drink with you: but I use an invisible meat and drink, which cannot be seen by men.
It is time therefore that I return to Him that sent me: but bless ye God, and publish all His wonderful works.
And when he had said these things, he was taken from their sight, and they could see him no more.
Then they lying prostrate for three hours upon their face, blessed God: and rising up, they told all His wonderful works (Tob. xii. 15–22).

Appearance of Angels in Groups in the New Testament. We read also of the visiting of angels in numbers or groups. A few of these appearances may be given.

1. After the announcement to the shepherds the account continues:

And suddenly there was with the angel a multitude of the heavenly army, praising God, and saying:
Glory to God in the highest; and on earth peace to men of good will (Luke ii. 13–14).

2. After Christ was tempted by the devil following the forty days of our Lord's fasting in the wilderness, we read:

Then the devil left Him; and behold angels came and ministered to Him (Matt. iv. 11).

Angels in Groups in the Old Testament. Only one instance of the appearance of angels in groups need be quoted from the Old Testament. The one from Daniel describing his vision of God's throne says:

A swift stream of fire issued forth from before Him: thousands of thousands ministered to Him, and ten thousand times a hundred thousand stood before Him: the judgment sat, and the books were opened (Dan. vii. 10).

Guardian Angels. Christ in His teaching often speaks of angels. One of the most famous references is to the guardian angels of children. In this case He begins by teaching His disciples that to gain the kingdom of heaven we must become as little children, and He promises that "He that shall receive one such little child in My name, receiveth Me" (Matt. xviii. 5). He continues:

> See that you despise not one of these little ones: for I say to you, that their angels in heaven always see the face of My Father who is in heaven (Matt. xviii. 10).

Christ indicates that life in heaven is life with the angels. The promises of reward for the just and the unjust are thus stated by Christ:

> And I say to you, Whosoever shall confess Me before men, him shall the Son of Man also confess before the angels of God.
> But he that shall deny Me before men, shall be denied before the angels of God (Luke xii. 8–9).

And the nature of hell is given more clear statement in that picture of the Last Judgment.

> Then He shall say to them also that shall be on His left hand: Depart from Me, you cursed, into everlasting fire which was prepared for the devil and his angels (Matt. xxv. 41).

These are only two references but they show clearly that there is an angel life that is in contact with human life, and it is part of the eternal scheme of things.

Our Knowledge of Angels. We get glimpses of angels in the Scripture. We see them deliver their message, and give their warnings. They come and they are gone. We know little about them. We know they are pure spirits. They are messengers of God. They sing the praise of God. They adore God. In their coming to the world they seem present to our senses or they assume human form. But that they are spirits we know from the suddenness of their appearance and the equal suddenness of their departure.

They are pure spirits without a body created to adore and enjoy God in heaven. From what we are told of them in the Scriptures we learn that they assist before the throne of God and minister unto Him, they have often been sent as messengers from God to man, and they are appointed as our guardians.

Evil Spirits. There are also evil spirits whom we see in the Garden of Eden tempting Adam, and in the wilderness tempting Christ. They are probably without much effect on human life because of the guardianship of good angels. The nature of this guardianship is not clear to us. We read of temptations of people, and there are instances recorded that seem certainly like temptations of the devil or evil spirits. They can be successful only if we coöperate with them. The advice of St. Paul is the advice for us. "Give not place to the devil" (Eph. iv. 27). The positive advice is: *Love God.*

The Fallen Angels. In the Garden of Eden we are told of the evil spirit, a fallen angel. Though God created the angels good and happy, all did not remain so. Some sinned, in a way we do not know exactly and were, as Christ tells us, cast into hell. The angels who had sinned and were cast into hell, we call devils, or bad angels. We know certainly that there are angels, but we do not know much about their life, their activities, or their nature, except such instances as are given in this chapter.*

Questions from the Catechism

Q. Which are the chief creatures of God?
A. **The chief creatures of God are angels and men.**

Q. What are angels?
A. **Angels are pure spirits without a body created to adore and enjoy God in heaven.**

Q. Were the angels created for any other purpose?
A. **The angels were also created to assist before the throne of God and to minister unto Him; they have often been sent as messengers from God to man; and are also appointed our guardians.**

---

*Cf. *Angels Good and Bad*, by Houck. B. Herder Book Company, St. Louis, Mo.

THE ANGELS

Q. Were the angels, as God created them, good and happy?
A. **The angels, as God created them, were good and happy.**

Q. Did all the angels remain good and happy?
A. **All the angels did not remain good and happy; many of them sinned and were cast into hell, and these are called devils or bad angels.**

Problem Questions

1. Make a list of the appearances of angels in connection with the life of Christ.
2. Make a list of some of the appearances of angels in the Old Testament. (A concordance might be used to answer this question completely.)
3. What were the names of angels who have appeared to men?
4. What did Christ say regarding our guardian angels?
5. In what ways does the guardian angel look after us?
6. Why do you think that at certain times hosts or multitudes of angels appear? Why would a multitude more fully express praise of God?
7. What is the basis for representing angels with wings? Have any angels wings? Have all angels wings?
8. Select two pictures of angels that you like. Tell why.
9. Why is the "Angelus" called by that name?
10. Find a poem on an angel that you like. Memorize it. What is its fundamental idea?

Quotations from the Bible

For each of the following quotations:
a) Identify the speaker.
b) State the conditions under which the statement was made.
c) Give the meaning.
d) Tell its significance.

"She shall bring forth a Son, and thou shalt call His name Jesus. For He shall save His people from their sins" (Matt. i. 21).

"Glory to God in the highest: and on earth peace to men of good will" (Luke ii. 14).

To what incident does the following description refer?
Who was present?
What is the significance of the event?

"It came to pass that night, that an angel of the Lord came, and slew in the camp of the Assyrians a hundred and eighty-five thousand" (IV Kings xix. 35).

"I am the Angel Raphael, one of the seven, who stand before the Lord. When I was with you, I was there by the will of God; I seemed indeed to eat and to drink with you: but I use an invisible meat and drink, which cannot be seen by men. It is time therefore that I return to Him that sent me. And when he had said these things he was taken from their sight, and they could see him no more" (Tob. xii. 15–21).

Chapter XLIV
THE END OF THE JOURNEY

Heaven. At the end of God's Highway are those mansions which Christ promised. "In My Father's house there are many mansions. If not, I would have told you: because I go to prepare a place for you" (John xiv. 2). Christ also refers to these places "which have been prepared from the foundation of the world" (Matt. xxv: 34). To those persons who followed the commandments and imitate Christ, this is their inheritance. It is to be with God. It is the beatific vision. It is heaven. It is life everlasting. It would be hard to describe it. Saints who have seen it in vision have not been able to tell us in words what it is. Even the Apostles cannot describe it:

> Eye hath not seen, nor ear heard, neither hath it entered into the heart of man, what things God hath prepared for them that love Him (I Cor. ii. 9).

And if we read about the vision of St. John in the last book of the Bible, we see it a little more clearly.

> God shall wipe away all tears from their eyes; and death shall be no more, nor mourning, nor crying, nor sorrow shall be any more, for the former things are passed away (Apoc. xxi. 4).

That is the end of the journey for those of us who have lived good lives. The end we think of too often is death. Death is a going over to the glorious life which we have described in the last paragraph. We feel at the time of death the very real, immediate sense of loss of dear ones. We should think of it in the language Christ used. He always spoke of death as sleep. "He sleepeth" meant he was dead. It is a sleep in which we may rise to a glorious tomorrow. Let us see what the steps and the possibilities are.

The Particular Judgment. St. Paul said it is given us once to die and after that the judgment. What is this judgment? It is a judgment of our words, our actions, our thoughts, and omissions. This judgment soon after death is called the Particular Judgment. It must not be thought that the soul is led before Christ in heaven. The judgment is made by Christ who is everywhere and knows all things. This judgment must come to the departed soul as a realization in a way we do not know. This judgment decides our destiny, heaven, hell, or purgatory.

The General Judgment. It is from the lips of Christ Himself that we learn the signs and the nature of the final or last judgment, and some of the signs of the General Judgment besides the coming of Antichrist, are:

For nation shall rise against nation, and kingdom against kingdom; and there shall be pestilences, and famines, and earthquakes in places (Matt. xxiv. 7).

For there shall be then great tribulation, such as hath not been from the beginning of the world until now, neither shall be.

And unless those days had been shortened, no flesh should be saved: but for the sake of the elect those days shall be shortened (Matt. xxiv. 21–22).

And the description and prophecy goes on with the appearance of the Son of Man coming in judgment:

And immediately after the tribulation of those days, the sun shall be darkened and the moon shall not give her light, and the stars shall fall from heaven, and the powers of heaven shall be moved:

And then shall appear the sign of the Son of Man in heaven: and then shall all tribes of the earth mourn: and they shall see the Son of Man coming in the clouds of heaven with much power and majesty.

And He shall send His angels with a trumpet, and a great voice: and they shall gather together His elect from the four winds, from the farthest parts of the heavens to the utmost bounds of them.

And from the fig tree learn a parable: When the branch thereof is now tender, and the leaves come forth, you know that summer is nigh.

So you also, when you shall see these things, know ye that it is nigh, even at the doors.

Amen I say to you, that this generation shall not pass, till all these things be done (Matt. xxiv. 29–34).

And the nature of the judgment which the Son of Man shall give, and the basis of it are shown in the following statement which is made just before the anointing of Christ's feet by Mary and the treason of Judas and the time when man, or rather evil men, are to sit in judgment of Him. This is the statement:

And when the Son of Man shall come in His majesty, and all the angels with Him, then shall He sit upon the seat of His majesty:

And all nations shall be gathered together before Him, and He shall separate them one from another, as the shepherd separateth the sheep from the goats:

And He shall set the sheep on His right hand, but the goats on His left.

Then shall the King say to them that shall be on His right hand: Come, ye blessed of My Father, possess you the kingdom prepared for you from the foundation of the world.

For I was hungry, and you gave Me to eat; I was thirsty, and you gave Me to drink; I was a stranger, and you took Me in.

Naked, and you covered Me: sick, and you visited Me: I was in prison, and you came to Me.

Then shall the just answer Him, saying: Lord, when did we see Thee hungry, and fed Thee; thirsty, and gave Thee drink?

And when did we see Thee a stranger, and took Thee in? or naked, and covered Thee?

Or when did we see Thee sick or in prison, and came to Thee?

And the King answering, shall say to them: Amen I say to you, as long as you did it to one of these My least brethren, you did it to Me.

Then He shall say to them also that be on His left hand: Depart from Me, you cursed, into everlasting fire which was prepared for the devil and his angels.

For I was hungry, and you gave Me not to eat: I was thirsty, and you gave Me not to drink.

I was a stranger, and you took Me not in: naked, and you covered Me not: sick, and in prison, and you did not visit Me.

Then they also shall answer Him, saying: Lord, when did we see Thee hungry, or thirsty, or a stranger, or naked, or sick, or in prison, and did not minister to Thee?

Then He shall answer them, saying: Amen I say to you, as long as you did it not to one of these least, neither did you do it to Me.

And these shall go into everlasting punishment: but the just, into life everlasting (Matt. xxv. 31–46).

So will be made clear the power, the justice, and the love of Christ to all men. To show this is the purpose of the Final Judgment, and to show that the justice of the Providence of God, which on earth often permits the good to suffer and the wicked to prosper.

The Resurrection of the Body. One special aspect of the Final Judgment is the general resurrection of mankind, and especially the resurrection of the body. Martha speaking to Jesus, who was to raise her brother Lazarus said:

> I know that he shall rise again in the resurrection at the last day (John xi. 24).

The resurrection of the body was prophesied and promised by Christ. He said:

> Wonder not at this: for the hour cometh, wherein all that are in the graves shall hear the voice of the Son of God.
> And they that have done good things, shall come forth into the resurrection of life; but they that have done evil, unto the resurrection of judgment (John v. 28-29).

He said also,

> He that eateth My Flesh, and drinketh My Blood, hath everlasting life: and I will raise him up in the last day (John vi. 55).

So the idea must have existed among the Jews. Job says:

> I shall be clothed again with my skin, and in my flesh I shall see my God (Job xix. 26).

Glorifies Body and Soul. The body will rise again because of Christ's divine power. But it will be immortal. "It was buried a natural body, it shall rise a spiritual body," says St. Paul. The bodies of the just shall be glorious; the bodies of the unjust, hideous. This immortal body will be joined to the immortal soul for its life of everlasting joy, or of everlasting judgment.

The Just. The just and holy shall see God face to face. In the words of St. Paul:

> Follow peace with all men, and holiness: without which no man shall see God (Heb. xii. 14).

And we know, nothing that is defiled shall enter heaven. The holy, the just, the undefiled, shall have those blessed joys which are so great and eternal which we call heaven. Heaven is the state of everlasting life in which we see God face to face, and are made like unto Him in glory and enjoy eternal happiness. St. Augustine, wondering how beautiful heaven must be, says, while gazing at the beauty of the world: "If, O my God, Thou dost give us such beautiful things here in our prison, that wilt Thou do in Thy palace?" We might repeat that passage from the Apocalypse:

And God shall wipe away all tears from their eyes: and death shall be no more, nor mourning, nor crying, nor sorrow shall be any more, for the former things are passed away (Apoc. xxi. 4).

And again,

And they shall see His face: and His name shall be on their foreheads.
And night shall be no more: and they shall not need the light of the lamp, nor the light of the sun, because the Lord God shall enlighten them, and they shall reign forever and ever (Apoc. xxii. 4–5).

The Unjust. The unjust shall be given eternal punishment. Those who fought against Christ, those who refused His grace, those who followed man rather than God, and continued in their willfulness, and loved not God, shall suffer eternal punishment in hell. It is pictured as a place of torment. Christ describes it as "unquenchable fire," as "outer darkness." The thought of it should keep us from sin.

Purgatory. There are some who died without grave sins on their souls, but they had not done complete penance for their offenses. They deserved neither heaven nor hell. They are sent to an intermediate place called purgatory, where they can cleanse themselves of any stain of sin remaining in them, and satisfy the justice of God for their offenses. This punishment or purging is not eternal, it is temporary. From purgatory the soul is taken to heaven. Purgatory may be defined then, as the state in which those suffer for a time who die guilty of venial sins, or without having satisfied for the temporal punishment due to their sins.

Helping the Souls in Purgatory. We have seen how the souls in heaven and those in purgatory and the faithful on earth are united in the Body of Christ, which we call the communion of saints. The faithful on earth can help the souls in purgatory by their prayers, fasts, almsdeeds, by indulgences, and by having Masses said for them.

Questions from the Catechism

Q. When will Christ judge us?
A. **Christ will judge us immediately after our death, and on the last day.**

Q. What is the judgment called which we have to undergo immediately after death?
A. **The judgment we have to undergo immediately after death is called the Particular Judgment.**

Q. What is the judgment called which all men have to undergo on the last day?
A. **The judgment which all men have to undergo on the last day is called the General Judgment.**

Q. Why does Christ judge men immediately after death?
A. **Christ judges men immediately after death to reward or punish them according to their deeds.**

Q. What are the rewards or punishments appointed for men's souls after the Particular Judgment?
A. **The rewards or punishments appointed for men's souls after the Particular Judgment are heaven, purgatory, or hell.**

Q. What is hell?
A. **Hell is a state to which the wicked are condemned, and in which they are deprived of the sight of God for all eternity, and are in dreadful torments.**

Q. What is purgatory?
A. **Purgatory is the state in which those suffer for a time who die guilty of venial sins, or without having satisfied for the punishment due to their sins.**

Q. Can the faithful on earth help the souls in purgatory?
A. **The faithful on earth can help the souls in purgatory by their prayers, fasts, almsdeeds; by indulgences, and by having Masses said for them.**

Q. If everyone is judged immediately after death, what need is there of a general judgment?
A. **There is need of a general judgment, though everyone is judged immediately after death, that the providence of God, which, on earth, often permits the good to suffer and the wicked to prosper, may in the end appear just before all men.**

THE END OF THE JOURNEY

Q. Will our bodies share in the reward or punishment of our souls?
A. **Our bodies will share in the reward or punishment of our souls, because through the resurrection they will again be united to them.**

Q. In what state will the bodies of the just rise?
A. **The bodies of the just will rise glorious and immortal.**

Q. Will the bodies of the damned also rise?
A. **The bodies of the damned will also rise, but they will be condemned to eternal punishment.**

Q. What is heaven?
A. **Heaven is the state of everlasting life in which we see God face to face, are made like unto Him in glory, and enjoy eternal happiness.**

Problem Questions

1. Where are you going?
2. What is heaven?
3. What is hell?
4. What is purgatory?
5. What is the Particular Judgment?
6. What is the General Judgment?
7. What judgment is expressed in the examination of conscience?
8. What is meant by the resurrection of the body? What reference is there to this doctrine in the Old Testament? What is the basis of our belief in this doctrine?
9. Will we all be judged alike? or will our capacity and our opportunity be taken into account?
10. Are there any clear descriptions of heaven?
11. What is the beatific vision?
12. Comment on the thirteenth chapter of the First Epistle to the Corinthians in the light of this chapter.

Quotations from the Bible

For each of the following quotations:
a) Identify the speaker.
b) State the conditions under which the statement was made.
c) Give the meaning.
d) Tell its significance.

"What doth it profit a man, if he gain the whole world, and suffer the loss of his own soul? Or what exchange shall a man give for his soul?" (Matt. xvi. 26.)

"Lord, save us, we perish" (Matt. viii. 25).

"In what day soever thou shalt eat of it, thou shalt die the death" (Gen. ii. 17).

"The hour cometh, wherein all that are in the graves shall hear the voice of the Son of God. And they that have done good things, shall come forth unto the resurrection of Life; and they that have done evil, unto the resurrection of Judgment" (John v. 28–29).

"Then shall the King say to them that shall be on His right hand: Come, ye blessed of My Father, possess you the kingdom prepared for you from the foundation of the world. For

I was hungry, and you gave Me to eat:
I was thirsty, and you gave Me to drink:
I was a stranger, and you took Me in:
Naked, and you covered Me:
Sick, and you visited Me:
I was in prison, and you came to Me.

"Then shall the just answer Him, saying: Lord, when did we see Thee hungry, and fed Thee; thirsty, and gave Thee drink? And when did we see Thee a stranger, and took Thee in? or naked, and covered Thee? Or when did we see Thee sick or in prison, and came to Thee? And the King answering, shall say to them: Amen I say to you, as long as you did it to one of these My least brethren, you did it to Me" (Matt. xxv. 34–40).

"If thy hand scandalize thee, cut it off: it is better for thee to enter into Life maimed, than having two hands to go into hell, into unquenchable fire: Where their worm dieth not, and the fire is not extinguished" (Mark ix. 42–43).

"It is written that eye hath not seen, nor ear heard, neither hath it entered into the heart of man, what things God hath prepared for them that love Him" (I Cor. ii. 9).

To what incident does the following description refer?
Who was present?
What is the significance of the event?

"What doth it profit a man if he gain the whole world, and suffer the loss of his own soul? Or what exchange shall a man give for his soul?" (Matt. xvi. 26.)

"As in Adam all die, so also in Christ all shall be made alive" (I Cor. xv. 22).

Chapter XLV
THE APOSTLES' CREED

The Apostles' Creed. The most convenient summary of what this book teaches is found in the creed or solemn profession of faith made by the Apostles and taught by them. This creed contains, too, the chief truths which the Roman Catholic Church teaches today, twenty centuries later. This we should know by heart. It is as follows:

I believe in God, the Father Almighty, Creator of heaven and earth; and in Jesus Christ, His only Son, our Lord; who was conceived by the Holy Ghost, born of the Virgin Mary, suffered under Pontius Pilate, was crucified; died, and was buried. He descended into hell; the third day He arose again from the dead; He ascended into heaven, sitteth at the right hand of God, the Father Almighty; from thence He shall come to judge the living and the dead. I believe in the Holy Ghost, the Holy Catholic Church, the Communion of Saints, the forgiveness of sins, the resurrection of the body, and the life everlasting. Amen.

The Twelve Articles of the Creed. The beginning of this creed is a belief in the Trinity, the Father, the Son, and the Holy Ghost. If we study the creed more carefully, we see that it is divided into twelve parts or articles. These are with the understood words, I believe, added:

Believe in God, the Father.

Article 1. I believe in God, the Father Almighty, Creator of heaven and earth.

Believe in God, the Son.

Article 2. I believe in Jesus Christ, His only Son, our Lord.
Article 3. I believe in Jesus Christ, who was conceived of the Holy Ghost, born of the Virgin Mary.
Article 4. I believe in Jesus Christ, who suffered under Pontius Pilate, was crucified, died, and buried.
Article 5. I believe He [Jesus Christ] descended into hell; the third day He arose again from the dead.

Article 6. I believe He [Jesus Christ] ascended into heaven, sitteth at the right hand of God, the Father Almighty.

Article 7. I believe from thence He [Jesus Christ] shall come to judge the living and the dead.

Believe in God, the Holy Ghost.

Article 8. I believe in the Holy Ghost.

Article 9. I believe in the Holy Catholic Church, and in the Communion of Saints.

Article 10. I believe in the forgiveness of sins.

Article 11. I believe in the resurrection of the body.

Article 12. I believe in life everlasting.

The Trinity as Foundation. The Creed is a profession of faith in the Trinity. The first article is a statement of faith in the nature of God. Articles two to seven are statements of faith in the facts of the birth, life, and death of God, the Son, our Redeemer. Articles eight to twelve are statements of faith in the Holy Ghost, and in His work in the sanctification of souls and in the Church.

The Nicene Creed. The Council of Nicea in A.D. 325 also wrote a creed which was revised by the Council of Constantinople

I believe in God the Father Almighty, Creator of heaven and earth; and in Jesus Christ, His only Son, our Lord, Who was conceived of the Holy Ghost, born of the Virgin Mary, suffered under Pontius Pilate, was crucified; died and was buried; He descended into hell; the third day He rose again from the dead; He ascended into heaven, sitteth at the right hand of God, the Father Almighty; from thence He shall come to judge the living and the dead.

I believe in the Holy Ghost; the Holy Catholic Church; the communion of saints; the forgiveness of sins; the resurrection of the body; and life everlasting. Amen.

(A.D. 381). It is called the Nicene Creed and is said at the end of the Mass of the Catechumens. Very properly does a later council say of this creed, "Let the *credo* resound." In that chant the true faith proclaims itself in a striking manner, and the soul of a Catholic people, with renewed faith, prepares to receive the Communion of the Body and Blood of Christ. It will be well to put the Nicene Creed and the Apostles' Creed in parallel columns.

Apostles' Creed

1. I believe in God, the Father Almighty, Creator of heaven and earth.

2. And in Jesus Christ, His only Son, our Lord.

3. Who was conceived of the Holy Ghost, born of the Virgin Mary.

4. Suffered under Pontius Pilate, was crucified, died and was buried.

5. Descended into Hell, the third day He arose again from the dead.

6. Ascended into heaven, sitteth at the right hand of God, the Father Almighty.

The Nicene Creed

1. I believe in one God, the Father Almighty, maker of heaven and earth, and of all things visible and invisible.

2. And in one Lord Jesus Christ, the only-begotten Son of God, born of the Father before all ages; God of God, Light of Light, true God, of True God; begotten not made; consubstantial with the Father; by whom all things were made.

3. Who for us men, and for our salvation, came down from heaven; AND WAS INCARNATE BY THE HOLY GHOST, OF THE VIRGIN MARY; AND WAS MADE MAN.

4. He was crucified also for us, suffered under Pontius Pilate, and was buried.

5. And the third day He rose again according to the Scriptures;

6. And ascended into heaven. He sitteth at the right hand of the Father;

7. From thence He [Jesus Christ] shall come to judge the living and the dead.	7. And He shall come again with glory to judge the living and the dead; And His Kingdom shall have no end.
8. I believe in the Holy Ghost,	8. And in the Holy Ghost, the Lord Giver of Life, who proceedeth from the Father and the Son, who together with the Father and the Son is adored and glorified; who spoke by the Prophets.
9. The Holy Catholic Church, and in the Communion of Saints,	9. And one holy Catholic and Apostolic Church.
10. The forgiveness of sins,	10. I confess one baptism for the remission of sins.
11. The resurrection of the body,	11. And I await the resurrection of the dead,
12. And life everlasting.	12. And the life of the world to come.

Glory to God in the Highest. And how may we better conclude this chapter and the book than with the "Gloria in Excelsis":

Glory to God in the highest, and on earth peace to men of good will.
We praise Thee,
We bless Thee,
We adore Thee,
We glorify Thee,
We give Thee thanks for Thy great glory.

The Father
O Lord God, heavenly King, God the Father Almighty.

The Son
O Lord Jesus Christ, the only-begotten Son. O Lord God, Lamb of God, Son of the Father, who takest away the sins of the world, have mercy upon us. Who takest away the sins of the world, receive our prayer. Who sittest at the right hand of the Father, have mercy upon us. For Thou only art holy. Thou only art Lord. Thou only, O Jesus Christ, art most high.

The Holy Ghost
Together with the Holy Ghost, in the glory of God the Father. Amen.

THE APOSTLES' CREED

Questions from the Catechism

Q. Where shall we find the chief truths which the Church teaches?

A. **We shall find the chief truths which the Church teaches in the Apostles' Creed.**

Q. Say the Apostles' Creed.

A. **I believe in God, the Father Almighty, Creator of heaven and earth; and in Jesus Christ, His only Son, our Lord; who was conceived by the Holy Ghost, born of the Virgin Mary, suffered under Pontius Pilate, was crucified; died, and was buried. He descended into hell; the third day He arose again from the dead; He ascended into heaven, and sitteth at the right hand of God, the Father Almighty; from thence He shall come to judge the living and the dead. I believe in the Holy Ghost, the Holy Catholic Church, the communion of saints, the forgiveness of sins, the resurrection of the body, and the life everlasting. Amen.**

INDEX

A.M.D.G., 4
Abstinence, 368; dispensation from, 368; fast and, 366
Accidents, 81
Actual grace, 245; matrimony and, 331
Actual sin, 104
Adam and Eve, 15 ff.; destiny of, before fall, 24; result of sin of, 18
Adults, baptism of, 257
Age of reason, 287
Almsgiving, 93
Andrew, called, 204
Angels, 391 ff.; announce birth of Christ, 128; appearance of, in Old and New Testament, 394; fallen, 396; guardian, 395; in Christ's life, 391; in Old Testament, 393; knowledge of, 395
Angel's announcement, to shepherds, 125; to Zachary, 121
Anger, 108; forbidden, 82
Anno Domini, 128
Annunciation, 123
Apostle of Gentiles, 213
Apostles, Christ and, 203 ff.; confirmation and, 321; descent of Holy Ghost upon, 219; effects of descent of Holy Ghost upon, 223; Mary with, 198; misunderstand, 210; Peter and, 211; teaching the, 209; twelve, selection of, 205
Apostles' Creed, 407 ff.; Nicene Creed and, 409
Apostolic, Church of Christ is, 229
Appearances of Christ, 184, 186, 187
Archbishop, 345
Articles, twelve, of the Creed, 407

Ascension, 188
Assisting at Mass, 314
Assumption, 200
Authority of Church, 230
Avoiding temptation, 45

Bad example, 83
Baptism, 254 ff.; administration, 255; children of God by, 263; ceremonies, 257; Christ prescribes words, 255; conditional, 258; God's mercy after, 263; lay, form, 259; necessary for salvation, 258; of adults, 257; of blood, 257; of desire, 256; sponsors, 255
Baptism of Christ by John, 133
Beatitude, 89
Beatitudes, eight, 154, 155
Beginning, in the, 8
Believe in God, the Father, 407; the Holy Ghost, 408; the Son, 407
Betrayal of Christ by Judas, 167
Birth of Christ, 124; angels announce, 128; divides time, 128; prophecy of, 193
Bishop, 345
Blasphemy, 51
Blood, baptism of, 257
Body, soul and, glorifies, 402; resurrection of, 402
Body of Christ organized, 228
Body of Church, 232
Books, immodest, 58
Bread of Life, I am, 298

Calvary, Last Supper, and Mass, 308
Canon Law, 359

413

Canon of the Mass, 290
Canonization, 385
Capital sins, 107
Cardinal virtues, 109
Cardinals, 346
Catechumens, Mass of, 311
Catholic Church, Roman, *see* Church, Roman Catholic
Catholic or Universal, Church of Christ is, 229
Ceremonies, baptism, 257; confirmation, 320
Channels of grace, 242
Charity, 83, 244; preventions, 101; promotions, 101
Child, expectation of, 132
Childhood of Christ, 203
Children, Christ's love of, 155
Children of God by baptism, 263
Chrism, 322
Christ, appearances in the world, 118; appearances, 184, 186, 187; Apostles and, 203 ff.; baptism, by John, 133; betrayal, 167; birth, 124; birth, prophecy of, 193; carrying on His work, 341; childhood, 203; Church and, 358; descended into hell, 179; desire for our spiritual welfare, 359; died, 176; divinity, 137 ff.; early life, 128; early life unknown, 130; expected Redeemer, 118; gives life or grace to Church, 227; Holy Eucharist and, 161 ff.; instituted confirmation, 322; instituted Holy Eucharist, 290; instituted penance, 267; is God, 142; is risen, 183 ff.; lead to death, 173; life, 203; life of, angels in, 391; love of children by, 155; memorable sayings, 154 ff.; mocked, 174; on earth, 358; power of, sacraments effective through, 244; present under either species, 301; public life, 144 ff., 203; public life of, beginning, 137; right hand of God, 189; soldiers of, 318; speaks to Nicodemus, 254; suffers under Pontius Pilate, 169; the Vine, 149; twelve years old, 132; urges us to pray, 351; who is, ?, 125; why He came, 341; with Church forever, 227; work continued, 358
Christian family, 329
Christian holydays, 62
Christian life, beginning of, 318
Church of Christ, *see* Church, Roman Catholic
Church, Roman Catholic, 225 ff., 341; Apostolic, 229; authority, 230; body and soul, 232; Catholic or Universal, 229; Christ gives life or grace to, 227; Christ and, 358; Christ with, forever, 227; commandments, 358 ff.; doctrine in, 301; fifth commandment, 375; first commandment, 360; forbids mixed marriages, 377; guardian of, 358; holy, 229; indefectibility, 230; infallibility of, 230; living members of, saints, 386; marks, 229; militant, 234; one, 228; organization, 345; organized, 227; persons to administer, 341; saints, and holiness, 383; second commandment, 366; sixth commandment, 376; suffering, 234; third and fourth commandments, 370; triumphant, 234, 386
Citizens, duty as, 72
Command, in sin, 111
Commandment, Eighth, of God, 98 ff.; Fifth, of God, 80 ff.; First, of God, 38 ff.; Fourth, of God, 70 ff.; greatest, 34, 157; Ninth, of God, 87 ff.; positive, 100; Second, of God, 50 ff.; Seventh, of God, 92 ff.; Sixth, of God, 87 ff.; Tenth, of God, 92 ff.; Third, of God, 59 ff.
Commandments of Church, 358 ff., 359; in general, 358
Commandments of God, ten, 28 ff., 29; failure to keep, 104; first three, what they command, 38; importance, 33; love of neighbor, 70; numbering, 34; division into, by God, 35
Commandments of love, 31

INDEX 415

Commands, negative, 99; obeying God's, 33
Communion, Holy, *see* Holy Communion
Communion of Saints, 234, 386
Concupiscence, 94
Conditional baptism, 258
Confession, 267; concealing sins in, 275; good, qualities of, 274; humanly helpful, 274; making a, 270; number of sins, 275; of sins, 270 ff.; penance after, 281; purpose to sin no more, 274
Confirmation, 318 ff.; Apostles and, 321; bishop's sermon at, 320; Christ instituted, 322; ceremonies, 320; Communion before, 319; day of, 318; form, 323; inward grace, 323; mark in soul, 323; outward sign, 322; sponsor, 319
Connivance in sin, 111
Conscience, examination of, 266, 271
Consent in sin, 111
Contrition, imperfect, 272; perfect, 271; sorrow or, 266; true, interior, 273; true, qualities, 275; true, sovereign, 273; true, supernatural, 273; true, universal, 273
Conversations, immodest, 88
Conversion, St. Paul, 212
Coöperating in sin, 110
Corporal works of mercy, 282
Councils, 231
Counsel or advice in sin, 110
Courts of justice, lies in, 98; perjury in, 52
Covenant, sealing, with blood, 32
Covetousness, 108
Creation, analogy of, 66; earth, 9; heaven, 9; light, 9; man, 11; steps in, 11; story, 8 ff.
Creator, God, 1 ff., 3
Creatures, of earth, 10; of waters, 10; worship of, 40
Creed, Apostles', 407 ff.; Nicene, 408; summary in, 179; twelve articles of, 407

Cross, sacrifice of, 307
Crucifixion, 173 ff.
Crucifixion, Peter's, prophecied, 188
Cursing, 54

Damascus, road to, 212
David, King, attitude toward God, 42; praise of God by, 2
Day, of the week, 64; what is a, 2, 12
Dead, men raised from, 140; sacraments of, 246; son of widow raised from, 142
Death, Christ and, 173; events following Christ's, 178
Defense of sin, 112
Denial of Christ by Peter, 168, 210; prophecy, 166
Descent of Holy Ghost upon Apostles, 211, 219
Desire, baptism of, 256
Despair, presumption and, 44
Destiny, Adam's, before fall, 24; man's, 25
Devotion to God, 65
Dinner, 187
Disobedience, punishment of, 23, 28
Dispensation, from abstinence, 368; from fasting, 368
Divine worship to God, 45
Divinity of Christ, 137 ff.
Doctrine in Church, 301
Doubting Thomas, 186, 211
Dreams, 41
Duty, citizens', 72; man's, 24

Early Church, Mass in, 361
Early life Christ's, unknown, 130
Earth, bringeth forth herbs, 9; creation of, 9; creatures of, 10
Easter Sunday, Good Friday and, time between, 183
Ecclesiastical year, division, 313
Eden, Garden of, man in, 15
Egypt, 196; flight into, 130; Jews in, 29; return from, 130

Eight Beatitudes, 154, 155
Eighth Commandment of God, 98 ff.
Ember days, 367
End of journey, 399 ff.
Envy, 109
Essentials of a sacrament, 241; holy orders, 344
Eternal, God is, 4
Eternal punishment, penance and, 281
Evil, 40
Eve, Adam and, 15 ff.
Everlasting life, 156
Evil spirits, 396
Examination of conscience, 266, 271
Example, bad, 83
Expectation, great, 115; of the Child, 132
Expected, King, 118
Extreme Unction, sacrament of, 335 ff.; delay and, 336; effects, 338; essentials of a sacrament, 336; fear of death and, 337; in form of prayer, 337; oil in, 337; preparation for, 336; St. James and, 335; St. Mark and, 335
Eye for an eye, 32

Faith in God, 42, 44, 244
Faithful, Mass of, 311
Fall of man, 16; destiny of Adam before, 24
Fallen angels, 396
Family, Christian, 329; importance, 87
Fasting, 366; abstinence and, 366; dispensation from, 368; Holy Communion and, 302
Fear of death, Extreme Unction and, 337
Father, God Our, 1
Father and mother, 70
Feed My lambs, feed My sheep, 188
Feeding multitudes, 139
Fellow man, love of, 39
Fifth commandment of the Church, 375
Fifth Commandment of God, 80

Final home, long journey to man's, 25
First commandment of Church, 360
First Commandment of God, 38 ff.
Fishing net, 147
Flight into Egypt, 130
Forbidden times, marriage, 379
Forgiveness of sins, 263 ff., 264; conditions, 265; opportunity to secure, 266; steps in securing, 266
Form of lay baptism, 259
Fortune tellers, 41
Forty days on earth, 184
Foundation, Trinity, a, 408
Fourth, third and, commandments of the Church, 370
Fourth Commandment of God, 70 ff.; promise of, 72; punishment and, 73; violations, 73
Free will of man, 18
Friendship, 80
Fruits of the Holy Ghost, 324

Gabriel greets Mary, 193
General judgment, 400
Genesis, 8; Jews and, 8; science and, 8
Gentiles, Apostle of, 213
Gifts of the Holy Ghost, 323
Glorifies body and soul, 402
Glorious mysteries, 201
Glory to God in the highest, 410
Gluttony, 108
God, Christ in, 143; Commandments of, 28 ff., 29; Creator, 1 ff., 3; divine worship to, 45; division into ten commandments by, 35; Eighth Commandment of, 98 ff.; eternal, 4; faith, hope, and love, 42; First Commandment of, 38 ff.; Fifth Commandment of, 80 ff.; Fourth Commandment of, 70 ff.; from, to God, 24; how to love, 31; instituted marriage, 330; is Love, 1; is One, 133; King David and, 2, 42; kingdom of, 147, 152; know, 23; love, justice, mercy, 5; love of, 23,

INDEX

73, 106; love of man by, 28, 240; love of truth for love of, 100; man and, 4; nothing impossible to, 13; our faith in, 44; our Father, 1; perfect, 5; power of, 12; Second Commandment of, 50 ff.; serve, 23; Seventh and Tenth Commandments of, 92 ff.; Sixth and Ninth Commandments of, 87 ff.; Pure Spirit, 5; resteth, 12; single devotion to, 65; the Father, believe in, 407; the Holy Ghost, believe in, 408; the Son, believe in, 407; things that belong to, 157; Third Commandment of, 59 ff., 361; what is?, 5; worship of, 39, 46

God's highway, keeping on, 66; signposts on, 115

Golden Mean, 88

Good Friday and Easter Sunday, time between, 183

Good Samaritan, 148

Good Shepherd, 150

Grace, actual, 245; channels, 242; Holy Communion and, 302; indulgence and, 283; inward, of confirmation, 323; Mary full of, 193 ff.; prayer and, 349; sacramental, 245; sacraments and, 240 ff.; sanctifying, 244

Greatest commandment, 34, 157

Guardian angels, 395

Guardians of Church, 358

Hatred forbidden, 82

Heaven, 25, 399; creation of, 9

Hell, Christ descended into, 179

Hidden treasure, 147

Hobbies, interests and, 88

Holiness, of Church and saints, 383; of Sabbath, 63

Holy, Church of Christ is, 229

Holy Communion, before confirmation, 319; fast and, 302; grace and, 302

Holy Eucharist, a true sacrament, 293; as a sacrament, 314; as a sacrifice, 306 ff., 314; Christ and, 161 ff.; effects of, 302; essentials of, 292; Christ institutes, 290; institution of, 166; names, 291; promise of, fulfilled, 300; reason for instituting, 315; sacrament, 287 ff.; St. Paul and, 300

Holy Ghost, descent of, upon Apostles, 211, 219; effects of descent of, upon Apostles, 223; effects of descent of, upon people, 221; fruits, 324; gifts, 323; names, 217; on Pentecost, 217 ff., 226; promise of, 217, 225; will come, 217

Holy Mass, see Mass, Holy

Holy Orders, 341 ff.; essentials of a sacrament, 344; mark on soul, 345; sacrament, 344

Holydays, among Jews, 62; Christian, 62; of obligation and Sunday, 362

Home, importance, 87; impurity destroys, 87

Honor, devotion and, to saints, 387; how to, 71; name of God, 54; owed to others, 71; parents, 70; spiritual superiors, 72

Hope, 244; in God, 42

House, building a, 146

Human nature, effect of original sin on, 19; restoration of, 254

I thirst, 174

Images, honor and respect to, 387

Immaculate Conception, 198

Immodesty, 88

Imperfect, contrition, 272; confession and, 272

Impurity destroys home, 87

Indefectibility of Church, 230

Indissoluble, marriage, 333

Indulgences, as satisfaction for sins, 283; state of grace and, 283; plenary and partial, 283

Infallibility of Church, 230

Institution of Sacrifice of the Mass, 308
Institution of the Holy Eucharist, 166; reason for, 315
Interests and hobbies, 88
Inward grace, penance and, 268
Irreverence, 51
Isaias, vision of, 392

James, St., called, 204; Extreme Unction and, 335
Jerusalem, women of, 173
Jesus Christ, see Christ
Jews, Genesis and, 8; holydays among, 62; in Egypt, 29; King of, 174
John, St., called, 204; testimony of, 178
John baptizes Christ, 133
Joyful mysteries of Rosary, 201, 134
Judas, betrayal by, 210; hangs self, 161
Judge of living and dead, 189
Judgment, general, 400
Just, 402
Justice, God is, 5

Keep holy the Sabbath day, 66
Keys, power of, to Peter, 264
Kill, thou shalt not, 80
Killing, contribution to, 82
King, expected, 118; of the Jews, 174
Kingdom, Head of, 148; members of, 148; not of this world, 118
Kingdom of God, 152; nature of, 147
Know God, 23
Knowledge, of angels, 395; tree of, 16

Lamb, Paschal, 288
Last Supper, Calvary, and Mass, 308
Lay baptism, form of, 259
Law, Canon, 359; in man's heart, 59
Leader, Promised, 115
Leaven, 147
Lent, 367
Lies, effects of, on society, 100; excuses for, 98; for or against neighbor, 99; in courts of justice, 98; wings of, 100
Life, everlasting, 157; preservation of, 80; natural and spiritual, 243; sacredness, 81; time and, 88
Life of Christ, 203; early, 128 ff.
Life of soul, 287
Light, creation, 9
Light of the World, 149
Living, matrimony, sacrament of, 331; sacraments of, 246
Living and dead, Judge of, 189
Living members of Church, Saints, 386
Lord, is My Shepherd, 38; ordinances of, 31
Lord's Day, servile works on, 64; works proper for, 66
Love, 80; commandments of, 31; God, 23; God is, 1, 5; how to, God, 31
Love of fellow man, 39
Love of God, 42, 106; prayers of, 46; supreme, 73
Love of man, God's, 28; God's penance and, 263
Love of neighbor, 83; commandments of, 70
Lust, 108

Magnificat, 194, 195
Major orders, 344
Man, creation, 11; destiny, 25; duty, 24; fall, 16; final home, journey to, 25; free will, 18; God and, 4; God's love of, 28, 240; heart of, law in, 59; in Garden of Eden, 15; making of, 15; Old Adam, in, 112; Paradise for, 22; what is ?, 22; why God made, 22 ff.; wonder of, 22
Mark, St., Extreme Unction and, 335
Mark in the soul, confirmation, 323; holy orders, 345
Mark of Church, 229
Marriage, before priest and two wit-

INDEX 419

nesses, 379; between close relatives, 379; forbidden times, 379; God instituted, 330; importance, 87; dissoluble, 332; mixed, Church, forbids, 377; mixed, conditions, 378; Old and New Testament, 329; solemnizing, 378; spiritual view of, 377

Mary, Apostles and, 198; at the foot of the cross, 174; ever Virgin, 200; full of Grace, 193 ff.; Gabriel greets, 193; memorial of, 201; Mother of God, 195; sorrows, 134

Mary Magdalen, Peter and, 211

Mass, Holy, 361; assisting at, 314; Calvary, Last Supper and, 308; Canon of, 290; early Church and, 361; Missal and, 362; Newman, Cardinal, and, 312; of Catechumens, 311; of Faithful, 312; order of, 310; sacrifice, institution, 308

Matrimony, 329 ff.; actual graces, 331; ministers, 330; outward sign, 331; preparation, 376; sacrament, 329; sacrament of living, 331

Matthew, St., called, 205

Members of the Kingdom, 148

Mercy, God is, 5; God's, after baptism, 263

Messiah, 115 ff.; prophecies, 116

Militant, Church, 234

Minimum, 372

Ministers of matrimony, 330

Minor orders, 344

Miracles, 137 ff.; performing, 144; power to perform, 137

Missal and Mass, 362

Mixed marriages, Church forbids, 377; conditions, 378

Monday, 165

Money changers driven from the temple, 161

Moon, 10

Mortal sin, 105; examples, 105

Moses on Mount Sinai, 29

Mother, father and, 70

Mother of God, Mary, 195

Mount Calvary, 173

Mount Sinai, Moses on, 29

Multitudes, feeding, 138

Mustard seed, 147

Mysteries, glorious, 201; joyful, 200; sorrowful, 201

Mystery of real presence, 298; anticipation of, 298

Name of God, honor to, 54

Natural, spiritual and, life, 243

Nature, His word controls, 139

Negative commands, 99

Neighbor, lies for or against, 99; love of, 83; who is, 99

New Testament, appearance of angels in, 394; marriage in, 329

Newman, Cardinal, Mass and, 312

Nicene Creed, 408; Apostles' Creed and, 409

Nicodemus, Christ speaks to, 254

Ninth, Sixth and, Commandments of God, 87 ff.

Nourishment for soul, 288

Numbering the Commandments, 34

Oaths, 52; false and injust, 53; rash and unnecessary, 53

Obeying God's commands, 23

Obligation to pray, 350

Observance, vain, 41

Occasions of sin, 94, 110

Oil in Extreme Unction, 337

Old Adam in man, 112

Old age, 71

Old Testament, angels in, 393, 394; marriage in, 329; Sabbath in, 60

One, Church of Christ is, 228; God is, 133

Order of Mass, 310

Orders, major, 344; minor, 344

Ordinances of the Lord, 31

Ordination of priests, 343

Organization of the Church, 345

Original sin, 18; effect of, on human

nature, 19
Our Father, 351
Outward sign, confirmation, 322; matrimony, 331; penance, 267

Palm Sunday, 161
Parables, 144 ff., 146
Paradise for Man, 22
Partial and plenary indulgences, 283
Parent to his son, 74
Parents, honor our, 70; responsibility, 74
Particular judgment, 400
Pasch, feast of, 164
Paschal Lamb, 288
Paul, St., conversion, 212; Holy Eucharist and, 300
Peace, 80
Pearl of great price, 147
Penance, 146, 267; a true sacrament, 267, 268; after confession, 281; eternal punishment and, 281; God's love of man and, 263; instituted by Christ, 267; inward grace, 268; need for, 265; qualities, 342; outward sign, 267; steps to, 343
Pentecost, Holy Ghost on, 217 ff., 227
Perfect, God is, 5
Perfect contrition, 271
Perjury in courts of justice, 52
Perseverance, 245
Peter, St., Apostles and, 211; called, 204; crucifixion of, prophesied, 188; denies Christ, 168, 210; Mary Magdalen and, 211; power of keys to, 264; prophecy of denial of, 166; rebuke of, 207
Pharisee, publican and, 148
Physician, 150
Pictures, immodest, 88
Plays, immodest, 88
Plenary and partial indulgences, 283
Pontius Pilate, Christ before, 168; Christ suffers under, 169
Pope, 231, 346; full power in, 232
Positive commandment, 100

Power in Pope, 232
Power, God's, 13
Power of sacraments, 247
Power of the keys to Peter, 264
Praise or flattery in sin, 111
Pray, Christ urges us to, 351; how to, 351; to whom, 352; well, 353; what for, 352
Prayer, 349 ff.; grace and, 349; meaning, 350; obligation, 350; of the love of God, 46; recommended, 355; time, 355; to Saints, 388
Preaching, 144; His daily, 163
Prepare ye the way of the Lord, 121 ff.
Preparation for matrimony, 376
Presence, real, 298 ff.
Presentation in temple, 128, 195
Preservation of human life, 80
Presumption and despair, 44
Pride, 107
Priest, two witnesses and, marriage before, 379
Priests, ordination, 343; services, 342; special training, 342
Principal sin, accessory sin may be, 112
Prodigal son, 151
Promise of Holy Ghost, 225
Promised Leader, 115
Prophecies of the Messiah, 116
Prophecy, destruction of temple and second coming, 164; fulfillment, 123, 220
Public life, Christ's, 144 ff., 203; beginning, 137
Publican, pharisee and, 148
Punishment, 18, 51; eternal, penance and, 281; Fourth Commandment and, 73; of disobedience, 23, 28; of sin, 281 ff.
Pure Spirit, God is, 5
Purgatory, 403; helping souls in, 403
Purpose to sin no more, 274

Quarreling, forbidden, 82

INDEX

Real presence, 298 ff.; mystery of, 298
Reason, age of, 287
Rebuke of Peter, 207
Reception of sacraments, 247
Redeemer, expected, Jesus Christ, 118; Savior of men or, 240
Relationship chart, 380
Relatives, close, marriage between, 379
Relics, honor and respect to, 387
Religions not the same, 45
Reputation, 99
Resolution, 266
Responsibility for sins, 105; of another, 105
Responsibility, of parents, 74; of superiors, 74
Restitution, 93
Resurrection, 183
Resurrection of body, 402
Return from Egypt, 130
Revenge, forbidden, 82
Reward, heavenly, 28
Right hand of God, Jesus at, 189
Risen, He is, 183 ff.
Roman Catholic Church, see Church, Roman Catholic
Rosary, 200; joyful mysteries of, 134; summary in, 179

Sabbath, holiness, 63; in Old Testament, 60; keep holy, 66
Sacrifice, Holy Eucharist as, 306 ff., 314; nature, 307; of cross, 307; of Mass, institution, 308; of Mass, and of Calvary, 309; old and new, 306; Old Law, 307; perfect, 307
Sacrament, baptism, 254 ff.; confirmation, 318 ff.; essentials, 241; extreme unction, 335 ff.; Holy Eucharist, 287 ff., 293, 314; holy orders, 341 ff.; matrimony, 329 ff.; penance, 267, 268
Sacramental grace, 245
Sacramentals, 247
Sacraments, 240; effective through power of Christ, 244; form and matter, 242; frequent the, 89; grace and, 240 ff.; of the dead, 246; of the living, 246; power, 247; reception, 247; sensible signs, 242; seven, 243
Sacredness of life, 81
Sacrilege, 46; confession and, 275
Saint, life of, 384
Saints, 383 ff.; Church and, holiness of, 383; communion of, 234, 386; enumerated, 383; honor and devotion to, 387; in every age, 383; living members of Church, 386; prayers to, 388; scripture, 383
Salvation, baptism necessary for, 258
Samaritan, good, 148
Sanctifying grace, 244
Satisfaction for sins, indulgences as, 283; trials as, 282
Saturday or Sunday, 61
Savior of men or Redeemer, 240
Sayings, memorable, of Christ, 154 ff.
Scandal, 83
Science, Genesis and, 8
Scripture, saints, 383
Second coming, prophecy, 164
Second commandment of Church, 366
Second Commandment of God, 50 ff.
Self-denial, ideal of, 368
Sensible sign of sacrament, 242
Serve God, 23
Servile works on Lord's Day, 64
Seven capital sins, 107
Seven Last Words of Jesus on the Cross, 176
Seventh Commandment of God, Tenth and, 92 ff.; forbids, 92
Shepherd, Good, 150; Lord is my, 38
Shepherds, angel's announcement to, 125
Sickness, 71
Signposts on God's highway, 115
Signs, in Old and New Law, 241; sensible, of sacrament, 241, 242
Silence in sin, 111
Simony, 46
Sin, 104 ff.; accessory, may be principal, 112; actual, 104; confession,

270 ff.; coöperating in, 110; defense of, 112; forgiveness, 263 ff., 264; important and less and important, 105; mortal, 105; mortal, examples, 105; occasions, 94, 110; original, 18; original, human nature and, 19; punishment, 281 ff.; responsibility, 105; responsibility for another's, 105; result of Adam's, 18; seven capital, 107; temporal punishment due to, 281; venial, 105, 106; venial, examples, 106
Six commandments of Church, 360
Sixth and Ninth Commandments of God, 87 ff.
Sixth commandment of Church, 376; prohibitions of, 377
Sixth to ninth hour, 176
Sloth, 109
Society, effects of lies on, 100
Soldiers of Christ, 318
Solemnizing marriage, 378
Son, parent to his, 75
Sorrow, contrition or, 266
Sorrowful mysteries, 201
Sorrows of Mary, 134
Soul, body and, glorifies, 402; helping, in purgatory, 403; life of, 287; nourishment for, 288; spiritual mark on, 247; value, 158
Soul of Church, 232
Species, Christ present under either, 301
Spirit, pure, God is, 5
Spirits, evil, 396
Spiritual mark on soul, 247
Spiritual and natural life, 243
Spiritual superiors, honor for, 72
Spiritual treasury, 283
Spiritual view of marriage, 377
Spiritual welfare, Christ's desire for our, 359
Spiritual works of mercy, 282
Spiritualists, 41
Sponsor for confirmation, 319
Sponsors for baptism, 255; duties, 319

Stars, 10
Stations of the Cross, 179
Storm, He stills the, 140
Superiors, responsibility, 74
Suffering, Church, 234
Sun, 10
Sunday, Saturday or, 61
Sundays, holydays of obligation and, 362; worship on, 360
Sursum corda, 349
Swearing, 53

Tables of stone, two, 34
Temple, destruction of, prophecy, 164; money changers driven from, 161; presentation in, 128
Temporal punishment of sin, 281
Temptation, avoiding, 45
Ten Commandments, 30, 271; division into, by God, 35
Tenth, Seventh and, Commandments, of God, 92 ff.
Thief, good, 174
Thieves, two, 174
Things that are God's, 157
Third and fourth commandments of the Church, 371
Third Commandment of God, 59 ff., 361; four parts of, 63
Thomas, St., doubting, 186, 211
Thursday, 165
Time, accepted, arrived, 121; birth of Christ divides, 128; definite, for special worship, 59; life and, 88
Tonsure, 343
Transfiguration, 209
Transubstantiation, 301
Treasury, spiritual, 283
Tree of knowledge, 16
Trials as satisfaction for sins, 282
Trinity, Blessed, 133; a foundation, 408
Triumphant, Church, 234, 386
Tuesday, 165

Undefiled hearts, 84

INDEX 423

Universal or Catholic, Church of Christ is, 229
Unjust, 403
Unstained hands, 84

Vain observance, 41
Venial sin, 105, 106; examples, 106
Vigils, 368
Vine, Christ is, 149
Virgin, Mary ever, 200
Virtues, cultivate, 109; four cardinal, 109
Vision of Isaias, 392
Visitation, 195
Vows, 51; keeping, 52

War, 81
Water, 254; changing, into wine, 138
Waters, creatures, 10
Way of the Lord, prepare ye, 121 ff.
Wednesday, 165
Whither?, 24
Widow, son of raised from dead, 142
Will, free, of man, 18
Wine, changing water into, 139
Wise Men, 129
Witnesses, two, priest and, marriage before, 379
Woman, making of, 16
Women of Jerusalem, 173
Wonder of man, 22
Word, His, controls nature, 139; be it done according to Thy, 193
Words for Baptism, Christ prescribes, 255
Works proper for Lord's Day, 66
World, Light of, 149
Worship, creature, 40; definite time for special, 59; divine, to God only, 44; God alone, 39; images and, 383; of God, 46; Sunday, 360; two changes in, 362

Zachary, angel's announcement to, 121

www.ingramcontent.com/pod-product-compliance
Lightning Source LLC
Chambersburg PA
CBHW060448170426
43199CB00011B/1134